Communication and Organizational Crisis

Communication and Organizational Crisis

MATTHEW W. SEEGER,
TIMOTHY L. SELLNOW,
AND ROBERT R. ULMER

PRAEGER

Westport, Connecticut
London

Library of Congress Cataloging-in-Publication Data

Seeger, Matthew W. (Matthew Wayne), 1957-
Communication and organizational crisis / Matthew W. Seeger, Timothy L.
Sellnow, and Robert R. Ulmer.
    p.   cm.
Includes bibliographical references and index.
ISBN 1–56720–534–8 (alk. paper)
1. Crisis management. 2. Communication in organizations. I. Sellnow,
Timothy L. (Timothy Lester), 1960- II. Ulmer, Robert R., 1969- III. Title
HD49.S44   2003
658.4'056–dc21   2003053575

British Library Cataloguing in Publication Data is available.

Library of Congress Catalog Card Number: 2003053575
ISBN: 1–56720–534–8

First published in 2003

Praeger Publishers, 88 Post Road West, Westport, CT 06881
An imprint of Greenwood Publishing Group, Inc.
www.praeger.com

Printed in the United States of America

The paper used in this book complies with the
Permanent Paper Standard issued by the National
Information Standards Organization (Z39.48–1984).

10 9 8 7 6 5 4

Contents

Illustrations   vii

Acknowledgments   ix

Part I: Introduction and Overview   1

  1 The Nature of Organizational Crisis   3

  2 Theories of Organizational Crisis   21

  3 Crisis Type   45

  4 Communication and Crisis   65

Part II: Stages of Crisis Development   83

  5 Crisis Development   85

  6 Communication and the Precrisis Stage   105

  7 Communication and the Crisis Stage   125

  8 Communication and the Postcrisis Stage   141

Part III: Crisis Management Functions   161

  9 Crisis Planning   163

  10 Crisis Teams and Decision Making   185

  11 Communication and Risk   201

Part IV: The Role of Crisis   217

12   Crisis and Ethics   219

13   Crisis and Leadership   239

14   The Role of Crisis in Society   257

References   275

Author Index   289

Index   293

Illustrations

FIGURES

5.1 Five-Phase Crisis Management Model   93

5.2 A Three-Stage Model of Crisis   98

7.1 Conditions and Features of the Crisis Stage   127

8.1 Consistent Stages in Effective Postcrisis Communication   142

8.2 Image Restoration Strategies   145

10.1 FEMA's Unified Command Structure   190

10.2 The Crisis Decision Model   195

11.1 Distinguishing Features of Risk Communication and Crisis Communication   203

11.2 Tensions in Connecting with the Public   206

14.1 Crisis as Resolving Social Issues   264

14.2 Reenvisioning Crisis   266

TABLES

3.1 Classification Systems for Organizational Crisis   47

4.1 Functions of Communication in Organizational Crises   67

5.1 Turner's Sequence of Failures in Foresight   89

6.1 Six Elements of the Precrisis Stage   106

6.2 Limitations on Crisis Warnings   109

6.3 A Precrisis Chronology of the Exxon *Valdez* Oil Spill   114

9.1 Coombs's Fifteen Characteristics of a Crisis
    Management Plan   170

9.2 Outline of FEMA Emergency Management Guide for
    Business and Industry   175

13.1 Factors in Crisis Leadership   242

13.2 Functions of Crisis Leadership   250

Acknowledgments

This work was initiated almost five years ago when we concluded that the body of work in organizational crisis and crisis communication had reached a point where synthesis and integration were required for further growth. Part of this conclusion was based on the recognition that the infusion of theory was necessary for the field to continue to expand and mature.

An additional part of this expansion involves the integration of substantial work from the fields of emergency management and risk communication. Increasingly, as we study and write about crisis, we conclude that the distinctions between organizational crisis and natural disasters are merely matters of degree and not of kind. We see crisis communication and risk communication as closely related rather than as two distinct forms. We believe that effective communication is at the very center of crisis avoidance and crisis management. Our thinking in these areas has been helped by our work with the Centers for Disease Control and Prevention and by our opportunity to meet and talk with many people whose business is emergency management and risk communication.

This work was initiated well before the September 11, 2001, terrorist attacks on the World Trade Center and the Pentagon and before the more recent round of corporate scandals involving Enron, WorldCom, and Tyco. We outlined this project before the sex-abuse scandal rocked the Catholic Church. We began writing chapter 1 before letters tainted with anthrax were sent through the U.S. mail, contaminating both mail-sorting machines and other letters. Before we finished our first draft, the tanker *Prestige* had set a new record for oil spills.

When we started, few people imagined an attack involving hijacked planes flown into two of the most prominent buildings in the world. In fact, although terrorism appeared on some lists of crisis types, it was regularly used as an example of unlikely crisis events. Now, of course, 9/11 is a dramatic illustration of the possibility of crisis. In many ways, 9/11 has already become the archetype for future discussions of crisis, illustrating dramatically the potential for things to go horribly wrong, the role of communication in disaster, and the widespread impact of crisis events. And it has created learning.

We have many colleagues, students, friends, and family to thank. Among these are Marsha Vanderberg, Barbara Reynolds, Bill Benoit, Dennis Gouran, Robert Heath, Dan Millar, Bethany Beebe, and Tim Coombs. Chandice Johnson's contribution in blending the styles of three authors into one voice was immeasurable. Elizabeth Ryan and Holly Petit helped in the proofreading of the manuscript. Keith Hearit sacrificed his Thanksgiving holiday to give us feedback; he helped us immeasurably by what he said and did not say. We express our appreciation to Ian Mitroff and Karl Weick for use of their models of crisis and enactment. Thanks to Hilary Claggett at Praeger for providing both support and a little extra time. We have been helped by dozens of committed students interested in crisis, including Mark Isbell, Jackie Crowder, Scott Walters, Thomas Wallace, Bethany Beebe, Sally Ray, Tony McGill, Steve Venette, Kym Overland, Donna Smith, Debra Snyder, Mike Lewis, and Debra Worely, to name only a few.

Finally, we would like to acknowledge the unique working relationship we have developed. Each of us has brought unique skills and talents to this project. We nurture and goad, encourage and critique, praise and needle one another. The ideas reflected in this book have been well-lubricated with dynamic conversation, hundreds of e-mails, and whatever happened to be on tap. We have used one another as sounding boards, constructive critics, helpful partners, and support systems. And we have managed to keep a sense of humor, maintain perspective, and stay friends.

We dedicate this project to that friendship and to the three supportive women, Beth, Deanna, and Stacy, who have helped us through this and many other projects. They have put up with not only our ridiculous antics but with the obsession to write.

We hope you find this book both interesting and useful.

Matthew W. Seeger
Timothy L. Sellnow
Robert R. Ulmer

PART I

Introduction and Overview

CHAPTER 1

The Nature of
Organizational Crisis

Increasingly, crises are common parts of the social, psychological, political, economic, and organizational landscape of modern life. They affect more people than ever before, are more widely reported in the media, and have a wider impact on increasingly interconnected, dynamic, and complex social–technical systems. Crises are sources of profound human loss, tragedy, and agony and are also the precipitating factors in radical, rapid, and often positive social change. They are stories of shortsightedness, hubris, greed, indifference, ignorance, and stupidity. Yet they are also stories of heroes, selflessness, hope, benevolence, compassion, virtue, and renewal. Understanding the complex dynamics of crises is imperative for both researchers and practitioners as they seek to reduce the frequency of crises and the level of harm they cause.

Our goal for this book is to provide a comprehensive discussion of crisis as an organizationally based phenomena with profound effects on individuals, institutions, communities, and society as a whole. We focus particularly on the communicative dimensions of crisis: how risk is discussed, how meaning is constructed, how explanations are offered and sorted out, and how blame is apportioned. We also focus on how crisis functions as a force for change. As described in chapter 2, our examination of crisis is grounded in contemporary theoretical orientations, including enactment, chaos theory, and organizational learning theory. Chapter 3 examines typologies of crisis.

In Part 2 we examine the three developmental stages of a crisis—precrisis, crisis, and postcrisis—to describe the features of these stages. Crisis- and risk-management functions and activities are described in Part

3. This discussion is grounded in the view that understanding the dynamic nature of crises is critical in avoiding, or successfully managing, these events.

THE CONCEPT OF CRISIS

The term *crisis* evokes a sense of threat, urgency, and destruction, often on a monumental scale. Crisis suggests an unusual event of overwhelmingly negative significance that carries a high level of risk, harm, and opportunity for further loss. For organizations, crisis often conveys a fundamental threat to system stability, a questioning of core assumptions and beliefs, and threats to high-priority goals, including image, legitimacy, profitability, and even survival (Seeger, Sellnow, & Ulmer, 1998). For managers, employees, community members, and victims, crisis often represents a profound personal loss. Careers may be threatened, livelihoods jeopardized, and health, well being, and sense of security and predictability shattered. Spills, floods, and explosions, for example, may fundamentally alter communities.

A crisis usually begins with some dramatic and surprising trigger event signaling its onset and ends with some resolution and return to near normalcy. Trigger events signal radical breaks with previous states of existence. The crisis state continues until there is some resolution. These events, then, are time ordered and occur within a specific and limited time frame. The development sequence of a crisis is important to understanding its larger character.

Crisis victims are often portrayed in the media as powerless and helpless, harmed by forces over which they have little or no control, exploited by economic structures and forces, and in need of some broader social support (Shirvastava, 1987). Victims who survive may suffer loss of comfort, property, income, earning potential, home, community, friends, family, or health, as well as their psychological sense of security and stability. Often, victims are depicted as casualties of corporate greed and irresponsibility (Shirvastava). This media portrayal sometimes generates broader support for crisis victims. Agencies such as the Federal Emergency Management Agency (FEMA) and the American Red Cross provide some basic support to the victims by meeting immediate needs for food, shelter, medical attention, and counseling. In the case of natural disasters and extensive man-made disasters, relief agencies also help in the immediate recovery and identification of bodies and the reconnection of survivors with families. Major crises often prompt large-scale efforts for mitigation, cleanup, repair, and return to normalcy. Broad national and international campaigns are sometimes mounted to raise funds to help those caught in the devastation of a crisis. The destruction created by Hurricane Mitch in October 1998 in Honduras generated an almost unprecedented outpouring of support from private agencies, churches, community groups, and social support agencies. The scale of the disaster, which left an estimated 900,000 dead from flooding and mudslides, created an overwhelming need. The humanistic ethic of providing support and care for those harmed by crisis is an ingrained value transcending national and cultural boundaries.

Survivors of a crisis are also usually central players in the intense post-crisis efforts to determine cause, blame, and legal liability and to ensure that no such event happens again. Legal systems often allow victims to seek compensation from those who caused, or were culpable in, the crisis. More-over, organizations seen as causing a crisis may lose legitimacy, credibility, reputation, and ultimately income. Competing claims about blame and responsibility usually dominate postcrisis discourse as various parties seek to position themselves strategically in relation to claims about cause. Public explanations seek to share blame, shift blame, create a scapegoat, or simi-larly reduce the organization's culpability (Benoit, 1995a). These explana-tions often become protracted public debates about fault, damage, and cost.

This view of organizational crisis as a narrative structure, with victims harmed by accidents or oversight seeking compensation through a dis-course of competing views of responsibility, is well ingrained in most por-trayals of crisis. This narrative structure frequently recurs in media reports of events such as toxic spills, product recalls, food-borne illnesses, and industrial accidents. As crises become more common and are more fre-quently reported, this view of crisis is continually reified. These general portrayals of crisis, however, are usually simplistic representations of a complex and highly dynamic social phenomenon. Organizational crisis is almost always the consequence of some unanticipated, complex, and long-term interaction(s) between social, psychological, and cultural fac-tors, on the one hand, and technical, structural, and standardized ele-ments on the other (Perrow, 1984). The complexities of these interactions are some of the most salient characteristics of organizational crisis and are becoming even more noticeable as organizational systems continue to evolve toward greater size, diversity, geographic dispersion, complexity, and technological sophistication. Pauchant and Mitroff (1992) viewed organizational crises "as normal events triggered by the complexity of the system itself and by faulty decisions as well as by the interrelationship between technological systems and the humans who attempt to manage them" (p. 20). As Perrow (1984) noted, "Human-made catastrophes appear to have increased with industrialization as we build devices that could crash, burn or explode" (p. 9). The diminished capacity of individu-als to comprehend complex and diverse systems, more centralization of decision making in organizational structures, increasing limitations on public access to information, growing control by experts, and greater sys-tem rigidity are factors enhancing the probability and scope of crises. The increasing complexity of these systems is compounded by unanticipated, unknown, and often unforeseeable interactions. Perrow argued that, in the last 50 years, society has added interactive complexity to a growing list of possible causes of crises.

In addition, the consequences of organizational crisis are more widespread and more comprehensive than usually suggested in the media. Crisis affects the core organization; its managers, employees, and stockholders; customers; suppliers; members of the community; and even its competitors. Primary victims (those affected directly) and secondary victims (their family, friends, and coworkers) may suffer immediate and long-term harm. Other stakeholders—hospitals, police and emergency agencies, the media, governmental agencies, communities, competitors, suppliers, customers, special interest groups, and the courts—are also affected. Often, crises are life-changing occurrences that become archetypal events for both individuals and communities. The Exxon *Valdez* oil spill, the Chernobyl nuclear disaster, the NASA *Challenger* explosion, and the 9/11 attacks have all become social icons, around which broader meaning is constructed, maintained, symbolized, and conveyed. The *Titanic* disaster has taken on iconic proportion as a story of tragedy and hubris. The Three Mile Island accident became profoundly meaningful as a cautionary tale and helped opponents of nuclear power make their case. The 9/11 terrorist attacks have taken on mythic proportions that overshadow many other crises. The meaning of these events, still being sorted out and framed within generalized lessons and beliefs, will filter through society, informing basic understandings about risk, threat, safety, and security. Airport security, building design, evacuation procedures, rescue and recovery methods, social support structures, and law enforcement policies of coordination and cooperation have all been modified according to the lessons of 9/11. The fact that these events disrupted the basic notions of normalcy and have become a lens for interpreting other events is captured in the phrase *a post-9/11 world*.

The consequences of a crisis, however, sometimes include positive outcomes. This "silver lining effect" is usually not immediately evident and may be far outweighed by overwhelmingly negative consequences. Meyers and Holusha (1986) described several potentially positive outcomes of crisis: heroes are made, change is accelerated, latent problems are faced, people are changed, new strategies evolve, new warning systems develop, and new competitive edges appear. Occasionally, organizations focus on victims' needs rather than on strategic explanations of cause designed to avoid blame. In these cases, there is an opportunity to transcend questions of cause and blame and bolster the organization's reputation and legitimacy (Seeger & Ulmer, 2001). Crisis may sometimes precipitate regeneration and renewal as outdated assumptions, procedures, resources, and structures are shed. Resources for change are made available, and resistance to change is reduced. In fact, public issues and events are frequently portrayed rhetorically as crises to justify changes. In this way, crisis may be seen as a fundamental force of social change, renewal, and, ultimately, growth.

For many organizations, crisis is a natural stage of development, grounded in the duality and paradox of deconstruction and construction, organization and disorganization, growth and decline, discord and harmony, decay and renewal, and chaos and "business as usual" (Seeger et al., 1998). This duality links the cycles and stages of system development, suggesting that one may be necessary for the other. "Disorganization is necessary to organization and the chaos of crisis is linked to the routines of business as usual" (Seeger et al., 1998, p. 232). Murphy (1996) argued that crisis acts as "bifurcation points that permanently redefine an organization in a new and unexpected light" (p. 106). Crisis is part of the natural organizational process, purging system elements that are outdated and inappropriate and creating new and unexpected opportunities for development and change, growth, evolution, and renewal. The postcrisis organization is often better matched to its environment and better able to compete.

DEFINING CRISIS

Chemical and nuclear disasters such as the Bhopal Union Carbide accident, the Love Canal and Three Mile Island accidents; major plane crashes such as those of Northwest Airlines Flight 255 and Valujet Flight 592; the sinking of ocean liners, such as the *Edmund Fitzgerald,* and the *Titanic;* space-program disasters such as the *Challenger* explosion; mining disasters such as the one at Buffalo Creek; public-health threats such as the *E. coli* bacteria outbreak at Hudson Foods and Jack-in-the-Box restaurants and the discovery of mad cow disease; public tragedies such as the shootings at Columbine High School; scandals such as the charges of sexual misconduct in the Catholic Church; product recalls and negative publicity such as those involving the Ford Pinto, Firestone's Wilderness XT tires, and the General Motors C/K7 pickup; corporate failures such as the Chrysler Corporation's near bankruptcy and the Enron and Arthur Andersen scandals, as well as many other misfortunes, represent a class of organizationally related events with similar characteristics and consequences.

The word *crisis* comes from the Greek *krisis,* which was used as a medical term by Hippocrates to describe the turning point in a disease, and from *krinein,* meaning to judge or decide. We define organizational crisis as "a specific, unexpected and non-routine organizationally based event or series of events which creates high levels of uncertainty and threat or perceived threat to an organization's high priority goals" (Seeger et al., 1998, p. 233).

Karl Weick (1988) suggested that crises are "low probability/high consequence events that threaten the most fundamental goals of the organization. Because of their low probability, these events defy interpretations and impose severe demands on sensemaking" (p. 305). During crisis, established routines, relationships, norms, and belief systems break down or no longer function. This collapse of sensemaking, which Weick describes as a "cosmological episode," may lead to confused, abnormal, and illogical behaviors that actually accelerate the level of harm. Pauchant and Mitroff (1992) distinguished between an incident, an accident, a conflict, and a crisis. An incident is a limited disruption. An accident is a systemic disruption, but one that does not affect basic assumptions and meanings. Conflict involves a disturbance of symbolic structures. A crisis is "a disruption that physically affects a system as a whole and threatens its basic assumptions, its subjective sense of self, its existential core" (p 12). Fearn-Banks (2002) noted that crisis "interrupts normal business operations and at its worse can threaten the existence of the organizations" (p. 480). In fact, crisis is a primary source of organizational mortality, making organizations vulnerable to takeover or, in some cases, forcing bankruptcy.

Charles Hermann (1963) developed one of the first and most widely used models of crisis through an examination of international political incidents. He argued that crisis includes three fundamental conditions: "(1) threatens high priority values of the organization goals, (2) presents a restricted amount of time in which a decision can be made, and (3) is unexpected or unanticipated by the organization" (p. 64). These three components have been used extensively in the analysis of many organizational crises.

Although all three conditions need not be present, the perception of a serious and credible threat is a requisite feature of all crisis events. Because an anticipated threat is usually avoided, crisis is most often unexpected or surprising. One of the interesting features of most crises, however, is that some participant in the organization is usually aware of the threat but is unable or unwilling to communicate that threat. Short or restricted response time is a consequence of the need to act immediately to manage a crisis and of the close media attention that inevitably follows. Responses are often required for remedial action, and delays in initial response often accelerate harm. Following the *Valdez* oil spill, for example, a number of delays in deploying cleanup equipment significantly enhanced the level of harm.

Media coverage of crisis has become more aggressive and frequent, with the proliferation of news magazines and 24-hour news programs. Typically, the media seeks information about scope of harm, cause, blame, responsibility, and remedial efforts. Generally, the broader the scope of harm and the more dramatic and visual the event, the more extensive the media coverage. The explosion of TWA Flight 800 over Long Island Sound received extensive news coverage because of the scope of harm and because its cause could not be identified.

Organizational crisis precipitates immediate changes and instability in the organizational system in several ways. First, the system is fundamentally disrupted in some basic way. Operations may cease, leaving facilities closed and key personnel distracted, incapacitated, missing, or dead. Although in some cases the impact of the crisis is contained, there is often widespread disruption. Systems disrupted in this manner are less stable, vulnerable to criticism, and susceptible to further crises. Second, the basic belief structures, premises, and assumptions of members are called into question (Pauchant & Mitroff, 1992). This fundamental questioning often concerns well-established beliefs about risk and its relationship to the organization, norms for risk avoidance, and probabilities for the failure of these norms (Turner, 1976). Such questioning may further destabilize the system. Third, organizational members, crisis stakeholders, and the public often experience intense emotional arousal, stress, fear, anxiety, and apprehension, which may compromise their ability to make effective decisions. These responses are often maladaptive and may significantly complicate the effects of a crisis by inhibiting crisis management and response capabilities.

The ability of managers to process information and make well-reasoned choices is often seriously reduced during crisis. Decision theorists note that stressful situations can result in a tendency toward isolation from important sources of information (Gouran, 1982). Decision makers, in effect, cut themselves off at the very moment when timely information is most critical. Following the Exxon *Valdez* oil spill, Chief Executive Officer W. D. Stevens appeared to intentionally disconnect from the situation and did not comment on the crisis for several days.

This phenomenon of reducing access to information during crisis is sometimes called a threat-rigidity response (Staw, Sandelands, & Dutton, 1981). Simply stated, organizations "behave rigidly in threatening situations" as a consequence of a "restriction of information processing" and "constriction of control" (p. 502). Snyder (2001) suggested that threat may result in (1) contraction or withdrawal of authority, (2) conflict, and (3) reduction in the channels of communication (pp. 61–82). Authority systems are often distracted and disrupted by the crisis. Conflict may arise over blame or over the best course of action. Managers often isolate themselves from important sources of information because they believe they need to focus on the crisis or because they simply feel overwhelmed.

Although many similarities exist, important conceptual distinctions are also evident when comparing organizational crisis with other disruptions, such as natural disasters. Natural disasters (earthquakes, floods, drought, severe storms, heat waves, blizzards, hurricanes, tornadoes, volcanic eruptions, mud slides, forest fires, and epidemics) are usually large-scale, environmentally based disruptions that affect entire communities and regions. Earthquakes and hurricanes, for example, periodically create massive destruction. The July 1976 earthquake in Tangshan, China, resulted in an official death toll of 255,000 and unofficial estimates of 650,000. Natural disasters involve normally occurring phenomenon, albeit unusually extreme in intensity, duration, and consequence. These extremes disrupt goods and services transportation; destroy infrastructure and property; and seriously threaten health, safety, and security. In some cases, such as the 1997 North Dakota floods, entire regions are affected. These crises are managed by community, governmental, or social groups such as the Red Cross, FEMA, or other state and local disaster-management agencies (Kreps, 1984). Most state, county, and community governments have professional disaster-management divisions that coordinate carefully with law enforcement agencies. Emergency managers monitor risk factors such as the weather, issue warnings, and help coordinate responses to disasters. Government emergency managers focus on natural disasters, but they may also coordinate responses to severe industrial accidents, such as explosions or toxic spills. In fact, one post-9/11 development has been the significant expansion of the capacity and role of government emergency-management services.

Organizational crises, in contrast, usually involve oversights or system deficiencies associated with a particular organization (Quarantelli, 1988). Organizational crises only occasionally reach the level of harm associated with natural disasters. The Chernobyl nuclear accident, for example, is generally recognized as the worst man-made crisis ever, with approximately fifteen thousand people affected from radiation in the near term and as many as five million affected long term, with at least moderately elevated risks of cancer. When an event is precipitated by the activities of an identifiable agent, such as in an organizational crisis, that agent may be held responsible for the harm (Benoit, 1995a). This responsibility translates into damaged image, legitimacy, and reputation, as well as potentially costly legal liability. By contrast, natural disasters are commonly portrayed as acts of God, consequences of fate that are beyond questions of individual blame, responsibility, and legal liability. Occasionally, organizations strategically seek to portray crises as acts of God. The computer industry, for example, portrayed the Y2K programming glitch as an act of God, rather than an industry flaw or oversight, as it sought immunity from legal liability. Airlines often seek to emphasize the role of weather in crashes, as weather conditions are natural phenomena beyond organizational control.

Organizational activities, however, frequently interact with natural disasters to compound or accelerate harm. Overlogging by timber companies increases the frequency and severity of mud slides. Inappropriate food processing or handling fosters the outbreak of food-borne epidemics.

Man-made greenhouse gases and the resulting global warming will accelerate a number of naturally occurring weather phenomena to the crisis stage. Controlling forest fires by extinguishing small blazes or limiting flooding by building dikes and dams may actually accelerate the harm when a large-scale disaster occurs. Changes in livestock feeding practices, including mixing slaughterhouse refuse with cattle feed, is associated with Creutzfeldt-Jakob, or mad cow, disease. These and many other events suggest that the line between natural and man-made disasters is increasingly unclear. Because these natural/man-made crises derive from the complex, unforeseen, and unanticipated interactions between natural phenomena and human activity, they are particularly difficult to predict, plan for, or control.

Natural disasters may also create extreme stress and threats to crisis-relief agencies. FEMA, for example, was severely criticized in August 1992 for mishandling the relief activities following Hurricane Andrew. Homestead, Florida, was devastated, and FEMA was overwhelmed with the needs of victims. The National Centers for Disease Control and Prevention (CDC) was criticized for its recommendations following the 2001 anthrax scare. The CDC did not immediately recommend that postal workers who might have been exposed to anthrax be placed on antibiotics. In other instances, the failure of relief agencies translates what might otherwise be perceived merely as a serious event into a full-blown disaster. Several city administrations have been severely criticized for inadequate responses to heavy snow storms. In 1999, for example, a storm that might otherwise have been considered a mere nuisance essentially shut down Detroit, Michigan, for nearly a week because the city's snow removal capacity was inadequate.

Finally, it is important to differentiate between organizational crises and two related areas of inquiry: risk communication and issue management. Issues are unresolved questions or perceived problems that arise in the public domain with the potential to affect an organization (Crable & Vibbert, 1985). Issue management is the strategic process of "issue identification, monitoring, and analysis" seeking to influence their resolution in a manner mutually beneficial to the organization and its stakeholders (Heath, 1997, p. 6). Public policy issues are related to crises in two general ways. First, an unresolved public policy issue may lead to crisis. Second, crises may create or reinvigorate public policy issues, particularly at the latter stages of crisis development. The Exxon *Valdez* oil spill, for example, provided significant impetus to the environmental movement. Gaunt and Ollenburger (1995) suggested that issue management is more proactive than crisis communication. Crisis is generally associated with a more restricted time frame than issue management. Risk communication concerns "risk estimates, whether they are appropriately tolerable, and risk consequences" (Heath, 1995, p. 257). Covello (1992) described risk communication as "the exchange of information among interested parties about the nature, magnitude, significance and control of risks" (p. 359). This form of communication is particularly relevant to precrisis stages and the evolving beliefs and norms related to risks.

CRISIS CAUSE

As crises become more common, much effort has been directed toward understanding their causes. The cause of any particular crisis is at some level unique, but a cause may also indicate a general risk factor, such as a faulty mechanical part or flawed procedure, for example, which may precipitate crises in similar systems if not corrected. Each crisis, then, is an important opportunity for system feedback and organizational learning. Usually, sorting out cause is also necessary for resolution and closure. Typically, cause is assessed in the postcrisis stage through careful examination of the facts of the case, including interviewing witnesses, examining direct evidence, and sifting through any crisis remains. Following the *Challenger* shuttle disaster, a presidential commission was charged with determining its cause. The National Transportation Safety Board (NTSB) investigates all civil air disasters, as well as accidents in rail, highway, marine, and pipeline transportation systems to determine probable cause and to issue general recommendations. Determinations of cause are then used to reduce the probabilities of the recurrence of a similar event (Ray, 1999). Three general views about patterns of crisis causality have been offered. These include (1) interactive complexity and normal accident theory, (2) failures in foresight, warnings, and risk perception, and (3) breakdowns in decisional vigilance.

Charles Perrow provided a general model of interactive complexity and crisis in his 1984 book, *Normal Accidents*. Perrow focused his analysis on high-technology systems that, when built on industrial scales, increase the probability of failure. Some forms of crisis are said to be normal in that they are regular expressions of those systems. The technology of flight, for example, when carried to the level of modern air travel, with millions of passengers and facilities and equipment at various levels of repair, is susceptible to occasional crashes. Two characteristics, according to Perrow, make these systems accident prone: interactiveness and tight coupling (p. 72).

Interactiveness is a feature of complex systems and limits the ability of managers to predict and control the system. Large geographically distributed systems such as globalized corporations, for example, cannot be tracked or managed by any single person. Thus, coordination and control is more difficult. Moreover, unforeseen, or "baffling," interactions often occur in such systems, creating the opportunity for crisis. As Perrow (1984) noted: "As systems grow in size and in the number of diverse functions they serve, and are built to function in even more hostile environments, increasing their ties to other systems, they experience more and more incomprehensible or unexpected interactions. They become more vulnerable to unavoidable system accidents" (p. 72). Interactiveness per se is not problematic. All systems are characterized by high levels of interactivity. Systems become vulnerable when interaction is no longer linear or predictable. Increasingly, for example, complex systems are characterized by common mode functions, where one device or structure serves multiple purposes. Many modern-aircraft designers, for example, use fuel tanks as mountings for air conditioner units. These units produce heat and vaporizing fumes, making tanks much more prone to explosion. In addition to common mode function, Perrow describes proximity and indirect information as additional sources of complexity. Systems in close proximity may interact in nonlinear ways. For example, the proximity of communities to the Union Carbide plant in Bhopal significantly enhanced the number of casualties. Feedback about systems performance is often indirect, particularly when it concerns an unforeseen interaction. The crew of the Exxon *Valdez*, for example, had no way of determining how quickly oil was leaking from the damaged tanker.

Tight coupling is the second feature of accident-prone systems. Perrow (1984) described system features where "there is no slack or buffer between two items. What happens to one directly affects what happens to the other" (p. 90). Tight coupling is associated with high levels of efficiency and direct service to markets. In such cases, fewer time delays are possible and less slack is built into the system. Just-in-time inventory systems reduce buffers in production systems. Loosely coupled systems, in contrast, tend to be more ambiguous and flexible. Supervisors, for example, may check to ensure that certain system coordinating functions occur. Tight coupling increases the probability of system failure and the system's ability to minimize damage and recover. Crisis is endemic to complex, tightly coupled systems, and efforts to reduce risk through new technologies, training, or safety devices are not solutions. New technologies always introduce more complexity, a fact that is particularly disturbing because modern organizational systems are evolving to higher levels of complexity.

A second view of cause describes crisis as the consequence of fundamental failures to observe or attend to some emerging risk. These "intelligence failures," or "failures in foresight," are a function of a wide variety of organizational and cultural phenomena (Turner, 1976, p. 381). Turner maintained that "disaster occurs because of some inaccuracy or inadequacy in the accepted norms and beliefs" (p. 381). Beliefs and norms about hazards, precautions, and risks allow members to manage most problems. Crisis, accordingly, involves the interaction of problems judged as insignificant or irrelevant with precautionary norms considered adequate (Seeger et al., 1998, p. 238). Many chemicals, such as PCBs, were once considered relatively safe and were disposed of in unprotected landfills, industrial sites, and even residential sewers. PCBs are now known to be unsafe, and contaminated sites, such as Love Canal, are now serious problems for chemical companies, governmental agencies, and residents.

Pauchant and Mitroff (1992) suggested that organizations become crisis prone when they are highly compartmentalized, emphasize narrow issues, and "fragment complex questions" while relying on restricted numbers of perspectives (pp. 3–4). They reported several instances in which managers were simply unable to admit a crisis was possible because to do so disrupted their sense of personal and organizational identity. The Enron collapse was characterized by a collective rationalization about the stability of this highly successful industry leader. Such rationalizations prevented senior managers from perceiving and understanding the risk.

Failure in foresight is also associated with ineffective communication about an emerging disaster or about the magnitude of the risk. Warnings may go unheeded because the one reporting lacks credibility or because the receiver discounts the report's veracity. Language or cultural barriers may impede warnings about emerging risks. In some cases, the organizational climate itself discourages members from communicating openly and honestly about risks. In many organizations, there is a widespread expectation that messengers bringing bad news will be punished. The tendency of subordinates to respond to this expectation by downplaying bad news is well documented and is associated with a threatening supervisory climate and low levels of trust (Jablin, 1979). This information distortion reduces the ability of a system to be self-reflexive and to recognize an emerging risk in a timely manner. According to Perrow (2001), systems should "solicit skepticism" and "open communication channels to let nagging worry through" (p. 7).

The organization's cultural framework in relation to risk also influences crises. The Exxon *Valdez* disaster may be understood by examining the shipping industry's values. Traditionally, the industry has valued risk, cultivating an image of the sailor as able to overcome the hazards of the sea. In similar cases, risk is seen as a hallmark of good management. The corporate culture of the investment firm Salomon Brothers in the 1980s encouraged greed, ambition, and unbridled competition. The result was a blurring of the legal and the illegal and an eventual crisis (Pinsdorf, 1999, p. 98).

Failures in foresight are almost-universal features of crisis because, in essentially all cases, postcrisis analysis indicates that some warning occurred. To avoid crises, organizations must not only receive warning signs but (also) learn to distinguish between signals that represent real threats and those that represent comparatively minor problems.

A final view of causal elements of crisis is associated with breakdowns in decisional vigilance. This view was popularized by Irving Janis (1972) in his analysis of public policy fiascoes, such as the Bay of Pigs invasion and the Pearl Harbor attack, using the groupthink hypothesis. He noted that many high-status groups made strikingly poor decisions. Janis argued that crises are a function of decisional failure, principally due to inadequate collecting, processing, and critiquing information. Normative group structures, such as pressures for consensus and conformity, may prompt members to discount important information and withhold criticism. Minutes before the NASA *Challenger* disaster, for example, NASA administrators, in a flawed decision, pressured contractor Morton Thiokol's engineers to approve the launch (Gouran, Hirokawa, & Martz, 1986). What is perhaps most striking about breakdowns in decisional vigilance is that in hindsight these decisions are so obviously wrong. The flawed *Challenger* launch decision was made in direct contradiction to elaborate safety protocols. Although specific actions and procedures may reduce the probability of a breakdown in decisional vigilance, organizations regularly continue to make poor, crisis-inducing decisions.

These three views of crisis causality—normal accidents, failures in foresight, and breakdowns in decisional vigilance—are not mutually exclusive. That is, elements of all three are often associated with a particular crisis. Crisis is almost always the consequence of multiple causes and develops over extended periods of time. Sorting out the causal elements of a crisis often becomes a matter of competing claims and interpretations; in some cases, the final cause is never fully determined.

CHARACTERISTICS OF ORGANIZATIONAL CRISIS

Although each organizational crisis is in some ways distinct, common features are usually present. In fact, much of the research to date has been done in an effort to provide detailed descriptions of common features. Specific industries, for example, typically face similar risks and experience similar crises. Airlines experience plane crashes; the food industry struggles with food-borne illnesses. These similarities, although not universal, allow for crisis-type classification and subsequent planning, management, and crisis response.

Many crises have common features in terms of cause, locus, source and location of the threat, and consequences. Product failures and defects, for example, have similar constituencies, threats, and responses, including product warnings and recalls. Transportation accidents are associated with specific industries (airlines, shipping, trucking, railways). Common exigencies include cleanup, questions of equipment failure and operator error, the role of the weather, and examination of procedures, norms, and rules. Similarly, food-borne illness is most closely associated with the meat-packing industry, in the midst of notable recent cases of *E. coli* 0157:-H7 at Hudson Foods and *Listeria* at Bil Mar Foods.

The examination of crisis by type has many advantages. First, it suggests that some specific risks are primarily a function of the organization's environmental contingencies and contexts. Potentially, determining such environmentally specific risks may increase the chances of avoiding a crisis. Second, examination of crisis type may allow for the development of well-matched precautionary norms and contingency plans. Such norms and plans have a much greater probability of effectiveness, given their greater sensitivity to crisis specific issues. Finally, industry or crisis-type sensitive-response contingencies can be developed with specific threats and stakeholders in mind.

Crisis planning reduces uncertainty by putting as much relevant information and as many resources and contingencies in place as possible. The organizational activities and departments relevant to an anticipated crisis—legal department, public relations, chief executive officer, operations, and security—are formed into a crisis-management team. Crisis teams often work with other support agencies to ensure that appropriate crisis-response resources are available and to coordinate response plans. In general, crisis planning and management are useful methods for accommodating the possibility of crisis. However, because crisis is by definition surprising and uncertain, crisis plans inevitably fall short. Nonetheless, comprehensive crisis planning, discussed in chapter 9, remains one of the most effective methods of mitigation.

A third feature of crisis concerns the organization's strategic response. Crisis responses include the communicative strategies employed by an organization in postcrisis conditions. Immediately following an organizational crisis, questions are asked about cause, blame, responsibility, remediation, scope, legal liability, and the need for new precautionary norms and rules (Benoit, 1995a). Depending on the seriousness of the crisis, the magnitude of harm, and the organization's apparent culpability, these questions may represent an intense attack on the organization's image and legitimacy. Postcrisis responses, then, seek to answer these questions and provide adequate interpretations and plausible explanations for the crisis while protecting the legitimacy and image of the organization, limiting legal liability, and restoring a positive image. During postcrisis, however, these goals are often seen as contradictory. Avoiding legal liability is often juxtaposed with the public-communication imperative to be open and honest and give complete explanations.

Examinations of postcrisis responses frequently employ the concept of apologia as a genre of public communication (Benoit, 1995a; Hearit, 1995). Elaborate typologies of postcrisis apologetic and impression-management strategies have been developed to help manage the interpretation of the event and limit its impact on the organization. The persuasiveness and efficacy of the organization's response is a critical factor in the development of the crisis. These typologies, described in greater detail in chapter

8, have been useful in outlining the repertoire of responses available to organizations facing a crisis.

In addition, several researchers have suggested that organizational crises have developmental features and identifiable stages or phases. The punctuation of a crisis event in this way is useful for analyzing and understanding the salient features of crisis, for clarifying interactive factors, and for strategic management. This approach is grounded in the notion that there are precrisis conditions related to the onset of crisis, at least in a temporal, if not a causal, manner. These antecedent conditions involve normative structures, procedural elements, environmental conditions and changes, systems complexity, and a combination of systems complexity in the form of interactive complexity. The actual onset of the crisis is also a discrete stage, and identifiable characteristics include a crisis-triggering event, the onset of threats, accumulation of damage, and the creation of victims. Following the immediacy of the crisis, additional stages develop, including an immediate cleanup phase, where crisis containment and triage occur, and a long-term repair and reconciliation stage, characterized by rebuilding, healing, and image restoration. Finally, postcrisis stages include a return to normal operations, predictability, and renewed system stability. These periods of normality, however, are usually described as the incubation periods for future crises. The developmental features of crisis are detailed in Part 2. The description of these crisis characteristics is important to a more comprehensive understanding of crisis. Specific theoretical frameworks are also useful for understanding crisis.

THEORETICAL APPROACHES TO ORGANIZATIONAL CRISIS

The study of organizational crisis is inherently multidisciplinary, drawing on management, organizational theory, political science, sociology, and psychology. In addition, specialized areas have grown, areas such as hazardous-waste management, logistics, food science, medicine, counseling, decision making, agriculture, and engineering. A large body of practitioner-derived, practice-based knowledge has been developed, including treatment of victims; identification and maintenance of crisis-response resources, equipment, and skills; crisis mitigation strategies for specific crises, such as chemical spills or transportation accidents; crisis logistics; and crisis communication, media management, and community relations. Only recently has a more general body of theory related to organizational crisis developed. Three theoretical frameworks, described briefly here and in greater detail in chapter 2, are useful in the examination of organizational crises. These include chaos theory, Karl Weick's theory of sensemaking, and organizational learning theory.

Chaos theory has only recently been applied broadly within the social sciences and organizational studies and to crisis communication (Murphy, 1996; Seeger, 2002). Chaos theory is an expansion and development of a general-systems theory that described the behavior of large, complex, non-linear systems, including those where social and technical elements inter-act. Despite the common belief that it rejects predictability, chaos theory does seek order, albeit not following established causal and deterministic patterns and models. Chaos theory points to both inherent disorder, ran-domness, and unpredictability and inherent order, patterns, and general predictability in its effort to understand the operation of large, complex systems. From this perspective, "disorganization is necessary to organiza-tion and the chaos of crisis is linked to the routines of business as usual" (Seeger et al., 1998). In complex organizational systems, moments of crisis are often followed by periods of renewal.

A second theoretical framework for understanding organizational crisis is Karl Weick's theory of sensemaking. Weick (1979, 1988) argued that action—including communication—defines, frames, and influences subsequent action. The fundamental exigency of organizing, according to Weick, is equivocality, or the various possible meanings or interpretations of informa-tion. Through communication, organizational participants collectively inter-pret and make sense of their informational environment. Those interpretations that prove useful are retained in a repertoire of responses and subsequent enactments. According to Weick, organization is a function of complex sets of expectations about the environment that influence percep-tions and guide subsequent action, not unlike self-fulfilling prophecies (Weick, 1988). These expectations derive from the industry, background of management, technology, past experiences, or similar influences on beliefs and assumptions. Because the expectation is that the future will look much like the past, new developments and new risks that do not fit existing inter-pretations may be overlooked or ignored.

Organizational learning theory is a third theoretical framework helpful to the examination of crisis. As with chaos theory and sensemaking, learn-ing theory embraces systems perspectives to develop a broad understand-ing of how organizations accommodate experience and information (Cohen & Sproull, 1996). Organizations learn through processes of knowl-edge acquisition, information distribution, information interpretation, and organizational memory (Huber, 1996). Crises, then, may prompt orga-nizational learning. New knowledge, understanding, and insights, for example, often arise as a consequence of a crisis. Crisis creates a time of intense self-reflection and debriefing as members actively seek to under-stand what went wrong and why. Information is rapidly distributed dur-ing a crisis as a consequence of heightened and unified attention. Because crisis creates high uncertainty by disrupting established expectations, it prompts the search for information. Common experiences, such as crisis, promote common interpretative frames, a common bond, and collective understandings. Finally, these crisis-induced interpretations and understandings are stored as stories, structures, procedures, and methods for response in the collective memory.

The processes described in chaos theory, sensemaking, and in organizational learning theory help clarify the dynamic and unanticipated elements that characterize crisis. Moreover, they are useful in constructing a set of plausible expectations related to the evolution and impact of a crisis. Specifically, these frameworks emphasize the role of information, its acquisition, dissemination, interpretation, and application. Taken together, these three perspectives create a rich framework for examining the role of communication in organizational crises.

THE ROLE OF COMMUNICATION IN CRISIS

Communication's role in the examination of organizational crisis roughly parallels the development of traditional approaches to crisis management and the relatively recent emergence of theoretically grounded views. Traditionally, communication (largely public relations, issue management, community relations, and media relations) is associated with postcrisis management and response. This includes disseminating risk mitigation information, such as warnings, to limit harm; communicating with various agencies so that logistics are coordinated; providing clarification of cause, extent of harm, and blame; responding to accusations of wrongdoing; and generally managing the unified public response to the crisis. In many organizations, communication practitioners, along with legal affairs and operations departments, are given the responsibility of creating, maintaining, and communicating the crisis-management plan. This includes media training for crisis spokespersons, establishing and maintaining both internal and external crisis-communication channels, and developing contingent responses and messages for anticipated crisis scenarios.

More recently, however, views about the role of communication in organizational crisis have significantly expanded. Drawing on the models suggested by Weick (1979, 1988, 1995), on notions of learning organizations, and on principles suggested by chaos theory, we argue that communication relates to all aspects of organizational crisis, including incubation in precrisis, manifestation in crisis, and postmortem and ultimate recovery during postcrisis. From this perspective, communication is epistemic, allowing organizational participants to come to know and understand various aspects of the system and its environment, including the existing dynamic relationships and their risks. The creation and retention of meaningful interpretations among organizational participants in response to equivocality is the general mechanism whereby crisis begins, develops, and is resolved. These interpretations are also critical in reaching consensus on cause, responsibility, and blame. These views of communication and crisis, described in detail in chapter 4, along with the emerging theoretical approaches to the organizational crisis outlined in chapter 2, create an opportunity to understand crisis in new and more-complete ways.

SUMMARY

The following chapters review and synthesize the rich and diverse body of theory, research, and practice concerning communication and organizational crisis. This review incorporates a broad view of organizational crisis and of the role of communication in the development and response to crisis. Organizational crisis is presented as a natural stage in organizational evolution, creating not only stress and threats but also opportunities for growth and development. Communication is viewed as the pivotal process in the creation and maintenance of organization and as central to the avoidance and/or management of organizational crisis.

The book is organized into four parts. In Part 1, we present the theory of organizational crisis, including a discussion of crisis type and the role of communication in organizational crisis. In Part 2, we discuss crisis development through various stages or phases, including precrisis, crisis, and postcrisis. Each stage is examined and its characteristics and their associated communication requirements are described, with extended examples. In Part 3, we examine pragmatic issues of crisis management, including crisis planning, crisis teams, and risk communication. In Part 4, we examine the role of crisis in light of other organizational issues, including ethics, leadership, and the larger role of crisis in society. Throughout the book, we draw on a number of examples and cases to illustrate features of crisis. We ground our discussions in the expectation that (at least theoretically) all crises can be avoided, but that the development of crises, given system complexity and emerging risks, is inevitable. Although crises are inevitable, a more complete understanding of them can reduce their frequency and improve their management when the inevitable occurs.

CHAPTER 2

Theories of Organizational Crisis

A number of general systems-based theoretical frameworks of organizations have been expanded and adapted to understand crisis. These views of crisis emphasize uncertainty, the novelty of the situation, and the potential threat to established routines and order. Theories of organizational crisis are most often grounded in systems perspectives, emphasizing the dynamic relationship between the organization and its larger social, technological, physical, legal, and cultural context. The theories discussed in this chapter are organized around the basic assumption that crises are recurring events that play a critical role in the life cycle of the organizational structures of businesses, corporations, governments, and communities. They seek to understand the factors associated with the onset of crisis, how organizations and social structures respond to and make sense of a crisis, and the impact of crisis on stakeholders, social systems, and on larger understandings of threat and risk. From these perspectives, crisis is understood as a broad class of events that are disruptive, unanticipated, and threatening and that have the potential to lead to both positive and negative outcomes.

This chapter explores three general organizational theories and their implications for crisis: sensemaking (Sutcliffe, 2001; Weick, 1979, 1995), chaos theory (Butz, 1997; Keil, 1994; Murphy, 1996; Seeger, 2002), and organizational learning theory (Huber, 1991; Senge, 1990; Weick & Ashford, 2001).

SENSEMAKING

Sensemaking has developed into a general theory of organization over the last three decades. Rather than adopting an approach whereby an established strategic structure influences behavior or where structure follows the behavior of members, Sutcliffe argued that structure emerges from the collective efforts of members to make sense of or construct their informational environment (Sutcliffe, 2001). Organizing is, therefore, a dynamic and ongoing process of social construction. Weick (1979) summarized his broad view of the socially constructed nature of the organizing process as, "How can I know what I think until I see what I say?" (p. 5). This process is inherently retrospective as members look back on events and construct their meanings. Communication is central to this process as members share meanings to create a collective sense of the informational environment. The principal problem for organizations, Weick suggested, is resolving or reducing environmental uncertainty, or equivocality. There is an ongoing need to determine how to know what to think. Equivocality concerns the various possible interpretations associated with some informational input. Those interpretations that prove most useful are retained in the form of structures, procedures, policies, methods, assumptions, and responses. This process of reducing or resolving equivocality through shared interpretations, or sensemaking devices and responses, represents the ongoing process of enactment leading to organizing. Enactment is a social process whereby a material and symbolic record of action is laid down and made available for subsequent action (Smircich & Stubbard, 1985, p. 726).

Weick (1979) identified specific phases or stages to organizing, including enactment, selection, and retention. Enactment, the first stage, occurs in acting toward something by saying something, or by choosing to notice some informational input. Organizations, for example, choosing to attend to, or frame, some information as a strategic contingency are forced to interpret or respond to that contingency. Therefore, organizations often choose to ignore information that may represent forewarnings of crisis until the crisis erupts and can no longer be ignored. This denial may be conscious or it may be a collective blindness manifest because the issue is too large, complex, threatening, or simply beyond control. Organizational enactment is by definition selective. Through boundary-spanning and environmental-monitoring activities, stimuli or informational inputs are made available. It is not possible, however, to attend to the entire body of available information. Factors such as history of attending to an issue; previous commitment; the relative prominence of information; the capacity to perceive; the perceived saliency of the information; background and experience of top management; and issues of access are all factors in enactment.

If, for example, an organization has a history of attending to a particular kind of information, it will do so in the future. Airlines, for example, continue to ask passengers highly standardized questions about luggage even when the usefulness of those questions in identifying threats has been largely discounted. Managers with technical backgrounds are more comfortable attending to technical matters than to human resource issues. Issues that are less familiar and less well defined, such as a nonspecific threat or warning, may be more difficult to frame, attend to, and make sense of. Capacity concerns the number of organizational members with the appropriate perspectives, background, and abilities. Following the 9/11 World Trade Center disaster, for example, a shortage of Arabic translators limited the amount of intelligence information that could be processed. Weick (1979) coined the phrase *requisite variety* to describe the relative variety of enactment capacity available within an organization. He observed that organizational variety is required to attend to and address variety in informational inputs. For example, organizations that include no highly placed female executives may have difficulty attending to and resolving issues of sexual harassment (Snyder, 2001). Finally, issues of access to top organizational decision makers influences enactment. Access is tightly controlled by gatekeepers who determine what kinds of information will be presented. If information is not available, it cannot be taken into account. Many crises, including the 9/11 terrorist attacks, the collapse of Enron, and the Catholic Church sex scandal, are characterized by failure to recognize or attend to some informational input. Weick's concept of selective enactment offers a plausible explanation for these failures.

Selection, the second stage, is the process of choosing a sensible interpretation for the informational input. Selection requires that members test various interpretations to determine which may reduce or resolve the equivocality. Following a crisis, for example, organizations are usually forced to offer explanations of cause, blame, and responsibility. Typically, they initially favor explanations that will cause the least legal and economic liability. If these explanations are adequate or effective, they are likely to be retained. The recent issue of defective Firestone Wilderness XT tires found on Ford Explorers, for example, involved competing sensemaking interpretations. Firestone, although acknowledging some problems with their tires, interpreted the rollover accidents of Ford Explorers as an automobile design flaw. Ford, in contrast, described these events as solely tire problems. Often, particular interpretations are retained until they are demonstrated as inadequate. Thus, Exxon's initial interpretation was that the *Valdez* oil spill was minor and that it posed no environmental risk. This interpretation was only replaced when the information, in this case reports regarding the volume of oil in the water, no longer accounted for the "no environmental risk" interpretation. Selection, then, has important implications for long-term decisions and actions, particularly as they are retained for subsequent decisions and actions.

Retention, the third step in Weick's (1979) model, involves using interpretations for subsequent sensemaking. Responses that have proved effective in reducing equivocality become part of the organization's established repertoire. When an event or input occurs that is similar to a previous event, the organization will survey its repertoire of retained responses and select those that may appear most helpful or appropriate. Thus, patterns of responses develop around common events. Retained responses eventually become the policies, procedures, routines, and methods of organizing. They are rooted in earlier interpretations that are subsequently carried on throughout the ongoing process of organizing. Organizations, then, can be thought of as complex sets of retained responses and the associated decisions and structures. As Weick (1995) noted, "The product of enactment is not an accident, an afterthought, or a byproduct. Instead it is an orderly, material, social construction that is subject to multiple interpretations. Enacted environments contain real objects such as reactors, pipes and values. The existence of these objects is not questioned but their significance, meaning, and content is" (p. 307). These enactments are "summarized internally by people in the form of a plausible map by which observed actions produce observed consequences" (Weick, 1988, p. 307). These "cause maps" are internal cognitive structures, if–then assertions, that influence perception about past and future events (Weick & Bougon, 1986). Members may have come to understand, for example, that calling attention to potential problems results in or causes superiors to view them less positively. As a consequence of member consensus and internalization of this cause map, management is buffered from bad news, and problems often go unaddressed (Weick & Sutcliffe, 2001, p. 11).

Organizations, then, exist both in the material environment and in the cognitions, beliefs, and cause maps of members. They are stable in the sense that consensual interpretations, retained responses, retained repertoire, and cause maps are semipermanent as they become enacted in the material environment. They are dynamic in that the informational environment and the various possible interpretations of it are in constant flux. Weick (1979) viewed organization as an ongoing, messy, and confusing jumble of changing and unchanging, competing and complementary interpretations.

Enactment and Crisis

Enactment as a consensual human process leading to organization is inherently dependent on human participants. These participants overlook things, ignore, forget, misrepresent and misspeak, have biases, blind spots, prejudices, and assorted other attributes that influence enactment. The enactment process is not logical, orderly, and systematic, but messy, illogical, and often incomplete. Weick (1979), for example, noted that organizational processes such as socializing, consensus building, and vicarious learning often result in a "pluralistic ignorance" about environments. The result is a kind of "stunted enactment," or collective blindness, that precludes the organization from enacting, or attending to, some (often critical) aspect of its environment. Weick (1988) has described three influences of enactment with particular relevance to crisis: enactment from commitment, enactment from capacity, and enactment from expectations.

Commitment concerns the fact that behavior often precedes understanding. During crisis, critical and irrevocable decisions often must be initiated without time to fully consider the implications. Decisions that are public, volitional, and irrevocable are often followed by retrospective explanations or tenacious justifications. Often, initial actions provide a necessary initial structure or interpretation to allow for subsequent, crisis-reducing action (Weick, 1988, p. 310). When Aaron Feuerstein, chief executive officer (CEO) of Malden Mills, announced immediately following a devastating plant fire that he would rebuild and continue to pay workers, the intensity of the crisis was reduced and participants began planning for rebuilding (Seeger & Ulmer, 2001). In other instances, however, commitment and tenacious justification can lead to crisis-enhancing positions. The decision by the State of Alaska not to approve chemical dispersants on the *Valdez* oil spill resulted in tenacious, public, and competing justifications on the part of the State of Alaska and Exxon.

Capacity is a fundamental influence on enactment. As noted earlier, background of top management and requisite variety limit the ability to initially perceive or enact an informational input. High turnover in top management and chronic understaffing also limit ability to perceive and understand an emerging risk. Systems may also be so complex and dynamic that the human capacity to perceive is overwhelmed. Capacity is clearly related to the initial perception of risk. Crises are usually accompanied by a sense of being blindsided, of having no warning. In retrospect, however, almost all crises are accompanied by warnings, albeit often subtle and outside established channels of communication. Capacity as an influence on crisis, then, is related to requisite variety and to structures and systems for monitoring risk and communicating that risk to appropriate decision makers.

On a more basic level, however, capacity concerns the perception among members that their actions can influence outcomes. As Weick (1988) noted, "[P]eople see those events they feel they have some capacity to do something about" (p. 311). Often a collective blindness develops with regard to some emerging threat because of perceived powerlessness. Simply stated, organizational members who feel helpless with regard to some issue may collectively ignore that issue. Comfort, Sungu, Johnson, and Dunn (2001), for example, observed that when a disaster is perceived to be an act of God and beyond control, members often take little action. In contrast, those who are empowered can afford to see more and do more. Weick (1988) suggested that seeing the larger picture may also be helpful in resolving a crisis: "[T]he more a person sees in a given situation, the higher the probability that the person will see the specific actions that need to be made to dampen the crisis" (p. 311). During a crisis, actors often undertake specific actions to reduce their perceived powerlessness and to create the impression that they are making a difference. Following the 9/11 terrorist attack, for example, hundreds of millions of dollars in donations were made to related charities by individuals seeking to help with the crisis. Immediately following the Exxon *Valdez* oil spill, commercial fishermen in the affected areas used their boats and nets to block the oil slick from damaging a critical fish hatchery. In preparation for the anticipated Y2K computer disruption, millions of households took at least the basic steps of stocking up on batteries, nonperishable food, and bottled water.

Capacity also concerns authority, its delegation throughout a hierarchical system, and its performance during crisis. In highly stratified hierarchies, the capacity to both perceive a crisis and act on it is similarly compartmentalized. The *Challenger* shuttle disaster was associated in part with a launch decision made from a management perspective as opposed to an engineering perspective. The compartmentalization of these two authority systems allowed information about potential safety problems to be ignored (Gouran, Hirokawa, & Martz, 1986). Compartmentalization allows members to construct plausible deniability regarding risks, so that members choose not to know about some issues. Moreover, in crisis situations, authority often contracts as the system struggles to refocus on the crisis. Authority may be cut off due to system disruptions or because leaders withdraw to focus on the crisis. Determining who is in charge becomes unclear, and action is consequently postponed. In the case of the Bhopal, India, Union Carbide crisis, CEO Warren Anderson was arrested and held by Indian authorities, seriously crippling the ability of the company to respond (Seeger & Bolz, 1996).

Finally, enactment from expectation concerns the assumptions of managers as a kind of self-fulfilling prophecy (Weick, 1988, p. 313). As with other crisis-related enactments, expectations influence crisis both at the pre- and postcrisis stages. In the Bhopal disaster, Union Carbide management viewed the plant as unimportant. Consequently, few resources and limited management attention was available, ultimately helping to precipitate the crisis. Similarly, during crisis, responses are often rooted in preexisting cause maps and sensemaking devices that are inadequate for the current situation. Managers often respond to nonroutine crisis events using routine response strategies.

Weick (1993) has also described a more generalized form of crisis related "collapse of sensemaking." These collapses are associated with the onset of some threatening situation and maladaptive responses that preclude appropriate action or accentuate harm. In his analysis of the Mann Gulch disaster, Weick points to the sudden loss of meaning that resulted in members of a smoke-jumper team abandoning well-established safety norms and procedures. Thirteen members of the team died in one of the worst disasters in the history of the National Forest Service. Weick called these losses of meaning "cosmological episodes...when people suddenly and deeply feel that the universe is no longer a rational, orderly system. What makes such an event so shattering is that both the sense of what is occurring and the means to rebuild that sense collapse together (p. 633). Cosmological episodes involve fundamental loss of understanding regarding what is happening and what can be done about it. Decision makers become so completely disoriented that they simply lose the capacity to respond. Such losses in sensemaking are not uncommon in the high-uncertainty, high-stress, and truncated-response window of crisis.

One of the implications of Weick's cosmological analysis is that previous experience with a crisis may enhance the ability of members to make sense of a related event. In others words, experiencing a crises may enhance the ability of participants to know how to respond. One of many ironies of the 9/11 World Trade Center disaster is that an earlier attempt to destroy the building enhanced the ability of occupants to know what to do. Having been through a similar, albeit less serious, episode, many knew how to react and were able to quickly evacuate the towering buildings. Conversely, however, members may also interpret a more serious event through the lens of a previous experience with a minor event. In this way, minor crises may create additional blind spots, particularly with organizations that routinely experience moderate threats and disruptions.

Crisis, due to its intensity and high equivocality, is well suited to enactment-based approaches, including interpretation and sensemaking. Crises are "low probability high consequence events that place severe demands on sensemaking" (Weick, 1988, p. 305). Crisis is a context of compressed time and consequence, where actions may intensify the crisis before understanding emerges. Enactment-based approaches focus attention on how messages and retained interpretations influence crisis development. One explanation for the value of immediate and open communication following a crisis is that it provides the necessary informational inputs for crisis stakeholders to engage in sensemaking. In addition, an enactment-based view empowers organizational actors to both prevent crises and reduce their intensity.

Organizations, however, often become trapped in enactments that preclude taking into account some emerging contingency. The Chrysler Corporation of the early 1980s continued to produce cars for shrinking markets, using methods and facilities that encouraged inefficiency. Following the onset of a crisis, new sets of sensemaking interpretations must be constructed and communicated. New understandings of risk and new precautionary norms and procedures were necessary following the 9/11 disaster. The need to make sense of a disrupting and unanticipated set of events is one of the most salient features of crisis. Weick's (1988) approach focuses researchers' attention on messages and how the interpretations and retained responses they include influence crisis development, including onset and resolution. Finally, enactment argues that actors construct the enacted environments, including crisis environments. Enactment highlights members' own actions and decisions as determinants of the conditions they seek to prevent (p. 316). Sensemaking can serve as the basis for an "ideology of crisis prevention and management" in which members are empowered to see the causes of crisis, to avoid them, and to reduce their intensity (p. 315).

CHAOS THEORY

Unlike enactment, which focuses on a socially constructed reality, chaos theory (CT) assumes objective structures and processes albeit existing in such a complex and dynamic form as to defy simplistic explanation. In fact, CT has been described as antithetical to traditional linear, mechanical, and static approaches of science (Gleick, 1987). Murphy (1996) even suggested that "chaos theory represents a postmodern departure" from social science orientations grounded in assumptions and epistemologies imported wholesale from the physical sciences (p. 96). CT describes a broad set of complex and loosely related theoretical and metatheoretical orientations to the behaviors of dynamic, nonlinear systems. Within these orientations are perspectives regarding predictability, scale and perspective, and the nature of order and organization.

CT has since emerged as a general framework for understanding complex system behavior in a number of fields. This includes psychology, economics, sociology, anatomy, medicine, political science, computer science, decision making, criticism, urban development, organizational studies, and crisis communication and management (Butz, 1997; Hayles, 1990; Matthews, White, & Long, 1999; Robertson & Combs, 1995). More recently, CT has been described as a powerful framework for understanding crisis, including how complex systems move in and out of crisis and the larger role of crisis in system development and evolution (Comfort et al., 2001). CT's utility in understanding complex systems is probably best illustrated by Charles Perrow's (1984) work on "normal accident" theory. As discussed in chapter 1, complexity, interactiveness, and tight coupling make systems inherently accident prone (p. 72). Although such complex systems can be designed in ways to enhance their reliability system, complexity is inherently related to nonlinearity. Moreover, systems and technology are increasingly characterized by interactive, tightly coupled complexity; nonlinearity; and instability. As Comfort et al. (2001) observed, many organizations increasingly face "permanent whitewater," characterized by "social, economic, and political environments fraught with risk and rapid change" (p. 144).

CT is a series of loosely related principles regarding the behavior of complex and dynamic systems. It does not offer specific predictions, largely because CT views systems as too complex and dynamic for such precision. The principles of CT are, therefore, inherently general, broad-based in scope, and spatially and temporally widely distributed. Murphy (1996) noted that unlike the worldview of traditional science, CT does not suggest that universal laws make it possible to generalize from small samples to entire systems (p. 98). Chaotic systems are complex, and the principals used to describe them must be sufficiently general and flexible to reflect these essential properties. The principles of CT discussed here include predictability within chaos, sensitive dependence on initial conditions, bifurcation as system disruption, and self-organization and renewal through fractals and strange attractors.

Predictability within Chaos

Most popular descriptions begin by suggesting that CT is a fatalistic portrayal of systems that rejects all predictability. CT, however, does describe systems as having a kind of pattern and general predictability although with an order, logic, and scale that does not conform to traditional causal and deterministic models (Hayles, 1990). Newtonian causal logic, linear proportionality of variables, and reductionist methods are viewed as too simplistic to explain the dynamics of complex systems (Kauffman, 1993; Matthews et al., 1999). Multidirectional and interactive causality, minor variance, inability to infinitely specify initial conditions, and unforeseen, immeasurable sources of variance affect system behavior in unforeseeable ways. General trends and patterns of chaotic systems may become evident over broad scales and wide time frames. Chaotic systems must, therefore, be viewed holistically and without assumptions of traditional causality.

The holistic order of chaotic systems derives from underlying structures and processes that function to constitute and reconstitute order, balance, and stability. Even following severe system disruption, what CT terms bifurcation, complex systems reestablish pattern, stability, structure, and eventually order (Kauffman, 1993). This ability to reorganize or regenerate derives from internal forces and processes. Moreover, this bifurcation "may be the necessary precursor of a higher level of order" (Keil, 1994, p. 4). This idea that disorder is necessary to order, decay a precursor to renewal, and collapse a step in rebuilding is one of the most appealing features of CT and is illustrative of the broad-based and generalized search for order that it proposes (Murphy, 1996; Seeger, Sellnow, & Ulmer, 1998).

Sensitive Dependence on Initial Conditions

Probably the best-known concept of CT is sensitive dependence on initial conditions. Sensitive dependence on initial conditions serves as the basic tenant regarding the difficulty of accounting for variance. Stewart (1989), in a popular example, described this principal by referencing the minor variance in weather systems created by a butterfly:

The flapping of a single butterfly's wing today produces a tiny change in the state of the atmosphere. Over a period of time, what the atmosphere actually does diverges from what it would have done. So, in a month's time, a tornado that would have devastated the Indonesian coast doesn't happen. Or maybe one that wasn't going to happen, does. (p. 141)

This description of complex systems emphasizes their openness and sensitivity to influences, many of which cannot be measured or understood using traditional methods. Minor variability, background noise, or error variance, in combination with absence of "infinite precision in the measurement of initial conditions" suggests that traditional concepts of predictability are impossible (Matthews et al., 1999, p. 446). What is perhaps best illustrated by Stewart's example is that the state of a system at any give time cannot be known, just as it would be impossible to quantify the impact of a butterfly's wings. Because the performance of a system is a function of its initial condition, its subsequent behavior cannot be predicted.

Kiel (1994) described the role of communication in the *Challenger* disaster as an example of this butterfly effect. "The butterfly—in this case an error in communication—generated amplifying effects that had unexpected outcomes, posing a new set of problems for the space agency...that still lingers today" (p. 7). The absence of clear measurement of initial conditions and understanding of their impact, along with the concomitant reduction in certainty and predictability, undermines accurate and confident forecasts. Similar examples of a small error being amplified into a systemwide crisis are associated with many crises. In Bhopal, India, the "butterfly" was the failure to insert a small metal plate during a pipe-washing procedure. For the flight crew of Northwest Flight 255, a failure to follow a preflight checklist led to crisis. In the case of Hudson Beef's *E. coli* contamination, an unknown quantity of contaminated beef entering the plant was amplified into a nationwide recall. "Reworking" procedures for broken or malformed patties amplified the error by cross-contaminating subsequent meat.

Bifurcation as System Breakdown

According to CT, organizational crises are points of system bifurcation. Bifurcation represents the flash point of disruption and change at which a system's direction, character, and/or structure is fundamentally altered. Bifurcations are the "abrupt, discontinuous, and divergent changes in the formal system" where the basic, established system equilibrium breaks down (Matthews et al., 1999, p. 445). Bifurcations are intersections that occur when system instability reaches a level where return to the previous order is increasingly difficult. Such systems face increasing disorder and eventually bifurcate from the previous pattern (Butz, 1997, p. 11). The onset of bifurcation may be predictable, given that it is a function of the level of variance and instability in the system. At moments of radical change, bifurcation is the point at which previous assumptions, methods, patterns, and relationships can no longer function. Therefore, crises become mechanisms of rapid system change and reorganization (Comfort et al., 2001).

Chaos theory suggests that within all complex systems, even those with the appearance of stability and order, there is the potential for bifurcation. In general, however, bifurcation occurs most often when systems reach higher levels of complexity and nonlinearity. At these levels, unanticipated, novel variance is more likely to be amplified and/or interact with other elements in ways that produce bifurcation. Systems with higher states of exchange with their environments are also typified by higher levels of instability and periodic bifurcation. Such systems must confront a wider array of variance. Crisis researchers often describe these open systems as functioning within more hostile and dynamic contexts and argue that such contexts increase the probability of crisis (Smart & Vertinsky, 1977). As organizational environments evolve toward even greater complexity, dynamism, and hostility, bifurcation will be more common. The phrase "change is the only constant" has become a common refrain for many managers.

Self-Organization

Self-organization is a "natural process" whereby the underlying order of the system reemerges from the randomness and chaos of bifurcation (Matthews et al., 1999). Self-organization seeks to understand how complex open systems can generate new forms of order out of chaos (Matthews et al., 1999). Following the chaos of the 9/11 terrorist attacks, for example, new kinds of order emerged in a number of affected systems, including the financial, airline, and tourism industries. New hierarchies, norms, policies, priorities, and markets emerged as resources were reallocated. Many systems, such as airline security, began operating with higher levels of complexity even as volume slowed. Comfort (1999) described self-organizing processes that emerged following the Whittier Narrows earthquake of 1987. After the collapse of traffic signals, self-appointed "citizen traffic cops" spontaneously left their cars and began coordinating traffic flow. Following the 9/11 attacks, Washington D.C.'s Dulles Airport was closed for security reasons. Many passengers were stranded, and some were forced to walk to other locations. Many of those leaving the airport by car began stopping and picking up pedestrians along the freeway, thus helping alleviate some of the disruption. Auf Der Heide (1989) suggests that rather than being paralyzed into inaction by a "disaster syndrome," most individuals are able to orient themselves relatively quickly, self-organize, and begin undertaking appropriate responses.

These reordering or reorganizing processes are sometimes characterized as the mirror image or antithesis of chaos (Matthews et al., 1999). Kauffman (1993), who referred to self-organization as a kind of antichaos, argues that highly disorganized systems often spontaneously solidify into a higher degree of order in a kind of system evolution. This new order arises from inner guidelines and principles rather than being imposed by external forces. Systems have some underlying drive or momentum for order, although the relationship between order and chaos is complex and dynamic. The self-organizing ability of systems is attributed in part to system continuity even at moments of bifurcation (Murphy, 1996, p. 100). While bifurcation denotes a breaking of the old order, the elements of that previous order serve as continuing reference points or components out of which the new order arises. The history of a system is a force, or attractor, of continuity in reconstituting organization.

As a quasi-evolutionary force, self-organization is continually impelling systems to higher levels of complexity and order following the collapse or bifurcation of lower-order systems (Kauffman, 1993). Through self-organization, new forms, structures, procedures, hierarchies, and understanding emerge, whereas outdated procedures, technologies, and assumptions are discarded, giving a fundamentally new form or shape to the system. In part, this is because the disruption of crisis vividly demonstrates the inadequacy of the previous system and allows for a suspension of the assumption of the status quo. In this way, much of the change-limiting inertia of systems is removed. Components may be refined or replaced when appropriate, or simply discarded. This principal is commonly accepted as critical to the health and development of many complex natural systems, such as forests and river deltas, where fires and floods are seen as both sources of destruction and renewal. Seeger and Ulmer (2001) described how fire can also become a renewing force for organizations. In the case of Cole Hardwoods, a devastating fire destroyed the company's facility and 14.5 million board feet of stock. The fire also created the opportunity to rebuild a much more efficient facility using new technology and more rational processes of work flow.

Self-organization is one of the most optimistic elements of chaos theory, suggesting that in many crises there is a sort of silver-lining effect, in which disruption creates renewal. It serves as the counterbalance to the inevitable disruption, disorder, and harm. It is important to emphasize, however, that self-organizing processes do not alleviate the damage created by crisis and in many instances do not function as significant forces of renewal. Crisis, for example, remains a major force in organizational mortality, usually occurring through the mismanagement of some crisis-related event. In some cases, self-organization processes lead to the abandoning of outdated components, operations, and divisions. Chaos theory suggests that embedded in every crisis is at least the potential for some form of self-organization.

Fractals and Self-Organization

Probably the most eloquent features of chaos theory are the elaborate self-repeating system patterns and forms known as fractals. These patterns were initially described in the measurement of geographic features, such as mountain ranges and shorelines. Fractals concern measurement of complex systems and the need for measurement to take into account the issues of complexity, perspective, and scale. Qualitative issues of perspective must be considered when examining complex systems. One's viewpoint on a complex system will fundamentally influence what is seen. Fractals argue that standard "quantitative units of measurement may be poor yardsticks" to describe a complex world (Murphy, 1996, p. 100).

In addition, self-similarity or correspondence exists within these qualitative perspectives. Although differing scales or perspectives yield different results, similar patterns of order appear. These "self-similar" structures, or "fractal sets," are repeated throughout the system, exhibiting constant patterns or similar "degrees of irregularity...over different scales," albeit at levels of high complexity (Gleick, 1987, p. 8). Fractal patterns are a function of bifurcation and self-organization in that each successive level is based on the order of the previous level. Fractals are, therefore, self-referential in a manner that establishes pattern and continuity (Murphy, 1996, p. 100).

The term *fractal* was derived from the Latin term *fractus*, meaning to break or to create irregular fragments. These fragmented and irregular forms do not correspond to established Euclidean geometric principles. As Mandelbrot (1977) stated, "Clouds are not spheres, mountains are not cones, coastlines are not circles and bark is not smooth, nor does lightening travel in straight lines" (p. 95). Standard methods of description and analysis, therefore, are not adequate for these complex fractal patterns and forms.

Fractals have been documented in a wide array of natural and physical phenomena: plant structures, economic trend data, stock market values, geographic features, cloud patterns, fluid dynamics, weather patterns, and artery, vein, and nerve structure (Butz, 1997; Gleick, 1987). The underlying pattern of fractals provides one important form of order and structure to chaotic systems. Fractals, in both their complexity and in their self-similarity, are part of the basic structure of order, complexity, and continuity of systems. As with the larger tenets of CT, fractals point to both inherent complexity and pattern in chaotic systems.

Strange Attractors and Self-Organization

A second level of system order and structure occurs through attractors. An attractor is a basic organizing or ordering principle, a deep structure, an inherent shape or state of affairs to which a phenomenon will always return as it evolves even through recurring bifurcation (Butz, 1997; Murphy, 1996). This underlying order in a chaotic system constrains variance and serves as a regulating force. Attractors also help reconstitute a system following bifurcation. In simple systems, a fixed-point attractor influences system performance over time as a kind of constant, uni-dimensional force. Simple gravitational pull is often cited as an example. A limit-cycle attractor governs and limits the performance of a system through multiple dimensions but does so in relatively predictable ways. Centrifugal force, gravity, and the force exerted by a pitcher limit and constrain the movement of a baseball in relatively predictable ways. Strange attractors, most closely associated with chaotic systems, operate on systems through multiple dimensions and in unanticipated ways. Attractors are strange in the sense that they do not operate from any fixed point or in linear ways (Butz, 1997). The point of attraction may be fragmented across time and several dimensions of space so that "an object in this attraction would move about unpredictably" (p. 13).

Strange attractors take the form of general and fundamental social assumptions, values, first principles, conflicting tensions, contradictions, or oppositional paradoxes to which a social system naturally and continually returns. They are the touchstones that pull complex systems toward order. Such order is evident when a river returns to the familiar oxbow shape following a flood, or when hierarchy and pyramidal forms of organizational structure reemerge. In other cases, attractors such as family, community, and economic ties and values, which can lead to rebuilding a city following a natural disaster, are more subtle. The near bankruptcy of Chrysler Corporation in 1982 attracted a diverse and wide-ranging coalition of supporters. This included banks, competitors, unions, state and local governments, dealers, suppliers, civil rights organizations, and even national sports franchises—all supporting federal loan guarantees for Chrysler. The attraction of common threat throws groups together and demonstrates commonalties and overarching goals. New patterns of interdependence and mutually beneficial relationships create new lines of attraction, cooperation, and order. Bifurcation creates a moment in which the status quo is suspended and established relationships are amenable to a fundamental reordering.

Crisis Communication and CT

As with general systems theory, CT as a framework for crisis functions best at the paradigmatic or metatheoretical level. The emphasis on the dual, ordered–disordered nature of highly complex and dynamic nonlinear systems makes chaos theory particularly useful for the study of crisis. Organizational crisis usually involves the radical failure of such systems due to unpredictable or unforeseen interactions and interdependencies. Moreover, CT outlines specific mechanisms for recovery and postcrisis reorganization that are helpful in crafting an understanding of renewing aspects of crisis. This silver-lining effect suggests that crisis is a force of renewal of systems, creating new higher-order systems following bifurcation. Chaos theory, then, has specific implication for understanding crisis and communication.

First, CT suggests that precise and confident predictions regarding system performance are not possible. Traditionally, postcrisis communication has emphasized precise messages as a way of reducing threat and uncertainty. Some have suggested, however, that such precision is not always warranted, nor indeed ethical (Ulmer & Sellnow, 2000). CT suggests that these predictions are simply not accurate. A precise message may create an unwarranted sense of security and accentuate harm. Unequivocal statements by scientists from the Centers for Disease Control and Prevention (CDC) regarding the risk of anthrax and exposure of postal workers were subsequently retracted. CDC staff members, having no experience with "weaponized" anthrax distributed through modern mail systems, had relied on decades-old epidemiological studies. Unanticipated anthrax hot spots on mail-sorting machines and cross-contamination of letters forced officials to admit that precise predictions about exposure and risk could not be made.

CT also suggests that communication may be a form of bifurcation-producing variance. Small variances in communication processes, message form or content, timing, or other factors may produce wide fluctuations and bifurcation. Keil's (1994) analysis of variance in patterns of communication between NASA and its contractors and its relationships to the *Challenger* disaster and Ray's (1999) examination of minor miscommunication between air traffic controllers and pilots and its role on airline disasters demonstrate that variance in communication, messages, and meaning produces crisis. Communication is a fundamental coordinating process in organized systems. Breakdowns in coordination, such as those described above, are often associated with crisis. In fact, almost all organizational crises have at their base some form of communication breakdown.

Third, CT's emphasis on longitudinal patterns of self-organization suggests that managers should focus beyond the short-term dynamics of crisis to larger patterns of crisis and self-organization. Current trends in management focus on the organization's quarter-to-quarter performance. Managers are pressured to maximize short-term profit even at the expense of long-term growth and renewal. In this climate, any disruption to constant and steady growth is seen as negative. Crisis, because it disrupts system stability and short-term stock value, is to be avoided whenever possible and resolved quickly with as few resources as possible. CT, however, focuses on long-term patterns of stability and growth and a dynamic relationship to instability and decline. Growth, resurrection, and renewal follow bifurcation, and the latter may be necessary for the former to occur.

Finally, underlying patterns and processes of communication are factors giving organizational systems stability and order, following the chaos of bifurcation. Crisis significantly changes the topics, the patterns, and the communicators. The common threat and hardship of a crisis may modify the tone and climate of communication. Crisis stakeholders often communicate in new ways, exhibiting higher levels of cooperation, creative problem solving, and collaborative decision making. Alternatively, crisis often creates tensions of conflict as crisis stakeholders offer competing interpretations of blame and responsibility. These patterns of cooperation and conflict suggest underlying forces of attraction and repulsion that, like fractal patterns, may help reconstitute organization.

As a general theory regarding the performance of nonlinear, complex systems, chaos theory views crisis as a natural stage of system evolution, ultimately leading to higher levels of organization. These disruptions and bifurcations are not abnormal accidents, but natural points of change. Crisis, then, is positioned differently and more centrally within the larger concept of organization. CT can serve as a powerful framework for a broad, conceptual understanding of crisis and its role in complex organizations.

ORGANIZATIONAL LEARNING THEORY

A third general framework for understanding crisis is organizational learning. Like enactment and chaos theory (CT), organizational learning theory is an extension and refinement of system perspectives. Learning theory cultivates a dynamic view of organizations as they seek to maintain a balance between stability and change. Organizations, accordingly, must be open to new insights, understanding, and skills while maintaining the knowledge, skill, and wisdom that have proved successful. Like other systems-based views, learning theory is a general view accommodating a variety of related perspectives, including organizational culture, the quality movement, and organizational development. Like CT, organizational learning cultivates holistic and organic views of organizations.

Organizational learning is described in a variety of ways: as a change in skill or knowledge (Brown & Duguid, 1996); as an adjustment in organizational culture (Normann, 1985); as "a change in the organization's enacted response repertoire" and sensemaking structure (Sitkin, Sutcliffe, & Weick, 1999, p. 7); and as the processing of information leading to a change in the range of behaviors (Huber, 1996, p. 126). Learning is both the process whereby members acquire new knowledge, responses, or skills and the systemwide modification of culture, procedures, and practices. Senge (1990) argued that organizations as purposeful collectivities must continually learn and adapt to their changing environments. This learning can take place quickly or slowly and over time. Additionally, learning may involve the entire organization or extend only to selected levels or divisions. A critical process in learning is the communication, knowledge diffusion, dialogue, and reflective openness of participants regarding their experiences (Weick & Ashford, 2001).

Organizational learning, then, concerns the processes of adaptation. It emphasizes system openness and flexibility as essential for accommodating changing conditions and for new understanding of existing conditions. By learning, the organization adds new know-how, competence, skills, and capacity, often replacing those previously learned. These learning events or experiences may be comparatively minor and routine, such as modest day-to-day changes in work schedules, or may involve more extreme disruptions, such as crises. As discussed earlier, crisis often demonstrates the inadequacies of established structures, procedures, and beliefs. Weick and Ashford (2001) noted that "[o]rganizations often discover faulty learning when they experience failures on a large or small scale" (p. 704). These experiences may be translated into histories that can be experienced richly for their implied lessons (Cohen & Sproull, 1996). Crisis events are often "critical incidents" with important lessons for organizations. For example, Cohen and Sproull cite the case where large sections of the sheet-metal skin of an Aloha Airlines flight peeled away in midair. This dramatic event created widespread and intense attention from airlines and regulators and new understanding of airline design and maintenance. A similar phenomenon occurred when many organizations examined their own accounting procedures in light of the Enron scandal.

Organizational learning, then, has particular implications for communication and for postcrisis adaptation. Postcrisis contexts are characterized by analysis of what went wrong, why, and what can be done to ensure that similar events do not occur again (Seeger et al., 1998). Within this environment, new understandings of risk, its relationship to the organization, and norms and procedures for risk avoidance develop (Turner, 1976). The post-9/11 environment was characterized by efforts to learn in a variety of domains—including air safety, immigration, border security, and law enforcement—and in how to issue warnings. Airline security firms, for example, had to learn new ways of searching passengers and luggage. Immigration services and port inspectors had to develop new methods of screening both people and goods. Law enforcement agencies have examined ways of sharing information and coordinating their activities.

Components of Learning Theory

One the most popular approaches to learning theory is the work of Peter Senge (1990). Senge has sought to subsume many traditional notions of organizational training, change, and development within the learning frame. Other efforts have positioned learning as a distinct process of organizational adaptation. These later approaches detail the processes and kinds of organizational learning (Huber, 1991), focus on aspects of history as critical learning events (Cohen & Sproull, 1996), and examine the relationship between work practice and learning (Brown & Duguid, 1996)

Senge's (1990) concept of the learning organization can be thought of as a reframing of other notions as opposed to an entirely new set of theoretical principles. He argued that "learning organizations" must first develop a shared vision or consensus that fosters a willingness to adapt or evolve in response to their environment. This strategic vision links learning to planning, where system openness is a prerequisite to learning. Senge also argued that although traditional organizational structures such as teams may function well with routine issues, when they confront crises their cooperative resolve tends to disintegrate. Conversely, learning organizations, as he described them, have the potential to emerge from crises with a renewed sense of purpose. Crisis events represent a chance for the organization to acquire new information, skills, insights, and capabilities.

Ultimately, organizations learn by using such feedback to "change the thinking that produced the problem in the first place" (Senge, 1990, p. 95). Organizations take action toward a goal. If the action is effective, the process continues. If the action fails, it is stopped or altered. Senge described this form of feedback as a "balanced effect" (p. 79). The balancing process allows organizations to regain stability in light of new information through adaptive feedback cycles. There is a danger, however, that organizations will "drown in the details" of the feedback they receive (p. 126). Rather than suffering from insufficient information, Senge, like Weick (1979), believes organizations are hampered by "too much information" (p. 129). To cope with the inevitable information overload, learning organizations emphasize wholeness, rather than focusing on the informational details.

Huber (1996) provided a detailed synthesis of the processes and kinds of organizational learning. An organization learns, he suggested, "if through its processing of information, the range of its potential behavior is changed" (p. 126). Learning, then, involves four related processes: (1) acquisition of knowledge; (2) distribution of information among various sources; (3) interpretation of information when commonly understood interpretations are available; and (4) storing of knowledge for future use, in organizational memory (pp. 124, 127). Within each of these process stages are embedded various subprocesses that detail specific forms of learning and influences on learning.

Knowledge acquisition, for example, may involve five specific learning processes: (1) congenital, (2) experiential, (3) vicarious, (4) grafting, and (5) searching (Huber, 1996, p. 127). Congenital learning represents knowledge available at the time of the organization's founding (p. 128). This first knowledge represents fundamental lessons regarding markets, products, services, and technologies. Experiential learning involves intentional or unintentional activities, such as market testing or research and development. Systematic experiments with new markets or new technologies are commonly used to acquire new knowledge. Self-appraisal or external critique is also a form of experiential learning. Vicarious learning is a kind of secondhand learning involving observing others and modeling behaviors accordingly. Organizations observe one another in a variety of ways, including participation in trade associations, review of business literature, dissection of one another's products, and even by industrial espionage (Pfeffer & Salancik, 1978). Grafting, the fourth kind of knowledge acquisition described by Huber (1996), involves the acquisition of new members for new stores of knowledge or skills. Many organizational mergers, such as the recent merger of Daimler Benz and the Chrysler Corporation, are justified on the grounds of acquiring new knowledge (Fitzgibbon & Seeger, 2002). The fifth kind of knowledge acquisition, searching, involves the conscious day-to-day processes of monitoring internal and external organizational environments. This may involve systematic boundary-spanning activities, specific problem-solving research, or monitoring and assessment of organization performance.

Information distribution among various sources is the second step in learning. Distribution of knowledge is a sign of learning and an indication of its organizational breadth. Huber emphasized the importance of distributions by suggesting that organizations often do not know what they know. Distribution, then, is the process whereby information acquired leads to more broad-based, organization-wide learning (1996, pp. 141–152). Huber also noted that information, when distributed widely, may result in synergistic understandings, in which information is used in unforeseen ways. Many organizational communication failures, inadequacies of networks, information overloads, various kinds of noise, beliefs about proprietary information, and attitudes toward communicators disrupt the distribution of information and make it inaccessible.

The third stage in Huber's (1996) model involves the interpretation of information. This may involve both "more and more widely varied interpretations" as well as when "more of the organization understands the nature of interpretations held by other units" (p. 143). In the former case, the organization has developed a wider set of skills, knowledge, and interpretations. In the latter case, greater congruence and understanding of the range of organizational interpretations enhances the level of coordination. In processes of socialization and the development and maintenance of organizational culture, for example, consensus around interpretations usually develops (Eisenberg & Riley, 1991). Huber described a variety of ways in which shared interpretations are affected, including cognitive mapping and framing, media richness, capacity and information overload, and unlearning. Cognitive maps, belief structures, interpretive schemes, and frames influence the interpretation of information. Media

richness concerns the efficacy of available channels for purposes of persuasion. Information overload reduces the ability of participants to interpret information. Finally, unlearning involves discarding or forgetting
knowledge that is outdated or no longer needed.

The final aspect in Huber's (1996) general model is organizational memory, the way in which knowledge is maintained or stored for subsequent
use. Organizational memory is a complex process involving human participants as well as storage and retrieval mechanisms. Huber identified
three observations regarding organizational memory. First, personnel
turnover results in losses in organizational memory, leading to information loss and a reduction in institutional memory. Second, failure to accu-
rately anticipate future needs results in more information being stored
than is needed and in some needed information not being stored. Information collection and storage are resource-intensive, and although organizations go to great lengths to collect and store information, future needs
cannot be anticipated. Third, the fact that information has been stored
does not mean that members are universally aware of that information,
that it is accessible, or that its form is useful. Information is stored in a
variety of ways: in procedures, routines, and methods; in formal storage
systems; in computer and paper files; in financial records and reports; and
in personnel. The fact that knowledge has been stored is necessary but not
sufficient for its use. Changes in technology, for example, have made
many computerized records inaccessible.

Huber's (1996) detailing of these processes demonstrates the complexities and comprehensiveness of organizational learning. Learning as an
adaptive organizational process is influenced by a wide array of organizational and human factors. Learning occurs by many routes, using diverse
methodologies for acquiring and distributing information and knowledge.
Moreover, learning is not merely the product of being exposed to, or having
access to, information; it also involves higher-level interpretive and institu-
tionalizing processes. Two specific approaches to organizational learning
operationalize these processes in ways that are useful in understanding crisis. In particular, crises as "critical events" represent postcrisis learning
opportunities, whereas analysis of work-related knowledge helps to identify crisis-producing fallacies and crisis-avoiding adaptive processes.

Organizational Learning and Crisis

Aspects of organizational history can become critical learning events.
Although some kinds of events are relatively infrequent, they nonetheless
may be experienced in ways that precipitate learning. Cohen and Sproull
(1996) argued that when histories are viewed as critical events, they are
dissected, elaborated, and repeated to extract information. Crises, particularly when their impact is severe and when mistakes or "faulty learning"

appear to be the cause, often become critical opportunities for learning (Sitkin et al., 1999). The story of Chrysler's near bankruptcy in the early 1980s, for example, took on the narrative structure of a saga as it was told and retold. For those employees who survived, the story was a way of remembering the mistakes of the past and a mantra for avoiding them in the future (Fitzgibbon & Seeger, 2002). Similarly, the *Challenger* disaster was examined in great detail for its lessons of human and technical failure (Gouran et al., 1986). One of the investigations was undertaken by a presidential commission, the Rogers Commission. This high-profile group helped to ensure that the lessons would be well-publicized, even beyond NASA. Detailed investigations in the courts, by commissions, or by other governmental bodies are common features of high-profile crises (Seeger, 1986a). Such postmortems are undertaken not only to apportion responsibility and liability, but also to ensure that the lessons of the crisis are learned and that similar events do not occur. Investigative boards and commissions in postcrisis situations serve to "collect, synthesize, summarize, and disseminate information; identify causes and associated factors;" and "suggest ways in which future crises may be avoided" (Ray, 1999, pp. 189–190).

Cohen and Sproull (1996) have identified three characteristics of organizational events that may make them "critical" (p. 4). First, events must have a significant place in history. That is, they must be associated with some important change or development so that they have implications for the future. Second, an event is critical when it "changes what is believed about the world" (p. 4). Often, crisis affects belief systems about the organization's vulnerability to risk, its probability of occurrence, and methods for avoidance. One of the most wide-ranging consequences of the 9/11 attacks was the dramatic demonstration of vulnerabilities. Third, Cohen and Sproull suggested that events become critical when they have metaphorical power. They noted: "Events that evoke meaning, interest, and attention for participants are critical incidents. Anecdotes and stories are standard features of pedagogical practice.... Critical incidents have a quality of simplicity and representativeness that is not entirely imposed on them" (p. 4). Crisis events frequently meet this test. They have dramatic features that demand attention and frame or embody larger organizational meanings and lessons. They often have a familiar and simplistic narrative structure that includes tragedy, victims, sacrifice, heroes, and villains, enhancing their ability to promote learning across time.

Sitkin (1996) has taken the notion of failure further, arguing that failure "is an essential prerequisite for learning" because it stimulates basic organizational experimentation (p. 542). Failures such as crises are beneficial to organizations to the degree that they promote seven interrelated outcomes. First, failure may create attention for a previously underrecognized problem. In fact, many events are framed as crises as part of a strategy to call attention to problems. Second, failure promotes ease of recognition and interpretation. A crisis event gives a clear definition to a problem, and the dramatic features of a crisis serve to promote broader recognition. Third, failures—particularly large-scale failures—stimulate the search for solutions by demonstrating the associated costs. Fatal airline crashes stimulate an intensive effort to identify the probable cause, in part because the cost of a crash is high—in legal liability, reduced profits, and loss of life. Fourth, crises are motivational. Crisis may result in a spirit of cooperation and motivation to rebuild among employees, members of the community, and management. Fifth, failure may result in an adjustment of risk tolerances. Sitkin suggested that such adjustments are beneficial because they enhance risk tolerance, but other views suggest that postfailure reduction in risk tolerance may be beneficial (Turner, 1976). The sixth outcome of failure that promotes leaning is that it stimulates "increased variation in organizational response repertoires" (p. 549). Finally, failure promotes experimentation and practice leading to an organizational "orientation that is more flexible and adaptive" (p. 550). Crises as critical incidents and as failures represent important opportunities for learning outside of established learning routines and structures.

One of the useful aspects of organizational learning theory is its detailed focus on how work is actually accomplished through learning routines and structures. Work is a reflection of skills, knowledge, insights, and understanding that members have acquired over time. As a tightly integrated body of practice, work evolves or changes slowly as members innovate. Learning, then, is the "bridge between working and innovating" (Brown & Duguid, 1996, p. 60). Moreover, Brown and Duguid pointed to two relatively distinct forms of work practice. Canonical practice is the espoused practice found in training programs and manuals. Noncanonical practice includes "the actual work practices of members" (p. 59). A strict "reliance on espoused practices can blind an organization's core to the actual and usually valuable practices of members," Brown and Duguid maintained (p. 59). Canonical practice is inherently an abstraction from the ways work is actually done. Organizations often assume that "complex tasks can be successfully mapped as a set of simple, canonical steps" easily replicated without deeper understanding, insight, or experience (p. 60). Thus, they may be said to "follow the map rather than the road conditions" (p. 61).

This form of organizational fallacy in reasoning about the operations of complex systems may lead to the lowering of skills for a position or downsizing the organization (Brown & Duguid, 1996). Such downsizing may be particularly common with skills and knowledge that are infrequently utilized, such as crisis-response capability. Cutting positions based on the canonical assumption that they are unnecessary or that skills or knowledge are not required is associated with both the onset of crisis and decay in response capacity. The Bhopal Union Carbide disaster, for example, was associated with canonical failures at several levels (Shirvastava, 1987). Training programs had been increasingly abstracted as the company relied on a "train the trainers to train" model and as resources were cut. The crisis failure itself was retraced to reductions in maintenance staff and the failure to oversee a simple pipe-washing procedure. Noncanonical knowledge represents deeper levels of system understanding based on practice, experience, and system literacy acquired over time. The ability to see and respond effectively to interactive complexity is often embedded in this noncanonical knowledge. It is in the operation of systems, as opposed to their design, that interactive complexity becomes evident.

Learning theory is an important addition to other system-based perspectives on crisis. The descriptions of fallacies in the espoused practices of work have important implications for the onset of many crises and for avoidance. Learning theory's explication of the processes whereby crisis translates into learning opportunities has direct relevance for postcrisis issues of adaptation, recovery, and renewal. It is plausible to expect that those organizations able to treat a crisis as a learning opportunity may recover more quickly, suffer less damage, and be able to capitalize more fully on the opportunities created by crisis than those that view these events as wholly negative.

SUMMARY

Broader theoretical frameworks are necessary to building more complete understandings of crisis events and for predicting their occurrence, development, and consequences. These frameworks may help in sorting out the crisis, inducing interactiveness of complex systems in ways that allow for crisis avoidance. They may also prove helpful in the management of crisis. Sensemaking, chaos theory, and organizational learning each make unique contributions to the understanding of crisis. Taken together, they complement one another and provide a comprehensive framework for crisis management. Each theory views organization as a complex process, existing in a dynamic relationship to its environment and using communication to constitute and reconstitute itself. Through communication, organizations learn what they know and how to think. They make sense of their experiences and construct consensual meaning around information and events, including crises.

CHAPTER 3

Crisis Type

Research on crisis type describes the breadth of organizational crises and classifies these events according to their common features. These typologies seek to detail the range of threats organizations face, describe common features, outline their general structure, and clarify the range of response strategies. Ultimately, the value in these approaches is to reduce the uncertainty associated with crisis and to help managers plan and respond more effectively. Although all crises are by definition unique, there are common traits. This chapter suggests an approach that more fully integrates the role of perception and communication into the examination of crisis type. The concept of crisis type is examined, followed by a discussion of three typologies by Meyers and Holusha (1986), Mitroff and Anagnos (2001), and Coombs (1999b). Finally, the relationship between crisis type and communication dimensions and exigencies is explored.

AN OVERVIEW OF CRISIS TYPOLOGY

Naming and classifying a crisis is important to addressing the uncertainty and confusion regarding causes and responsibility, particularly during the initial moments of the event. An initial definition frames both action and meaning. Moreover, classification is closely connected to questions about how both organizations and stakeholders should respond. Classifying a crisis as a particular type or form reduces the initial uncertainty. Initial examinations of crisis, for example, usually focus on naming and defining the event so that organizations and others know how to respond and think. The events of 9/11 were initially reported by many news outlets as an accident. Later, they were defined as a terrorist attack. Later still, they were described as an act of war. This naming, defining, and classifying crises, then, is instrumental in managing crises and determining a response. Definition also implies both causality and responsibility. What one organization defines as an accident, a primary stakeholder may define as a case of organizational malfeasance. Organizations often define crises strategically to absolve themselves of responsibility or to shift the blame. Competing narratives of responsibility often arise and affect how the crisis is ultimately resolved. The ability to define and classify crisis is an important first step in crisis management.

Beyond responding to these events, crises must be named and defined to determine which regulatory agencies are involved. Classification helps in understanding who is responsible for regulatory enforcement, oversight, or even cleanup. Varying issues may place a crisis under the purview of local, state, or national law enforcement agencies. In addition, local, state, and national regulatory agencies such as the Centers for Disease Control (CDC), the Federal Emergency Management Agency (FEMA), and the Department of Energy (DOE) handle some forms of crisis, whereas local health departments or state emergency-management agencies handle others. Insurance is also related to basic issues of definition and labeling. For instance, part of the response to the World Trade Center bombings of 9/11 was contingent on whether the event was an attack or an accident. Insurance companies handle payments differently by virtue of how the event is defined. If the 9/11 events were defined as an act of war, then the insurance companies might face reduced liability. Interestingly, the U.S. government's initial response to the event was to describe it as an act of war without much thought regarding the impact of the definition.

Much of the research on crisis type focuses on developing exhaustive lists of the various crises that an organization might face. This approach also classifies crises according to causes, consequences, and response strategies. Classifications enable organizations to understand the connections between organizational conduct and crisis, to reduce risk, and to prepare for common crises. In addition, they offer organizations the opportunity to learn from similar crises and prepare to meet the needs of specific kinds of events. Three typologies of crisis are described below.

CLASSIFICATION SYSTEMS FOR ORGANIZATIONAL CRISIS

Research on crisis type emphasizes a list of potential crises organizations should consider (Coombs, 1999; Meyers & Holusha, 1986; Mitroff & Anagnos, 2001). In addition, much of the work on crisis focuses on case studies to illustrate particular crises types. Other approaches take a more macro approach by emphasizing a synthesis of these types into mutually exclusive categories according to some common feature (Coombs, 1995). Regardless of the specific approach, this work helps in understanding potential crises.

Meyers and Holusha's Classification System

Meyers and Holusha (1986) described nine crises representing general forms of crisis, with common causal features and some shared response contingencies (see Table 3.1). Their approach is particularly useful in encouraging organizations to brainstorm crises they may experience and to expand their perspectives regarding what might be done. Meyers and Holusha's list of nine common types of crises organizations may face includes crises of public perception, sudden market shifts, product failures, management successions, cash crises, industrial relations crises, hostile takeovers, international events, and regulation or deregulation. This initial list, they argued, includes those crises for which all organizations should at least have some minimal level of preparation.

Table 3.1
Classification Systems for Organizational Crisis

Meyers and Holusha, 1986	Coombs, 1999	Mitroff and Anagnos, 2001
Public perception	Natural Disasters	Economic
Sudden Market Shift	Malevolence	Informational
Product failure	Technical Breakdowns	Physical—Loss of key plants and facilities
Top management succession	Human Breakdowns	Human Resource
Cash crises	Challenges	Reputation
Industrial relations	Megadamage	Psychopathic Acts
Hostile takeover	Organizational Misdeeds	Natural Disasters
Adverse international events	Workplace Violence	
Regulation/Deregulation	Rumors	

Sources: Adapted from *When It Hits the Fan: Managing the Nine Crises of Business*, by G.C. Meyers and J. Holusha, 1986, Boston: Houghton Mifflin; *Ongoing Crisis Communication: Planning, Managing, and Responding*, by W.T. Coombs, 1999, Thousand Oaks, CA: Sage; and *Managing Crises Before They Happen: What Every Executive and Manager Needs to Know about Crisis Management*, by I.I. Mitroff and G. Anagnos, 2001, New York: AMACOM.

A crisis in public perception, their first type, can affect stock values and the sale of goods and services. Stakeholder perception may contribute to a loss of legitimacy, a lowered image, and a tarnished reputation. Organizations need to be sensitive to how they are perceived and should address any deficiencies that may lead to crisis. Sudden market shifts, the second type, can have severe repercussions for organizations that are unprepared. Netscape experienced a market shift when Microsoft gave away its Internet Explorer browser. Netscape, in this case, was obviously not prepared for a competitor giving away a competing product. Product failures, a third type, appear to be increasingly common. Products as diverse as automobiles, pharmaceuticals, and toys in children's meals are often identified in media reports as defective. The repercussions from these failures can range from mere nuisances to customer injuries and death. International events include such disruptions as the Organization of Petroleum Exporting Countries (OPEC) oil crisis or the Gulf War, events which can have a profound impact on entire industries, particularly when critical resources such as oil are affected. Management successions, such as Al "Chainsaw" Dunlap's taking over Sunbeam, can create crises, particularly if the new leaders have a reputation for downsizing. Many organizations have at one point experienced cash crises, a sixth type, and have realized the debilitating impact of reduced cash flow. Cash crises may be short-term problems or may signal larger organizational or market problems. Industrial relations crises are events that most often develop out of poor management or poor employee relations and can take the form of grievances, work slowdowns, or strikes. Hostile takeovers occur when management loses control of the organization. Low stock prices are typically associated with this form of crisis. In addition, organizations that experience other forms of crisis may face hostile takeovers as a result of depressed stock prices or may encounter adverse international events. Regulation and deregulation, Meyers and Holusha's (1986) final type, involve major shifts in the organization's operating environment. Changes in regulations may profoundly affect how organizations produce and sell their products and meet economic goals.

Mitroff and Anagnos's Classification System

Mitroff and Anagnos (2001) examined the role of crisis type specifically in relation to planning (see Table 3.1). They suggest that organizations are far too narrow in their perception of the types of crises they may experience. Organizations typically prepare for crises such as natural disasters that are "least threatening to the 'collective ego' of organizations," according to Mitroff and Anagnos (p. 32). Fires, earthquakes, and floods, for example, affect all organizations equally and are not caused by internal decisions or management oversights. Mitroff and Anagnos contended that if organizations are to prepare for crises more effectively they must assess the risk for at least one crisis in each of the following seven categories: economic, information, physical, human resource, reputational, psychopathic acts, and natural disasters.

Economic crises include internal exigencies such as labor strikes and illegal accounting practices or external pressures such as labor shortages, market crashes, or stock fluctuations. Informational crises involve a loss of proprietary information, discovery of false information, or tampering with records. Physical crisis refers to major plant disruptions, breakdowns of equipment, or loss of materials or supplies. Workplace violence, absenteeism, or loss or succession of key executives or personnel exemplify human-resource crises. The fifth type, reputational crises, includes gossip, slander, rumors, or any damage to the corporate reputation. Psychopathic acts refer to product tampering, hostage taking, terrorism, or kidnapping. These intentional acts of destruction are particularly difficult to anticipate. The final crisis type, according to Mitroff and Anagnos (2001), is natural disasters, including earthquakes, fires, floods, and hurricanes.

Mitroff and Anagnos (2001) pointed out that many organizations are myopic in their perception of potential crises and should broaden their consideration of risks. For this reason, risk analysis that weighs risk based on crisis probability should be avoided. They suggested that "it is precisely those crises that have not yet occurred to an organization that need to be considered" (p. 38).

Coombs's Classification System

Coombs (1999b) combined these lists into systematic crisis types, including natural disasters, malevolence, technical breakdowns, human breakdowns, challenges, megadamage, organizational misdeeds, workplace violence, and rumors (see Table 3.1). This synthesis of crisis types differentiates between human and technical breakdowns and crises that originate within and outside of the organization. For instance, natural disasters, malevolence (i.e., product tampering), challenges (i.e., discontented stakeholders), and megadamage (i.e., oil spills) are typically external events. Technical breakdowns (i.e., product recalls), human breakdowns (i.e., human error), and workplace violence are usually internal crises. Rumors and organizational misdeeds (harming internal or external stakeholders) can bridge both internal and external organizational boundaries. Clustering crises this way provides some indication about management strategies. Organizations can usually exert more control over internal crises, although they are also more likely to be responsible for internal events. External events are beyond the organization's control and create less organizational responsibility.

CAUSE, CONSEQUENCE, AND CRISIS TYPE

Several common features of crisis are evident when examined according to type. First, common underlying causes may be evident, suggesting that some risks are common to all organizations. Second, responses may also be evident across various types of crisis. Most often, responses are negative and structured along patterns of cause–blame, although some responses are more forward-looking. Third, classes of consequences indicate how crisis events are resolved. This is particularly important for organizations planning responses for various kinds of events. Finally, classes of mitigation strategies may be evident when examining types.

Common Causes and Crisis Type

Causes of crisis vary widely, but many share an underlying complexity. This complexity is largely associated with new technology and the interaction of technologies (Perrow, 1984). Technology introduces new variables and is often so tightly coupled that a change in one part of a system can have unforeseen consequences in another. Moreover, some organizations, such as nuclear power plants, large chemical processing facilities, or complex computerized systems, are so complex they defy understanding. In this case, several managers must work together to create a consensual understanding. In general, the primary causal variable in a significant proportion of crisis types is the additional complexity created by humans interacting with complex technological systems—actions resulting in defective products, product breakdowns and recalls, technological breakdowns of various kinds, plant explosions, industrial accidents, transportation accidents, and environmental spills.

When considering causes of a specific type of crises, the list of factors is surprisingly short. For instance, Ray (1999) suggested that causes of airline disasters include pilot or other human error, problems related to weather, equipment failure, or the interaction of these factors. Similarly, food-borne illness involves a limited set of typical infectious agents, including *Campylobacter, Escherichia coli* O157, *Listeria monocytogenes, Salmonella, Shigella, Vibrio,* and *Yersinia enterocolitica salmonila*. Moreover, these agents are introduced into food in limited ways: in the field, in processing plants, and in food preparation. Mining disasters most often involve floods, collapses, explosions, and equipment failures. Schools face violence-related crises, bomb threats, bad weather, transportation accidents, and fires. Any particular industry, then, is likely to have a well-defined set of industry-specific risks. These derive from the products they produce and the methods and technologies they employ. Moreover, although organizations and industries are more susceptible to crisis due to the specific technology used and products or service provided, no organization is exempt.

Responses and Crisis Type

As noted earlier, organizational responses to crisis are most often designed to avoid liability, shift blame, diffuse responsibility, transcend the crisis, bolster image, and, occasionally, to accept blame and compensate victims. Organizations typically focus on getting beyond the crisis with as little cost and disruption as possible. These strategies of postcrisis communication, described more fully in chapter 8, have also been linked to crisis type.

Coombs (1995), for example, suggested four general causes of crises—faux pas, accidents, terrorism, and transgressions—and connects them to particular postcrisis communication strategies. According to Coombs, a faux pas is "an unintentional action that an external agent tries to transform into a crisis. The second crisis type, accidents, "are unintentional and happen during the course of normal organizational operations." Terrorism is "an intentional act taken by external actors." Transgressions are "intentional acts taken by the organization that knowingly place publics at risk or harm" (p. 455). Those making decisions about communication should consider five variables: (1) type of crisis, (2) evidence or proof, (3) whether the damage was major or minor, (4) victim status, and (5) performance history of the organization. Organizations that commit a faux pas should generally use mortification (publicly accepting blame) or apologies and strategies designed to gain public approval, such as image bolstering. Organizations that have accidents should consider mortification, public-approval strategies, and in some cases strategies that distance the organization from the crisis. When organizations commit transgressions, the most appropriate actions are mortification, justification, and strategies to enhance public approval. Finally, after terrorism, organizations should use mortification, suffering, and ingratiation strategies. Coombs's type-specific crisis response suggests that mortification and public-approval strategies are used most often. In addition, organizations should be aware that corporate performance, history, and reputation have an impact on response capability.

The type of crisis can also affect the communication options available to an organization (Fitzpatrick & Rubin, 1995). The level of responsibility the organization is perceived to have creates different options for postcrisis communication. Denial, for example, is unlikely to be a successful strategy in cases where crisis type indicates that the organization is at fault. When the crises type suggests organizational culpability, denial will increase the harm by reducing credibility and creating the impression that something is being hidden. Susskind and Field (1996) also suggested that responses grounded principally in the evasion of responsibility have led to erosion of confidence in public organizations. In such cases, a message accepting blame and announcing corrective action is more appropriate. An organization's precrisis communication may also affect the types of response available in postcrisis (Ulmer, 2001). Similarly, Tyler (1997) and Fitzpatrick and

Rubin (1995) suggested that legal restrictions typified by some kinds of crisis tightly constrain the latitude of an organization's postcrisis responses.

Classes of Consequences

Crises of all types cause harm to stakeholders, including customers, workers and their families, retirees, stockholders, creditors, suppliers, competitors, the community in which the organization operates, and the environment. Organizations routinely suffer massive losses, merge, downsize, or go out of business following a crisis. Legal costs in the aftermath of a crisis often are tremendous. Litigation over asbestos continues decades after its manufacture was halted. Exxon spent at least $1 billion on cleanup and legal claims following the *Valdez* spill. Moreover, such litigation can continue to regularly distract the organization, keeping it from paying attention to other important issues.

Consequences of crisis, regardless of type, may have internal and external manifestations. The company may lose profitability, customers, and market share. Employees may lose jobs, health insurance, and pension plans. Stock values may plunge and the company may face hostile takeover. In addition, communities suffer lost tax bases and the costs of cleanup and helping displaced workers. The environment may be harmed. Suppliers often suffer as they lose markets for their products. These consequences may be immediate and long term. It should also be noted, however, that consequences need not be entirely negative. Meyers and Holusha (1986) have identified several potentially positive outcomes: heroes are born, change is accelerated, latent problems are faced, people are changed, new strategies evolve, new warning systems develop, and a new competitive edge appears.

Classes of Mitigation

An additional form of consequence concerns mitigation strategies to reduce, contain, respond, and offset the harm. Disseminating warnings, for example, may help members of the community take appropriate actions in the event of a chemical spill. Organizations often provide support to employees and their families when an industrial accident has caused injury or death. Counseling is sometimes provided in cases of serious trauma. In some cases in which fire destroyed plant facilities, organizations have extended employee health benefits and pay. Airlines usually have standing policies for mitigation following a crash. Many pay medical or funeral expenses and provide travel, lodging, and counseling for families, and many automatically offer cash settlements. Schools may be forced to evacuate students, provide counseling, and hold memorial services in cases of trauma. Schwan's, a food company, took extraordinary cor-

rective efforts to lessen the impact on their customers following an outbreak of salmonellosis. Rather than waiting for the courts to determine
appropriate actions, Schwan's proactively took steps to lessen the potential impact on consumers.

As these examples indicate, mitigation strategies may be both generic to
most crises or matched to the specific event. In general, organizations mitigate harm to stakeholders by disseminating as much information as possible about the event. Although caution must be exercised to ensure that
information is accurate and that messages acknowledge the inherent
equivocality of the situation, disseminating information serves three
goals. First, it helps to reduce rumors. Second, it helps to ensure that the
organization maintains control of the message. Third, it enhances credibility and creates the impression of accessibility. Beyond being open and
honest, an additional general mitigation strategy involves being supportive to victims. In general, acknowledging the harm, offering support and
condolences to victims, and doing everything within reason to assist them
is recommended as a universal response strategy.

Specific crisis types, however, may require a diverse set of mitigation
and response strategies and specialized expertise. Industrial and mining
accidents, for example, may require heavy equipment as well as personnel
trained in rescue and recovery. Oil and chemical spills require specialized
containment equipment and knowledge. Releases of radiological materials are particularly challenging in terms of the technical equipment and
specialized knowledge required. Both generic and type-specific mitigation strategies should be identified in the crisis-planning stage.

Crisis Type and Organizational Learning

One of the advantages of examining crisis by type is that this approach
creates some structure to what appears to be a wholly novel circumstance.
Crisis is most often thought of as an isolated event that affects a single
company or community. Corporations are often unaware of the types of
crisis that affect others in their industry and even fail to attend to generic
risks. In some cases, however, individual organizations appear to learn
from prior crises and are able to improve avoidance and hone their
responses. For instance, Johnson & Johnson's response to its second
Tylenol tampering episode was in part a function of the company's experience with the first episode. In this case, Johnson & Johnson was able to
learn from its experience. Malden Mills was able to learn from earlier
crises and apply those lessons to a fire that devastated the organization's
manufacturing facility. One explanation for the comparatively successful
evacuation of the World Trade Center following the 9/11 terrorists attack
was the experience of the 1994 car bombing of the center. Occupants had
learned from this experience how to evacuate the facility. These learning

processes are all grounded in the assumption that crises of particular types will have common characteristics and follow established patterns.

CRISIS TYPOLOGY

Much of our understanding of what causes a crisis and its affects is derived from the examination of different types of crises. Generally, understanding of these events is facilitated by looking for common features. Nine crisis types based on common features include crises in public perception, natural disasters, product or service crises, terrorist attacks, economic crises, human resource crises, industrial crises, airline crashes, and crises that originate in the organization's environment.

Crises in Public Perception

Crises in public perception can range from news stories depicting the organization negatively to destructive rumors appearing in e-mail, on rogue Web sites, or by word of mouth. These perceptions may concern the nature of a product, the conduct and credibility of management, the financial health of the organization, or its conduct with regard to specific issues, such as use of animals in testing, treatment of women employees, or its record on diversity or environmentalism. Crises in public perception can have particularly devastating consequences when they undermine investor confidence and stock values. Regardless of the form or transmission of a negative public perception, crises in public perception result in an increase in negative attention directed at the organization. A lack of communication from the organization may contribute to the severity of these crises. Managers are often frustrated by the way the media covers a crisis compared to what they perceive to be the reality of the situation. Meyers and Holusha (1986), however, noted that "[r]eality is what your customers, suppliers, bankers, regulators, and other constituencies believe" (p. 83). Managers must pay attention to stakeholder perceptions to successfully manage crises in public perception.

Organizations must also be vigilant in monitoring their environment and must be prepared to respond to even the most ridiculous of rumors. Fearn-Banks (2002) described some common rumors that organizations have worked to alleviate. For example, K-Mart was the subject of a rumor that it was regularly experiencing kidnappings. The Snapple Beverage Company was rumored to support the Ku Klux Klan, with the label on its popular ice tea drink depicting a slave ship. The company spent thousands of dollars to correct these false, but destructive, rumors. Proctor and Gamble has consistently fought a rumor that their logo, a Man in the Moon and stars, was a disguised satanic sign. Although organizations frequently work to quell such rumors, the rumors are often reinvigorated at specific times. Known as birthday rumors, these recurrences can create ongoing difficulties in public perception. In the case of Proctor and Gamble, rumors regarding their satanic connection recurred so many times that the company eventually changed its logo. The Internet has now made many rumors both easier to disseminate and more persistent. Coombs (1999b) suggested that organizational credibility and an immediate response is vital to combatting such rumors.

Natural Disasters

Natural disasters have received comparatively little attention in the organizational crisis literature, although they create very high levels of destruction and disruption for organizations. Natural disasters are generally assumed to be beyond the control and responsibility of most organizations. Rather, preparation and management of these events usually falls to governmental agencies. Organizations often seek to have crises classified as natural disasters, therefore, to avoid responsibility for the associated harm. In this way, weather-related airline accidents are more advantageous to the industry than strictly human error or mechanical failures. Natural disasters clearly have a debilitating impact on organizations. Floods, earthquakes, mud slides, hurricanes, tornadoes, and blizzards often limit an organization's ability to meet its goals. Pearson and Clair (1998) explained that organizations should be conscious of natural disasters for four reasons. First, these events may affect a product or service. For example, heavy snowfall often limits the transportation of goods, services, parts, and people. Second, natural disasters can destroy the organization's information base. In July 1999, for example, when New York City experienced high temperatures and humidity, "[m]any research laboratories lost their electricity, killing lab specimens and seriously impeding research" (Barton, 2001, p. 182). Third, natural disasters may damage corporate facilities: 1997 flooding in North Dakota created so much damage that it took years for many organizations to rebuild. Among the structures destroyed was the Grand Forks *Herald* building, along with printing presses, computers, and its archives of news stories and photographs documenting much of the region's history. Finally, natural disasters may harm key stakeholders. People lose homes, neighborhoods are destroyed, and families are displaced as a result of natural disasters.

Many organizations now spend considerable resources to create disaster-proof buildings. It is not uncommon for buildings in earthquake areas to be built on massive shock absorbers to help limit earthquake damage. Concrete designs are being replaced with lighter, more-flexible steel structures so that the possibility of building collapse is lessened. In addition, computerized data is often protected and backed up regularly at off-site locations. Mitroff and Anagnos (2001) suggested that even though organizations may not be responsible for earthquakes, they are responsible for developing relatively safe buildings. Similarly, organizations are responsible for designing appropriate recovery efforts for the potential victims of these events. Some organizations have planned alternative transportation systems in case established routes are disrupted. In addition, weather monitoring has become a critical factor in crisis management. Moreover, many organizations have developed elaborate plans for creating operating continuity following a natural disaster. Governmental agencies, such as FEMA, have also encouraged businesses and industry to prepare for these kinds of crises. Illustrative of organizational learning, the widespread disruption from the Loma Prieta earthquake in 1989, Hurricane Andrew in 1992, and the western U.S. wildfires of 2001–2002 convinced many organizations that contingencies must be in pace for natural disasters.

Product or Service Crises

Product failure is a surprisingly common crisis. Today, the product and service industry, with its customer focus, is under increased scrutiny. Indeed, regardless of the organization's goals, regulatory agencies such as the Food and Drug Administration (FDA) or the Consumer Product Safety Commission (CPSC) have some jurisdiction. In addition to these regulatory agencies, organizations must be aware of print and television media "watchdogs," such as *Consumer Reports* magazine and television newsmagazines *Dateline NBC, 60 Minutes,* and *PrimeTime Live,* whose reporters regularly test products and services, claiming the public's right to know. Product liability lawsuits also play a key role in product and service crises and have enhanced the frequency and severity of this form of crisis.

Organizations are particularly sensitive to crises that affect their products because, fundamentally, this is the way organizations interact with customers. Long-term damage can take place while a defective product is "out there," even when it has been recalled. A Web site that focuses on the impact of drug recalls (www.recalleddrugs.com) suggests that some 250,000 side effects linked to prescription drugs are reported each year and that some drugs have caused deaths. Crises that stem from an organization's product or service can have a severe impact on the organization's fundamental ability to operate. It may experience product or service boycotts, forced recalls, lawsuits, and intense media scrutiny, as well as a damaged reputation. Once it is known that an organization's product has caused injury or death, it may be difficult for the company to reestablish that product. Finally, organizations must be aware that, as in the Johnson & Johnson's Tylenol case, their products may be tampered with by external agents. Several forms of product or service crises are described below.

Product Recalls

Product recalls, either undertaken voluntarily or mandated by regulatory agencies or the courts, are common. Not all product recalls result in a crisis, particularly when a product does not create widespread harm. These routine recalls rarely cause crises if the company provides an avenue to exchange or repair the product and if the defect has not done extensive harm. However, defective products can create crises. Johnson & Johnson experienced two recalls, in 1982 and 1986, both relating to their Extra Strength Tylenol capsules. The first tampering episode resulted in seven deaths. The second left two people dead after they took capsules laced with cyanide. In the first case, Johnson & Johnson immediately withdrew Extra Strength Tylenol capsules from the market and advertised new triple-safety-seal packaging. This helped to move the company beyond the crisis. After the second tampering episode, however, Johnson & Johnson was forced to replace the capsule with a new tamper-proof caplet. In both cases, the company appeared to put their customers ahead of profits, garnering them high public-approval ratings for their handling of the crises.

Food-Borne Illness

Food-borne illness may take a wide variety of forms in a myriad of food products, including fresh and frozen meats, prepackaged and canned goods, and fresh and processed produce. A common crisis faced by restaurants, meat-packing plants, and food distributors is that food-borne contaminants such as *E. coli* or *salmonella* bacteria make consumers ill or, in some cases, cause death. Events such as Jack-in-the-Box's and Hudson Food's *E. coli*-infected hamburgers, *Lysteria* contamination in Bil Mar Foods, and Schwan's *Salmonella*-contaminated ice cream are common and have the potential to create widespread harm. The CDC describes food-borne illness as a significant health problem. The agency suggests that although the food supply in the United States is one of the safest in the world, some "76 million people get sick, more than 300,000 are hospitalized, and 5,000 Americans die each year from food-borne illness" (CDC, 2003, www.cdc.gov/foodsafety/default.htm). Beyond identifying the scope of contamination, finding the source and determining treatment is also challenging. The CDC explains that food-borne infections "can spread through contaminated food, contaminated drinking water, contaminated swimming water, and from toddler to toddler at a day care center." Measures to stop the spread can include "removing contaminated food from stores, chlorinating a swimming pool, or closing a child day care center" (CDC, 2002, www.cdc.gov/ncidod/dbmd/diseaseinfo/foodborneinfections_g.htm#foodbornedisease). Contaminated food may also be frozen for later consumption, creating an ongoing potential for harm. Food-borne illnesses are common and complex and demand multiple agencies to coordinate efforts and protect the public.

Media-Induced Product or Service Crises

One of the increasingly common product or service crises involves media investigations. Journalists generally take their job as a public watchdog quite seriously and are zealous in uncovering organizational malfeasance, typically in the form of defective products or services. Moreover, as discussed in chapter 2, more media outlets means greater competition to uncover these stories. In addition, crisis stories often have high potential for audience ratings. Media-induced crises sometimes involve undercover investigations such as *PrimeTime Live's* investigation of Food Lion supermarkets for unsanitary food-handling practices (Kernisky & Kernisky, 1998). Food Lion sued, citing invasive and deceptive media practices. The now-classic case of deceptive investigative journalism is *Dateline NBC's* accusation that General Motors (GM) was selling pickup trucks that caught fire following side impacts. In its story, *Dateline* presented viewers with two demonstrations in which certain GM pickups ignited following side impact. However, *Dateline* failed to disclose that it had rigged incendiary devices to cause these fires. When GM discovered that *Dateline NBC* had rigged these fires, it immediately held a public press conference and threatened to sue. GM was able to successfully defend itself in the media. *Dateline* was forced to retract its accusations regarding the pickups and apologize to GM (Hearit, 1996; Ulmer, 1999).

Another interesting and more successful example of investigative journalism involved the *Dateline NBC* examination of Wal-Mart's "Buy American" campaign. *Dateline* levied several accusations against Wal-Mart: that it was selling foreign goods under "Made in USA" labels, that it was exploiting child labor to produce its products, that it had shifted from American to foreign suppliers, and that its products violated import quotas. Wal-Mart was subsequently forced to change many of these practices (Benoit & Dorries, 1996).

The media generally plays a very important role as watchdog in uncovering organizational wrongdoing. Without the media, most issues of corporate wrongdoing, including many with the potential for serious harm, would go unaddressed. The media is also instrumental in distributing warnings about products and services. The successful recall of Hudson Foods' *E. coli*-tainted beef was a consequence of the rapid media attention given the issue. Nevertheless, these cases also illustrate that the media sometimes crosses the line between serving as the public's watchdog and engaging in deceptive reporting. Interestingly, this unethical behavior often creates a media-induced crisis for the media company.

Terrorist Attacks

Some of the most devastating crises in U.S. history were the terrorist attacks of September 11, 2001. Although such acts are not necessarily uncommon worldwide, particularly in developing countries, few have occurred in the United States. The Middle East has a long history of terrorist attacks. Terrorist bombings were once common in the United Kingdom, and Colombia is well known for the abduction of executives for ransom. These attacks, often described as random acts of violence, are difficult to anticipate and prepare for. They have typically been framed as governmental issues, although the nature of the 9/11 attack created clear and profound effects on a number of private organizations and industries, including air transportation, insurance, financial services, and tourism. Little research regarding terrorist attacks and/or communicating in their aftermath had been conducted before 9/11. However, since 9/11 much attention has been given to information needs, coping and support strategies, warnings, and media coverage in the aftermath of terrorism.

Coordination of information following the 9/11 attacks was a critical issue. For instance, medical teams, fire departments, police departments, hospitals, and federal and state government agencies all needed to maintain contact. Communication was difficult to maintain, however, due to cellular and landline telephone disruptions. Ironically, a significant proportion of the cellular telephone infrastructure was located on top of the World Trade Center. Maintaining coordination under these circumstances takes considerable foresight and planning. Keeping track of employees, allocating appropriate resources, and establishing timelines for completing tasks require effective coordination and information sharing. In the aftermath of 9/11, New York police and fire departments and other first responders are reexamining their communication networks and methods to enhance their capacity for coordination. Moreover, wide-ranging planning for related events, such as bioterrorism attacks, so-called dirty bombs, chemical attacks, and attacks on infrastructure has been undertaken. In this way, 9/11 has promoted both significant organizational learning and more-complete planning and preparation.

Economic Crises

Arguably, all crises eventually become economic. However, cash crises are typically signals of other significant organizational problems. Chrysler Corporation in the early 1980s is the prototypical example of this crisis type. The cash crisis was symptomatic of other, more broad-based problems, including outdated products, marketing, and manufacturing techniques. Meyers and Holusha (1986) explained: "It had—all at the same time—bad product, marketing, regulatory, public perception, and other crises. But in 1980 it all came down to cash" (p. 133). The cash crisis then became the trigger event for the recognition of widespread deficiencies. Until the cash crisis was addressed, the company could not resolve its other problems.

Hostile takeovers are potential economic crises for any publicly traded company. When stock prices are low, organizations are particularly susceptible to takeover. Obviously, the goals, direction, and often the personnel of the organization acquired in a takeover will change dramatically. There is at least an implied threat to the very identity of the organization, its culture, values, and the jobs it provides. Interestingly, there is often debate as to whether the takeover is actually hostile. This again illustrates the importance of naming and defining a crisis.

Sudden market shifts are a common crisis in the current competitive business environment. This type of crisis concerns an organization's ability to understand and identify dynamic customer demands. Such crises are difficult to prepare for because many factors may affect a shift. For instance, a newly energy conscious public had a negative impact on domestic auto sales in the early 1980s. At the time, the auto industry was introducing automobiles with large engines, but consumers, due to rising gasoline prices, were more interested in smaller cars. Meyers and Holusha (1986) noted, "When the demand for your product dies, you die" (p. 96). In the case of the auto industry, such vehicles as the AMC Pacer were discontinued, and entire companies, such as Chrysler, faced the possibility of bankruptcy. Auto companies have responded to these events by diversifying products to spread the risk of downturns in any one market, shortening product development timelines, and aggressively collecting information to predict market trends.

In early 2002, Enron, the seventh-largest company in the United States, experienced a crisis due to deceptive and illegal accounting practices and artificially inflated stock values. The company filed for bankruptcy shortly after this information was made public. Among other consequences, Enron workers and retirees lost retirement benefits. Although corporate economic scandals have occurred in the past, the scope of the Enron deception and the resulting collapse was unique. Within months, the telecommunications giant WorldCom experienced a similar crisis due to improper accounting practices. With the emphasis of corporate America on short-term profitability, organizations are more susceptible to economic crises than ever before. Organizations such as Enron and WorldCom exemplify why organizations that place short-term profitability and stockholder value over corporate ethics, stakeholder responsibility, and long-term profitability are likely to experience similar crises in the future.

Human Resource Crises

Human resource crises take a variety of forms, such as strikes, sexual harassment, discrimination, and workplace violence. Even top-management succession can create a crisis. The public often very strongly identifies with the leadership of an organization. Lee Iacocca came to personify the Chrysler Corporation in the 1980s; Jack Welch was the powerful symbol of General Electric, and Michael Eisner personifies Disney. When changes occur in such visible and dynamic leadership, both workers and the public may lose confidence and loyalty. In other cases, leadership may be synonymous with the actual product. John F. Kennedy, Jr., was the driving force behind *George Magazine*. After his death the magazine soon ended publication because the entrepreneurial drive was lost. Crisis can also create changes in top management in order to scapegoat some of the blame. Organizations also at times try to change their image by focusing on a change in leadership. Ford, for example, replaced CEO Jack Nassar with Bill Ford, grandson of the founder, after the tire crisis associated with Ford Explorers. Probably the most damaging form of succession, however, is a public fight over leadership.

Another kind of human resource crisis usually involves lower-level workers. Some of the most notorious examples involve workplace violence. Shootings by postal workers were so well publicized in the 1990s that the phrase *going postal* came to represent an extreme form of employee violence. Shootings in high schools have occurred in Jonesboro, Arkansas; Littleton, Colorado; and Paducah, Kentucky; at an elementary school in Mount Morris, Michigan; and also at universities, including Iowa State University, Wayne State University, and the University of Arkansas. Ford and General Motors have both experienced dramatic episodes of shooting rampages by disgruntled workers at manufacturing plants. Such extreme human resource crises can be devastating to the morale of the organization because so much of the violence happens in front of employees. Despite careful pre-employment screenings, support structures, warning systems, and supervision, these types of crises are not likely to subside in the future because employees are sources of high variability in organizations.

Industrial Crises

Industrial disasters, including plant explosions, fires, collapses of facilities and mines, and releases of toxic substances, account for some of the most-dramatic organizational crises. Shirvastava, Mitroff, Miller, and Miglani (1988) explained that industrial crises "are caused by two interacting sets of failures. Inside organizations, a complex set of human, organizational, and technological (HOT) factors, lead to the triggering event" (p. 290). This makes an industrial accident the quintessential organizational crisis. Human factors, Shirvastava et al. suggested, may include

operator and managerial errors, purposive acts such as sabotage and terrorist acts or acts of war.... Organizational factors include policy failures, inadequate resource allocations for safety, strategic pressures which allow managers to overlook hazardous practices and conditions, communication failures, misperceptions of the extent and nature of hazards, inadequate emergency plans, and cost pressures which curtail safety....Technical systemic factors include faulty design, defective equipment, contaminated or defective materials or supplies, and faulty technical procedures" (p. 290).

Industrial crises may also be triggered by natural disasters. These crises exemplify the role of complexity. As manufacturing technologies become more complex, the potential for crisis increases. Although this increase is often accompanied by heightened vigilance, training, and new safety technologies, the increasing size and complexity of such systems makes them inherently more prone to failure.

Oil and Chemical Spills

Oil and chemical spills most often occur during transportation of the product. They are typically related to shipping, trucking, rail, or pipelines and have the potential for a profound impact on communities and the environment. The classic example of a failed crisis response is the Exxon *Valdez* spill of 11 million gallons of oil in Prince William Sound, Alaska. Although oil spills happen on a regular basis, the Exxon event created the most media exposure of an oil spill in recent memory. Almost universal criticism followed Exxon's response. As described in chapter 5, Exxon Chief Executive W. D. Stevens was criticized for his delayed response, unsympathetic reaction, and failure to accept responsibility for the crisis (Williams & Treadaway, 1992). This response failure was in part a result of the characteristics of this crisis type. Crises related to spills include the difficulty of cleanup, the explanation of scientific procedures to the public, and the immediate environmental impact. Moreover, any delay in response compounds the harm.

Transportation Disasters

Transportation disasters are related to spills and may involve airlines, trains, automobiles, ships, and trucks. Amtrak has experienced derailment resulting from a range of triggering events from operator error to overheating of the rails. Airlines experience operator error, weather problems, and technical failures. Ships experience inclement weather and a variety of technical failures. Although trucks are regularly inspected by external agencies for safety, truck transport accidents, as with many crises, are associated with equipment failure, human error, or the interaction of the two.

Airline disasters are often associated with poor coordination arising from ineffective communication (Cushing, 1994). Communication between airline pilots and airline traffic controllers, misunderstanding based on technical jargon, ambiguity, and even speakers' accents all play a role in airline disasters. Ray (1999) argued that air travel requires a high degree of coordination between a variety of groups and agencies, such as the various airline companies, the Federal Aviation Administration, and airplane manufacturers. After disasters, these agencies usually offer competing views of cause and responsibility. In these cases, the role of communication, along with the interactive complexity of airline technology, plays a major role.

Crises That Originate in the Organization's Larger Environment

To some extent, all crises concern the organization's larger environment. However, a distinct type of crisis has primarily external, national, or even international origins. These include adverse international events such as the OPEC oil crisis in the 1970s and the Asian market meltdowns of 2000. During the OPEC oil embargo, automobile companies suffered and eventually changed the way they produced cars. These events often require national legislation for effective management. In the case of OPEC, gas rationing and import quotas for fuel-efficient Japanese cars were instituted. Typically, these kinds of events have industrywide, regional, or national implications and are managed at broader national levels. Regulation or deregulation is another form of environmental crisis. The 2001 California power crisis was instigated at least in part by the deregulation of the power industry and by a lack of foresight regarding the impact. The result was a crisis that not only inconvenienced millions but nearly crippled the power industry in California. As a result, other states have either postponed deregulation efforts or revised their initiatives substantially.

Additional Features

Two additional features of crisis types are worth noting. First, to some extent all crises combine two or more of these types. Economic crises affect public opinion. Natural disasters may become economic crises and may create spills or transportation accidents. Some forms of human resource disasters represent a kind of terrorism and may involve sabotage leading to industrial accidents or chemical spills. Rail disasters may involve both spills and the loss of human life. Crises almost always evolve in unexpected ways and often precipitate secondary shocks or crises. In this way, the crisis types described here are almost never mutually exclusive.

Second, risk is inherently dynamic, and new crisis forms will continue to emerge in unexpected ways. New diseases and new forms of infection, such as West Nile virus, Lyme disease, and deer chronic wasting disease continue to emerge. Natural disasters can take new and unexpected forms, particularly as they interact with human technology and development. The impact of climate change cannot be anticipated. Unforeseen human resource challenges will create new crisis forms. Although crisis typologies are very helpful crisis learning and management tools, they cannot predict when an event will occur, what specific features it will have, or how the crisis will evolve.

SUMMARY AND CONCLUSION

These nine crisis types provide a general characterization of the threats organizations face. Although risk varies with the type of organization, its environment, products, technology, employees, location, stakeholder relations, culture, and history, it is clear that the potential for crisis is always present. Moreover, the potential impact of any of these events is tremendous. Natural disasters fundamentally alter organizations and communities. Product and service crises may have an impact on the basic way a company does business. Terrorist attacks affect our basic sense of security and change the way we live and travel. Economic crises change the way organizations do business and the way employees view their retirement plans. Industrial crises change the way companies do business and how technology is viewed. Airline crises change our view of technology, safety, and travel. Environmental crises illustrate the impact organizations have on their environment and how environments and organizations relate in the future.

Ultimately, the value of understanding crisis type is that it reduces the uncertainty associated with crisis and helps managers respond more effectively. All crises are by definition unique and chaotic events, but the common traits manifested across type offer helpful patterns, structures, and a general predictability within chaos.

CHAPTER 4

Communication and Crisis

Communication and organizational crisis intersect at many points. Communication is an ongoing process that enables organizations to monitor their environments before and during crisis, to understand and respond appropriately, to construct a consistent interpretation, and to resolve the crisis and reestablish order. As discussed in chapter 3, crises take many forms, yet communication is the common thread among these forms. If an organization is faced with a false, destructive rumor, accurate communication by the organization is essential. During natural disasters, communication is essential in coordinating recovery. The confusion, ambiguity, and potential legal consequences surrounding crises complicate this communication (Coombs, 1999b). Adding to the confusion are crisis-induced time constraints. Audiences in crisis situations are also complex. An organization is expected to simultaneously communicate with customers, stockholders, residents in the surrounding area, special-interest groups, and regulatory agencies (Schuetz, 1990).

In crisis situations, overcoming the prevalent communication constraints is essential if organizations are to respond effectively. Poor communication or reticence can intensify the magnitude of a crisis to a point where recovery is impossible. In this chapter, the functions of communication during crises are explored. Initially, the traditional view of crisis communication is described; it is followed by a discussion of an expanded notion of the function of communication in crisis. Each function is explained, and associated communication strategies are described.

TRADITIONAL VIEWS OF CRISIS COMMUNICATION

Communication, usually in the form of public relations, is a traditional function of postcrisis management or, in many cases, postcrisis spin. This position derives from the need for skilled communicators to strategically defend and explain the organization in the face of crisis-induced criticism, threat, and uncertainty. During crises, public relations practitioners providing accounts of what went wrong and why typically face a hostile and inquisitive press. Thus, historically, crisis communicators served as both spokespersons and buffers (Seeger, Sellnow, & Ulmer, 1998). Crisis communication, from this venue, is one manifestation of public relations as press agentry. This perspective involves two broad strategies: "deny that a crisis exists, refuse to answer media questions, and resist involvement by appropriate government agencies" or release "partial, often inaccurate and delayed information while concealing unfavorable facts" (Wilcox, Ault, & Agee, 1986, p. 310). This view of communication as spin has contributed to a cynical view of organizations and public relations and has made achieving crisis resolution more difficult.

As the role of public relations has expanded and as crises have become more common, so too has the notion of crisis communication. One fundamental change involves a cardinal tenet among public relations practitioners that an honest, candid, prompt, accurate, and complete response to a crisis is always called for (Small, 1991). A more-dynamic relationship between organizations as senders and stakeholders as audiences is also reflected in current approaches. Contemporary notions of public relations call for ongoing two-way symmetrical relationships. From this perspective, postcrisis may be a period of intense cooperation that allows for building and repairing relationships. In some cases, this form of cooperation translates into long-term organizational structures. Specifically, four functions of crisis communication are explored in this chapter: (1) environmental scanning, (2) crisis response, (3) crisis resolution, and (4) organizational learning (see Table 4.1).

COMMUNICATION AS ENVIRONMENTAL SCANNING

Organizations cannot evolve and sustain themselves without the support of their larger environments. The environment is a source of critical resources: raw materials, human resources, energy, and information. Society makes judgments about the appropriate use of these resources (Pfeffer & Salancik, 1978). Organizations are considered legitimate when they "establish congruence between the social values associated with or implied by their activities and the norms of acceptable behavior in the larger social system of which they are a part" (Dowling & Pfeffer, 1975, p. 122). Environmental scanning is essential for organizations to establish and maintain this consistency and legitimacy. There are four means by which organizations monitor their environment: (1) sensemaking, (2) issue management, (3) boundary spanning, and (4) risk communication.

Table 4.1
Functions of Communication in Organizational Crises

Environmental scanning	(Monitoring and maintaining external relationships)
	Sense making
	Issue management
	Boundary spanning
	Risk communication
Crisis response	(Planning for and managing crises)
	Uncertainty reduction
	Coordination
	Information dissemination
	Strategic ambiguity
Crisis resolution	(Restructuring or maintaining relationships after crises)
	Defensive
	Apology
	Explanative
	Renewal
	Grieving/memorializing
Organizational learning	(Emerging from a crisis with an enhanced knowledge base)
	Dialogue
	Epistemology
	Hierarchies

Sensemaking

Weick (1979) defined organizing as "a consensually validated grammar for reducing equivocality by means of sensible interlocked behaviors" (p. 3). From this perspective, it is "behaviors that are organized, not individual people" (Pfeffer & Salancik, 1978, p. 30). Behaviors, as discussed in chapter 2, are coordinated through the communicative act of sensemaking. Sensemaking is composed of four parts: (1) ecological change, (2) enactment, (3) selection, and (4) retention. Key to Weick's view is enactment. Ecological changes, such as emerging risks, foster equivocality and uncertainty. To comprehend and respond to these changes, organizations engage in ongoing processes of enactment. Enactment occurs when individuals take action and observe the subsequent response both inside and outside the organization. Because crises represent a radical change in the status quo, organizations cannot fully understand the crisis situation or their ability to resolve it without taking some initial action. These actions are usually selected from a repertoire of previous experiences. Organizations take action, observe the results, and decide whether to continue the initial line of action or to pursue another strategy. Until action is taken, an organization has no tangible evidence regarding its capacity to relieve the tensions surrounding a crisis.

The enactment process also concerns the ways organizations attend to ecological changes in the informational environment. The environment is potentially so large, confusing, and complex that it is simply not possible to attend to all elements. Rather, some selective attention must occur. Selective attention involves bracketing some aspect of the environment for attention. In this way, the organization chooses to act toward some aspect of its environment. This selection may be a function of top-management background, history, previous commitments, capacity, ease, or prominence of some environmental feature. Crisis can be understood, then, as a failure to attend to or enact some information input, which in turn develops into a crisis-inducing threat. From this perspective, a failed, incomplete, or "stunted" enactment is the basis of all organizational crises.

Issue Management

Issue management is a dominant paradigm in public relations. It concerns "the identification, monitoring, and analysis of trends in key public's opinions that can mature into public policy and regulative or legislative constraint" (Heath, 1997, p. 6). An issue is a contestable claim about a matter of fact, policy, or value. In managing issues, organizations seek to influence the ways in which these claims are resolved. By monitoring such issues, organizations have the potential to predict difficulties and to influence the development of public policy (Heath, 1997; Johnson & Sellnow, 1995; Jones & Chase, 1979). Whereas the fundamental facts of a crisis, such as an explosion or an airplane crash, are rarely in dispute, questions of cause, responsibility, blame, relative harm, and remedial action are almost always present (Seeger et al., 1998). Issue management, therefore, should be part of the organization's environmental scanning and postcrisis communication.

To manage issues effectively, organizations first must identify incubating issues that have a potential impact on the organization. If potential problems exist with a group, organizations should seek to establish some rapport. Failure to do so can either foster or exacerbate a crisis. Similarly, organizations can use their resources to persuade governing agencies to establish policies that are favorable to organizational goals. Failure to monitor such policy development leaves organizations vulnerable to regulatory whims. Heath (1997) argued that effective issues management, along with an appropriate sense of corporate responsibility, may lessen crisis conditions (p. 290). Similarly, a crisis may inflame public interest, making it necessary for an afflicted organization to argue on behalf of an entire industry for a reasonable response from governing agencies. For example, following the Exxon *Valdez* oil spill, angry environmentalists and concerned citizens demanded that government regulations be enacted to prevent future spills. In response to this pressure, Exxon's chief executive officer (CEO) W. D. Stevens, delivered a series of speeches warning against more-restrictive oil transportation legislation. Stevens successfully argued that such constricting policies would cripple the industry, causing a rapid rise in gas prices. Thus, through his public communication, a crisis-induced issue was resolved in a way that was conducive to Exxon's goals.

Boundary Spanning

The concept of boundary spanning views organizations from a "resource dependence perspective" (Pfeffer & Salancik, 1978, p. 262). Organizations cannot function without acquiring resources from their environments. This dependence on resources grants the organization's environment some degree of influence over the organization's operations. The more limited access to essential resources becomes, the greater this external influence. To maintain normal operations, organizations must sustain relationships with stakeholders who provide the needed resources. Thus, agents outside the organization's boundaries have the ability to influence the organization's activities. Organizations work to limit this "influence and constraint by restricting the flow of information about them and their activities, denying the legitimacy of demands made upon them, diversifying their dependencies, and manipulating information to increase their own legitimacy" (p. 261). Organizations also seek to collect and interpret information from external sources in order to predict and strategically influence stakeholder behavior. This movement of messages and information back and forth across organizational boundaries is critical to monitoring and maintaining external relationships.

From the boundary-spanning perspective, crises have the potential to disrupt an organization by limiting its access to essential resources. For example, Exxon suffered an immeasurable loss of resources following the *Valdez* oil spill. First, the crisis disrupted the flow of oil to Exxon's refineries, limiting its ability to meet its distribution goals, after frustrated government agencies suspended oil transportation in the region. Second, special-interest groups rallied against Exxon, resulting in diminished credibility and lost business. Third, the crisis fostered a congressional inquiry into oil transportation policies for the entire industry. In short, this single crisis threatened Exxon's access to the vital resource of transportation as well as its social legitimacy.

In coping with crises, the boundary-spanning perspective suggests that organizations should maintain effective relationships with relevant stakeholders prior to crisis. Crisis also creates a need to resolve any tensions that develop between the organization and those who provide essential resources. Organizations engage in boundary spanning to facilitate the process of mutual influence and accommodation, which allows for the development and maintenance of effective relationships with relevant environments. Crises may compromise legitimacy, strain these relationships, and ultimately deny organizations access to critical resources. Rebuilding these relationships is a part of the crisis recovery process.

Risk Communication

Another important function of communication between an organization and its environment concerns risk. Risk communication suggests that organizations should encourage an "exchange of information among interested parties about the nature, significance, or control of a risk" (Covello, 1992, p. 359). Organizations that fail in this function inhibit the ability of constituents to make rational choices about how organizational activities may affect them. Successful risk management reduces the uncertainty surrounding organizational products or technologies that have the potential to cause harm. Effective risk communication reflects an "information exchange and shared knowledge model" grounded in disseminating messages regarding the relative magnitude of risk, precautionary norms, and risk reduction strategies (Heath, 1995, p. 257). Risk communication is closely associated with the precrisis stage, in which perceptions of risk contribute to the development of precautionary norms; the crisis stage, in which timely information about risk may mitigate harm; and the postcrisis stage, in which new perceptions of risk are institutionalized in new precautionary norms and practices.

The need for risk communication has intensified as the development of high-risk technologies has intersected informed and activist stakeholders. Essentially, stakeholders claim a freedom of information based on the right to know about the potential harms associated with products, services, manufacturing facilities, technology, transportation, and many other organizationally constituted processes and outcomes. The information-exchange and shared-knowledge model, then, has important implications for what and with whom an organization communicates.

CRISIS MANAGEMENT

Communication is vital to supporting organizational operations in both the planning and recovery stages of crises. Communication is the primary means for organizations to reduce uncertainty and coordinate actions. In the crisis-planning process, described in chapter 9, organizations detail the communication procedures designed to coordinate activities and disseminate information during crises. Strategic choices about coping with and capitalizing on the inherent ambiguity of crises are also management functions. Four communication management functions are described below: (1) uncertainty reduction, (2) coordination, (3) information dissemination, and (4) strategic ambiguity.

Uncertainty Reduction

Uncertainty is the sine qua non of crisis. Uncertainty reduction enables organizations to diminish ambiguity, build consensual meaning, and coordinate efforts. During crisis, organizations can anticipate uncertainty related to the cause, consequences, legal and regulatory implications, and the public reaction. Berger and Bradac (1982) have contended that the human need for uncertainty reduction intensifies when the behavior of others is deviant, when repeated interaction with others is likely, and when there is a high probability of receiving rewards or punishment from others. Two of these factors help explain how crises intensify uncertainty. First, crises often stem from inappropriate, deviant, and abnormal behaviors. Second, employees and consumers seek information during crises in an effort to determine whether or not to maintain their ongoing relationship with the organization. More generally, the public seeks information to determine whether the crisis will affect them, how they should think, and what they should do. Simultaneously, then, organizations must engage in uncertainty reduction to ascertain the causes of the crises, to communicate interpretations to the public, and to monitor how crisis management efforts are received.

Routine responses are usually of little value in coping with crisis uncertainty. Weick (1995) explained that organizations must take novel actions and evaluate those actions before they can fully understand the crisis and the merits of management efforts. This is because "people often don't know what the 'appropriate action' is until they take some action and see what happens" (p. 306). Yet, an initial crisis response that is inappropriate can actually intensify public outrage. "There is," Weick noted, "a delicate tradeoff between dangerous action which produces understanding and safe inaction which produces confusion" (p. 305). He explained that it is the shock of crises that often inspires organizations to engage in uncertainty reduction: "[P]eople frequently see things differently when they are shocked into attention, whether the shock is one of necessity, opportunity, or threat" (pp. 84–85).

For employees, customers, and other stakeholders, uncertainty reduction is accomplished by monitoring and evaluating the situation. This process includes the general media coverage and the reactions of regulating agencies and officials. If the organization fails to provide stakeholders with a consistent flow of information regarding the crisis, the organization risks having its stakeholders depend exclusively on the assessment of the media and regulatory agencies. In other words, the organization runs the risk of allowing others to interpret the event and frame its meaning. In these cases, the organization is left in a reactive stance. Without the flow of information between the organization and its stakeholders, organizations cannot establish and fortify those relationships that are essential to effective crisis management.

Coordination

Crises usually create an intense and immediate need for organizations to coordinate their activities with internal and external groups. Internally, crises often halt or disrupt standard procedures. Accordingly, employees often must undergo some degree of reorganization. Similarly, crises are seldom solved through standard procedures and responses. Even when crisis plans are in place, organizations typically must adopt some form of novel solution to convince all stakeholders that similar crises are less likely to occur in the future (Sellnow & Seeger, 1989). All of these changes require coordination through communication. This coordination requires the allocation of resources and subtle or major changes in infrastructure. Additional coordination includes complex crisis logistics such as the strategic movement of personnel and resources to create the response capacity necessary for mitigation.

The complexities of the coordinating process can best be understood from the systems perspective of wholeness. Wholeness suggests that because all parts of the systems are interconnected, repercussions of failure in one aspect will reach others. For example, the Union Carbide Bhopal disaster prompted the company to shut down operations at a number of facilities worldwide until their safety was assessed. Airline disasters often prompt systemwide assessments that may delay flights. Coordination, then, must occur throughout organizations as they seek to contain the damage and begin the crisis recovery process. Messages clarifying the situation and directing actions produce the coordination that is essential for containment and recovery.

Coordination may also be necessary between the organization and its environment. For example, natural disasters create turmoil in the lives of entire communities, regions, or, in some instances, countries. Relief personnel such as emergency management, medical, and search-and-rescue teams, as well as fire and police departments, coordinate preparation, rescue, and warning during the disaster. This often necessitates complex logistics of equipment, manpower, and technical expertise, especially when the crisis site is inaccessible and communication is difficult. Such coordination is rarely possible without the cooperation of the media. For example, when the 70,000 residents of Grand Forks, North Dakota, were evacuated due to flooding, the local newspaper remained a vital form of communication. Although the newspaper's presses and offices were destroyed, the journalists acquired the services of a printing press in another community and created a means for distributing the paper. The newspaper, then, became the primary means for locating displaced people, announcing cleanup procedures, and scheduling meetings with the Red Cross and federal agencies such as the Federal Emergency Management Agency (FEMA). For its efforts, the *Grand Forks Herald* won a Pulitzer Prize. In Fargo, a local AM radio station devoted nearly all of its air time to providing minute-by-minute updates on river levels and announcing areas where volunteers were needed for sandbagging assistance. During crisis, communication is vital and often functions in novel ways through nonstandard channels to help coordinate an effective response.

Information Dissemination

Coordination and mitigation processes during and after crises are likely to fail unless organizations have a means for effectively disseminating information. Organizations that distribute information in a timely and efficient manner are better able to address concerns raised by the press, employees, customers, and other stakeholders. Moreover, clear information about what actions to take, such as avoiding certain meat products during *E. coli* outbreaks, is critical to limiting harm. In cases of toxic spills, residents may need to be instructed to take shelter or evacuate. A key strategy in the information dissemination process is selecting a primary spokesperson prior to the crisis. Crisis management plans typically identify a single spokesperson responsible for communicating or approving communication to all relevant audiences for the duration of the crisis (Seeger, Sellnow, & Ulmer, 2001). This spokesperson should be a credible source and an authority figure. Crisis creates a need to hear from authority figures in part to signal that the established authority structures are functioning.

When the space shuttle *Challenger* exploded, media sources scoured NASA and the contractor Morton Thiokol in an effort to find explanations for the explosion. Some of the first stories released by the media included comments from engineers at Morton Thiokol speculating that the crisis was caused by a malfunction in the large fuel tank. The public was showered with conflicting stories regarding the cause and reasons why there was no opportunity for the crew to escape. The resulting confusion and frustration could have been avoided if NASA had identified a crisis spokesperson. Although it is not possible to control all messages, designated spokespersons can help an organization centralize and coordinate its response. Eventually, all NASA and Morton Thiokol employees were asked to defer questions to NASA's leadership. The cause of the crisis was ultimately linked to the booster rockets. Ironically, this was not one of the theories initially shared following the crisis.

A single spokesperson is also valuable for internal communication. Customers and shareholders are likely to experience frustration, alienation, or confusion when messages are inconsistent. A single spokesperson allows for all inquiries to be noted and for all official responses to be consistent. Individual employees are often approached by the media for information about a crisis. Employees who receive clear and consistent information are able to act on and share that information more efficiently. Thus, personnel become another resource that may assist with crisis resolution. If employees do not receive clear and consistent information, they may also feel confused and frustrated.

Strategic Ambiguity

The public generally demands that organizations in crisis situations share information clearly and immediately (Schuetz, 1990). The surprise and complexity of many crises make such precise and expeditious communication impossible, at least in the initial stages. Hence, crisis management usually begins as a process of managing or coping with ambiguity. For example, when a plane crashes, the names and exact number of victims cannot be released until passenger lists are consulted and families notified. Cause and responsibility for the crash may not be known for months. Airline officials are initially forced to manage the crisis without these details. The interdependent nature of organizational elements and the interaction between an organization and its environment also makes determination of consequence complex. For example, following the initial collapse of Enron, many questions were asked about consequences. How would the accounting firm Arthur Andersen be affected? What effect would this collapse have on investors, employees, the industry, and on the economy generally? Questions such as these are reasonable and inevitable following a crisis. In short, the complexity of organizational systems makes ambiguity an inherent component of crisis communication.

Although ambiguity is inevitable, organizations can use it to their advantage. Eisenberg (1984) maintained that, when used strategically, ambiguity "promotes unified diversity in organizations" (p. 230). For example, "[W]hen organizational goals are stated concretely, they are often strikingly ineffective" (p. 231). Strategic ambiguity is a "political necessity" to create an interpretation that is sufficiently broad to meet the needs of various stakeholders and to reflect the inherent uncertainty of the situation. Although "clear communication of intended meaning usually is one major aim of an ethical communicator," in some situations "the intentional creation of ambiguity or vagueness is necessary, accepted, expected as normal" (Johannesen, 1996, p. 108). Eisenberg and Witten (1987) cautioned that organizational activities that have "safety or legal implications, require clear, complete communication" to avert the "worsening of some problems over time, making them less manageable if confronted in the future" (p. 423). However, overreliance on strategic ambiguity in organizations "minimizes the importance of ethics" and "is often used to escape blame" (Eisenberg & Goodall, 1997, p.

26). In general, strategic ambiguity may be both ethical and warranted in some crisis situations.

COMMUNICATION AS CRISIS RESOLUTION

After the urgency of the crisis has dissipated, organizations must respond to and accommodate the conditions created by the crisis. This involves offering plausible accounts, interpretations, apologies, explanations, descriptions, and narratives. These responses must be enacted and integrated into new organizational operations, norms, procedures, beliefs, structures, and values so that they can address multiple and conflicting audiences. Generally, the organization addresses its external publics, but internal stakeholders also demand a response.

Communication is the means whereby organizations respond to criticism and rebuild their images after a crisis (Coombs, 1999a). Crisis creates an exigency for the organization to explain and defend its actions, to clarify its role in the crisis and the cleanup, and in some cases apologize and seek forgiveness. The feedback organizations receive following a crisis response is particularly valuable in assessing how the response is being received and determining if modifications are needed. When the response is adequate and remaining questions are answered, the organization is able to move past the crisis. Communication, then, is the essence of crisis resolution. Communication as crisis resolution involves defensive messages, apologies, explanations, grieving and memorializing, and reconstituting normalcy.

Defensive Messages

An organization's defensive communication is made difficult by the characteristics inherent in organizational crisis situations. As discussed in chapter 1, crises creates three characteristics: threat, surprise, and short response time. Not only must an organization respond quickly to an event it could not or did not foresee, it must do so while under the pressure of an impending loss of profit, legitimacy, or both. When faced with a crisis, organizations have three general options: inaction, routine solutions, and original solutions (Sellnow & Seeger, 1989). Inaction involves no response. Routine solutions depend on precedence or precrisis planning. Original solutions "are created specifically for a particular crisis situation" (p. 10). Although routine responses to crisis—such as blaming and firing individuals—can salvage an organization's legitimacy, original solutions that signal change can "enhance a perception of preventive, long-term change and renewed social legitimacy" (p. 17). The willingness of Johnson & Johnson to change the form of its capsule and packaging techniques was an original solution. In this case, the company was able to recover quickly from a devastating case of product tampering with its reputation intact, if not enhanced.

Apology

Organizational response to crisis is referred to as corporate apologia (Benoit, 1995a; Ice, 1991; Sellnow, 1993). As detailed more fully in chapter 8, the apology process for organizations is more complex than for individuals. As Ice (1991) noted, "[P]lacing responsibility for a corporate action is more difficult than for an individual act, because there are multiple layers of acts and interactions which can cause a corporate accident" (p. 6). Matters of authorship, attribution, and responsibility for messages from organizations are equally difficult to ascertain. Corporate messages "tend to 'decenter' the self, the individual, the acting subject" (Cheney, 1991, p. 5). This tendency can be seen in the conventions typical of corporate messages such as using the passive voice, synecdoche, or personification. Statements such as "Ma Bell decided" or "the Pentagon reacted" leave observers wondering, "Decided by whom?" (Cheney, 1991, p. 5). The nature of organizations creates an opportunity to deny and diffuse responsibility in crisis situations that is not generally possible for individuals (Schultz & Seeger, 1991).

During crises, apologia, as rhetoric, involves strategies designed to repair image, respond to criticism or accusations of wrongdoing, and move past the crisis as quickly and easily as possible. This approach seeks to synthesize comprehensive typologies of apologetic strategies. Benoit (1995a), for example, has developed a comprehensive list of strategies for both organizational and individual speakers. He has described five general image-restoration strategies: denial, evading responsibility, reducing the offensiveness of the event, corrective action, and mortification. Hearit (1995) argued that in apologia, organizations employ three prototypical appearance/reality disassociations. These include (1) denial of guilt through opinion/knowledge disassociation, (2) differentiation of guilt by scapegoating through individual/group disassociation, and (3) distancing from guilt through act/essence disassociation. These strategies, described in more detail in chapter 8, can be invaluable for organizations seeking to find their way out of a damaging crisis situation.

Explanative Messages

A message that may or may not have been part of the organization's apology is an explanation. An explanation addresses the fundamental question What happened? The immediacy of crises demands that organizations cease standard operations and focus almost entirely on explaining an event it did not anticipate. Because of this, the entire organizational communication process is sometimes transformed by crises. Often, leaders are initially unaware of the specific factors leading to the crisis. They must rely on lower-level members to inform them of what happened. As a result, there is often a momentary transpositioning of the typical top-down communication structure as organizations struggle to acquire the necessary information.

As organizations seek to explain to themselves and others what happened, the value of information may outweigh authority. For example, the expertise of an engineer describing a malfunction in a factory may have considerably more explanatory power than the organization's leader expressing regret. Explanations of this sort are an essential first step in knowing what to do, determining cause and blame, and moving beyond a crisis. Although the public explanations may come through a single spokesperson, information about what happened is acquired from all levels of the organization. In short, expertise in areas related to the crisis and firsthand knowledge of the event become paramount.

Grieving and Memorializing

There is a powerful human drive to remember, build memorials to, and commemorate events of great tragedy and loss. Victims of crises share their losses through a variety of communication channels, ranging from face-to-face interaction to communication through Web sites. Although there is little research regarding this form of crisis communication, commemorative events, media features, and Internet activity have all functioned as part of the postcrisis communication process of grieving and remembering.

Memorial events are the most obvious form of postcrisis communication related to grieving, remembering, and learning. Communities that have undergone a particular hardship often commemorate the date. For example, each year, Grand Forks, North Dakota, commemorates the flood that destroyed its city by unveiling further progress in the greenway it is creating. The greenway is designed to control future floods and to provide a recreation area for residents. In this manner, city residents are able to regularly reconstruct the meaning of the flood into a vision for a renewed and improved community. The memorializing process is also a form of learning. Communities work to maintain the memory of tragic events, not just as part of the grieving process, but also as a reminder that the community must remain vigilant in preparing for and, if possible, preventing similar crises in the future.

Other victims of crisis turn to the media for catharsis. In the wake of the Enron collapse, many individual investors and employees repeated their stories of lost retirement savings on television and in the press. These victims appear to take some comfort when their stories of loss and grief are shared in this manner. Through sharing the story, vicarious learning occurs. Others may take actions to avoid similar losses. Consequently, the loss incurred from the crisis is not in vain. Many crisis victims indicate that they seek out media attention for this reason. The degree to which this relief is also based in retribution, vindication, or as an admonition for others depends on the individual. Nevertheless, media exposure appears to assist many individuals in the grieving process.

There was a unique manifestation of this public grieving following the horrors of 9/11. The chaotic devastation of that day left thousands of people separated from families and friends. Some were hospitalized. Some were simply unable to get home or to contact family or friends. Many had died. In an effort to coordinate contact between these missing persons and their loved ones, several Web sites were created. Those who were missing a loved one were encouraged to post the missing person's name, photo, and contact information. Early in this process, the Web sites served this coordinating function. Hospital and social workers searched the sites in an effort to find the injured or displaced and to identify the dead. As time passed, however, the Web sites took on other roles. First, those who had survived the attacks, including friends and family who lived elsewhere but had friends working in the World Trade Center or the Pentagon, used these sites to determine if their coworkers or acquaintances were reported missing. A second shift occurred involving the individuals who had posted missing persons data. As the days passed and families became increasingly aware that their loved ones had died in the attacks, the sites evolved into public tributes rather than sites for inquiries. Friends and family members began to embellish their initial Web information with obituaries that honored the lives of the people who had died. Pictures, poems, and eulogies were posted. In the end, the Web sites evolved into public memorials of pain, human grief, and senseless loss. Various forms of postcrisis communication are related to grieving and memorializing and are important to both learning and resolution.

Reconstituting Normalcy

A final crisis resolution function of communication is to help reconstitute normalcy. During crisis, patterns of communication are disrupted. Contact with friends, family and coworkers is lost. The established channels of communication, such as newspaper and television, often are unavailable. New topics and themes are introduced into public communication and filter into conversations with friends and family. Changes in communication patterns and forms are continual reminders of the crisis. When communication returns to some form of normalcy, information is again available from familiar sources and voices. These reconstituted channels and forms help to reestablish a sense of normalcy. Normalcy is also signaled when the channels of public communication no longer feature the crisis as a primary part of their agenda.

A dramatic illustration of the return to normalcy occurred following the 9/11 attack on the World Trade Center. The nationally syndicated television talk show *Late Night with David Letterman*, which originates from New York, was cancelled for several days following the attack—a vivid reminder of the disruption. When the show was again aired, on September 17, host David Letterman indicated that, despite the overwhelming pain, he felt obligated to help people "go back to their lives—to go on living" and return to a sense of normalcy. This return to normalcy function suggests that moving the crisis off the media agenda and reestablishing familiar channels and patterns of communication facilitates crisis resolution.

CRISIS COMMUNICATION AS ORGANIZATIONAL LEARNING

As discussed in chapter 2, a principal framework for understanding crisis is organizational learning. Ultimately, learning is a perspective that encourages organizations to develop a shared vision that fosters a willingness to adapt or evolve in response to their environment. Senge (1990) argued that organizational teams may function well with routine and familiar issues, but when they are confronted by crises their cooperative resolve tends to disintegrate. Conversely, organizations that are able to learn have the potential to emerge from crises with a renewed sense of purpose. Learning as both the process whereby members acquire new knowledge, responses, or skills, and the systemwide modification of culture, procedures, and practices depends on communication. In this section, the role that crisis communication plays in organizational learning is discussed through the perspectives of dialogue, epistemology, and organizational hierarchies.

Dialogue

Communication in the form of dialogue is essential for organizations to recondition their processes. When dialogue is effective, knowledge and insights are pooled (Senge & Kleiner, 1994, p. 239). Moreover, dialogue may also be self-reflexive, allowing members to examine, critique, and more fully understand their beliefs, knowledge, values, and assumptions. In a manner similar to retrospective sensemaking, Senge and Kleiner's notion of dialogue allows "people to become observers of their own thinking" (p. 242). For dialogue to be successful, participants must suspend assumptions, regard one another as colleagues, and maintain a consistent view of the context during the interaction. Discussion is the "necessary counterpart to dialogue." In discussion, "different views are presented and defended," whereas in dialogue "different views are presented as a means toward discovering a new view." Both dialogue and discussion "can lead to new courses of action, but actions are often the focus of discussion, whereas new actions emerge as a by-product of dialogue" (p. 247). In short, organizations cannot learn effectively without dialogue.

Crisis as a learning opportunity involves translating events into a history and defining the event as a "critical incident." Histories are narrative, interpretive schemes of past events that allow for meaning and lessons to be transposed to current circumstances. Histories told as stories allow current members to richly experience the past. Critical incidents are those that are recognized as having important lessons for the organization. Learning can be part of the crisis resolution process as well as the means for developing a plan to avoid similar crises in the future. Most importantly, an organization cannot learn from a crisis without communication. Communication distributes the knowledge of the critical incident throughout the organization. The discussion is most effective when it takes the self-reflexive form as with organizational dialogue.

Epistemology

Although crises have the potential to disrupt organizations, this disruption, if managed effectively, is also an opportunity to create fundamentally new knowledge and understanding. In experiencing and making sense of a serious crisis, organizations frequently must communicatively construct a quintessentially new understanding of self, environment, risk, opportunity, markets, stakeholders, products, and technology. This perspective is best described as corporate epistemology or as a way of knowing and creating knowledge (Von Krogh, Roos, & Slocum, 1994). The communication associated with severe crises is epistemic in that it allows members to collectively construct this new knowledge base. Members do so through a variety of processes. Selection and enactment allows interpretive knowledge to be tested against the emerging equivocality. As with learning, a severe crisis may prompt a systematic search for a new knowledge base. Crisis often forces organizations to confront entirely new sets of stakeholders and interact with them in ways that create novel insights, perspectives, and, occasionally, functional relationships

Viewing crisis communication as epistemic is similar to self-organizing following bifurcation, as described in chaos theory (see chapter 2). Self-organizing may require a fundamental new understanding of what the organization is, what markets it serves, and how it does business. Often, following bifurcation organizations find that they are functioning in new, smaller markets. Alternatively, organizations that are taken over following crises may discover they have become part of much-larger organizational structures. In either case, communication serves the role of allowing members to construct the new knowledge and understanding necessary to continue serving the organization.

Organizational Hierarchies

An organization's approach to epistemology and learning has implications for the hierarchical distribution of power. Traditional methods of information gathering in organizations are highly routinized and follow a standard set of hierarchies, procedures, and assumptions (Knights, 1992). The development of new activities or perspectives is limited within such hierarchies as dominant views become "normalized" and controversial actions or individuals are objectified or stereotyped (p. 518).Von Krogh et al. (1994) warned that "new distinctions often vanish simply because they are not understood or further debated" (p. 63).

Relying on the work of French philosopher Michel Foucault, Knights (1992) suggested that organizations reach this form of stagnation by relying on positive forms of knowledge. Positive knowledge involves a dependence on the methods of natural sciences to develop laws, rules, and probabilities which, in turn, create the standards and truths of organizational life.

Creativity and flexibility are often lost when positive knowledge dominates because such knowledge is "self-fulfilling" (Knights, 1992, p. 532). To break free from this quiescent view, organizational members must "at the cost of their own demise...continue to unsettle, to disturb, and ultimately to undermine the stability and reputability of positive forms of knowledge" (p. 520). Yet "until a major crisis occurs, or new top management replaces the old team, a change in rigid knowledge structures cannot be expected" (Von Krogh et al., 1994, p. 57).

Crises create the opportunity for publicly questioning long-held beliefs or the positive knowledge of organizations. "Massive criticism," such as that following crisis, can foster "changes in the core of the knowledge structures" (Von Krogh et al., 1994, p. 57). Investigating agencies may force organizations to defend standard procedures that, for decades, went unquestioned. Because crisis modifies beliefs about risks, norms, and procedures in the organization by suspending the assumption of the status quo, new stakeholders may demand that the organization consider alternative bases of knowledge. Similarly, crisis situations often place pressure on those who are most dominant in the organization's hierarchy. Frequently, crisis forces old managers out, making room for fresh perspectives and new voices.

By their nature, crises foster communication that departs from the normal patterns and hierarchies, creating room for the kind of creative thinking and "multiperspectivism" that can advance an organization's knowledge system (Tsoukas & Papoulias, 1996, p. 77). This process often involves careful scrutiny of feedback from all levels of the organization. Crisis may create the opportunity to privilege a new set of voices and perspectives.

SUMMARY

Crises are by nature shocking events that have the potential to traumatize an organization, its employees, stakeholders, and leadership. Traditional notions of communication as merely postcrisis spin have given way to a recognition that communication has a broader and instrumental role. Crises place severe demands on sensemaking and thus require communicative processes to construct consensual meanings. Communication is essential for sensing risk, for coordinated and effective response, for reducing uncertainty, for apologizing, for memorializing, and for returning to normalcy. These functions of communication are not mutually exclusive; that is, some messages may serve multiple functions in a process of creating dynamic interactions among crisis stakeholders.

Optimally, communication enables organizations to monitor their environments before and during a crisis, to understand the event and respond appropriately, to construct a consistent interpretation of the event, and to resolve the crisis and reestablish order. In many other cases, however, communication is less than optimal and harm is accelerated, uncertainty remains high, the meaning is unclear, and the crisis is extended. A fuller recognition of the instrumental role of crisis communication may help increase its effectiveness.

PART II

Stages of Crisis Development

CHAPTER 5

Crisis Development

One of the most useful approaches to understanding crises describes these events as series of interrelated phenomena developing over time. These developmental approaches involve longitudinal analysis to understand how in crisis a class of antecedent conditions is associated with a class of subsequent events (Coombs, 1999b; Seeger, Sellnow, & Ulmer, 1998). This approach describes a series of relatively general and discrete stages or phases that can be used to describe the development of a crisis, regardless of the industry or crisis type. Developmental models have been outlined by a number of researchers and represent one of the most-common tools for crisis analysis (Fink, 1986; Guth, 1995; Shirvastava, Mitroff, Miller, & Miglani, 1988; Sturges, 1994).

This chapter begins with an examination of the assumptions of the developmental approach and its contribution to the larger understanding and management of crisis. Three developmental approaches are discussed, including Turner's (1976) six-stages sequence of failure in foresight, Pauchant and Mitroff's (1992) crisis management-crisis phase model, and the three-phase model of crisis development (Coombs, 1995; Ray, 1999). These approaches are used to identify and examine specific stage-related features of crisis. The application of the three-phase model is illustrated further through the examination in chapters 6, 7, and 8 of three crises: the 1989 Exxon *Valdez* oil spill, the outbreak of salmonellosis traced to Schwan's in 1994, and the North Dakota floods of 1997.

ASSUMPTIONS OF DEVELOPMENTAL APPROACHES

Embedded within developmental approaches are assumptions about crises and systems. First, there is an inherent tendency to describe crisis in simplistic terms as the consequence of a single cause. Most descriptions of systems, for example, view them as the outcomes of single decisions and choices by individual managers rather than as complex interactive structures in which outcomes are systemic and involve multiple actors. There is a strong tendency, for example, to attribute both system successes and failures directly to formal leadership structures (Seeger, 1986a). Moreover, an isolated cause may allow the organization to compartmentalize and limit blame and responsibility in a way that protects the larger system. Scapegoating, for example, is a common postcrisis strategy. Individual managers are often blamed for the failure of an entire system even though they may have little direct control over day-to-day operations. Developmental views of crisis, however, expand beyond the specific moment, the single decision, and the individual manager associated with the immediate aftermath of the crisis, to events, decisions, and changes that occurred long before the trigger event and to adaptations and adjustments that occurred long after.

A second assumption of developmental approaches is that crises are both time-ordered and time-sensitive events. These two characteristics, evident in any close examination of crisis, account for the developmental view's popularity among both researchers and crisis managers. Crises occur at a particular point in the ongoing and dynamic operations of a system. System theory often takes a cyclical view of operations, but crisis clearly marks a point of radical departure. The bifurcation disrupts the repetitive cycles of input-throughput-output in distinct ways. Crisis researchers and participants often describe these events as "points of departure," or "moments of change" at which the world—or our understanding of it—shifts in important and dramatic ways (Murphy, 1996). Crisis, therefore, is experienced as a moment in time that is distinct from "normal." Participants in crisis often describe a fundamentally altered sense of what is normal following a crisis and often describe a "new normal." In some dramatic cases, those experiencing a crisis report that their fundamental sense of security is shaken. Worldviews are turned upside down, continuity with the past is lost, and old assumptions are broken at the moment of a crisis.

The time-ordered dimensions of crisis are also reflected in the ways these events are recalled. Often, events of particular significance are remembered, recounted, and commemorated on the anniversary of the event. In this way, the event is memorialized and the passing of time since the event is marked. Anniversaries are used to assess progress toward strategic changes initiated after a crisis. As discussed in chapter 2, the telling and retelling of critical histories creates opportunities for organizational learning (Huber, 1996). Marking a crisis anniversary makes it possible to reiterate the fact that the crisis is in the past and to recall the lessons learned from the crisis.

A third time-ordered dimension of crisis concerns the time-sensitive nature of these events. Crisis compresses the interval between decision, actions, and antecedent conditions on the one hand and outcomes, reactions, and consequences on the other. Time compression is associated with high uncertainty within an environment of high risk (Gouran, 1982). Decision makers in these circumstances must act quickly to reduce the threat of crisis, without the requisite information about cause or about how the system will behave under crisis (Weick, 1988). Thus, actions designed to reduce the severity of the crisis sometimes serve to accentuate harm. Moreover, crisis often creates a tighter coupling between various aspects of system operation by reducing available slack resources. Managers or technical experts who might have served as buffers between systems, for example, are often distracted or cut off. Access to records, personnel, decision systems, and support structures may be limited. During the Union Carbide Bhopal disaster, for example, decisions had to be made about how to treat victims without having precise information regarding what chemical compounds had been released (Shirvastava, 1987).

Time compression is also associated with the intense media scrutiny that follows a crisis. News is inherently a time-sensitive product; increasingly, the news media closely covers crisis events (Greenberg & Gantz, 1993). The proliferation of 24-hour news services and newsmagazines has created an intense need for news. Journalists, in fulfilling their social-watchdog function, actively seek stories of defective and unsafe products and corporate wrongdoing, adding an additional layer of crisis-induced threat. Moreover, the media often seeks immediate explanations regarding cause and blame and disseminates this information very broadly. The harm created by a crisis, often revealed in victims' stories, is dramatically represented in the press. During a crisis, this pressure for immediate explanations about cause and consequences—and the broad public dissemination of those messages—intensifies the consequences of decisions and public statements made by the organization.

Finally, developmental approaches also assume such an evolution of system behavior that Event A @ T1 is followed by and influences Event B @ T2, which in turn influences Event C @ T3, and so on. System behavior at any point is a consequence of previous conditions. Although it is not possible to specify initial conditions with enough precision to predict outcomes, these outcomes are antecedent to and dependent upon initial conditions. In some cases, at least, it is possible to retrospectively trace the antecedent influences on a crisis. These developmental approaches, therefore, can also help to clarify how dynamic and interactive sequences of events and interpretations may, through long and unanticipated cause-effect linkages, result in crisis. Such efforts are often necessary for retrospective sensemaking, for organizational learning, and for the resolution of the crisis. Some level of consensus regarding a probable cause, blame, responsibility, and what will be done to ensure that a similar event does not occur is generally necessary for crisis resolution.

Developmental approaches are useful in helping to clarify how dynamic and interactive sequences of events and interpretations may, through long and unanticipated cause-effect linkages, result in crisis. The

goal of these approaches—to identify a series of relatively discrete stages
or phases that can be used to describe the development of a crisis regardless of the industry or crisis type—is particularly useful for crisis management (Pauchant & Mitroff, 1992). If the broad and general outlines of crises
can be drawn, managers may have a much better sense of what to expect
during a crisis. This, in turn, facilitates planning and the selection of
appropriate response strategies. Although all crises are by definition
uncertain (and often involve the erratic behavior of complex systems),
patterns, trends, and a kind of consistency are evident as a crisis evolves.

DEVELOPMENTAL VIEWS

Three approaches to crisis development are described here: Turner's
(1976) six-stage sequence of failure in foresight; Pauchant and Mitroff's
(1992) five-phase crisis management model; and the three-stage model of
crisis development (Coombs, 1995; Ray, 1999; Seeger et al., 1998). These
approaches are compared and used to identify, examine, and cluster the
specific time-ordered features of crises. The three-phase model is then
developed as a general analytical framework for understanding and
managing crisis.

Six Stages of Failure in Foresight

One of the most-comprehensive models of crisis stages was developed
by Barry Turner (1976), based on his analysis of public inquiries into disasters. Turner identified a sequence of six relatively discrete stages. He
argued that crises may be understood as "large scale intelligence failures"
or "failures in foresight." Turner wrote, "A disaster occurs because of
some inaccuracy or inadequacy in the accepted norms and beliefs" that
"rarely develops instantaneously" (p. 381). Beliefs about the world, its
hazards, and what constitutes reasonable precautions allow organizations
to manage many day-to-day problems. At any point, Turner argued, these
established beliefs help constitute a sense of normal operations. In fact,
most crises are effectively resolved with little or no attention through
these routine and normal structures. One fundamental difficulty organizations face, then, is to determine which problems can be safely ignored
and which should be attended to. When an organization misses some critical cue regarding an emerging threat, it experiences what Turner called a
"failure in foresight" or "collapse of precautions which have hitherto been
regarded culturally as adequate" (p. 380). Crisis often involves an interaction between problems considered unimportant and precautions that
were considered adequate. Crisis, then, is the result of a widespread and
dramatic failure in the adequacy or veracity of shared belief systems,

rather than a short-term failure in technology, a momentary lapse in managerial or operator vigilance, or flawed decision making.

As discussed in chapter 3, a system's communication procedures are associated with these failures in foresight in two specific ways. First, the messages and cues regarding risk may not be heard, noticed, or attended to. This represents a kind of detection or reception problem. A number of factors limit this ability to detect cues, including cues that are subtle or ambiguous and belief systems that preclude seeing a deficiency. Rarely, if ever, does a crisis occur without any warning. Second, even an issue or problem that is recognized may not be effectively communicated in a way that fosters action. Poor levels of management-employee trust and related problems in upward communication are often associated with the failure to effectively communicate crisis warnings. The organization may simply not be able to accept or believe a problem-signaling message because it is so inconsistent with established beliefs and values. Whistle-blowers, individuals who explicitly identify and communicate a problem, for example, are frequently ignored and sometimes punished for calling attention to problems (Jensen, 1987; Near & Micelli, 1986).

Table 5.1
Turner's Sequence of Failures in Foresight

Stage I.	Point of normal operations
	(a) Culturally accepted beliefs about the world and its hazards
	(b) Associated precautionary norms (set of laws, codes of practices, mores, and folkways)
Stage II.	Crisis incubation period
	Unnoticed accumulation of events that are at odds with accepted beliefs about hazards and their avoidance.
Stage III.	Precipitating event
	First sensing of crisis and realization of the inadequacy of fundamental beliefs
Stage IV.	Onset of crisis
	Period of direct impact and harm
Stage V.	Rescue and salvage
	Recognition of collapse of beliefs and initiation of ad hoc adjustments to begin rescue and mitigation
Stage VI.	Full cultural readjustment of beliefs
	Full readjustment based on inquiry and assessment; return to a new Stage I

Source: Adapted from "The Organizational and Interorganizational Development of Disasters," by B. Turner published in *Administrative Science Quarterly,* 21 by permission of *Administrative Science Quarterly.* Copyright © 1976 Cornell University.

In Turner's Stage I (see Table 5.1), a point of normal operations and procedures, members have (a) a set of culturally accepted beliefs about the world and its hazards, and (b) associated precautionary norms set out in laws, codes of practices, mores, and folkways, which are generally considered adequate (p. 381). Accepted beliefs, policies, and procedures, for example, may govern handling of dangerous chemicals, dealings with agitated employees, or accounting methods for reporting profits and losses. These beliefs, norms, and attendant procedures are highly interdependent, so that a change in *a* would necessitate a change in *b*. The widespread belief of the 1930s and 1940s, for example, was that asbestos was a safe, convenient, and technologically superior product. Its flame retardant and insulating characteristic made it particularly useful for a variety of applications. Subsequent changes in belief structures surrounding asbestos, however, resulted in a dramatic change in the accompanying precautionary norms, codes, and practices. Asbestos is now itself a major hazard, with elaborate accompanying norms, codes, and practices for its safe handling and disposal.

In Stage II, the crisis incubation period, events that are outside the parameters of and/or at odds with the accepted beliefs about hazards and the norms for their avoidance accumulate, usually unnoticed. Turner argues that either the events are unknown or are known but not fully understood. Often a collective blindness, similar to Weick's concept of stunted enactment, allows minor problems to grow to overwhelming proportions. A problem incubates, grows, and perhaps interacts with other unnoticed problems. Turner (1976) suggested that incubation often occurs because a problem or issue is poorly structured or defined and, consequently, cannot be attended to easily. In other instances, the problems are known and understood but are not communicated in ways that garner the attention and action of decision makers. Enron Corporation's collapse is a vivid example of Stage II incubation. Cues about the company's problems were evident long before the dramatic collapse and in fact were widely reported in the business press. These cues were largely unrecognized, judged as unimportant, or simply ignored by Enron executives. In part, this was due to the complexity of the energy-trading business and its poorly understood accounting practices. Even the overt actions of Enron whistle-blower Sherron Watkins failed to elicit a response. Rather, Enron executives actively sought to deny the veracity of these claims.

In Stage III, the crisis is first sensed through a "trigger event" that signals the fundamental inadequacy of the accepted beliefs about hazards and avoidance norms. A trigger event—some dramatic occurrence such as a consumer harmed by product failure, a lawsuit, some dramatic disruption of operations, an explosion, a violent act, or a media report—signals the eruption of a threat into a crisis (Billings, Milburn, & Schaalman, 1980). These trigger events are the dramatic points of bifurcation at which the distinction between normal, routine operations and what is happening is so clear that it cannot be ignored. The crisis, however, is still difficult to define or understand. There is an immediate sense that something is dramatically wrong, but the exact nature of the event is not clear, nor are the consequences. At the moment when the *Challenger* space shuttle exploded in a ball of flame over southwest Florida, the NASA announcer continued his laconic narration by stating simply, "Obviously, a major malfunction."

In some cases, the first person to perceive a trigger event must convince others that a crisis actually exists. Many crises first become evident to lower-level operators, who must then alert senior managers. Sometimes, an outside agency or watchdog group first becomes aware of a triggering event and must convince the organization that a problem exists. Often, the initial response of managers is to try to frame the crisis within the parameters of normal operations, particularly when the event is distant or lacks dramatic features. Plant supervisors may discount readings from gauges because they are outside norms of safe operation. Problems may be described as merely "blips on the radar screen," misunderstandings, overreactions, or mistakes until enough evidence has accumulated to create the general recognition of the crisis. Until mutual agreement about the crisis is created, a coordinated organizational response is unlikely (Billings et al., 1980).

The severity of the perceived threat is related to two factors. The first concerns the nature of the compromised organizational goals, and the second is the perceived probability of loss (Billings et al., 1980). In some instances, a crisis may only slightly reduce profitability but have a high probability of occurring. In other instances, the organization's viability is at risk, but the probability of crisis is low. In almost all instances, the exact nature and implication of the threat is not immediately evident. Managers must sort through possible outcomes and responses before some sense of the severity is known. At any time during the crisis, the nature of the response, probabilities, and values of a loss may change as new information becomes available. A third factor, time pressure, further complicates estimates of severity. During Stage III, interpretations of earlier stages first begin to be modified so that decision makers can define and structure what is now seen as a problem. This is an important first step in the readjustment of beliefs about hazards and avoidance.

Stage IV involves the onset of the crisis and its immediate, direct, and unanticipated consequences. Damage varies widely in intensity and scope from crisis to crisis. Stage IV may be described as the crisis in operation or that period where the direct impact or harm occurs. In many instances, such as the crash of Valujet Flight 592 or the *Challenger* disaster, the Stage IV interval may last only a matter of minutes, but within that time, significant harm accumulates. In the case of an outbreak of food-borne illness, such as in the Hudson Foods case, Stage IV is much more extended. Damage continued until the source of the outbreak was identified, warnings were issued, and the tainted meat was recalled. Reducing the Stage IV interval is a goal of most crisis managers. Crisis containment means that some level of control has been reasserted and the major risks are past, although secondary risks and outbreaks are possible. The conclusion of Stage IV, however, often goes unrecognized or is prematurely declared. Because crisis events represent novel circumstances, it is often impossible to know when containment has been successful or if risk is still high. Many who witnessed 9/11 believed that the crash of American Airlines Flight 11 into the World Trade Center's Tower One represented the major crisis event. Much more damage, however, was yet to come.

Stage V is rescue and salvage, where the immediate collapse of beliefs about the world, its hazards, and its avoidance norms is fully recognized. This recognition allows for initial and rapid ad hoc adjustments and initiation of rescue and salvage. At this point, the organization may activate its crisis plan and begin to strategically manage its crisis response to rescue threatened individuals and assets while mitigating harm. Efforts to mitigate harm, provide treatment to victims, recover bodies, cordon off dangerous areas, and assess the level of damage are undertaken. These responses often require high levels of coordination between the organization and outside agencies. This Stage V coordination requires some consensus about the nature of the crisis and appropriate mitigation strategies. Coordination also requires channels for communication, which are often disrupted during crisis. Phone lines may be down and established reporting relationships broken. Crisis plans often address these potential breakdowns by establishing prearranged channels for communicating, such as phone trees or hot lines. In other cases, channels may emerge spontaneously during rescue and salvage. During the aftermath of 9/11, for example, thousands of paper flyers describing missing persons and family members and providing contact information were posted around the disaster site. As the immediate effects of the disaster dissipate, more time is available for a carefully thought out assessment. During Stage V, the intensity and stress of the crisis begins to wane, allowing for consideration of what happened. This is also the stage at which participants first begin to try to understand the crisis and its implications. This understanding involves untangling the "incubating network of events" associated with the crisis (Turner, 1976, p. 382).

Stage VI, Turner's (1976) last, involves a full cultural adjustment regarding beliefs about the world, its hazards, and its avoidance norms, so that they are compatible with the new insights and understanding. New norms, policies, and procedures are instituted so that similar events do not occur. This final stage requires some general consensus about cause, blame, and responsibility. Often, a formal inquiry or assessment into the crisis is undertaken by outside agencies to identify the network of events associated with the crisis. Stage VI creates an exigency regarding communication of a plausible explanation and attendant issues of blame, responsibility, and legitimacy. Image restoration, for example, may be necessary as an apologetic response to the crisis. This may include denial, evasion of responsibility, reduction of the offensiveness of the event, corrective actions, or mortification (Benoit, 1995a). Legitimacy is a status conferred by the external public and constituencies and concerns the larger social value and justification for an organization (Metzler, 2001). Strategies for rebuilding legitimacy during Stage VI may include excuses, justification, ingratiation, denouncement, and distortion (Allen & Caillouet, 1994). In terms of organizational learning, Stage VI is also the point where a critical event becomes a narrative history about risk, its potential for crisis, and its avoidance. In some instances, the process of learning from crisis is highly structured, such as in the National Transportation Safety Board's issuing of "probable cause" findings and recommendations for enhanced safety. In other instances, Stage VI adaptations are more informal as members reach a new consensus regarding risk and choose to behave differently. In either case, Turner argues, a new understanding regarding what constitutes normal arises. This new understanding is reflected in postcrisis adaptive responses that become standardized parts of the organization's operations.

Turner (1976) also suggested that Stage VI leads back to Stage I, a point of normal operation and procedures. Crises, then, are understood as long-term and broadly cyclical processes, with Stage VI, full cultural readjustment, leading to a new Stage I, accepted beliefs about the world and its hazards and their avoidance. One of Turner's most important contributions is his suggestion that crises incubate over extended periods of time. The onset of crisis, in his view, does not occur until the third stage. As he noted, "Small-scale failures can only be produced very rapidly, but large-

Figure 5.1
Five-Phase Crisis Management Model

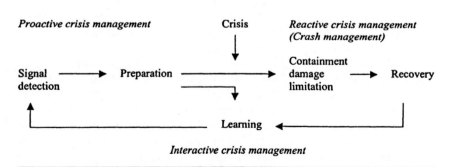

Source: Adapted from *Transforming the Crisis-Prone Organization*, by T. C. Pauchant and I. I. Mitroff, 1992, San Francisco: Jossey-Bass.

scale failures can only be produced if time and resources are devoted to them" (p. 395). Turner's notion of Stage VI as cultural readjustment is also an important contribution, allowing for integration of a number of post-crisis exigencies such as apology, reestablishing legitimacy, learning, and the construction of a new consensus regarding risk.

Five-Phase Crisis Management Model

Pauchant and Mitroff (1992) have created a five-phase model that links developmental features of crisis to three larger strategies of crisis manage-ment (see Figure 5.1). They began their analysis with the assumption that some organizations are more prone to crisis than others. Organizations that are less prone to crisis are "able to confront the anxiety of the crisis and to act decisively...they are able to be ethically, emotionally and cog-nitively responsible" to various stakeholders (p. 5). Responsibility, in this sense, concerns the choices and actions of organizational participants. Cri-sis, then, is largely a question of effective organizational management. This view places organizational participants' actions and choices at the nexus of crisis. Thus, a crisis can be anticipated, avoided, and prevented by the responsible actions of management. Pauchant and Mitroff also made cogent arguments about the role of participants in crisis and the importance of responsibility:

People who manage destructive crisis-prone organizations believe it is their fun-damental right to exploit any resource—human, financial, or physical—without limitation. They admit no wrongdoing, no necessity for change. If a crisis occurs, they are likely to blame others. They are incapable of empathizing with others, and they exhibit little concern for issues of human dignity or ethics. (Pauchant & Mitroff, 1992, p. 5)

This fundamental assumption regarding the role of managerial discretion and the associated view of responsibility in the development of crisis, then, influences the ways in which Pauchant and Mitroff described crisis development. Specifically, five stages are described and related to three broad classes of strategic crisis management behaviors: proactive, reac-tive, and interactive. The five phases of crisis are (1) signal detection, (2) preparation/prevention, (3) containment/damage limitation, (4) recov-ery, and (5) learning. Signal detection concerns the reception of early-warning signals, identification of cues, or recognition of forewarnings of crisis. Pauchant and Mitroff (1992), like Turner (1976), argued that crisis "usually sends off a persistent trail of early warning signals, or symptoms, announcing a probable occurrence" (p. 136). They also suggested that in crisis-prone organizations, managers and employees are "very skilled in blocking out the signals of impending crisis," whereas crisis-prepared organizations "are able to sense even very weak signals" (p. 137). It is the failure to receive, enact, or attend to these signals that allows a crisis to erupt. The phenomenon of organizational members distorting or ignoring messages signaling potential problems is a kind of systematic information distortion. This distortion is most common with upward communication in organizations that have defensive climates and low levels of superior-subordinate trust. Signal detection, then, can be expected to function most effectively in a context of high superior-subordinate trust and supportive climates of communication.

Preparation and prevention, Pauchant and Mitroff's (1992) second stage, also relates to crisis management. Prevention is possible where the signals have been detected and where the crisis is controllable. Prevention, in this sense, represents a strategic adjustment in activities, processes, products, and services so that the risk of a crisis is reduced. Preparation involves "designing various scenarios and sequences of actions for imagined crises, and testing them fully until those involved are familiar with their roles" (Pauchant & Mitroff, 1992, p. 137). Effective crisis management involves the construction of crisis plans and the development of crisis-mitigation expertise.

Despite comprehensive preventative efforts, however, some crises inevitably erupt. Pauchant and Mitroff's (1992) third phase, then, involves "damage limiting mechanisms" (p. 138). These mechanisms, often outlined in the prevention component of the second stage, are designed to contain and limit damage. The ability to prevent damage from spreading to other parts of the system is highly contingent on the kind of crisis. Toxic spills, for example, typically spread out from a centralized point over time. Rapid containment in this case is highly beneficial. Explosions and crashes, in contrast, typically create damage within a very short time frame, allowing little opportunity to contain the harm. Pauchant and Mitroff have suggested that the width of diffusion of information about a crisis, such as through the media, can extend damage. Part of the damage-control process, therefore, may involve limiting or controlling this diffusion.

The fourth phase of crisis management is recovery. Recovery, like containment, is highly contingent upon the preparation described in Stage 2. The goal of this stage is to "recover what has been lost," including both tangible and intangible items (Pauchant & Mitroff, 1992, p. 138). Recovery allows for the return, as soon as possible, to normal business operation. Prioritization and backup plans from the preparation stage. as well as improvising with available resources, are crucial components in recovery. Pauchant and Mitroff also noted that recovery can be a time of exhilaration, in which participants exhibit high levels of cohesion and motivation in achieving what is an "undeniably crucial task" (p. 138). This exhilarating aspect of the recovery stage may allow recovery to occur more quickly and may be part of the larger renewing force of crisis described in chapter 2.

Finally, they suggest that in considering recovery, managers should focus on external relations with key stakeholders as well as internal operations.

Learning is the final process described in Pauchant and Mitroff's (1992) model. Unlike the other stages, learning is presented as both an outcome and as a variable in earlier stages (see Figure 5.1). Learning is a process of "reassessment to improve what has been done in the past." Learning seeks to "review and critique, without assigning blame, so as to learn what was done well and what was done poorly so that the organization can handle crises better in the future" (p. 107). In this way, learning interacts with earlier stages, such as signal detection and preparation/prevention. This characterization of learning processes as dynamic outcomes of earlier stages is a much more flexible view of crisis than that proposed by Turner. Whereas Turner described learning as "full cultural adjustment" occurring after crisis is resolved, Pauchant and Mitroff portrayed crisis as a more malleable, dynamic, and controllable process. Three kinds of strategic management processes in particular may influence crisis development. These include proactive, reactive, and interactive crisis management.

Proactive crisis management involves the activities associated with Stage 1, signal detection, and Stage 2, preparation/prevention. Proactive strategies allow the organization to change its behaviors and activities to effectively detect crisis signals, prevent crisis through risk reduction, or prepare for response. Proactivity assumes that the organization recognizes the need to change, has the motivation to change, and has the ability to change. Reactive management involves Stage 3, containment/damage limitation, and Stage 4, recovery. These management strategies are reactive in the sense that they occur after the crisis. Because it is no longer possible to avoid harm, management strategies at this stage concern containment and resumption of normalcy. The success of these strategies is often contingent on activities undertaken in Stages 1 and 2. Interactive strategies involve learning and making continual adjustment of plans and preparation in the absence of crisis or as the consequence of experiencing a crisis. Pauchant and Mitroff (1992) described interactive strategies as reaching across the various stages and integrating proactive and reactive approaches.

The developmental model offered by Pauchant and Mitroff (1992) views crisis as a more controllable and manageable process, where the onset of harm is not inevitable. Learning occurs at various points, allowing for adjustments to avoid the crisis or for preparation and more successful crisis resolution. Organizations characterized by "responsibility" are, accordingly, able to reduce their vulnerability to crisis, limit the frequency of these events, respond more successfully, and recover more quickly and fully. Pauchant and Mitroff's model, then, challenges managers to be more responsible in proactively avoiding and preparing for crisis. "Reactive crisis management strategies" or "having no strategy at all" is, in their view, simply not acceptable (p. 141).

Three-Stage Model of Crisis

A third approach involves three discrete stages of crisis: precrisis, crisis, and postcrisis. The three-stage model is not associated with any particular theorists, but it appears to have emerged from several research efforts as a general analytical framework (Coombs, 1999b; Guth, 1995; Ray, 1999; Seeger & Bolz, 1996; Ulmer, 2001). Ray (1999), for example, used this approach to examine a series of major airline disasters and the involvement of federal regulatory agencies. The Federal Aviation Administration (FAA) and the National Transportation Safety Board (NTSB) oversee safety norms and procedures in precrisis stages and conduct investigations to determine probable cause in postcrisis stages. The involvement of the NTSB as an outside agency, Ray concluded, is helpful in rebuilding organizational legitimacy during postcrisis stages. These investigations then return to FAA guidelines and policies as part of the cultural readjustment leading to a new precrisis state.

The three-stage model offers three broad stages that may encompass other, more limited, less apparent, and more variable substages (Coombs, 1999b, p. 13). These three phases, then, can be generalized, regardless of the specific manifestation of an individual crisis. As summarized in Figure 5.2, the three-stage model collapses Turner's Stage I and Stage II and Pauchant and Mitroff's (1992) first two stages into the macro precrisis stage as the time of normal operation, preparation, and sensing before the onset of a trigger event. The crisis stage, then, involves the crisis trigger event and the onset of harm and continues until such time as the system returns to near normal operations. It encompasses, therefore, Turner's Stages III and IV and Pauchant and Mitroff's containment/damage limitation stage. The postcrisis stage encompasses Turner's last two stages by including postmortem, system modification and adjustment, and resolution. Pauchant and Mitroff's last two stages, recovery and learning, are also within the postcrisis stage. Postcrisis includes the postmortem and cultural adjustments and learning and leads back to the precrisis state of near normal operations. These processes are outlined in Figure 5.2.

The precrisis stage, described more fully in chapter 6, is characterized as a state of normalcy in which worldviews, interpretive schemes, and sense-making structures—including procedures and policies—are considered adequate to avoid risk. In this way, precrisis is also a point of strategic preparation, reflecting an understanding of risks and procedures for crisis mitigation. Some planning and development of teams can be highly detailed and carefully structured to create a robust crisis avoidance and response capacity.

Assumptions about crisis and risk typically dominate during this precrisis stage. For example, the organization believes that risk can be known, contained, and controlled. Moreover, the organization typically believes that it understands its exposure to risk, that risk is at an acceptable level,

Figure 5.2
A Three-Stage Model of Crisis

---

1. Pre Crisis ⟶ Incubation Period

Beliefs and associated enactments about risk,
    its levels and nature
Associated policies, procedures, structures
    Safeguards for avoidance
    Crisis plans/procedures

Failure in foresight/signal detection ⟶ Critical uncertainty
Failure to perceive event, critical uncertainty,   grows/interacts in
Issue, problem, and/or emerging threat   unanticipated/nonlinear
    disproportional ways
    ↓
Failure to communicate effectively   Growth of threat and/or
    shrinking of response
    capacity

2. Crisis→Onset of harm ⟶ Initiation of mitigation
    activities/plans

Threat→Heightened stress/emotion→Rigid response→Lost decisional vigilance

    Uncertainty about cause and consequence/
        Loss of sensemaking structures/predictive relationships
        Previous understanding of risk judged as inadequate

    Restricted response time→Inability to assess situation and options

    Initial self-organizing→Return to near normalcy

3. Postcrisis→Assessing cause→Image restoration/relegitimation

Return to near normal operations/recovery

Restablished pattern/routines ⟶ Apologia/image restoration
    Reconstituted sense of normalcy   Cultural adjustment in beliefs
    about risk
    New norms, behaviors,
    procedures
    Changes in preparation

    Opportunity for renewal/learning ⟶ Establishment of crisis as a
    historical/critical event

    Suspension of status quo; critical event ⟶ Organizational learning

    Continue on crisis themes of
    self-organizing/potential for
    renewal

and that appropriate safeguards, policies, precautions, and procedures are in place. In addition, networks of safety procedures, security, and training are the tangible manifestations of precrisis beliefs and assumptions regarding risk. These assumptions, however, may limit the ability of the organization to perceive or enact some signal of an emerging threat, critical uncertainty, or contingency. The variety of failures in foresight discussed by Turner (1976), the limitations on enactment identified by Weick (1988), and the lapse in processing novel information may account for such failures. In addition, crisis signals or cues may be so subtle that they defy detection. In other cases, the signals may be clear and understood but are not communicated in ways that prompt action. For example, Roger Boisjoly, a Morton Thiokol engineer, expressed his serious reservations about launching the *Challenger* space shuttle, given the cold temperatures and a lack of information regarding how the shuttle would respond. His warnings went unheeded by NASA managers.

During precrisis, an emerging threat of precritical uncertainty, then, develops and interacts with other aspects of the system. This process is typically described as incubation, where gestation includes growth in the magnitude of the threat and in its dynamic nonlinear interaction with other aspects of the system. Often, this incubation involves a disproportional and nonlinear impact of what has been judged as "insignificant" or "minor" variance. In some cases, threats converge or connect and interact with other failures in foresight or fallacious assumptions about risk. Another common interaction concerns the level of threat preparation interacting with other system needs. Expensive crisis training, for example, may be reduced as other budget contingencies emerge. Crisis response equipment may even be cannibalized to maintain operating capacity. Positions may be eliminated, reducing slack and buffers, and thereby enhancing tight coupling. The general tendency to discount anticipated risks if they do not become manifest often accounts for a general decay in vigilance. Thus, during precrisis, risk of a serious threat often grows while crisis response and mitigation capacity shrink.

The crisis stage, as discussed earlier, begins with the trigger event and the larger recognition that a crisis has occurred. This recognition is often accompanied by extreme emotional arousal, stress, fear, anger, shock, and general disbelief. Panic in the form of extreme maladaptive responses, although a feature of some situations, is uncommon. More often, it is the overwhelming confusion about what is happening that disrupts the capacity to understand. Crisis is also the stage at which harm is initiated and where a majority of the direct harm occurs. Harm may take many forms and may extend beyond the boundaries of the organization to affect stakeholders. In other cases, the harm may be more limited. Mitigation activity, containment, and damage limitation during the crisis stage may significantly reduce harm. For example, containment booms are usually deployed around oil spills. Product recalls and warnings serve to remove dangerous products before they do additional harm. Rapid organizational responses can help limit damage to reputation, image, and legitimacy.

As discussed earlier, crisis immediately creates three conditions. First, there is the perception of the probability of loss to some high-priority item or goal. Second, there is surprise and uncertainty about cause and consequences and about previously held assumptions regarding crisis. Finally, crisis creates decisional pressure through contraction in response time. The perceived threat of loss initiated by a trigger event may be both institutional and personal. In extreme cases, the organization's very existence is threatened. In almost all cases, profitability, stability, and reputation are at risk. Individual managers may face the threat of lost jobs, serious career damage, or legal liability. The threat usually creates heightened levels of stress and reduced decisional vigilance and may precipitate a rigidity response and decisional paralysis. In many cases, organizational authority systems are distracted and contract as they struggle to focus on the crisis. The novelty of the situation and the general bifurcation of established patterns and relationships intensify uncertainty. The demonstrated inadequacy of established assumptions, basic worldviews, and interpretive schemes further enhances response uncertainty. Complicating this uncertainty is a third condition in the crisis stage: contraction in decisional and response time. Organizations are forced to respond to the crisis, offering explanations about cause, blame, responsibility, and consequence, at the very moment when their ability to do so is seriously compromised.

The crisis stage, then, is a moment of great emotional turmoil, drama, and confusion. Moreover, the structures and devices necessary to make sense of the situation often collapse at the very moment they are necessary to reconstitute order. Slowly, however, through self-organizing processes and the reemergence of basic sensemaking processes, order reemerges. Often, order reemerges from a precrisis plan with preestablished contingencies, responses, and prepared plans. Outside agencies, such as firefighters and law enforcement and emergency-response teams, converge to contain harm and reestablish order. Frequently, a senior manager or designated leader helps to reassert some order and authority. Recovery may be accompanied by heroic efforts and extraordinary cooperation. The recovery period may also be a time of exhilaration for participants. The crisis stage ends, then, when this order is reestablished and the system again begins to function in some kind of nearly normal way. This may be a matter of hours for some crises or a matter of months for others. Fink (1986) noted that the Three Mile Island crisis was called "the accident without end" (p. 24). Toxic spills, defective products, or cases of mismanaged toxic waste, in particular, may have extended crisis stages. The Chernobyl disaster is expected to affect several generations of residents living near the plant. Often, a crisis precipitates an extended backlash through the reemergence of a public policy issue. Three Mile Island reinvigorated the anti–nuclear power movement, and the Exxon *Valdez* incident brought environmentalism back onto the public agenda.

The final stage, postcrisis, is a time of intense investigation and analysis that includes efforts to create plausible explanations of what went wrong, why, how, who is to blame, and what should be done to prevent a recurrence. These processes are fundamentally efforts to make sense of the crisis by looking retrospectively at what happened and constructing and testing plausible interpretations (Weick, 1979). Often, these investigations are undertaken by outside agencies, regulatory bodies, and sometimes by the courts. Much of the postcrisis determination of blame and responsibility involves elaborate arguments, explanations, excuses, and apologies. These strategies, described more fully in chapter 7, are grounded in the assumption that "restoring or protecting one's reputation" is a primary goal (Benoit, 1995a, p. 71). These approaches are helpful in describing the range of strategic options available to organizations during postcrisis. Apologetic and image-restoration strategies are largely defensive and reactive responses to the uncertainty and threat of the crisis. They are designed to symbolically position the organization more favorably regarding questions of cause and blame and to move beyond the crisis with minimum cost and disruption. The overriding goal is to return to a precrisis state quickly, with as little damage to the organization's image and reputation, and as little cost, as possible. In some cases, these strategies of image restoration are used in a misleading and even deceptive way as organizations seek to diffuse responsibility about blame, interject uncertainty about cause, and discount the relative level of harm (Ulmer & Sellnow, 2000).

Sitkin (1996) argued that "failure is an essential prerequisite for learning" (p. 542). The explanations of cause and blame usually inform a set of critical postcrisis changes and adjustments, including new understandings of risk and their associated procedures, policies, norms, and behaviors. Postcrisis investigations are often justified on the grounds that they help to ensure that a specific kind of failure does not happen again. In some cases, new industrywide policies and controls are instituted. Crisis plans may be amended, response procedures adjusted, and crisis training added or modified. New sources of crisis warnings may be identified for future monitoring. In this way, postcrisis, is an important time for organizational learning.

The postcrisis stage may also be a time to continue the momentum of self-organizing and renewal initiated in the crisis stage. Usually, this involves building on themes, trends, and motivation established in the crisis phase. Those individuals and agencies that helped to resolve or contain the harm during the crisis stage may be celebrated as heroes. Firefighters, police officers, individual employees, managers, and bystanders sometimes become crisis heroes. New cooperative relationships that emerged during the crisis may be strengthened and formalized. Leaders who helped to reduce the uncertainty by their actions and statements during the crisis may be recognized and rewarded. These leaders may capitalize on their status by calling for renewal and offering a vision of the renewed organization that incorporates crisis-induced changes. The role of leadership in crisis is examined more closely in chapter 13. Intense energy, motivation, creativity, and resources are sometimes available during postcrisis for cleanup, recovery and rebuilding, and ultimately for renewal. As chaos theory suggests, the new postcrisis organizational forms and structures emerging from a crisis often operate at a higher level as a consequence of this renewing affect.

A final component of the crisis stage is the larger systemic vulnerability it induces. Systems shocked by bifurcation may be weakened or vulnerable and particularly susceptible to subsequent crisis-induced trigger events. An organization distracted by a crisis may be ripe for a hostile takeover. Sometimes, bifurcation creates secondary interactions or stresses leading to secondary harms in the core system or related systems. The intense media scrutiny created by the initial crisis may reveal other problems or perceived wrongdoings. These secondary shocks may reignite a crisis phase or may extend the postcrisis stage. Within one 12-month period, for example, Ford Motor Company experienced a public dispute with Firestone over defective tires and Explorer rollover accidents, a series of high-profile law suits, a major market downturn, and changes in top leadership. Many of these trigger events were closely interconnected and in some ways built upon one another. Crises, in this way, may occur in such staggered and interrelated sequences that they become relatively common features of organizational life. Ford, like so many large and complex organizations, faced "permanent whitewater," where threat and risk are constants (Comfort, Sungu, Johnson, & Dunn, 2001).

As with the models proposed by Turner (1976) and Pauchant and Mitroff (1992), the adjustments that occur in the postcrisis phase ultimately bring the organization back to precrisis, where risk is again assumed to be understood, contained, and largely static and where avoidance norms and procedures are viewed as adequate. The organization again faces a set of conditions it considers largely normal, although this state is often described as a "new normal." At this point, a new set of threats, critical uncertainties, dynamic risks, or unobserved contingencies may emerge, go unrecognized, interact in unanticipated and disproportional ways, and begin leading the system into crisis. These cycles of crisis, from the stability of normalcy to the instability of a trigger event and the onset of threat, function as dynamic forces of radical system learning, adaptation, and transformation.

CONCLUSION

No single developmental model has yet emerged as sufficient for all types of crisis. The three-phase model is valuable in broadly capturing general process characteristics, yet is sufficiently general and flexible to be adapted to specific conditions. This model is grounded in the crisis-related communication activities that organizations undertake at particular times as they face particular contingencies. It views crisis as part of the larger ongoing cycle of organization, yet it suggests that crises may be managed, both in terms of avoidance and successful recovery.

Examination of crisis development has great promise in interrelated behaviors, beliefs, and system features of crisis, its onset and resolution. These models help to capture the dynamic tendencies of organizations and the disruption and harm they regularly face. They describe organizations as complex, interactive, and adaptive systems that change and learn in relation to dynamic and evolving environmental contingencies and new understandings of risks. Most importantly, development views may help crisis managers anticipate the general development of these events in ways that enhance the organization's capacity to respond to crisis in proactive, harm-reducing ways.

CHAPTER 6

Communication and the Precrisis Stage

Crises begin with a period of incubation during which an organization is operating in what is seen as an essentially normal, routine manner. Worldviews, interpretive schemes, sensemaking structures, procedures, rules, norms, and policies are considered adequate to avoid risk. In many cases, precrisis is characterized by the subtle decay of vigilance regarding risk and the erosion of crisis mitigation and response capacity. This decay, in turn, interacts with the incubation of some minor, yet dynamic, variance and emerging threat. Cues regarding the impending crises are overlooked, allowing for the development of a crisis trigger event. Precrisis ends with the onset of serious harm.

This chapter details the development of the precrisis stage and describes six primary features: (1) the establishment of belief structures regarding risk, (2) norms for mitigation and crisis response, (3) the decay of those structures, (4) processes of incubation and complex interaction, (5) missed warnings, and (6) a crisis trigger event. These conditions are used to examine the development of the 1989 Exxon *Valdez* oil spill, the costliest and one of the most damaging oil spills in U.S. history.

THE PRECRISIS STAGE

Organizational environments are the primary source of risks that lead to the development of crisis (Meyer, 1982) Uncertainty and the inability to completely monitor and communicate with the environment are central to most crises (Smart, 1985). The precrisis stage, then, involves existing organizational deficiencies in operations, perceptions, structures, norms, or policies interacting with emerging and often unobserved or uninterpreted environmental threats. These conditions incubate over time until some aspect of the organization is radically misaligned with an important contingency. Crisis often involves problems judged as unimportant interacting with precautions that were considered adequate (Turner, 1976). Ultimately, a trigger event occurs, leading to the onset of a crisis and a shared recognition of the problem. The six general processes associated with the precrisis stage are presented in Table 6.1 and described below.

Organizations develop belief systems about risks and threats and the associated structures of risk mitigation, crisis avoidance, and response in several ways. Industry standards, for example, often develop around areas of clearly identified risk. Through processes of vicarious learning, organizational approaches to risk often become highly standardized across an industry. Industry norms are sometimes formalized in elaborate governmental regulations and guidelines. Detailed procedures for food handling, for example, are outlined by the Food and Drug Administration (FDA), the United States Department of Agriculture (USDA), and state and local health boards. The Occupational Safety and Health Administration (OSHA) outlines elaborate procedures for maintaining health and safety in manufacturing organizations. According to the mission statement on the OSHA Web site, OSHA is charged with enhancing safety "by encouraging employers and employees to reduce the number of occupational safety and health hazards at places of employment" (http://www.osha.gov). Organizations may also develop an understanding of particular risks through reports of other crises. For example, following the Enron collapse, a number of organizations examined their own accounting practices. The Columbine (Colorado) High School shootings prompted careful reassessment of school safety policies and procedures throughout the United States. Organizations also develop specific understandings of risk, norms, and procedures for avoiding crises from their own experiences. A crisis usually serves to vividly demonstrate an area of risk and motivates managers, employees, and even society at large to mitigate against that risk.

Table 6.1
Six Elements of the Precrisis Stage

1. Established belief structures regarding risk and the probability of crisis
2. Development of norms and structures of risk mitigation including crisis plans
3. Decay in structures of mitigation and crisis plans
4. Incubation and complex, nonlinear interaction of emerging environmental contingencies and minor system variance
5. Missed warnings, failure to perceive and/or act upon crisis cues
6. Trigger event, the onset of harm, recognition of crisis

Crisis often prompts an organization to update its crisis plan and develop more-elaborate mitigation strategies. An organization that has recently experienced a crisis, therefore, is more likely to be vigilant toward risk. As a result, organizations are often best prepared for the kind of crisis they have most recently experienced. During the precrisis stage, however, the belief systems and attendant norms and structures of risk tend to decay and become misaligned with emerging risk areas. Simply stated, it is difficult to maintain a heightened state of risk vigilance when beliefs about risk do not become manifest and when risk is highly dynamic. A record of safety, therefore, often has the unintended consequence of actually reducing crisis vigilance by creating the belief that safeguards are adequate. This decay in belief systems usually occurs in three interrelated ways.

First, these shared precautions and belief systems about risk, technology, structures, markets, suppliers, competitors, and associated operating norms are set out in relatively rigid laws, codes, practices, policies, and procedures. As the environment changes, these static precautionary norms often are no longer adequate. Even crisis plans are often outdated and do not reflect basic changes in facilities, personnel, telephone numbers, resource availability, or the current size and scope of a potential crisis. Second, precautionary norms and structures tend to decay over time, particularly when they are not used or regularly practiced. During the precrisis stage, initial beliefs about risk become less salient as the system operates in a crisis-free context. Elaborate precautionary norms and structures are often created when a system or technology is new. These are sometimes developed in response to criticism that a new plant or new technology is too risky or that much about its operation remains unknown. As the pressure dissipates over time and the fears do not become manifest, these systems are frequently not maintained. This decay in precautionary norms and the attendant structures of risk mitigation and response—in such areas as training, personnel, procedures, and equipment—is accelerated in the presence of cost constraints. When faced with budget constraints, for example, risk mitigation strategies and structures are often seen as unnecessary luxuries and are reduced or eliminated. Third, low-level crisis events may become routine and serve to normalize both risk and threat in the perceptions of organizational members. When activities are no longer considered novel or exceptional, they generate less attention and often less vigilance. When risk is viewed as routine, vigilance decays and is responded to in similar routine ways.

The fourth major component of the precrisis stage involves incubation, or the largely unforeseen, disproportional, and nonlinear interaction of various environmental and system elements in ways that lead to crisis. Often, incubation is the consequence of long and unanticipated dynamic networks of what were previously seen as minor events and unimportant forces. Incubation also involves entropy, the natural decay and disorganization of systems. Natural processes of entropy, aging, and decay, such as metal fatigue; friction-induced fraying of wire insulation; hairline cracks; worn tires, brake pads, and suspension systems; oxidation of electrical switches; spalling of concrete due to freeze-and-thaw cycles; corrosion of metal parts exposed to road salt and water; and human fatigue, poor eyesight, poor hearing, and memory loss are among many factors associated with crises. Decay may be delayed through careful maintenance, such as replacing worn parts and updating training. In many cases, however, systems continue to be used far beyond their design life, and regular maintenance procedures are not followed. Moreover, as resources become scarce or as industries become more competitive, there is a tendency both to use systems beyond their design life and to delay maintenance of those systems. The U.S. Department of Transportation (DOT) reported on their Web site, for example, that roughly 30 percent of highway bridges are deficient (http://fhwa.dot.gov/ohim.hiqsep00). Given the replacement expense, there are strong motivations to continue using bridges, even when they are inadequate.

Systems may also incubate risks when they are pushed beyond the capacity or longevity for which they were designed; when they do not fail, they are presumed to be safe. Transportation systems are regularly overloaded. Technologies, procedures, and even an understanding of risk are often generalized from one context to another, although the conditions are not analogous. Solutions that work on a small scale for a short term may also lead to incubation of risk when replicated for a longer term or on a larger scale. A temporary solution, designed in the 1950s and 1960s to save computer memory storage space, involved using two digits to record the year rather than a full four-digit designation. Ultimately, this shortsighted solution led to the Y2K problem.

One common aspect of incubation involves the interaction of an emerging threat with a reduced capacity for risk mitigation. Turner (1976), in his analysis of failure in foresight (see chapter 5), suggested that among the most-common features of crisis incubation are failures to comply with existing regulations (p. 390). This may involve failure to understand the regulations, failure to recognize that regulations apply, failure to recognize their importance, and, in some cases, an attitude of What can we get away with?

As discussed in chapter 1, Charles Perrow (1984) identified complex, usually nonlinear, interactiveness and tight coupling as incubation factors. Interactiveness refers to a relationship between system elements in which actions of one element affect the others. Larger systems, systems that are more diverse in terms of the functions they serve, and those functioning in complex environments are likely to experience more complex, unplanned, and unseen interactions. Perrow (1999) has identified a number of other specific system features related to complexity and nonlinear interaction. These include close physical proximity, common mode functions, unfamiliar or unintended feedback loops, multiple control parameters, indirect information, and limited understanding of some processes (pp. 85–87). Letters stored close to one another or processed through mechanical sorters, for example, were cross-contaminated by anthrax spores in New Jersey mailrooms during the 2001 anthrax crisis.

Tight coupling is a second incubating factor (Perrow, 1999). Systems may be so tightly connected or coupled that there is no slack or buffer. In mechanical systems, for example, various components may be close in terms of proximity and thus interact in unanticipated ways. An ignition switch mounted too close to a car's manifold may overheat and malfunction. In terms of time, tight production schedules and just-in-time inventory controls may not allow sufficient intervals for correcting defects. One of the factors in the *Challenger* disaster was an implicit pressure to launch at a particular time. The time sequences in tightly coupled systems are typically invariant, often requiring a particular order of events separated by particular intervals (Perrow, 1999, pp. 92–94).

In addition to these processes and factors in incubation, precrisis is often associated with a failure to receive or attend to a threat signal or message. Mileti and Sorensen (1990) suggested that "[t]he ability to recognize the presence of an impending event is determined by the degree to which an indicator of the potential threat can be detected and the conclusion reached that a threat exists" (p. 4). As described in chapter 4, risk monitoring is a critical communication function associated with crisis avoidance. Missed warnings, failed interpretations, and/or failure to act on warnings, then,

Table 6.2
Limitations on Crisis Warnings

1. Weak or subtle crisis signal
2. Presence of strangers as distraction
3. Source of crisis signal not viewed as credible (i.e., from outside source, or from whistleblower)
4. Inadequate channels for communicating risk or threat
5. Signal of threat embedded in routine messages
6. Risk/threat messages systematically distorted
7. Organizational or professional norms against communicating risks and warnings
8. Risk/threat messages discounted because of inconsistency with dominant beliefs
9. Signals that do not coalesce, are not compiled, or do not reach appropriate persons

Source: Adapted from "The Organizational and Interorganizational Development of Disasters," by B. Turner published in *Administrative Science Quarterly*, 21 by permission of *Administrative Science Quarterly.* Copyright © 1976 Cornell University.

are the components of the fifth precrisis stage. Crisis is a systemic adaptive failure in which feedback messages fail to produce corrective actions. The limitations on crisis warnings are presented in Table 6.2.

Failure to perceive may involve a variety of signal features as well as the organization's general reception, detection, and interpretation ability. Threat signals are often quite subtle, or they may take forms not easily detected and interpreted. Threat signals often involve novel, nonroutine messages that do not have well-defined audiences, channels, or responses. In other cases, threat signals may be embedded in routine messages that do not call attention to the impending problems. The veracity of the message and the credibility of the source are often in question. Threats of school violence, for example, are common. In fact, almost every high school must deal with bomb threats. Fortunately, only a tiny portion of these warnings have validity. School administrators, however, must attend to all such warnings and determine which are sufficiently credible to prompt action. In many cases, however, warnings never reach school administrators. They are heard by parents or students and are not passed on. In other cases, the signals regarding violence are so subtle that they are simply overlooked or may be interpreted as part of the larger routines of teen behavior. In still other cases, appropriate channels for communicating risk are simply not available. Many schools have created safety hot lines so that established warning channels are available.

Signal detection may also be disrupted by the presence of novel circumstances or the presence of strangers (Turner, 1976). The tragic collision of the Japanese fishing boat *Ehime Maru* with the submarine, USS *Greenville*, was attributed to distractions that allowed signals of problems and standard risk mitigation activities to be overlooked. Visitors in the cramped quarters of the submarine distracted the crew from its established procedures and routines for surfacing. In other cases, the warnings themselves are issued by outsiders and discounted by the organization. Warnings regarding many auto defects come from industry watchdog groups, such as the National Highway Transportation Authority or the Insurance Institute for Highway Safety and are easily discounted by the industry.

Organizations also create impediments to the communication of crisis signals and messages. As Pauchant and Mitroff (1992) have suggested, organizations that ignore messages signaling problems are more prone to experience crises. In general, most organizations find warnings difficult to process and disruptive to well-established belief systems about risk and threat. In other cases, the warning may compromise careers or company profitability. Whistle-blowers, a common source of critical information regarding impending threats and serious organizational problems, are often labeled as disloyal employees, muzzled, or even fired (Devine & Aplin, 1988). In many of these cases, however, whistle-blowers are seeking to call attention to and rectify serious crisis-inducing deficiencies.

Information distortion by lower-level employees is an additional impediment to communication of crisis signals and risk messages. As discussed in chapter 5, distortion of messages originating at lower levels of the organization is a well-documented phenomenon (Plantly & Machaver, 1952; Roberts & O'Riely, 1974). Jablin (1979), in summarizing the research on distortion, concluded that subordinates tend to tell their superiors things that reflect positively and avoid those things that reflect negatively. Warnings of impending crises have a strong potential to reflect negatively on the person issuing the warning. These distortion tendencies, then, limit the ability of accurate information about risks or emerging threats to flow to upper-management levels, where remedial activities and strategies can be initiated. Norms and values against "rocking the boat," or calling attention to problems, also limit warnings. These norms often function to encourage members to overlook and ignore risks and to avoid calling attention to emerging threats.

One of the most striking features of many organizational crises is that they are not surprising to some organizational participants. Following 9/11, for example, reports emerged that forewarnings of an attack received by the intelligence community did not coalesce or reach appropriate sources. The Enron crisis was not surprising to many employees. In cases of employee violence, the attacker is often known to be unstable. In most cases, crisis and threat signals exist at points in a system but are not synthesized in ways that allow threats to be recognized, understood, assessed as credible, and acted on.

The final element of the six pertaining to the precrisis stage (see Table 6.1) is the occurrence of a crisis trigger event followed by the immediate onset of harm and the recognition of a situation as a crisis. A crisis trigger event is usually a dramatic occurrence, such as a consumer being harmed by a product failure, as in the Tylenol poisoning or the outbreak of *E. coli* from hamburgers produced by Hudson Foods. In other instances, the trigger event is a dramatic disruption of operations, such as the plant explosion at Malden Mills, or, as described below, the grounding of the Exxon tanker *Valdez*. Managers often initially believe that the person breaking the news must be confused or has the facts wrong. Independent confirmation is often required before the circumstances are seen as a crisis.

Trigger events that rise to the level of crisis create several conditions. First, the trigger event gives initial cues as to the type and magnitude of the crisis. These cues, in turn, give some nascent definition to the crisis and some rudimentary indication regarding appropriate response. As discussed in chapter 3, merely defining a crisis as an explosion, a shooting, or a product recall indicates something about initial response, including what resources might be required and what agencies might be involved. Responses are by definition contingent upon the nature of the threat and its magnitude. Second, trigger events also call both internal and external attention to the crisis (Billings, Milburn, & Schaalman, 1980). Depending on magnitude and newsworthiness, they often prompt publicity and media attention that may enhance, or in some cases reduce, the intensity. Publicizing an event sometimes reduces threat by initiating immediate mitigation activities. The 1997 outbreak of food-borne illness associated with Hudson Foods was quickly contained, largely because of immediate and widespread media coverage. Alternatively, the media played a crisis-enhancing role in Valujet Flight 592's crash into the Florida Everglades. The national media fixated on the gruesome details of body recovery for several days following the crash, resulting in extended and extremely negative publicity. Media attention also functions to publicize initial interpretations of the event, repeating and enhancing the impact of these interpretations.

Finally, trigger events often prompt strong emotional and psychological responses, including stress, fear, confusion, anger, and sadness. In some rare cases, these responses are maladaptive and reflective of a failure to make sense of a threatening situation. Staw, Sandelands, and Dutton (1981) described a generalized threat-rigidity response that involves restricting access to information by centralizing authority and control. The result is less-variable, flexible, and adaptive structures at the very moment when adaptability is required. A trigger event often disrupts basic belief systems and sensemaking devices, creating cosmological episodes or a fundamental break in their worldview. Participants often report high levels of confusion following a crisis as they sort through the event and collect information. The initial response to a major crisis is often one of disbelief and rejection of the information.

These six precrisis features of established belief structures—development of norms and crisis plans, decay, incubation, missed warnings, and, finally, the trigger event—constitute the primary aspects of the precrisis stage. These processes are the principle variables that move an organized system toward bifurcation and crisis. They also represent factors that if strategically managed may allow organizations to avoid some crises. Systematic decay need not always occur. Organizations are not destined to miss warnings and signals of impending problems. Incubation is not inevitable. Vigilance is often maintained in organizations, even in the presence of high risk and tight budget constraints and without the reinforcing occurrence of crisis or a near miss. Weick and Sutcliff (2001) described organizations "that have less than their share of accidents" as "mindful" (p. 10). "By this we mean that they organize themselves in such a way that they are able to notice the unexpected in the making and halt its development...containing it...for swift restoration of system functioning" (p. 3).

The six features of precrisis are illustrated in the remainder of this chapter through a close examination of the precrisis stage preceding the Exxon *Valdez* oil spill. On March 24, 1989, 240,000 barrels of North Slope crude oil were spilled in Prince William Sound, Alaska, by one of Exxon's newest and best-equipped tankers. This was one of the costliest and most-damaging oil spills ever, even though it was relatively small compared to some other spills. This episode is characterized by precrisis conditions of unrealistic sets of beliefs about the risk of shipping oil, development of complacency about the risk, failure to recognize or attend to a variety of cues about an emerging threat, and significant and sustained decay of risk mitigation, navigational support systems, and reliability of human operators.

THE EXXON *VALDEZ*

In many ways, the events of March 24, 1989, in Alaska's Prince William Sound could be understood as a quintessential transportation accident. It is possible to explain the grounding of the Exxon *Valdez* as simply poor judgment by a captain who was most likely intoxicated. Captain Joseph Hazelwood had turned the piloting of the ship over to an inexperienced and fatigued third mate who had run it aground onto a well-marked reef. The simple explanation, in fact the one initially offered by Exxon, was human error. A more comprehensive examination, however, suggests that the Exxon *Valdez* spill, like most organizational crises, involved a complex web of precipitating factors (see Table 6.3).

The Exxon *Valdez* is arguably the subject of the most famous oil spill in recent history, even though it ranks surprisingly low in terms of volume of oil spilled. The worst oil spill in history occurred in January 1991 in the Persian Gulf War, as Iraqi forces destroyed the Kuwaiti oil fields. Some 240 million barrels of oil were spilled. The worst tanker spill involved the *Castillo de Bellver*, which lost 78.5 million barrels of crude oil off the coast of South Africa in 1993. The *Valdez* spill ranks only 53rd, but it ranks much higher in terms of cost, environmental damage, and negative publicity. The cost of the spill has been estimated at around $8 billion. An analysis of the enduring affect of the spill on its 10-year anniversary concluded that several affected animal species had still not recovered, including common loons, harbor seals, cormorants, several species of fish, and killer whales (http://www.oilspill/state/ak.us). The *Valdez* generated such negative publicity that Exxon Shipping was renamed the Sea River Shipping Company to disassociate the company from the disaster.

Oil is transported in bulk to refineries close to final markets, usually via tankers or pipelines. Oil tankers ply many domestic waterways, including the Great Lakes, the Ohio and the Mississippi Rivers, and U.S. seacoasts. Some are massive, as much as a quarter of a mile long and weighing almost 500,000 tons (Perrow, 1999, p. 196). This size increases overall complexity and significantly limits maneuverability. Tankers are flagged by many different countries and operate under widely differing standards. Intensive performance pressures, as well as the "traditions of the sea,"

Table 6.1
A Precrisis Chronology of the Exxon *Valdez* Oil Spill

1968	Discovery of large oil reserves ↑ in Alaska's North Slope.
1973	Senate votes to approve Trans-Alaska Pipeline to Valdez.
	Construction begins on 800 mile Pipeline
1977	DEC questions adequacy of response plans.
1985	Oil begins flowing through Trans-Alaska Pipeline. Alaska Department of Environmental Conservation issues first reports that Alyeska's oil-spill contingencies are inadequate.
1984-89	Joseph Hazelwood, youngest tanker captain at Exxon, establishes pattern of drinking problem, including three driver's license suspensions.
1982	Alyeska disbands stand-alone response team due to budget cuts. State Inspector reports spill response capacity has "regressed to a dangerous level."
1985	DEC memo warns that inadequacies exist in Alyeska's response training, communication, dedicated cleanup personnel, spill reporting and monitoring, and equipment readiness. Reduction in Coast Guard budget forces reduction in radar tracking of shipping traffic in Prince William Sound.
1988	Routine inventory finds response equipment inadequate.
March 24, 1989, 12:09 A.M.	The tanker Exxon *Valdez* grounds. Eight of the 13 tanks are ruptured; tanker begins losing about 20,000 barrels of oil per hour.
March 24, 1989, 12:27 A.M.	Hazelwood reports the accident to the Coast Guard, which begins notification process. Spill described as minor.
March 25, 1989, 2:30 P.M.	Response Team arrives at the grounded *Valdez* with booms and skimmers. Begins to skim oil and deploy containment boom. Equipment is not sufficient to control the volume of oil.
March 25–26	Extent of spill and potential environmental impact becomes known. Exxon prepares to spray dispersants, although amount available is unclear, but does not receive approval from the Coast Guard.
March 28, 1989	A spring storm hits Prince William Sound, dispersing the oil and making the use of chemical dispersants ineffective.

encourage risky behavior. Often, tankers are operated with ridiculously narrow margins of safety. Perrow described the marine transportation system as "error-enducing" and noted that about four hundred ships a year are lost, with most losses attributed to operator error. Pipelines carrying oil, as well as those carrying natural gas, crisscross the country and cannot be constantly monitored or protected. This extensive network of tankers and pipelines is one aspect of the industry's complexity that enhances the potential for crisis. In 2001, for example, in another episode involving alcohol, an intoxicated man fired a gun into the trans-Alaska pipeline, causing a spill of 80,000 gallons of oil.

Oil is also difficult to contain and to clean up. It is extremely tenacious in the environment and, although not as poisonous as many other industrial chemicals, it is toxic to a variety of plants and animals. It is viscous and adheres to other materials and is easily absorbed into porous substances, such as vegetation, rocks, and soil. It does not easily mix with water, although many of its components are volatile and readily vaporize. In general, oil spills are easiest to deal with when they are contained slicks, on calm water. Over time, spills disperse, making mechanical cleanup using skimmers more difficult and in situ burning, another common response strategy, impossible. When seas become rough, slicks tend to spread out and break up. At this point, chemical dispersant becomes the only viable method of response. Dispersants are chemical agents, similar to detergents, that allow oil to break up more quickly, mix with water, and disperse into the environment. However, even dispersants lose their effectiveness as a spill spreads out. Immediacy of response is, therefore, absolutely critical to successful cleanup, something widely acknowledged throughout the industry. If oil contaminates beaches, cleanup becomes an overwhelming task, and the impact on the environment becomes more visible and pronounced. In these cases, cleanup crews often turn to high-pressure steam washing to dislodge the oil, to wiping down rocks by hand, or to simply leaving the oil to uncertain natural weathering. Sea birds and mammals are particularly vulnerable to oil spills, although fish populations are also affected. Sea otters and birds become coated with oil and die from hypothermia because their coats and feathers lose insulating properties. They also lose buoyancy and drown. Often, they ingest the oil while grooming and are poisoned. Scavengers such as bears and eagles eat the carcasses and are poisoned. Fish may be affected directly by the spill or by contamination of their food supply.

Established Belief Structures Regarding Risk

The system of beliefs regarding the production and transportation of oil through Alaska was characterized by two sets of competing values. First, oil is a valuable commodity promising great profits for those involved in its exploitation. The industry has generally developed a freewheeling culture described by some as arrogant. "Big oil" in particular has had a mixed record in terms of the environment and questionable business practices (Davidson, 1990). The development of the domestic Alaskan oil fields in the 1970s was framed as contributing to energy independence, which was increasingly important following the oil embargoes of the early 1980s. Oil production in Alaska was also close to the gasoline-hungry West Coast markets while at the same time contributing significantly to the Alaskan economy. Eventually, revenues from oil and gas leases would swell state budgets by about $1.5 billion a year. Oil revenues allowed the state to distribute an additional $400 million a year directly to Alaskan residents (Deakin, 1989). The small fishing village of Valdez, Alaska, saw a huge development and construction boom and became known as "the home of the supertankers" (Davidson, 1990, p. 4).

A second set of values came from the environmental community, which objected to oil exploitation of the Alaskan wilderness. When the North Slope Alaskan fields were first being developed and the Trans-Alaska Pipeline was being considered, significant opposition was mounted by the environmental community and the fishing industry. Cautions included the direct damage done by construction, the disruption of migratory routes for animals, and the specter of an oil spill. Environmentalists argued that the Arctic tundra was a particularly sensitive ecosystem and that drilling would have irrevocable harm. The environmental insult was enhanced by the way in which the oil would be transported. A pipeline was to be built over 400 miles of the frozen tundra to move oil to the Port of Valdez. This also meant roads, fuel stations, and movement of heavy equipment across the tundra. The commercial fishing industry, also important to Alaska, worried about the potential contamination from oil and about the increased traffic from supertankers in Prince William Sound (Davidson, 1990). Seven oil companies with heavy investments in Alaskan oil and gas leases formed a consortium, called Alyeska, and lobbied congress for approval. The North Slope oil field eventually was opened to drilling, following a 49–49 vote on the plan in the U.S. Senate. Vice President Spiro Agnew broke the tie.

Construction began in December 1973 on one of the most expensive private construction projects ever undertaken (Davidson, 1990). The construction of the Alaskan pipeline and the facilities at the Port of Valdez were undertaken by the same consortium of oil companies, now called the Alyeska Pipeline Service Company. At a total cost of around $8 billion, the pipeline and port were depending on efficiency, economies of scale, and continued high gasoline prices to achieve profitability. Alyeska provided hundreds of well-paying jobs and contributed significantly to the Alaskan economy. As part of the federal and state government-approved plan, assurances were given that oil could be extracted and transported safely and that procedures and structures were also created for responding to a possible spill. This plan was characterized by several assumptions about the probability of a spill, its size, and the ability of Alyeska to respond.

First and foremost was the assumption that a spill was simply unlikely. The transportation of oil in U.S. waters by U.S. ships was viewed as safe. American crews were generally well trained, and American equipment was technologically superior and well maintained. Shipping lanes and hazards were well marked, and navigational aids, such as mandating pilots in the dangerous 900-yard-wide harbor entrance known as the Valdez Narrows, were considered more than adequate. Most domestic tankers did not, however, have double hulls, first proposed in 1973 and considered the final insurance against spills. The industry had successfully argued that double hulls reduced the carrying capacity of tankers and raised costs. Ironically, it was the *Valdez* spill that finally pushed through federal double-hull legislation.

Norms, Structures, and Plans for Risk Mitigation and Crisis Response

The 1,800-page Alyeska crisis plan had been developed primarily as a response to criticism from environmentalists. Compromises worked out to allow drilling to go forward specified that contingency plans be in place for safe transportation of oil and for spill response. Because the oil industry had argued successfully that a spill was unlikely, the dominant belief system was that a plan was largely unnecessary. As such, the plan was optimistic in its assumptions and minimalist in resources and details. It would later be criticized as a lesson in overly optimistic spill contingency plans, inadequate risk assessment, risk oversight, and overreliance on technology (Jones, 1989; Eplar, 1989; Davidson, 1990; Exxon *Valdez* Oil Spill Trustees Council, 2002). For example, the plan assumed best-case scenarios such as spills of limited size, on calm seas, and accessible to response teams within hours. One of the most interesting arguments was based on a risk analysis suggesting that a spill in the 200,000-barrel range could happen only once in 241 years. It estimated that a spill of 100,000 barrels could be contained and cleaned up within 48 hours, before reaching beaches. The plan also assumed that 80 percent of any spill would be contained and recovered by mechanical means, leaving only a small proportion for subsequent cleanup (Davidson, 1990, p. 23).

Alyeska's initial contingency plan did include a designated spill-response team and mandated specific containment procedures and equipment. The team was composed of 12 responders who trained regularly and maintained spill-response equipment, including containment booms and buoys and skimmers used to recover oil from the surface. Ships were maintained for the rapid transportation of equipment to a spill site. During the 12 years preceding the Exxon spill, there had been few instances in which the recovery team was called into service, and those had involved spills under 2,000 barrels (Davidson, 1990, p. 40).

Norms and structures regarding the safe transportation of oil included state and federal regulations as well as industry practice and company policy. The Coast Guard, for example, licensed tanker officers and established a set of minimum standards for safety, including shipping lanes for inbound and outbound traffic, maximum speeds for areas considered dangerous, minimum crew size, and required periods of rest. Exxon had policies regarding minimum requirements for piloting a ship, a requirement for lookouts, and a variety of detailed procedures for specific conditions, such as the presence of ice. As tankers called on Valdez without major incident, however, these minimum standards began to be systematically violated as complacency replaced vigilance (www.oilspill.state.ak.us). The operation of the Valdez port with its supertankers became "extremely routine" (Davidson, 1990, p. 40).

Decay in Structures of Mitigation and Crisis Plans

As early as January 1977, the Alaska Department of Environmental Conservation (DEC) warned that the cleanup contingencies were inadequate. Again, in March 1977, the DEC warned that Alyeska had an insufficient containment boom, that its maximum spill assumption of 74,000 barrels was too optimistic, and that its containment and cleanup crew was too small. The DEC's specific recommendations for improving the plan, however, were largely ignored. In addition, relatively minor spills had become routine to the point where they were almost overlooked. This included occasional oil spills while loading the tankers and the more common discharge of "mousse" in ballast water. Tankers carried seawater in their empty cargo tanks. The water would mix with the oil residue in the tanks, creating an emulsification called mousse. Although federal law required that mousse be siphoned off before water was discharged, this procedure was regularly ignored. Alyeska had also learned to manipulate water testing to remain within the legal limits of discharge set by the Environmental Protection Agency (McCoy, 1989).

In 1982, Alyeska took a dramatic cost-cutting step by disbanding its stand-alone 12-person spill-response team. The team had conducted response drills and maintained equipment and was on 24-hour call (McCoy, 1989, p. A1). This high level of vigilance helped to ensure that a response would be timely and have the requisite expertise and equipment. The team, however, had essentially not been called, so Alyeska redesigned its response. The new team drew on workers with other port assignments. Alyeska argued that it had in actuality bolstered its response capacity by replacing the 12-member crew with a 120-member team. These members, however, had little or no training. After witnessing a chaotic drill, a state inspector sent a memo indicating that Alyeska's response capacity under the new system had "regressed to a dangerous level" (McCoy, 1989, p. A1). Alyeska appeared to be relying more and more on the magic bullet of chemical dispersants in the advent of a large spill. The oil industry has generally argued that dispersants are cheap and effective ways to deal with spills. Environmentalists claim that dispersants simply compound the harm.

Procedures for safe operation had similarly begun to decay. Policies requiring minimum levels of rest for crew, for example, were largely ignored. Fatigue is a common source of unpredictable variance in the form of human error and is a frequent factor in marine accidents (Perrow, 1999). Exxon appeared to have knowingly violated existing regulations regarding the required amount of rest by systematically reducing crew sizes during the early 1980s to minimum required levels. The inbound and outbound shipping lanes and their zones of separation in and out of the harbor were regularly violated so that tankers would not need to slow down when ice was present. Required reporting of ship positions and speed to Valdez harbor traffic control was haphazard (www.oilspill. state.ak.us). Budget cutbacks had forced the replacement of a 100,000-watt station with a 50,000-watt system that could not completely track ships or ice through the sound. In addition, in 1981, the Coast Guard had recommended an additional radar site near Bligh Reef.

Incubation and Nonlinear Interaction of Minor System Variance

The incubation leading to the grounding of the *Valdez* included small variances in the human and technical aspects of the system. Human errors were not recognized or corrected, allowing a minor problem to rapidly escalate. The piloting of a 987-foot oil tanker requires both art and technical skill. These vessels are slow to respond to course corrections and impossible to stop quickly. While the Prince William Sound shipping channel is well charted and marked, it is a challenging environment, with dangerous reefs, high and unpredictable winds, and strong currents. Ice conditions often force ships to take alternative routes and sometimes move outside established shipping lanes. The captains generally are highly skilled and very vigilant. In the case of Captain Joseph Hazelwood, however, his drinking appeared to interfere with his judgment.

Incubating factors in the actual grounding involved violation of several company policies and procedures, imprecise information, fatigue, and Hazelwood's poor judgment. The designated harbor pilot, required under Coast Guard rules for navigating in and out of the harbor, left the *Valdez* at 11:24 P.M., after steering the ship through the Valdez Narrows. Soon thereafter, Hazelwood increased the ship's speed to "sea speed." He also notified Valdez Vessel Traffic Control that he would "probably divert from the TSS [traffic separation scheme] and end up in the inbound lane if there is not conflicting traffic" (Davidson, 1990, p. 13). This course correction was to avoid slowing for ice in the established outbound lane. By this time, the Coast Guard tracking station could not precisely track the ship. At 11:39 P.M., Hazelwood directed that the ship be placed on autopilot on a due south heading. The *Valdez* continued on course through the inbound traffic lane for about 20 minutes to avoid ice. At about 11:53 P.M., Hazelwood ordered a further increase in speed, conferred with the third mate, Gregory Cousins, regarding when and how to make a course correction back to the outbound lane and retired to his cabin. It appears that the correction Hazelwood outlined for taking the tanker between the ice and Bligh Reef allowed little room for error. Cousins, not fully trained for piloting the ship and probably fatigued, was left in control. It was Cousins's failure to make this difficult course correction in a timely manner, perhaps because he did not know precisely where the Exxon *Valdez* was in relation to Bligh Reef, that led directly to the grounding. By the time the fix for the course correction was plotted, a lookout had already warned that the Bligh Reef light was off the bow, indicating that the *Valdez* was far outside the safe-shipping lane. Moments later, the *Valdez* grounded on Bligh Reef, with a series of sharp jolts (Davidson, 1990; Exxon *Valdez* Oil Spill Trustees Council, 2002).

The event itself could easily be described as the consequence of small errors. The *Valdez*, which had traversed thousands of miles of open seas, strayed only a few thousand yards outside the safe-shipping lanes. Hazelwood had been out of the control room for only 11 minutes when the ship ran aground. The ship itself had only been out of the designated sea lanes for a matter of about 20 minutes. The tolerances of oceangoing vessels, however, are often quite small, with only a few feet of clearance (Perrow, 1999). Oil tankers respond slowly, and even though Cousins tried to turn the ship before it grounded, he was simply too late—perhaps only by a matter of minutes.

Missed Warnings: Failure to Perceive and Act on Crisis Cues

A consistent pattern of warning and cues existed regarding the possibility of a major spill and the inadequacy of response contingencies. As discussed earlier, many of these warnings about the decay of response capacity had come from the DEC. These included a series of memos directed toward Alyeska about the inadequacy of its spill-response plan, beginning when the port first opened. In 1982, the DEC warned that the response plan was "superficial at best." In 1985, a DEC memo cited inadequacies in training, communication, dedicated cleanup personnel, oil-spill reporting and monitoring, and equipment readiness (GPO, 101–5, I, 1989). Drills observed by state inspectors in the 1980s were described as "comic." A 1984 drill was cancelled because the containment boom sank. In another, the response boat ran aground. A routine inventory of response equipment conducted in 1988 found only about half the lighting equipment used to respond to spills. The rest, reportedly, were being used in the Valdez winter carnival (McCoy, 1989). It is likely that many of these warnings and cues were more easily ignored because they came from outside regulatory agencies. Warnings were at odds with both the 12-year record of safe operation and the dominant public position that oil transportation was safe.

Warnings also existed about Hazelwood's drinking problem. Hazelwood's driver's license had been suspended in his home state of New York three times between 1984 and 1989 for driving under the influence of alcohol. In fact, at the time of the grounding, Hazelwood did not have a valid driver's license. Moreover, as early as 1982, Exxon had been officially aware that Hazelwood had a serious drinking problem, following an incident in which he was accused of assaulting another crewman while intoxicated. In 1985, following another episode, Exxon gave Hazelwood a 90-day leave of absence and suggested that he attend Alcoholics Anonymous (Davidson, 1990; Exxon Valdez Oil Spill Trustees Council, 2002).

In addition, evidence suggests that Alyeska employees had learned to ignore and avoid discussing various safety and environmental violations for fear of being punished. Response team members reported that they feared losing their jobs for speaking out and that Alyeska had retaliated against employees for identifying problems (Davidson, 1990, p. 82). A similar phenomenon had developed within the DEC. Some employees who were particularly critical and outspoken about Alyeska's operations had been transferred. In one case, a DEC inspector was removed from Alyeska premises after videotaping operations (McCoy, 1989, p. A1) Eventually, an implicit understanding had developed that public criticism by DEC employees was to be avoided (Davidson, 1990, p. 300).

Trigger Event, Onset of Harm, Recognition of Crisis

Captain Hazelwood had been notified by Third Mate Cousins moments before the grounding that the ship was in trouble. Following the grounding, Hazelwood returned to the bridge and took command. Eighteen minutes after the grounding, Hazelwood radioed the Coast Guard in Valdez and notified them of the accident: "Yeah. It's Valdez back. We should be on your radar there. We've fetched up, run aground, north of Goose Island, around Bligh Reef. And evidently were leaking some oil. And we're going to be here awhile. And if you want to, say you're notified" (Davidson, 1990, p. 19). Officials of Exxon were notified in Houston, Texas, at about 12:30 A.M.

Exxon's initial efforts to communicate about the incident were hampered by incomplete information and a decentralized corporate structure. Little information was available about the nature or volume of the spill, and Exxon's corporate public relations offices and spill-response divisions, located in Texas, initially let local managers handle the crisis. The statement released by Exxon and Alyeska on March 24 was low key:

The [*Valdez*] ruptured several cargo tanks and oil is reported in the water. The amount of the spill is undetermined. An inbound tanker—the Exxon *Baton Rouge*—has been diverted to the area for possible assistance. The Coast Guard and the Alaska Department of Environmental Conservation are on the scene. Oil Spill cleanup equipment is being mobilized at the pipeline terminal and is being dispatched to the scene. (Exxon Company USA, March 24, 1989)

The specialized equipment needed to respond to the spill was scattered throughout the Port of Valdez and disorganized. The oil-containment boom was in a warehouse buried under tons of other equipment. Skimmers were not loaded on the spill-response barge, and the barge itself was undergoing repairs (Davidson, 1990). The response team, expecting a relatively minor spill, finally left Valdez harbor 10 hours after the grounding and arrived at the spill about 14 hours after the grounding.

When the team arrived, it was clear that they were not adequately prepared to respond, given the size of the spill. Oil was described as "boiling" out from the *Valdez*. Skimmers siphoned oil from the water but had no place to store the reclaimed oil. The containment boom was too light for the choppy open waters of the sound and for the volume of oil (Davidson, 1990). This failure to respond to the spill in a timely and appropriate manner significantly accelerated the harm and moved the spill to the level of a major environmental disaster. It soon became apparent that other options had to be explored. Exxon officials concluded that the only alternative involved spraying very large quantities of chemical dispersants over the slick. Dispersants are most effective if used while slicks are contained.

Even though the area around the *Valdez* grounding had been preapproved by the Alaskan DEC for dispersant use, approval was also needed from the Coast Guard. Coast Guard officials believed that mechanical retrieval via skimmers should be fully explored before permission was granted to use dispersants and that dispersants should initially only be used in limited tests to assess their effectiveness. This failure to agree among Exxon, the U.S. Coast Guard, and the state of Alaska, created uncertainty and the opportunity for each side to shift blame to the other.

By the third day, the full extent of the spill was becoming more widely known, and perception of the spill as a major environmental catastrophe was beginning to take hold. The dramatic environmental harm became clear as oiled sea birds and otters began to wash up on beaches. At this point, the U.S. Coast Guard granted Exxon permission to use dispersants. Exxon, however, even three days after the disaster, did not have enough dispersants on-site for the treatment of the spill. Before adequate dispersants could be shipped to the site and applied, a spring storm broke up the slick and spread it over a wide area, making cleanup impossible. The crude oil was now diluted to the point where dispersants would not be nearly as effective or as easily applied.

Eventually, the spill cost Exxon an estimated $7 billion in direct compensation to Alaska and to fishermen, in costs of cleanup, and in ongoing environmental mitigation. The *Valdez* incident was the worst environmental accident ever for Alaska and a public relations disaster for Exxon and the oil industry. It also reinvigorated the environmental movement and significantly modified understanding of the risks of transporting oil.

CONCLUSION

The tragic case of the Exxon *Valdez* illustrates the precrisis factors of belief systems, incubation, and missed warnings, followed by a crisis trigger event and the onset of serious harm. It also demonstrates the systemic connections, often unanticipated and unnoticed, between these elements. The safe transportation of oil for 12 years and the relatively minor spills that had occurred contributed to a sense of complacency. The possibility of a spill and the inadequacy of response contingencies, however, were well known and were the basis of repeated warnings. The Exxon case also demonstrates how a set of assumptions and attendant statements about risk translate into enacted structures of risk avoidance and response. The larger arguments about the safety of oil exploration and transportation used by the industry to garner political support influenced the kinds and levels of crisis response contingencies that were created. Alaskans were repeatedly assured that oil development could be undertaken in an environmentally safe manner. Incubation coupled with minor variance created a catastrophe on a scale that was previously considered impossible. The ability of Alyeska to respond to a spill had decayed so badly that its limited contingencies and capacities were overwhelmed. Only between 3 and 13 percent of the Exxon *Valdez* spill was recovered. The crisis was initially defined as not serious, further slowing a response when timing was recognized as critical to containment. In this case, the precrisis stage clearly foreshadowed the onset of harm and the development of the second stage of the crisis.

CHAPTER 7

Communication and the Crisis Stage

The crisis-triggering event marks the beginning of the crisis stage, the second stage of crisis development. The most immediate and salient conditions of this stage are high levels of uncertainty, confusion, disorientation, surprise, shock, and stress. High levels of emotional arousal, including fear, anger, sadness, and loss, accompany the event. Organizations must also act toward or respond to the crisis under these intense and uncertain conditions. In retrospect, the initial impact of a crisis is usually indisputable. Yet organizations often lose valuable time by failing to recognize the severity of the events. This may include tenaciously clinging to routine responses and procedures, which are rarely effective because of the novel circumstances and the intense confusion and urgency. Crises are often associated with high levels of turmoil and stress that cannot be managed with conventional practices. Hence, crisis forces organizations to resolve a fundamental tension between the urgency of the moment and the long-term complications their responses may foster.

What follows is a discussion of the conditions of the crisis stage and the initial organizational responses. Crisis recognition, which is typically characterized by both urgency and denial, is also discussed. Problems associated with managing crisis-induced uncertainty are examined, including information needs, collection, and use. Finally, the comprehensive nature of crisis is explored. This section concludes with an examination of a crisis involving Schwan's Sales Enterprises of Minnesota and an outbreak of food-borne illness associated with its trademark product, ice cream.

THE CRISIS STAGE

Crisis, the shortest of the three stages, is the stage of greatest intensity, where the radical bifurcation of the system becomes evident. It begins with crisis sensing, usually through a crisis trigger event, and continues until the organization returns to some sense of normalcy. Within this period, sometimes only lasting for a matter of minutes or hours, intense confusion, uncertainty, and emotional arousal occurs. Harm to the organization and to stakeholders accumulates. Decisions must also be made and actions taken under conditions of high uncertainty, which will subsequently structure both understanding and additional action. In general, the goal of crisis managers is to limit and contain harm and move past the crisis stage as quickly as possible. The crisis stages ends when the organization is able to return to a nearly normal state of operations, although secondary shocks may occur. The general conditions of the crisis stage and the process of response are outlined in Figure 7.1.

Initial Conditions of Crisis

Crisis, as described earlier, creates a novel and threatening set of conditions for the organization and its stakeholders. These conditions must both be attended to and interpreted. Following the onset of crisis, the organization must respond to the crisis conditions very quickly, with little information about the nature of the event and often under conditions of extreme emotional arousal. Crisis is perceptual—organizational participants receive and interpret the signal of a crisis as representing a serious threat. Various cues, such as the way others are responding to the event and the presence of obvious crisis markers, such as sirens and emergency workers, may facilitate the interpretation of an event as a crisis. Such obvious cues of crisis are often not present or may be visible to only a small number of organizational members. In some case, members must persuade others that an event is a serious threat and should be seen as a crisis. It often falls to the organization's leadership to formally recognize an event as a crisis. General agreement that an event is a crisis is usually necessary before the organization can respond in an effective and coordinated manner.

Billings, Milbourne, and Schaalman (1980) suggested that initial recognition "involves perceiving an event in the environment which triggers the crisis" (p. 302). A disruptive event may be perceived merely as a serious issue or may be interpreted as a full-blown crisis. The level of perceived seriousness is determined by three factors: perceived value of possible loss, the probability of loss, and time pressure (see Figure 7.1). The value of possible loss concerns which specific aspect of the organization is threatened and its relative value. Losses such as an easily replaced resource or a loss resulting from a minor accident may be judged as having little relative value. Second, the probability of loss involves a projec-

Figure 7.1
Conditions and Features of the Crisis Stage

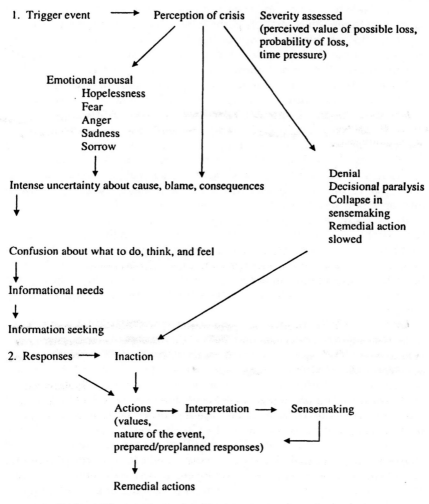

1. Trigger event ⟶ Perception of crisis   Severity assessed
   (perceived value of possible loss,
   probability of loss,
   time pressure)

   Emotional arousal
        Hopelessness
        Fear
        Anger
        Sadness
        Sorrow

Intense uncertainty about cause, blame, consequences   Denial
                                                        Decisional paralysis
                                                        Collapse in
                                                        sensemaking
                                                        Remedial action
                                                        slowed

Confusion about what to do, think, and feel

Informational needs

Information seeking

2. Responses ⟶ Inaction

        Actions ⟶ Interpretation ⟶ Sensemaking
        (values,
        nature of the event,
        prepared/preplanned responses)

        Remedial actions

3. Harm ended/contained; organization returned to near normalcy
   (Possibility of secondary shocks)

tion based on what is currently known. Three factors affect perceived probability of loss: accuracy of the perception, plausible explanations for the event, and response uncertainty. Perception about the loss may be inaccurate. The explanation of the crisis, particularly with regard to cause and blame, may enhance the threat. Finally, the appropriateness of various responses may be more or less clear. Time pressure, the final variable in the perceived seriousness of a crisis, refers to the perceived amount of time available to respond and correct the negative outcome. These factors contribute to the interpretation of the relative seriousness of an event. In addition, the relative familiarity of the event and the way it is initially named and described, as outlined in chapter 3, influences the perception of seriousness. Familiarity allows organizational participants to refine their estimates of seriousness. Moreover, some kinds of events, such as accidents, are inherently seen as less serious than others, such as attacks.

One of the most common psychological and emotional responses to crisis is denial. It is also one of the most problematic psychological responses for organizations. Denial is an important part of the crisis stage, because denial increases the probability that remedial action will be postponed. The Centers for Disease Control (CDC) suggests that people may respond to a crisis warning in various ways. Some people avoid getting the warnings or action recommendations, some people may become agitated or confused by the warning, some people may not believe the threat is real, some people may not believe the threat is real to them (Reynolds, 2002). In all of these cases, risk-reducing actions and crisis responses are postponed. In fact, a common problem in natural disasters is getting the public to take such warnings seriously. Residents in threatened areas often ignore evacuation warnings and even hold "hurricane parties" during dangerous storms.

When the signals of crisis are subtle or the probabilities of loss are seen as remote, participants sometimes must persuade others that a crisis is indeed occurring. Initial reports of a crisis are often discounted as overstatements or mere misunderstandings. It is not uncommon for an organization to seek additional information or independent confirmation from credible sources before accepting that a crisis has occurred. Sometimes, an initial downplaying of severity is a strategy designed to influence subsequent interpretations of the event. Exxon, as described in chapter 6, initially sought to describe the *Valdez* spill as minor. Kenneth Lay, chief executive officer (CEO) of Enron, initially sought to deny the presence of problems and even encouraged employees to buy more stock. Although this strategy of downplaying seriousness may sometimes work, particularly if the event is subsequently judged as minor, it has the potential to result in an inadequate response that allows crisis harm to accumulate.

In other cases, the nature of the threat may be so overwhelming that a sense of hopelessness and helplessness is created. This emotional response can be debilitating for those affected by a crisis and in extreme cases may contribute to crisis paralysis. It often falls to a designated leader to initially act toward a crisis in a way that empowers others. Simple decisions, such as notifying others of the crisis, moving people away from the source of harm, or attending to victims, can alleviate helplessness. The initial framing of an event, or sensemaking, may help others take actions to reduce harm. Moreover, basic information about mitigation activities may further reduce helplessness. For example, simple actions such as boiling water during a flood or putting a damp cloth over the face or nose during a fire may both reduce harm and alleviate a sense of helplessness. During many chemical accidents, simply removing and discarding clothing and immediately showering may significantly reduce contamination. These actions, empowerment, and reduction in a sense of helplessness encourage acting toward a crisis in ways that contain harm and facilitate a return to a sense of normalcy.

Other kinds of intense emotional arousal also accompany a crisis. One study, conducted within five days of the 9/11 attacks, found that the most common emotional responses were feeling sorrow, sadness, anger, and confusion. Older individuals were more likely to be sad, whereas younger respondents were more likely to be angry. Women reported more intense emotional responses, particularly being sad, sorrowful, and frightened (Seeger, Vennette, Ulmer, & Sellnow, 2002). A number of reports suggested that many Americans experienced serious depression following these attacks. Intense emotional responses both help individuals interpret and make sense of events and influence subsequent actions. Crisis-induced fear and threat are often very personal and are associated with the loss of something of value. Anger often accompanies the perception of some wrongdoing. When the consequences of a crisis begin to set in, sadness and feelings of loss may follow. Sympathy may facilitate external support of those harmed by the crisis. Occasionally, crisis may also be exhilarating, accompanied by feelings of pride, accomplishment, and camaraderie.

Related to emotional arousal is an intense need for information resulting from the high uncertainty of the crisis stage. The crisis trigger event disrupts the status quo in ways that render established interpretive frameworks inoperative. In one study of 9/11, respondents indicated that they spent 8.34 hours the first day collecting information primarily about cause, threat, scope, and damage. Those with the closest connections to the event had the greatest informational need (Seeger et al., 2002). Despite the emergence of the Internet, television remains the most widely used channel for collecting information during a crisis, probably because of the speed with which information can be disseminated (Greenberg, Hofschire, & Lachlan, 2002). Moreover, crisis creates intense needs for information while often disrupting the established channels of communication. For example, during the World Trade Center disaster, much of lower Manhattan's communications technology infrastructure for cellular telephone and police and emergency services, as well as broadcast television, was also destroyed. Those experiencing a crisis also appear to favor interpersonal encounters and contexts. During 9/11, many watched the television coverage in small groups and discussed the events as they were reported. In fact, the amount of interpersonal activity was positively related to greater worry about the personal implications of the event and to heightened psychological anxiety (Greenberg et al., 2002).

Acquiring information facilitates two sets of remedial processes. First, information allows participants to observe how others are behaving, hear interpretations of the event, and engage in sensemaking processes. There is some evidence that formal leaders may have a particularly important role in helping others to learn what to think about a crisis (Seeger et al., 2002). Those experiencing a crisis may also seek out groups to discuss what is happening. Basic cues are often available, allowing for refinement of judgments about the severity of the threat. The type of crisis and how it is named and described by others may also help make sense of what is happening. Second, information facilitates specific remedial responses. The ability to "do something" in the face of a crisis facilitates empowerment and creates the impression that the circumstances are within a participant's control. This reduction in perceived powerlessness allows participants to begin to act toward the event in a way that facilitates sensemaking. This ability to respond, however, requires some basic understanding of the event.

Although crises are fundamentally perceptual, they also clearly have significant real-life consequences. As Weick (1988) explained, crises are "low probability/high consequence events that threaten the most fundamental goals of the organization" (p. 305). This may involve the economic viability of the organization and its fundamental stability. The ability to understand and make sense of a crisis is severely hampered by the threat, surprise, and associated uncertainty. Moreover, basic assumptions, patterns, rules, and even relationships are disrupted. This disruption also compromises the fundamental ability to predict outcomes and make sense of events. In extreme cases, failure to make sense results in a collapse of sensemaking, cosmological episode, or decisional paralysis. In these cases, the organization may not be able to respond in a coordinated and strategic manner.

CRISIS RESPONSE

Organizations are confronted with an intense sense of urgency following a crisis trigger event. Managers often have an overwhelming feeling that they must "do something," particularly when the situation is judged as severe; that is, when harm is evident and threatens to increase. The specific response, however, is highly contingent on a number of factors, including the nature of the event, the presence of a response capacity such as a crisis plan, and the organization's core value system (see Figure 7.1).

Historically, organizational responses to crisis have generally been more negative than positive. Specifically, organizations tend to put a narrow set of interests regarding profitability, protection of the organization's stability, and avoiding legal liability over other values, such as the needs and well-being of stakeholders. Interests of other groups and stakeholders are often overlooked in these reactive responses that seek to protect the organization. Union Carbide's response to an explosion at its pesticide plant in Bhopal, India, is typical of these failures. In the crisis stage, Union Carbide failed to communicate appropriate information to stakeholders about the nature of the chemicals involved, making medical treatment more difficult. In the *Challenger* space shuttle explosion, NASA initially sought to impound all news videotape of the disaster, supposedly to help with the investigation. These reactive knee-jerk responses to a crisis trigger event most often compound harm by compromising the organization's integrity and legitimacy. In contrast, most crisis experts suggest that an organization's first impulse should be to acknowledge those harmed and do everything possible to assist them. Unfortunately, a consistent theme in crisis management is to avoid responsibility for the crisis and minimize the potential legal damage to the organization. Markus and Goodman (1991) noted that whereas some organizations take responsibility for their actions, others have "consistently denied wrongdoing, even in the face of overwhelming evidence to the contrary, perhaps because their lawyers have warned that admissions [of guilt] could be used against them in court" (p. 282). However, organizations that avoid responsibility in their crisis response risk increasing the adverse effects on stakeholders already affected by the crisis and damaging the image of the organization as well.

How an organization initially reacts to the crisis influences subsequent interpretations and actions (Weick, 1988). As Weick noted, "To sort out a crisis as it unfolds often requires action which subsequently generates the raw material for sensemaking and affects the unfolding of the crisis itself" (p. 305). Despite the information collection discussed earlier, organizations are usually forced to take some action without adequate information about the nature of the crisis, the scope of harm, or how those actions may affect crisis development. Although these initial actions may enhance the harm, they also may assist in the selection of subsequent actions. As Weick (1988) explained, "There is a delicate tradeoff between dangerous action which produces understanding and safe inaction which produces confusion" (p. 315). "From the standpoint of enactment, initial responses do more than set the tone; they determine the trajectory of the crisis. Since people know what they have done only after they do it, people and their actions rapidly become part of the crisis" (p. 309). Three forms of enactment are particularly relevant to these initial responses: (1) public commitment, (2) capacity, and (3) expectation.

Public and irrevocable actions are harder to undo. When those actions are also volitional, they become harder to disown (Weick, 1988, p. 310). Initial responses and interpretations, therefore, may become public commitments to positions that subsequently must be tenaciously defended. Managers often go "on record" by making irreversible assertions about technology, operators, and capabilities that are difficult to undo, deny, or even amend. These responses may include tenacious justifications for how the crisis started or was instigated. Spokespersons often make public commitments and offer interpretations of responsibility, harm, and repair of the damage, including cleanup and aid to victims. Once these statements are made and disseminated, the organization often feels compelled to vigorously support and defend them. When a statement is communicated widely and with certainty, it is even harder to retract or reinterpret.

Capacity, a second influence, concerns the relative ability to interpret information. "Capacity and response repertoire affect crisis perception, because perception has a very broad influence on enactment. People see those events they feel they have the capacity to do something about" (Weick, 1988, p. 311). Following a trigger event and the onset of harm, perceptions of powerlessness are common. Finally, expectations influence crisis responses. Most people expect events to follow predictable patterns. Although crises disrupt predictability, they create a search for new patterns of predictability. Managers, for example, may interpret a specific crisis within the framework of an earlier, similar event. In some cases, this expectation can be critical to successful crisis management. In other cases, expectations may prove inaccurate and serve to enhance harm.

One particular challenge of the crisis stage is to respond in ways that are specific enough to empower subsequent interpretation and action, yet flexible enough to accommodate what is obviously a dynamic and uncertain condition. In other words, the relative equivocality in initial responses must be sensitive to the equivocality of the situation. Managers often seek to be decisive in the face of a crisis and respond in unequivocal ways. Such responses may then become tenacious justifications. In other cases, organizations may be pressured by the media or by other stakeholders to offer immediate explanations and interpretations, even when the situation is inherently equivocal. Statements such as "to the best of our knowledge" and "based on what we currently know" may help organizations avoid the pitfalls of tenacious justification while acknowledging the limitations on capacity that occur during the crisis stage.

Comprehensive Nature of Crisis

Crisis results in lost jobs, reduced profitability, damaged careers, injury or death, damaged or destroyed equipment and facilities, damage to the company's image and infrastructure, and damage to the environment. The impact of crisis is also comprehensive in the sense that a crisis affects all aspects of the organization and may extend to the industry, the community, and a diverse set of stakeholders. Crisis may even create new stakeholders, such as individuals or communities harmed by the crisis. Moreover, the impact of a crisis may be long-term, affecting workers, community members, or the environment for years or even decades.

The stakeholder model provides a framework for examining the far-reaching effects of organizational crises. It identifies a diverse set of agents with relationships to the organization, including customers, suppliers, employees, members of the community, government, regulatory agencies, media, retirees and owners, and other individuals, groups, and agencies. Because these groups have some relationship to the organization, they have a stake in how the organization operates—its processes, products, activities, and outcomes. The needs and values of these stakeholders should, therefore, be taken into account in organizational planning, problem solving, and decision making (Deetz, Tracy, & Simpson, 2000; Freeman, 1984). The stakeholder model moves organizational communication and sensemaking from a narrow focus on profitability and organizational issues to a greater awareness of how the organization's actions affect the composite audience. The stakeholder model may also be useful in assessing the organization's larger responsibility to its community and constituencies (Seeger, 1997). This involves balancing the competing needs of stakeholders, maintaining flexible stances, and communicating openly, honestly, and frequently with stakeholders (Ulmer & Sellnow, 2000). In essence, the model can be used to generate a map of mutual obligations, networks of support, and systems of dependency between an organization and its stakeholders.

Stakeholder views are important throughout precrisis, crisis, and postcrisis stages. Positive stakeholder relations established before a crisis can translate into networks of support during a crisis. During crisis, however, stakeholder relations are often rapidly and fundamentally altered. Pauchant and Mitroff (1992) contended that organizations in crisis should adapt their views beyond typical stakeholder analysis to fit the special needs of the crisis situation. For example, a toxic spill may push environmental issues to the top of a set of stakeholder concerns. In addition to causing many deaths, the Union Carbide Bhopal crisis created chronic health problems for thousands of others.

The crisis stage is generally resolved when the harm has been contained and the organization is able to return to nearly normal operations. Nearly normal usually means some form of regular business activity, such as reopening a plant or office, shipping products, or beginning the rebuilding process. In general, the longer the crisis stage lasts the greater the possibility of harm and serious damage to the organization.

SCHWAN'S AND THE OUTBREAK
OF SALMONELLOSIS

The conditions of the crisis stage are clearly illustrated in the Schwan's food-borne illness outbreak of 1994. Unlike many organizations facing a crisis stage, however, Schwan's was particularly responsive to its stake-holders and was able to move beyond the crisis quickly. It did so by acting to contain the harm, even before the nature and extent of the crisis was fully known. Schwan's Sales Enterprises is a privately held company located in Marshall, Minnesota. Founded in 1952 as a convenience to farmers who made infrequent trips into town, the company is the largest in Marshall and the second largest in Minnesota. Schwan's is a diversified company, princi-pally in the business of selling frozen foods such as ice cream, pizza, egg rolls, prepared meals, frozen meat, and juice drinks under a wide variety of brand names. However, the company is best known for its trademark ice cream products, which prominently display the Schwan's name and logo.

Schwan's describes itself as "the Uncommon Company" (Feder, 1994). One way Schwan's exemplifies an uncommon approach to the food busi-ness is through its advertising, promotion, and distribution of products. Schwan's spends very little money on publicity and advertising. Instead, the company relies on direct door-to-door sales and word-of-mouth advertising. Schwan's route drivers make regular visits to the homes of their customers, delivering a variety of ice cream and frozen-food prod-ucts. Without the cost of extended distribution channels, company profits have benefited from this direct-sales strategy. Today, Schwan's provides convenience to busy families with limited shopping time. The company uses highly recognizable yellow trucks and places a high value on cus-tomer satisfaction, loyalty, and repeat sales. Drivers work strictly on com-mission and, therefore, rely on positive long-term relationships with customers to ensure their profits. Drivers typically stop by homes once a week and often refer to their customers by first name.

In 1994, Schwan's experienced the largest outbreak of illness caused by the food-borne bacteria *Salmonella* in U.S. history. *Salmonella* causes salmo-nellosis, with symptoms of nausea, vomiting, diarrhea, and fever. Its symp-toms are most severe in infants, the elderly, and people with weak immune systems. The crisis posed a serious threat to the company because of the extent of the outbreak and because the infected product was their trademark ice cream. The fundamental trust between company and customer—the basis of Schwan's success—was at risk. The crisis began on October 7, 1994, when the Minnesota Department of Health, after tracking 67 cases of salmo-nellosis over a two-week period, announced, "We do have a very strong association between Schwan's products [its trademark ice cream] and the salmonella outbreak we have been seeing" (Sievers & Yost, 1994, p. A1).

Trigger Event

Dr. Michael Osterholm, an epidemiologist with the Minnesota Depart-ment of Health explained that, as word of the tainted ice cream spread, the department received a "flurry of calls" from customers who were ill as a result of eating Schwan's ice cream (Sievers & Yost, 1994, p. A5). This information-seeking behavior is characteristic of the crisis stage. Immediately after the Minnesota Department of Health connected Schwan's ice cream to the salmonellosis outbreak, local, state, and federal health inspectors converged on the Marshall, Minnesota, plant. These officials included investigators from the U.S. Food and Drug Administration (FDA), the Centers for Disease Control and Prevention (CDC), the Minnesota Department of Health, and the Minnesota Department of Agriculture as well as such local officials as city sanitation and health inspectors.

The announcement of the *Salmonella* link to Schwan's created high levels of perceived threat for the company, its managers, workers, and the extended network of stakeholders. First, the economic impact was simply not clear. Although ice cream is not Schwan's most profitable product, it is closely associated with the company's identity. As a staff writer for the *Marshall Independent* noted, "Ice cream has stood as a symbol of the company's 42 year history...since the corporation started with one delivery truck transporting dairy products" (Muchlinski, 1994, p. A1).

There was also considerable uncertainty regarding how the outbreak would affect customers and about the extent of the outbreak. When the Minnesota Department of Health signaled the crisis, Schwan's perception of the severity and the threat was largely a function of the number of customers affected and the severity of their illnesses. A large number of cases involving serious illness could severely hurt the organization. Other cases of foodborne illness have resulted in deaths. In addition, the number of cases can rise dramatically, depending of the amount of food infected. For example, at the outset of the Schwan's outbreak, estimates ranged from 2,400 cases one week after the crisis, roughly 13,000 cases one month after the crisis, to 224,000 cases nearly two years after the crisis. Moreover, widespread consumer harm raises the specter of extremely costly and extended legal action.

Uncertainty and Initial Enactment

At the time of the crisis, information about cause, responsibility, and consequences was scarce. All Schwan's initially knew about the crisis was that there was a strong correlation between their ice cream products and the salmonellosis outbreak. Rather than responding to these events with denial and evasion of responsibility, however, Schwan's responded by allowing all public health inspectors full access to their Marshall plant and aided the investigations as much as possible. Detailed inspections, sampling, and culturing of samples for infectious agents are all part of the investigative process used to track the source of food-borne illness. As a result of the investigation, Schwan's was initially forced to close its Marshall plant.

Thrust into the uncertainty of this crisis, Schwan's immediately reacted to the crisis by taking responsibility for the harm caused to its customers.

This response was striking, given the fact that the source of the outbreak at this point was still not clear. At the time of the crisis, Dave Jennings, Schwan's director of human resources, explained: "Our philosophy was a simple one. We did not wait for the complete scientific research to be completed. At the first point where we believed there was a possible connection between our product and the illnesses reported, we took action (personal communication, November 17, 1997). Schwan's response was to prioritize the interests of their customers, their key stakeholders. Jennings explained that "Our guiding principle for the actions we took was one simple question. If you were a Schwan's customer and knew what we know, what would you do?" (personal communication, November 17, 1997).

During the crisis, Schwan's focused its communication in two directions. First, the company worked to indicate clearly to their customers that they were the organization's highest priority. Second, Schwan's communicated to stakeholders its plans to alleviate future outbreaks of salmonellosis. One feature of the company's communication was the immediacy of communication. Immediacy is particularly important in containing the harm of an outbreak of food-borne illness. Schwan's was able to use both the media and the personal contacts of route drivers to assist in the recall. Customers were sent packages of information, including information about how to be tested for salmonellosis and assurances that Schwan's would pay for these tests.

As discussed earlier, determining monetary compensation for pain and suffering as a result of a crisis is a difficult, divisive, and time-consuming aspect of crisis management. Legal tensions and threats of crisis litigation often go on for years, or decades in some cases, depending on the type and extent of the damages and lingering questions about responsibility. Moreover, the threat of extended legal action often serves to preclude organizations from taking corrective action for fear of creating additional legal exposure. Schwan's initial response to its crisis was novel in that it compensated customers as quickly as possible by paying for their medical tests and by providing refunds or credits for contaminated ice cream. Schwan's took this corrective action even before a definitive source of the outbreak was identified.

Another distinguishing aspect of Schwan's response was that the company began to settle with many customers immediately, without the intervention of court proceedings or attorneys. Soon after the crisis, four national class action lawsuits were filed against Schwan's. Customers had the choice, however, of settling directly with Schwan's or taking part in the class action lawsuits. By November, 15, 1994, Schwan's had voluntarily begun settling roughly fourteen thousand claims. At the time, it was reported that compensation worked "out to an average of $158.45 for each settlement" (Sievers, 1994b, p. A9). Roughly 2,600 reports were settled with gift certificates, although nearly 7,000 reports remained unresolved (Sievers, 1994b).

The fact that Schwan's was settling with customers so quickly was seen by many as a uniquely responsive approach to crisis management. However, class action lawyers were uncomfortable with Schwan's efforts to pay customers so quickly. As a result, the class action attorneys actually sought a temporary restraining order to prevent the company from settling with its customers. The restraining order was denied by a Minnesota judge, who said, "A strong public policy in favor of settlements exists.... Individuals should be allowed to enter into settlements with defendants if they voluntarily choose to do so" (Sievers, 1994b, p. A9).

In another highly unusual twist to this crisis, the plaintiff's lawyers sought to have the trial moved from Marshall, Minnesota. This was highly unusual; typically, plaintiff lawyers would want the trial to take place as close to the crisis event as possible because that is where public outrage is usually highest. However, Schwan's attention to the needs of its customers served to repair its image quickly and even strengthened its relationships with customers. The lawyers for the plaintiffs, in arguing to move the trial, pointed to a "4 1/2 page newspaper ad from the *Independent* [newspaper] bearing more than 1,000 signatures of Marshall area residents expressing support" for Schwan's. The lawyers also claimed that Schwan's was using its responsive stance and strong public image in the community "in an attempt to take advantage of the situation" (Kuebelbeck, 1994, p. A1). The judge, however, ruled a lack of sufficient justification for the change of venue.

The result of the lawsuits was a settlement that "calls for claimants to receive anywhere from $80 to $75,000, depending on how severely they were affected" (Seely, 1995, p. A1). The litigation was not prolonged and consensus was achieved quite quickly. Karl Cambronne, a lawyer for the plaintiffs, "commended Schwan's on its responsiveness and approach in handling the ordeal" (Seely, 1995, p. A5). He also commented that "Schwan's has behaved in a uniquely responsible way.... It's as a result of their corporate attitude that this case has been resolved so quickly, fairly, and equitably (Seely, 1995, p. A5).

Schwan's initial response to the crisis put its stakeholders at the center of its crisis management strategy. The crisis created a unique class of stakeholders: customers harmed by Schwan's products. Schwan's initial goal and guiding philosophy was to meet the expectations and needs of its customers. This response was informed by the company's long-standing values of direct customer service. This case illustrates the importance of paying attention to key stakeholders, particularly emergent stakeholders, during the crisis stage.

Local, state, and federal health agencies working in the Marshall plant eventually traced the source not to the plant but to the trucks used to transport ice cream mix from suppliers to the plant. The report from the investigation explained that Schwan's received its ice cream mix from two independent sites where the mix was pasteurized. However, Schwan's contract company, Cliff Viesman Trucking, apparently carried "raw eggs . . . in a tanker truck before the truck hauled pasteurized ice cream mix to Schwan's" ("Schwan's Cleared of Wrongdoing," 1995, p. A1). Schwan's did not pasteurize the incoming mixes as some other ice cream manufacturers had been doing. However, the company was clearly in compliance with state and federal food-manufacturing regulations.

As a result of the investigation and the determination of the source of the outbreak, Schwan's changed its practices. First, the company began construction of an on-site plant to pasteurize ice cream mix. Schwan's ice cream would still be pasteurized by the supplier but would then be repasteurized at the Schwan's plant before distribution, thus neutralizing any accidental contamination between supplier and plant. Until the new repasteurization plant could be built, the company instituted a policy called test and hold (Sievers, 1994a, p. A1). The process involved holding distribution of each day's products until each passed a test that cleared it from containing any *Salmonella* bacteria. Second, Schwan's publicly announced that it would dedicate a fleet of tanker trucks to carrying only Schwan's products. Schwan's management explained that when the tankers are empty they will be sealed so that they could not be used for any other purposes. These decisions, taken soon after the source of the outbreak was determined, allowed the company to quickly return to nearly normal operations.

Schwan's crisis is unique in that the company was successful in moving quickly to contain the harm, resolve the threat, and return to nearly normal operations. Several factors allowed the company to quickly move beyond the trigger event to a crisis response. First, the nature of the event was not uncommon in the food industry. In fact, merely describing the event as a salmonellosis outbreak associated with ice cream significantly reduced the relative levels of uncertainty. Second, Schwan's was able to respond even before the extent of the crisis was fully known. The company acted from a well-developed sense of customer values and long-term direct customer relationships. Acting from values in this way allowed for a much faster response. Moreover, acting toward the crisis from familiar value positions and long-established relationships allowed the company to quickly interpret and make sense of the crisis. Third, Schwan's experience clearly demonstrates that positive stakeholder relationships developed in the pre-crisis stage can help organizations manage the crisis stage.

This case also illustrates the role of crisis management during the crisis stage. For the organization, this is the most uncertain and stressful stage. It is also a point at which effective crisis management can significantly limit harm. Moreover, interpretations created in the crisis stage often significantly influence the postcrisis stage and subsequent developments. A fundamental goal of crisis management is to try to reduce the uncertainty of potential harm for both the organization and its stakeholders. How an organization deals with the crisis plays an important role in how the crisis will be resolved and the overall trajectory of the crisis. In this case, Schwan's chose to deal with the crisis fundamentally in terms of customer safety and well-being. Management determined that its actions following the crisis would be framed by the question of what is best for Schwan's customers. As a result of this attention to stakeholders, the typical legal wrangling, which may extend harm, was quickly resolved. Settlements were expedited by Schwan's aggressive approach to moving beyond the crisis, which included plans to ensure that in the future its products would be safe.

CONCLUSION

The crisis stage is the second major stage of crisis development. It is usually the shortest, but it is the phase of greatest intensity, emotional arousal, and harm. The crisis stage is the point of highest uncertainty, when the status quo is disrupted and the ability to collect and process information is reduced. It is also the point at which timely, effective, and strategic intervention has the greatest probability of containing the harm and limiting the impact of the crisis. Doing so allows the organization to move into the postcrisis stage, to a return to nearly normal operations. The decisions and positions taken during the crisis stage profoundly affect the development of the postcrisis stage. Often, however, the organization cannot assess its success until the crisis stage is over because of the intensity and time pressure of the crisis stage. The Schwan's case illustrates how a crisis stage may be managed effectively. The outbreak of food-borne illness was a familiar threat, and the company was able to respond from a well-established pattern of relationships and clear values. Most crisis stages, however, are characterized by denial, high levels of uncertainty, limited ability to make sense of the situation, conflict with stakeholders, and failure to act in harm-reducing ways. In these cases, the crisis stage is extended, harm accumulates, and the postcrisis stage is more likely to be characterized by continued conflict and secondary shocks.

CHAPTER 8

Communication and the Postcrisis Stage

As described in chapter 7, the intensity of the crisis stage results in a variety of communication exigencies. When the intensity of the crisis stage recedes, however, the postcrisis stage fosters more deliberate inquiry and long-term recovery. In contrast to the frantic, yet short-term, crisis phase, the postcrisis stage may linger for years. At worst, crisis victims and their families may see the postcrisis period as a protracted impediment to justice. Conversely, organizations may see postcrisis communication as distraction in the form of seemingly endless litigation and criticism. At best, however, postcrisis communication generates the information and resolution necessary to move beyond a crisis. When postcrisis communication functions effectively, organizations can emerge having learned important lessons, with improved risk management and with social legitimacy intact. Optimally, postcrisis is a time of rebirth and renewal.

This chapter discusses three essential stages for exemplary postcrisis communication. As Figure 8.1 illustrates, effective postcrisis communication moves chronologically through three stages: (1) salvaging legitimacy, (2) learning, and (3) healing. Organizations may move laterally within these stages as a postcrisis investigation unfolds. An organization's communication strategies may also fit into two or more stages simultaneously. If an organization is to move beyond a crisis mended rather than marred, all three stages, in varying degrees, are essential. This chapter examines these postcrisis processes in two sections. First, the outcomes and procedures for each of the three postcrisis stages are detailed. Second, a case study of how these stages functioned in the postcrisis communication following the massive 1997 flood in the Red River Valley of Minnesota and North Dakota is presented.

Figure 8.1
Consistent Stages in Effective Postcrisis Communication

I. Salvaging Legitimacy
   • Affirming Social Responsibility
   • Issues Management
   • Image Restoration
II. Learning
   • Retrospective Sensemaking
   • Reconsidering Structure
   • Vicarious Learning
III. Healing
   • Explanation
   • Remembering
   • Forgetting
   • Renewal
IV. Return to Crisis Planning and Pre-Crisis State

SALVAGING LEGITIMACY

In the wake of a crisis, salvaging legitimacy may be the single most important organizational objective. The intense media coverage and crisis-induced controversy places organizations "on the defensive to show the legitimacy of themselves or their actions" (Brummer, 1991). Organizations are judged as legitimate when they "establish congruence between the social values associated or implied by their activities and the norms of acceptable behavior in the larger social system of which they are a part" (Dowling & Pfeffer, 1975, p. 122). Crises instill public doubt as to the whether an organization's behavior is acceptable. Hearit (1995) explained: "a clear indicator of a social legitimacy crisis is the emergence of public animosity toward the corporation." In crisis situations, "public hostility is a form of social sanction" from stakeholders that demands a response" (p. 3).

Affirming Social Responsibility

Regaining legitimacy is a complex process whereby an organization's objectives and public sentiment are in harmony. Profitability, although essential to organizational survival, is not sufficient for legitimacy. Organizations must also reaffirm a larger social purpose or value. In addition to satisfying social norms, organizations often emphasize their social contributions as employers, taxpayers, and philanthropists (Seeger, 1997). Similarly, winning legal battles does not ensure a victory in the court of public opinion (Epstein & Votaw, 1978, p. 76). In fact, an organization's legal victories often frustrate the public and further diminish credibility. For example, Nike did not violate the Vietnamese standards for air quality in its Vietnam shoe factories. Outrage by the American public, however, convinced the company to employ the much-higher American standard for air quality (Sellnow & Brand, 2001).

Audience diversity is another dimension of social legitimacy (Nakra, 2000). A diverse array of stakeholders constitute the relevant audience for maintaining or improving an image. According to Ulmer and Sellnow (2000), viability for an organization during postcrisis depends on its ability to maintain a positive relationship with "stockholders, workers, consumers, suppliers, creditors, competitors, government agencies, professional groups, and the local community" (p. 144). Schuetz (1990) explained that organizations in crisis situations must structure a complex campaign in response to the crisis and direct different elements of the case to different audiences. Ironically, "in some cases, companies must advocate new policies and defend old ones in the same message" (p. 283). Ultimately, "the belief is that communication (words and actions) does affect how stakeholders perceive the organization in crisis" (Coombs, 1999b, p. 121). During the postcrisis analysis period, an organization's foremost purpose is to convince its relevant audiences that the organization can and will function within or exceed the norms of society. Failure to do so typically results in serious harm (Hearit, 1995; Seeger, 1986a).

Issues Management

Issues management is "the strategic use of issues analysis and strategic responses to help organizations make adaptations needed to achieve harmony and foster mutual interests with the communities in which they operate" (Heath, 1997, p. 3). Issues management is a means through which organizations can establish or regain social legitimacy. Although crises are not necessary for organizations to commence an issues management campaign, the protracted investigation and social commentary associated with postcrisis communication usually necessitates an issues management approach. Issues such as public or environmental safety, adequate warning, or new limits on organizational operations often arise, to which the organization must respond. Failure to engage in the debate about these public issues may mean that they are resolved in ways that compromise the organization's ability to operate.

After the acute crisis phase subsides, organizations face an "onslaught" of "why, how, what, when," and "where" questions (Fink, 1986). Organizations must answer these questions throughout the postcrisis phase. Initially, they must answer in ways that address questions of social responsibility and legitimacy. To do so, organizations must be active participants in the postcrisis investigation and debate. Later, as the fervor of the postcrisis investigation lessens, answers to these questions assume the form of organizational learning. Legitimacy and learning, then, may both require an ongoing issues management initiative.

Image Restoration

Following accusations of wrongdoing, such as those often made in the aftermath of a crisis, organizations must engage in defense and image restoration. This process of image restoration is usually framed as apologia, or a genre of public apologetic discourse (Benoit & Brinson, 1994; Benoit & Lindsey, 1987; Ice, 1991). For organizations, apologetic communication "is corporate rather than individual centered" and employs a variety of strategies (Schultz & Seeger, 1991, p. 51). Benoit (1995a) offers the most comprehensive and widely applied typology of image restoration strategies.

His five image restoration strategies include denial, evading responsibility, reducing offensiveness of the event, corrective action, and mortification. Denial may involve simply denying responsibility for an event or shifting the blame from the organization to outside individuals or agencies. Organizations evade responsibility for a crisis by claiming they: were provoked, lacked sufficient information, had an accident, or, despite the crisis, were acting with good intentions. Corporations can reduce the perceived offensiveness of the crisis event with three variants: bolstering, differentiation, and transcendence. Bolstering may "mitigate the negative effects" of the wrongdoing by strengthening the audience's "positive" feelings toward the organization (Benoit, 1995a, p. 77). Differentiation occurs when the communicator "attempts to distinguish the act performed from other similar but less desirable actions" (p. 73). Transcendence involves suggesting "a different frame of reference" for the act in question (p. 74). To these, Benoit adds minimizing the crisis, attacking the accuser, and compensating the victims. In taking corrective action, the accused pledges to follow one of two alternatives: "restoring the situation to the state of affairs before the objectionable action and/or promising to 'mend one's ways' and make changes to prevent the recurrence of the undesirable act" (p. 79). Mortification is shown when the accused accepts responsibility for its wrongdoing and asks to be forgiven.

Coombs's (1999b) strategies of image restoration (see Figure 8.2) are most closely associated with public relations. His typology accounts for the most common strategies on a continuum between defensive and accommodative responses to crises. The first two strategies involve denial that a crisis exists. Coombs's strategy of attacking the accuser is the most-extreme defensive stance, whereby the organization "confronts the person or group who claims that a crisis exists" (p. 123). The organization, for example, may threaten lawsuits as part of its attack on the accuser. In

Figure 8.2
Image Restoration Strategies

Benoit	Coombs
Denial	Attack the Accuser
Simple Denial	Denial
Shifting Blame	Excuse
Evading of Responsibility	Justification
Provocation	Ingratiation
Defeasibility	Corrective Action
Accident	Full Apology
Good Intentions	
Reducing Offensiveness of Event	
Bolstering	
Minimization	
Differentiation	
Transcendence	
Attack Accuser	
Compensation	
Corrective Action	
Mortification	

denial, Coombs's second defensive strategy, the organization contends "that there is no crisis" or that "the organization has no responsibility for the crisis" (p. 125). Offering an excuse is a third defensive posture. Excuses enable organizations to deny "any intention to do harm" or to claim that "the organization had no control of the events that led to the crisis" (p. 123). Coombs places justification at the center of his defensive versus accommodative continuum. Justification is similar to Benoit's (1995a) minimization strategy. When applying justification, an organization "accepts the crisis but tries to downplay the perceived severity" (p. 125). Coombs warned, however, that justifying arguments may create the problematic perception that the organization is "trivializing victim concerns" (p. 125). Ingratiation, the first of Coombs's accommodating strategies, is similar to what Benoit (1995a) called bolstering. Organizations ingratiate during crises by praising a stakeholder or by emphasizing "good deeds of the past" (Coombs, 1999b, p. 123). A second ingratiating strategy, corrective action, parallels Benoit's category of the same name. Organizations take corrective action by "seeking to repair the damage from the crisis" or by taking "steps to prevent a repeat of the crisis" (Coombs, 1999b, p. 123). Coombs's final strategy, full apology, is the most ingratiating. A full apology occurs when the organization publicly takes full responsibility and "asks forgiveness for the crisis" (p. 123). Some forms of victim compensation may also be included in this strategy.

The image restoration strategies described by Benoit (1995a) and Coombs (1999b) combine to present an extensive typology for understanding the initial postcrisis response of organizations. Depending on the context of the crisis and the organization's ultimate goal, each strategy has potential relevance as the postcrisis investigation begins. If the investigation lingers on, organizations are often asked to publicly articulate the extent to which the organization has changed or been renewed by the crisis. Thus, the initial investigation and organizational response gives way to a more sophisticated discussion of the organization's long-term plans for preventing similar crises in the future. This heightened inquiry takes the form of organizational learning.

LEARNING

Although most organizations engage in constant self-analysis, postcrisis situations create a period of heightened awareness. Even if an organization can argue successfully that external agents such as terrorism caused a crisis, stakeholders still demand explanations regarding the organization's vulnerability, ineffective crisis management, and ways similar events may be avoided in the future. Although organizations may describe corrective actions in their image restoration claims, organizational learning requires that the changes are actually made and evaluated. To accomplish this postcrisis objective, organizations engage in three general forms of learning: (1) retrospective sensemaking, (2) structural reconsideration, and (3) vicarious learning.

Retrospective Sensemaking

Initially, the slower pace of the postcrisis period affords organizations time to reconsider questions of causation. To do so, organizations engage in what is called retrospective sensemaking. According to Weick (2001), this "process of learning occurs when people notice some of what was previously overlooked and overlook some of what was previously noticed." The organization engages in a form of "biased hindsight" in an effort to understand how previously unchallenged assumptions contributed to the crisis (p. 305). Ironically, Weick has explained that learning and the explanation process are inextricably linked. For example, as organizations enact image restoration strategies, they are, in essence, establishing an argument to explain the organization's actions. Some claims may be well received, but others may be rejected. Weick (1995) explained that "in the process of developing and criticizing explanations, people often discover new explanations, which is why argument can produce adaptive sensemaking" (p. 139). Thus, postcrisis messages and organizational responses evolve, in part, based on the reactions of stakeholders.

Postcrisis inquiry also expands an organization's repertoire of potential responses. For example, when NASA proceeded with its ill-fated *Challenger* launch, the organization gave limited consideration to the impact of temperature on the booster rockets. This lack of attention occurred despite warnings by engineers. The postcrisis period made clear that temperature was a critical variable. In this manner, the postcrisis investigation contributed directly to NASA's knowledge base and how that knowledge was prioritized. Postcrisis communication, then, is far more than a form of public apology. Rather, the dialectic of public explanation and stakeholder response contributes to the organization's knowledge base. This expanded repertoire, then, influences the organization's understanding and future behavior.

Reconsidering Structure

Postcrisis learning may also lead an organization to reconsider its structure. In chapter 4, the epistemic role of crisis communication was explored. Crisis, accordingly, offers a means of knowing which assumptions about the organization's structure are valid and which are flawed. Over time, an organizational structure inevitably becomes stagnated. Structural patterns grant influence and power to some organizational members and the simple comfort of predictability to others. Consequently, major changes in structure are difficult to accomplish without a disruption of some kind. Crises pose such a disruption, suspending the status quo and creating opportunities for change. During postcrisis, criticism is often directed toward the organization's most influential members (Von Krogh, Roos, & Slocum, 1994). Changes in leadership, mission, and general practices are sometimes necessary to regain legitimacy. These changes may be subtle, such as increased security or a redistribution of personnel. More often than not, however, crises produce conspicuous structural changes, such as new leadership, major changes in operations, or unprecedented means for sensing and averting crises. The Department of Homeland Security, created in 2001, is an example of a structural change that probably would not have been accomplished without a precipitating crisis such as 9/11.

Huber (1996) characterized reconsideration of structure as "unlearning" (p. 147). Ironically, organizations learn by discarding knowledge that was previously held in high regard. Specifically, "unlearning opens the way for new learning to take place" (p. 147). Because crises inherently introduce a need for change at some level, unlearning is often necessary in postcrisis recovery. Huber also suggested that changes in an organizational hierarchy rarely occur without disruption. Such disruptions are an unfreezing of the organization's assumptions and leadership. Huber suggested that "an extreme form of intentional unlearning by organizations is the discharge of employees, especially managers who are unable to move from outdated ways of doing things" (p. 147). In short, crisis creates doubt in an organizational structure that has previously been unquestioned. This doubt serves an epistemic function of revealing weaknesses.

Vicarious Learning

The public nature of crises makes vicarious learning viable for many organizations. Weick and Ashford (2001) suggested that "by watching what happens to individuals when they engage in different behavior patterns, the learner comes to understand that a certain strategy leads to success while another leads to failure, without engaging in either strategy personally." Similarly, organizations learn vicariously "what practices to adopt by watching successful firms in their industries" (p. 712). Sellnow and Brand (2001) extended this definition to include the possibility of organizations learning vicariously through the mistakes of similar organizations. Organizational crises may establish some organizations as antimodels whose behavior should be avoided. Conversely, some organizations respond to crises so effectively that their crisis response serves as a model for others. Organizations reduce uncertainty by scrutinizing the successes and failures of other organizations in attempting to avoid or to recover from a crisis. In this manner, crises can be "a catalyst for affirmative change" (Crable & Vibbert, 1985, p. 13).

The past two decades are replete with examples of crises that produced vicarious learning. Responses to the Tylenol poisoning incidents have long been considered a model for crisis management. Exxon's delay and seeming nonchalance in coping with its *Valdez* spill is widely referenced as an antimodel. Aaron Feuerstein, owner and chief executive officer (CEO) of Malden Mills in Lawrence, Massachusetts, was praised by President Bill Clinton as an icon of ethical management for his decision to continue paying employees as he rebuilt his textile factory after a devastating fire. State health directors have scrambled to learn from states that encountered letter-borne anthrax. In each of these cases, organizations were able to reduce their uncertainty by observing the actions of others. Organizations may observe the crisis circumstances of their peers in hopes of learning from them. The postcrisis learning process also gives organizations the knowledge and expertise needed for the organization and its stakeholders to engage in the healing process.

HEALING

Postcrisis healing is a multifaceted process that allows the organization and stakeholders to reconstitute themselves and move past the crisis. Both the organization and its stakeholders seek to simultaneously remember some aspects of the crisis and forget others as they embrace the future. Healing involves constructing a meaning for the event. In some cases, the healing process may usher in a sense of renewal for the organization. In others, it is merely relief that the crisis is over. Regardless of the approach, healing begins with a narrative of explanation.

Explanation

The explanation process, if successful, helps stakeholders construct some understanding of causation. Explanation answers the fundamental question, What happened? Understanding cause typically enables an organization or a community to plan for similar crises in the future. Isolating the cause enables organizations to establish countermeasures that will thwart or reduce the risk of similar crises. For example, the highly visible changes in airline security following the 9/11 terrorist attacks vividly created the impression that airlines and government had fortified previously vulnerable points. These observable changes in response to publicly stated causes of the crisis are essential for the healing process to begin.

Forgetting

Explanations that produce changes in the status quo are essential to correcting systematic errors or risks. These changes, however, also contribute to emotional healing in the form of forgetting. Forgetting, in this case, refers to the ability to replace feelings of urgency, anxiety, and loss with positive emotions such as patience, confidence, and optimism. This process is essential, because crises deprive their victims of a sense of control over their environment (Freedy, Kilpatrick, & Resnick, 1993; Rubonis & Bickman, 1991). Freedy et al. explained that feelings of diminished control and lost predictability combine with high personal threat to delay posttrauma adjustment. Simply stated, stakeholders have a more difficult time moving beyond a crisis if they remain fearful that sufficient measures have not been taken to avoid similar crises in the future. In their work with natural disasters, Freedy, Kilpatrick, and Resnick found that "planning and protective actions" have the potential to "reduce anticipatory anxiety by enhancing a sense of personal control" (p. 52).

Failure to relieve feelings of vulnerability and helplessness may result in extended psychopathological conditions. In their extensive metanalysis of psychological impairments fostered by crises, Rubonis and Bickman (1991) found a "consistently positive and practically meaningful relationship between disasters and psychopathology" (p. 395). Specifically, they identified nine symptom domains in the postdisaster literature:

a) stress or posttraumatic stress syndrome, b) depressions, including manic symptomatology, c) anxiety, including panic disorder, or nervousness, d) somatization or physical health symptomology, e) phobia, f) psychosexual dysfunction, g) alcohol dependence or abuse, h) drug dependence or abuse, and i) psychosis, including schizophrenia or thought disorder. (pp. 388–389)

Research generally estimates a 17 percent psychopathology incident rate in postcrisis. To promote recovery, Rubonis and Bickman argued for "techniques that help victims understand the cause of the disaster" (p. 397). This approach is most appropriate when the cause of the crisis is natural as opposed to human. If human error, incompetence, or corruption is the cause, victims are less likely to fear a similar event once the perpetrator is removed. In the case of a natural disaster such as a flood or tornado, with no identifiable human agent, victims are likely to continue to feel a heightened sense of vulnerability and have more difficulty forgetting past feelings of urgency, anxiety, and loss.

Remembering

While releasing, forgetting, or contextualizing the emotional responses to a crisis is essential for healing, so, too, is the effort to recall those elements of the crisis that provide unity and resilience. Simply shunning or denying a failure stunts organizational learning. In fact, Sitkin (1996) argues that failure "is an essential prerequisite" for learning (p. 542). In the case of large failures, there is a danger that an organization's response is "more likely to be protective than exploratory" (p. 548). In extreme cases, a crisis can foster a form of learning in which reminders of the crisis, such as the anniversary, "may become conditioned stimuli that [regularly] activate negative emotions" (Freedy et al., 1993).

To overcome such unproductive reactions, organizations and communities seek to reframe the crisis so that their recollection creates a positive or optimistic frame of reference. Payne (1989) described this reframing process as therapeutic persuasion: when a population suffers a trauma, therapeutic discourse may help victims to "recover an identity that has been denied" by the crisis event. Through discourse, victims must "create a new identity capable of dealing with one's new reality, and one must be able to get support for this new identity through effective communication techniques" (p. 29). To establish this renewed identity, organizations and communities often stage events for crisis victims and other stakeholders that typically generate considerable media attention. Crisis survivors and casualties are often portrayed as heroes who endured hardship for the sake of the organization or community. The identity that emerges from such ceremonies for crisis stakeholders is one of sacrifice, bravery, persistence, and resourcefulness. The crisis stakeholders thus engage in a form of healing by releasing retrospective self-perceptions of helplessness and fear and adopting a prospective attitude rich in community and capability. Communities often erect statues or memorials to commemorate the organization or community's recovery from the crisis. Similarly, heroes are held up as symbols of the organization or community spirit. At Pearl Harbor, Hawaii, for example, the bullet holes from strafing attack planes are preserved in the walls of Air Force buildings. Tourists are ferried to a floating shrine above the sunken USS *Arizona*, where hundreds of American sailors are entombed. Rather than a symbol of failure and vulnerability, Pearl Harbor serves as a symbol of the courage and perseverance with which Americans rose to the challenge of World War II. More recently, the one-year anniversary of the 9/11 attacks was observed, with both civic and religious ceremonies throughout the United States. The first anniversary was also marked with monuments throughout the nation, many incorporating pieces of the destroyed World Trade Center. These types of ceremonies portray the crisis as more than a senseless loss of life, emphasizing lessons learned and a commitment to going forward. Remembering a crisis may be less ceremonial in cases when corruption of an individual or group is to blame. Still, some form of epideictic rhetoric and a call for a renewed sense of community is likely to occur even in these cases. Both the WorldCom and Enron collapses, for example, have been characterized by this public commitment to learn the lessons of the past and go forward.

Renewal

In some postcrisis contexts a form of healing emerges that is not concerned with image restoration, explanations, or causation. Some organizations are able to embark on rebuilding with little or no hesitation. Organizations that adopt such a strategy are able to bypass much of the image restoration, remembering, and forgetting processes and move directly toward renewal. Two recent examples involved Aaron Feuerstein, owner and CEO of Malden Mills, a textile firm in Lawrence, Massachusetts, and Milt Cole, owner and CEO of a hardwood lumber company in Logansport, Indiana. In both cases, the CEOs' responses to devastating fires were not consistent with the predictions of the postcrisis literature. Both CEOs responded to the destruction of their factories not by apologizing or investigating but by immediately and publicly committing to continue paying workers and rebuild their facilities, even when the economic justification for this action was suspect. The responses offered by Feuerstein and Cole were widely reported as powerful examples of management virtue and commitment to the community (Seeger & Ulmer, 2001). This public pledge to rebuild and to maintain support for employees eliminated the need for discourse salvaging legitimacy and the need for extended discussions of lessons learned. Moreover, media interest

in the crises shifted from investigating causation and blame to praising committed and responsible CEOs. Healing was almost immediate, because the
employees were not asked to endure financial hardship while waiting for the
mills to reopen. Further, because both organizations were privately held, neither CEO had to wait for support from a governing board to engage in
rebuilding.

Cases of organizational renewal, although rare, offer four implications
for postcrisis (Seeger & Ulmer, 2001). The first focuses on issues of direc-
tionality in postcrisis discourse. Postcrisis discourse typically begins as
retrospective in nature, primarily because the organization is looking back
to explain and justify past acts. In contrast, the postcrisis renewal focuses
on the future, on how previous limitations can be overcome, and on new
opportunities that can be explored. Second, the natural role of crisis, at
least in some instances, is for organizations to transform and restructure
themselves in ways leading to growth and renewal. Third, a discourse of
renewal emphasizes the positive possibilities in crisis over other issues
such as cause, blame, and culpability. Stories of support, rebuilding, and
renewal are more compelling than stories about questions of cause.
Fourth, this discourse of renewal reaffirms the leader's role in enacting
and framing the meaning of crisis.

Clearly, crisis does not typically have this renewing effect. The literature
includes dozens of examples of crises that lingered on through claims and
counterclaims of cause, responsibility, and wrongdoing and through legal
maneuvering over victim compensation (Hearit, 1995; Seeger & Bolz, 1996;
Williams & Treadaway, 1992). Although it is not clear why some crises result
in decline and others result in renewal, it is likely that the nature of the organization, the nature of the crisis, the nature of the response, and the immediacy of the response all play a role. In the case of the Red River Valley flood,
described below, some communities were able to create postcrisis renewal,
whereas others used the event primarily as an opportunity to learn.

THE 1997 RED RIVER VALLEY FLOOD

The spring of 1997 made the Red River Valley, the region along the border between Minnesota and North Dakota, a media focal point for the
nation. The most devastating flood in the region's history coiled around
the communities in the region, constricting all activity and, in some
instances, essentially destroying entire cities. Ultimately, the 1997 flood
became the first time in modern history that entire communities were con-
sumed by the flow of the Red River. When the water eventually receded,
damage and home buyouts caused by the flood surpassed $5 billion, mak-
ing it one of the most expensive natural disasters in U.S. history. This case
vividly illustrates many of the postcrisis strategies described earlier.

Context of the Flood

The fact that the Red River surged to flood levels in 1997 did not come as a surprise. More snow—a staggering total of 119 inches—fell in the winter of 1996–1997 than ever recorded in the region (Pantera, 2002b, p. A1). As Fargo, North Dakota, drivers inched their way through intersections, peering around towering snowbanks, every resident knew that a flood was looming. In fact, some residents living along the river referred to the annual process of constructing sandbag dikes in their backyards as a spring ritual.

Calculating the 1997 crest of the river based solely on snowfall was impossible. Ground moisture prior to the onset of winter, melting rates, water released from reservoirs upstream, and spring rains made such long-range predictions pointless. Instead, residents relied on a series of gauges that provided specific measurements of water depths along the Red River. In 1997, however, this traditional approach failed to account for the overwhelming enormity of the runoff. The combined pressure caused by rapid melting and overland flooding created an unparalleled strain on the traditional measurement system. Floating ice jammed the river, causing flash floods and blocking or damaging gauges. Further, the calculating formulas were compromised by heavy rain and widely fluctuating temperatures. The National Oceanic and Atmospheric Administration's (NOAA) weather service forecast office could not keep pace with fluctuating water levels ("Ice Jam Could Worsen Flood," 1997).

Early in April, officials from NOAA warned residents to prepare for flood crests as high as 38 feet, considered a generous prediction. On April 10, neighborhoods along the river received their first warning that this flood would exceed records. On that date, NOAA predicted that the crest would hit between 39 and 39.5 feet (Gilmour, 1997a, p. A1). Two days later, work on the dikes was interrupted by news that the "predicted crest dropped from a top height of 39.5 feet to a low of 37.5 feet" due to the discovery of "a faulty automated gauge upriver" (Hilgers, 1997a, p. A1). Although residents were relieved to hear the lower prediction, they were also frustrated by the two-foot disparity.

The U.S. Geological Survey, which monitors the gauges, claimed the faulty reading was an isolated incident, attributing the malfunction in the gauges to extreme temperatures and damage produced by floating ice. Because NOAA considers the data provided by the gauges when making predictions, the discrepancies in its readings were blamed on the faulty gauge readings. Manual gauges back up the automatic versions; however, the manual gauge in this case was attached to a bridge that was inaccessible because it was covered with ice (MacDonald, 1997).

By April 14, Fargo's NOAA operations manager said it was unlikely that the Red River would crest again in Fargo. An unofficial crest reading of 37.61 feet, the second highest on record, reflected a slow drop. The next day, all hope for a quick finish to the flood was lost. The operations manager's prediction was based on what was the second faulty gauge reading in a week. Floodwaters were actually rising and were expected to climb above 38 feet (Hilgers, 1997b). With this second failure, NOAA abandoned its automated gauges.

On April 17, the Red River surpassed the 100-year-old record by climbing to 39.12 feet. Fargo's operations manager noted, "We are at river stages that exceed the 1897 level. No one has ever seen this much water in the Fargo area, ever. All we can do is react" (Gilmour, 1997b, p. A1). The record crest in Fargo created even greater concern for Grand Forks, North Dakota. The residents of Grand Forks, located 75 miles north and downriver from Fargo, knew that they too were about to see record water levels. During the night of April 18, Grand Forks' dikes were overwhelmed by water levels that were as much as two feet higher than expected. Emergency officials evacuated the entire city of more than fifty thousand residents. One reporter described the scene: "With sirens screaming over the river, helicopters circling overhead and National Guard trucks rumbling down the streets, the city felt like a war zone" (Condon, 1997, p. A1). Water rushed into the sewer system, and residents reported seeing manhole covers shooting eight feet in the air while the city flooded from within.

Flooded electrical systems caused the upper floors of a historic section of downtown Grand Forks to burst into flames. Fire raced from building to building while city firefighters sat by in fishing boats watching helplessly. The water was simply too deep to deliver equipment to the blaze. Residents watched as black smoke rumbled through the sky above their flooded city. In a scene reminiscent of a forest fire, airplanes and helicopters circled the city for hours, dropping water and chemicals on the flooded conflagration.

Receding floodwater, contaminated with chemicals and untreated sewage, left devastation. In some cases, water had almost entirely covered houses; many were condemned. Even homeowners who experienced comparatively minor flooding had to replace drywall, appliances, and furniture. Mounds of water-soaked refuse began piling up on curbs, waiting to be hauled away. Several public buildings were destroyed. Because numerous businesses in the area had lost both buildings and equipment, many residents lost jobs. The *Grand Forks Herald* lost printing presses, computers, and its irreplaceable archive of historic photos and back issues spanning the history of the area.

As the tedious and extraordinary cleanup process began in earnest, mental-health officials encouraged residents to take time to express their emotions. They explained that, after experiencing a disaster, victims go through many stages. The experience may begin with shock and numbing, moving to a heroic stage of being supportive and coming together with other victims. After a brief honeymoon stage of pledging to overcome any hardship, victims begin to feel severe disillusionment and anger. One clinical social worker explained that "anger is a legitimate emotion...to bottle that anger up is not good" (Angeles, 1997, p. 15).

Salvaging Legitimacy

City, state, and county leaders were praised for their united recognition of an impending flood and their deployment of all available resources to prepare for an extended battle. Similarly, residents were praised for the countless hours they volunteered to battle the flood. Many community leaders, however, were highly critical of NOAA for its inconsistent and inaccurate crest predictions. Simply stated, some blamed NOAA for the destruction of Grand Forks. This sustained public anger and criticism necessitated a public response in the form of image restoration from NOAA.

Residents insisted they could have saved Grand Forks if they had known how high the water would rise. Officials accused NOAA of misleading them. Grand Forks' mayor said, "we were told absolutely 49 feet by the weather service," and she insisted that, had the city known how high the waters would rise, the devastation "would have been preventable" (Produs, 1997, p. A7). The hydrologist in charge of the regional forecast center defended his agency by claiming that the flood conditions were so volatile that precise crest calculations were not possible. He said, "We were dealing with an unprecedented flood and you're dealing with Mother Nature and you just have to roll with the punches.... It's extremely complex and under the circumstances I think we did a very credible job" (Produs, 1997, p. A7). This response represents what Benoit (1995b) labels defeasibility. The agency simply did not have the capacity to provide the type of information that Grand Forks' mayor demanded. Similarly, this explanation could be viewed as an excuse in Coombs's (1999b) typology. NOAA argued that the conditions were such that it simply could not make accurate predictions.

The postcrisis investigation of the agency provided the evidence to establish what Hearit (1997) has called an opinion/knowledge dissociation. Following the flood, an extensive investigation into NOAA's forecasting procedures yielded no evidence that the agency had "bungled" its crest predictions ("Newspaper: No Evidence Feds Bungled Flood Forecast," 1997, p. C1). One study did find, however, that "government officials worked at the edge of scientific knowledge and made extraordinary efforts—occasionally risking their lives—as they tried to monitor and predict the river's behavior" ("Newspaper: No Evidence," 1997, p. C1). In the end, Weather Service officials explained that the bridges in Grand Forks created an unanticipated damming effect, forcing water levels higher than predicted. The report also indicated that NOAA had "never suggested its original 49-foot crest prediction was something Grand Forks residents could rely on; however, the agency did admit that "forecasters could have stressed the uncertainties of their prediction in stronger terms" ("Newspaper: No Evidence," 1997, p. C1). In the end, NOAA based much of its defense on the claim that it could not have known the crest level and that it never intended for the cities to rely on its predictions.

Learning

On the fifth anniversary of the 1997 Red River Valley flood, community leaders and residents alike emphasized the learning that had occurred as a result of the disaster. Newspaper stories featured interviews with flood victims and city officials. Headlines included "Learning from the Past" (Gilmour, 2002b, p. B1) and "Painful Lessons: 1997 Flood Teaches F-M Officials about Vulnerability, Weak Spots" (Pantera, 2002a, p. A1).

Organizational learning manifests itself in a response to inadequacies or to what was previously overlooked. This learning process develops over time and is shaped by the participation of multiple stakeholders. The post-crisis period in the Red River Valley included continuous public debate. In Grand Forks, $171 million in federal aid was spent to prevent future flooding and to rebuild the city's infrastructure to more flood-proof standards. This rebuilding has occurred despite ongoing debates over how and where rebuilding should occur and how and where new dikes and diversion systems should be built. Some residents were embittered by the city's decision to condemn their homes. Businesses lobbied for favorable treatment, causing conflicts throughout city government. For example, the Grand Forks mayor, who had been praised for her courage and tireless leadership, lost her bid for reelection, largely due to conflicts regarding her plans for the city's recovery (Froslie, 2002). Fargo had extensive public debates over which of three flood-control plans would be undertaken on its southern border (Zent, 2002). Most important, the continued debate and the associated changes have expanded the region's crisis-response repertoire.

Effective learning during postcrisis also requires organizations to reconsider their structure. Huber's (1996) emphasis on unlearning is particularly relevant to the Red River Valley's postcrisis state. The shock of the flood's magnitude, the inconsistent crest predictions, and the catastrophic failure of Grand Forks' dikes inspired the region's leaders to reconsider their long-standing flood plans. Fargo's city engineer explained that, because of the old system, "[W]e may have been a little bit too conservative in making our preparation based on the flood predictions" (Pantera, 2002a, p. A8). Dikes had been built based on maximum crest figures provided by NOAA. On several occasions, Fargo officials had reduced the recommended dike levels due to lower-than-anticipated crest predictions. When the river surged to unrivaled levels, residents felt that the city engineers had failed them. Yet, as discussed above, NOAA had never intended for the crest predictions to be taken as absolute. This realization prompted learning in the form of two changes in how NOAA is perceived in the structure of the communities' flood-management system. First, communities are now generally less dependent on forecasts of maximum crest levels. Second, "Since 1997, the weather service now gives a percentage of risk that the river will reach given levels so local jurisdictions have a better idea of how to plan" (Pantera, 2002a, p. A8).

The shocking damage prompted those communities in the region that had escaped damage to learn vicariously. Specifically, even though they had escaped the floods, communities throughout the Red River Valley wanted to be part of the solution. Officials from South Dakota and Canada joined Minnesota and North Dakota in forming the International Red River Task Force. The task force was charged with recommending cooperative solutions to the flooding problem. After three years, the task force released its report. Principally, the report recommended consistent and extensive coordination. Although cities in the Red River Valley were advised to individually take swift action to prepare for the inevitable recurrence of a major flood, they were asked to do so while "keeping in mind how each city's action will affect others along the river" (Gilmour, 2000, p. C3). To accomplish this coordination, the report advised communities to build and maintain communication networks that would allow rapid sharing of information during floods. This improved communication was presented in the report as the primary means for maintaining a comprehensive capacity for monitoring potential floodwater. In a general sense, the enhanced communication network was designed to ensure that vicarious learning would continue as future floods develop. The extensive learning during the postcrisis period of the flood ultimately contributed to the continued healing by demonstrating that lessons had been learned.

Healing

Healing begins with an explanation of the vulnerabilities that allowed the crisis to occur. The knowledge acquired in the learning phase of postcrisis, then, sets the healing process in motion. Initially, the flood victims were challenged to forget or move beyond feelings of anguish and despair. As part of this healing process, residents were challenged to rebuild their flooded homes and the city infrastructure. For healing to be successful, this rebuilding process needed to be reframed in the residents' memories to accentuate their resilience and the recovery.

The 1997 floods caused a wide variety of reactions. The forgetting process required residents to struggle with psychopathological responses such as depression, anxiety, and substance abuse. Remnants of these emotions still linger among many residents. For example, East Grand Forks did not sound sirens as part of a statewide tornado drill near the anniversary of the flood, to avoid "bringing up those memories that aren't real pleasant for some people" ("Grand Forks Recalls '97 Flood Disaster," 2002, p. A18).

The psychopathological effects of the flood in Grand Forks were painfully apparent to the local medical community. In the month following the flood, Grand Forks medical and law enforcement officials offered some startling statistics:

- Complaints of mental health problems such as depression increased 45 percent.
- The number of domestic violence incidents increased 43 percent.
- Driving under the influence (DUI) violations increased 129 percent.
- Drug and narcotics violations increased 275 percent. (Anderson, 2000, p. B1)

Residents also experienced higher rates of divorce and bankruptcy after the flood. The study summarized the situation by saying: "It's true no one died directly from the flood, but it's the opinion of many ministers, mental health providers and health care providers that the death of many citizens was hastened by the flood" ("Grand Forks Recalls," 2002, p. A18).

On the fifth anniversary, at least one Grand Forks psychologist reported some evidence of emotional healing. Although "long-term depression, addiction and employment problems remain," most of the population has a new outlook ("Grand Forks Recalls," 2002, p. A18). Moreover, the scope of the disaster created some unique opportunities for emotional recovery. Because the entire community experienced the flood, it was socially acceptable for residents to express their feelings:

That was something a lot of people, especially men, hadn't been able to do before. Without talking about the loss and grieving, healing wouldn't have happened. Talking is part of the healing process. They were able to see how far they came and see their growth in recovery. As tragic as it (the anniversary) was, it forced us to look at the flood again. ("Grand Forks Recalls," 2002, p. A18)

One lingering feature of the flood is the high rate of drug and alcohol abuse by area teens. The increase started when "kids lost their last boundaries—their structures—in life. And they were left alone a lot because their parents were so busy" ("Grand Forks Recalls," 2002, p. A18).

Many individuals have, however, successfully reframed the crisis. Their healing process involved forgetting or moving beyond the negative emotions and embracing the future with pride and optimism. Some use humor in describing the flood. One resident whose home and possessions were destroyed had an optimistic recollection of the flood: "My wife has been hauling this stuff from house to house for years, and I can finally get rid of some of it" (Baird, 2002, p. A8). A Fargo resident quipped, "I enjoy snow. I just don't enjoy it here anymore" (p. A8). In Grand Forks, "Some observers even joke that the mid-April flood and fire were a blessing in disguise, clearing away much that was old and tired in downtown to make way for the new and fresh" (Knutson, 2002, p. A22). The city lost 40 downtown buildings in the flood and fire, many of which were old and poorly maintained. Grand Forks' current mayor, however, expressed optimism by claiming that his city's "downtown is back all the way. Grand Forks is back all the way" (p. A22). Residents frame the tremendous recovery and rebuilding as evidence of "pride in the community and hope for our future" (Gilmour, 2002a, p. A21).

The healing process often involves ceremonies that honor both community and individual heroes. On the fifth anniversary, Grand Forks unveiled 12 bronze plaques that tell the story of the flood. The plaques are located on the site of the downtown fire. The Grand Forks celebration also included a parade and a prayer breakfast. One of the event's planners noted, "I understand, for a lot of people, five years is not enough to heal those wounds. But I also think five years is an important landmark and once we get past five years, it's almost like we're looking forward" ("Grand Forks Recalls," 2002, p. A18).

When East Grand Forks replaced its flood-damaged city hall, the new building was designed as a symbol of the town's survival. The exterior pinnacle of the new city hall is precisely 97 feet high, to represent the year 1997. Inside, the domed ceiling is 54 feet high, to represent the river's crest. Three steps and three flags at the entrance of the building represent the combined efforts of the community, the state of North Dakota, and the federal government. Finally, a heart-shaped monument near the city hall symbolizes East Grand Forks' appreciation for the assistance that it received from surrounding communities. The East Grand Forks mayor noted that the city hall symbolizes the courage of the entire community. "The real heroes," the mayor said, "are the people who were on the sandbags until the last minutes to try to save our community" ("Grand Forks Recalls," 2002, p. A18).

In contrast, Fargo, which was far less damaged, chose not to erect a monument or to hold a ceremony of any kind. City leaders stress the importance of the community's spirit by reemphasizing, with "both astonishment and pride," that 20,000–30,000 volunteers handled 3.5 million sandbags to aid in constructing 10 miles of levees (Pantera, 2002b, p. A1). The mayor argued, however, that the city should not dwell on the anguish and drama of the flood. "The flood's over. It's no longer an excuse. So don't use that excuse.... It's a done deal. Move on instead of keep bringing it up" [sic] (personal communication, June 28, 1999).

The communities that endured the worst of the Red River Valley flood experienced some forms of renewal. Cities such as Grand Forks have re-created their downtown areas and attracted new businesses. Grand Forks has created an extensive new greenway along the river, not only to help in flood control, but to make the city more inviting. Many other buildings and homes were extensively updated and modernized. Still, many of the residents remain troubled by the unyielding threat of floods. Some residents lost homes they had hoped to live in for rest of their lives. Possessions accumulated over a lifetime were destroyed. Other residents faced lost jobs and bankruptcy. Residents have learned from the crisis, and they continue to revitalize their community. The losses and emotional scars, however, are deep and are underscored by the continued threat of flood.

SUMMARY

The actions of an organization or community during postcrisis have the potential to turn a crisis into an opportunity for improvement and renewal. Initially, organizations may need to restore a damaged image by arguing publicly that their crisis response was appropriate. The positive potential for crisis recovery rests primarily on the organization's ability to learn from the crisis. This learning begins with understanding the cause, which then enables organizations to alter their physical and leadership structures to address points of vulnerability. The learning process also serves as a foundation for healing. During postcrisis, stakeholders rely on the learning process to gain confidence in the organization's ability to manage or avoid similar events. Ultimately, crisis stakeholders heal by moving beyond memories of vulnerability and toward renewed confidence. Ceremonies, memorials, and epideictic discourse are often a part of rebuilding a culture of self-assurance in organizations or communities that have endured a crisis. In short, the postcrisis period, despite its sometimes extensive length and complexity, is an essential component of successful crisis management.

PART III

Crisis Management Functions

CHAPTER 9

Crisis Planning

Of the various strategic activities organizations can undertake to deal with crisis, planning is the most critical. Planning, as a management activity, involves projections of future conditions and strategic allocation of resources to attain goals. Crisis planning involves projecting the condition of a crisis and identifying the resources, structures, and strategies necessary to resolve the crisis with as little disruption, cost, and harm as possible. Planning helps to ensure that necessary resources and capacities are available. It also reduces decision time, uncertainty, and stress; reduces the probability that important contingencies or stakeholders will be overlooked; and reduces the time interval of response and recovery (Barton, 2001; Coombs, 1999b; Gottschalk, 1993).

This chapter begins with a description of crisis management and describes how crisis planning relates to the stages of crisis development. The current state of crisis planning is assessed. Factors associated with crisis planning are described, including a discussion of the rationalizations and fallacies that hinder planning. A detailed examination of two crisis planning structures is also offered: the Crisis Planning Model (Barton, 2001; Coombs, 1999b) and the Federal Emergency Management Agency's (2003) *Emergency Management Guide for Business & Industry.*

CRISIS PLANNING AND CRISIS MANAGEMENT

Crisis management is "a set of anticipatory measures that enables an organization to coordinate and control its response to an emergency" (Nudell & Antokol, 1988, p. 21). Pauchant and Mitroff (1992) have suggested that crisis management is a function of four interrelated factors: characteristics of the organization's personnel and its culture, structure, and strategies. Moreover, crisis management reduces the frequency of crisis and limits the harm. As such, it involves three general strategic goals. The first is to reduce the frequency of crises, usually by more careful monitoring and information collection as well as recognizing, evaluating, and responding effectively to warning cues. These activities occur in the precrisis stage and relate to preestablished notions of risk and threat, risk communication, and norms and structures for risk avoidance. A second goal is to limit the harm, duration, severity, and intensity of a crisis. Because the onset and accumulation of harm occurs in the crisis stage, this is the point at which harm may be reduced through strategic intervention. Successful intervention usually requires that some predetermined set of resources and decisions is available during the stress, uncertainty, and restricted response conditions of a crisis. Reduction of harm is most effectively undertaken when plans and structures have been established, practiced, and carefully maintained. As discussed in chapter 8, harm may also carry over to the postcrisis stage, particularly if there are widespread perceptions that the crisis was not managed adequately or appropriately and if unresolved questions of blame, responsibility, and accountability linger. Finally, a third goal of crisis management is to identify ways to use the crisis as a learning opportunity and as a force in system renewal in postcrisis. Crisis management, then, is an ongoing process and set of interrelated activities with specific manifestations in the three stages of precrisis, crisis and postcrisis (Coombs, 1999b). It is proactive in the sense that it identifies risks, seeks to reduce them, anticipates the conditions of crisis, and seeks to prepare for them. It is reactive in the sense that, when crisis occurs, it responds directly to the dynamic conditions of the crisis.

THE STATE OF CRISIS PLANNING

Observers of crises and crisis managers universally advocate developing and maintaining crisis plans (Andriole, 1985; Fink, 1986; Gottschalk, 1993; Mitroff, 1986). In many contexts, crisis planning is a highly developed set of professional activities with a body of well-established principles, structures, procedures, and resources. Governmental emergency management agencies, such as the Federal Emergency Management Agency (FEMA) and state, county, and municipal emergency management agencies, generally constitute a high level of standing crisis response capability, focused largely on natural disasters or similar threats to the general public (FEMA, 2002, www.fema.gov). FEMA advocates crisis mitigation planning for a wide variety of community-based risks such as floods, earthquakes, severe weather events, transportation accidents, hazardous-material spills, radiological incidents, power interruptions, and, recently, terrorist attacks.

Several studies, however, suggest that many private organizations fail to take even the most basic precautionary crisis planning steps. Pinsdorf (1995) reported that in a 1984 study of *Fortune* 1,000 industrial and *Fortune* 500 service firms, only 53 percent had crisis plans. Most were created in response to specific incidents. Fink (1986) reported that only 50 percent of the *Fortune* 500 firms he examined had crisis plans, even though company leadership believed a crisis of some sort was inevitable. He also found that lack of planning resulted in a more extensive or chronic postcrisis phase. Guth's (1995) survey of public relations practitioners found a general lack of adequate crisis planning. He concluded that a relationship exists between an organization's experience with crisis and its tendency to view public relations as a crisis management function. He also found that larger, more complex organizations were more prone to crisis. Seeger, Barton, Heyart and Bultnick (2001) found that 30 percent of a sample of public schools in a large Midwestern state did not have crisis plans until such a plan was mandated by state law. Moreover, larger, more established schools were better prepared for crisis, although they also faced more risk. A 1993 study examining issues of workplace violence found that only 28 percent of the responding organizations reported having formal crisis management programs (Anfuso, 1994). Barton (2001) reported that 13 percent of the companies that developed crisis plans did so only after experiencing a crisis. Probably a larger proportion of organizations with crisis plans have not updated them regularly or maintained crisis response capacity. The Exxon *Valdez*, discussed in chapter 6, illustrates that merely having a plan does not ensure appropriate responses. Plans that are not maintained or regularly updated and that are based on unrealistic assumptions and projections are unlikely to help contain and reduce harm. In fact, such plans may actually accelerate harm by creating confusion and distracting decision makers. Recent events, such as the 9/11 attacks, have encouraged many organizations to consider planning for crisis or updating plans by virtue of vicariously experiencing the crisis. However, many impediments to crisis planning exist.

By definition, crisis is always uncertain and surprising. Although crisis planning can help reduce time pressure by predetermining some decisions and procedures, it does not alleviate risk. Moreover, little empirical evidence exists to suggest that crisis planning or experience in crisis management necessarily reduce harm. Quarantelli (1988) has suggested that planning is only indirectly related to good crisis management. In contrast, Benson (1988) argued that Johnson & Johnson's successful management of the second Tylenol tampering incident was in part a function of its experience with the first episode. Similarly, Ray (1999) concluded that airlines learned from disasters and were able to manage subsequent events more successfully. A number of organizations have reported that experiencing a crisis is an important motivation and learning opportunity for enhanced preparedness (Doughty, 1993; Lovejoy, 1993). As described in chapter 2, crisis creates new understanding of risk and often demonstrates the inadequacy of crisis-related assumptions, beliefs, and attendant structures and plans (Turner, 1976). The continued emergence of new types of crises, new technologies of communication, the globalization of organizations, and new risks and associated threats continue to create new crisis contingencies. Risk is dynamic and crisis plans, to be effective, must be sensitive to these fluid conditions and contingencies.

FUNCTIONS OF CRISIS PLANS

The fundamental function of a crisis plan is to reduce risk and help an organization respond to crisis in a timely and effective manner. Crisis often overwhelms an organization's normal decisional and response capacity. Without planning, the urgency and confusion of a crisis often results in inconsistent and delayed responses, maladaptive reactions, failure to contain and reduce the harm, an extension of the crisis stage, adversarial relations with stakeholders, and a protracted and damaging postcrisis stage. In short, crisis plans help to offset the potential for harm by enabling organizations to craft timely, accurate, and strategic crisis responses. In addition, however, crisis plans serve other, more specific functions.

In making the case for encouraging organizations to engage in crisis planning, FEMA describes several functions. First, planning helps companies fulfill their moral responsibility to protect employees, the community, and the environment. For example, organizations have obligations to keep employees and customers safe, and crisis planning and risk mitigation may help fulfill that goal. Second, crisis planning facilitates compliance with regulatory requirements. A complex network of regulations governs issues of safety, including hazardous materials, fires, building codes, transportation regulations, and requirements for worker safety. A third function of crisis planning is to enhance an organization's recovery ability by reducing the time interval of disruption and the level of harm. In this way, crisis preparation is increasingly framed as "business continuity planning," the identification of "strategies to sustain vital business functions during a stabilization period" (Myers, 1999, p. 217). Planning, FEMA has suggested, may also reduce legal exposure following an incident. As discussed in chapter 8, issues of responsibility and accountability, and their attendant questions of legal liability, often dominate postcrisis stages. Careful planning may allow an organization to reduce the damage, and thus the liability, and to demonstrate its overall risk vigilance. Fourth, planning enhances an organization's reputation, image, and credibility with stakeholders.

Planning for crisis demonstrates that the organization is concerned about employees, customers, suppliers, and the community. It suggests that the organization is careful, prudent, aware of its environment, and proactive in dealing with risk. Finally, from a merely pragmatic standpoint, FEMA noted that crisis planning may reduce a corporation's insurance premiums. Safety records and programs may demonstrate to an insurance provider that the organization has a lower exposure to risk.

FACTORS IN CRISIS PLANNING

Because crises are by definition surprising, it is difficult to anticipate their particular timing, structure, and form. However, a number of features give some indication of how crises will develop. As discussed in chapter 3, crises in specific industries typically follow similar patterns, although the specific form and level of threat varies widely. Crises of a particular type, such as workplace violence or hazardous spills, will have common features regardless of the industry. Organizations have their own experiences with crises, which give clues to what future trigger events might bring. These inferred structures and forms of an anticipated crisis allow organizations to develop plans.

Several specific factors are related to the ability and motivation of organizations to plan. First, many organizations simply are not able to see the need for crisis planning (Pauchant & Mitroff, 1992). Individual managers may believe that they are capable of avoiding or managing crisis. New technologies are often described as universal solutions to established and emerging risks (p. 33). Fink (1986) reported that even organizations without crisis plans believe they would be able to respond to a crisis successfully (p. 67). Many organizations believe that standard business safeguards, such as fire extinguishers, workman compensation, and liability insurance, are adequate.

A second factor is the relative ability of management and the larger organization to recognize and accept risk. Meyers and Holusha (1986) wrote, "Most organizations are reluctant to prepare for adversity. Leaders in any field find failure distasteful" (p. 3). Some school districts, for example, are reluctant to undertake planning for student-initiated violence, because doing so acknowledges that such an attack is possible (Seeger et al., 2001). Even when schools do plan, some seek to keep knowledge of their activities from the public to avoid creating the perception that a real threat exists. Acknowledging a risk may be seen as reflecting negatively on the image of the organization and may call public attention to its deficiencies. Exxon, as described in chapter 6, mounted an extensive media campaign to convince Alaskans that their operation posed minimal environmental risk. This failure to acknowledge the risk likely contributed to the breakdown and decay of the spill-response plan. Some managers believe that acknowledging a risk enhances the probability that a crisis will occur.

A third factor related to crisis planning involves external regulatory agencies, oversight, or advisory groups. These groups may encourage or require crisis planning. The Y2K threat, for example, was widely publicized, and many governmental regulatory agencies required "Y2K compliance" among their vendors. In high-risk areas, such as air travel, the transportation or handling of dangerous substances, or the use of risky or potentially dangerous technology, plans are often mandatory. Toxic-spill recovery plans, for example, are often required by state departments of transportation as a condition of licensure. Sometimes mandated planning includes conducting annual simulations and drills. The Nuclear Regulatory Commission mandates that all nuclear power plants develop and maintain crisis plans. Such plans are often elaborate and detailed and may include evacuation contingencies for entire communities. The Federal Aviation Administration requires that air carriers conduct at least a minimum level of contingency planning. In addition, insurance companies are increasingly willing to pressure organizations to consider undertaking contingency planning. Insurance carriers argue that a vigilant position, reflected in safety programs and contingency plans, decreases the organization's risk exposure.

In addition to issues of perceived need and outside pressures, organizations must also have the necessary resources for crisis planning. Two kinds of resources are required: expertise and slack resources. Crisis planning requires specialized knowledge and, in some fields, technical expertise. While these skills and areas of expertise are not always available within the organization, a wide variety of public and private agencies are available to help in crisis planning. The American Red Cross, for example, offers several kinds of crisis training to assist in preparedness and offers lists of resources for various kinds of disasters such as floods, hurricanes, blizzards, and earthquakes on its Web site, www.americanredcross.org. Specialized training in emergency-response vehicles, establishing emergency shelters, disaster service and control centers, dealing with mental health issues, and responding to the media is also offered. FEMA, although principally focusing on governmental disaster management, provides a wide variety of resources for earthquakes, floods, storms, hazardous materials, fires, nuclear power plant emergencies, and terrorism on its Web site, www.fema.gov. Many professional associations, such as the National Education Association (school crisis programs) and the National Association of Manufacturers, offer specialized crisis management resources. The Public Relations Society of America and the International Association of Business Communicators both sponsor workshops and training focusing specifically on crisis communication. In addition, the body of research- and practice-based literature on crisis planning has expanded dramatically in the past decade (Barton, 2001; Gottschalk, 1993; Mitroff & Anagnos, 2001; Myers, 1999).

Crisis planning also requires slack resources, including time, personnel, and budget for acquiring and maintaining materials and equipment and conducting training and simulations. As discussed in chapter 6, prioritizing the acquisition of resources for an event that has a low probability of occurring is difficult. Nudell and Antokol (1988) have suggested that crisis planning, as a systemwide activity requiring "What if?" scenarios may be particularly challenging for highly divisionalized, operationally focused organizations. Managers usually have much more immediate and tangible concerns competing for their attention and budgets. Budget constraints, economic downturns, downsizing, and cost cutting may deflect attention and resources, making crisis planning almost impossible (Pinsdorf, 1987). Crisis mitigation resources are frequently diverted to production, particularly when they have not been used. The problem of getting management to take crisis planning and associated risks seriously is almost universal. The organization must perceive a performance gap between current crisis mitigation systems or capacities and the anticipated conditions of some future, although realistic, crisis scenario. It is often the direct crisis experience or the vicarious experience of observing others in crisis that convinces an organization that crisis planning and mitigation capacity is not an expendable budget item.

Crisis planning as a management activity, however, is neither complex nor necessarily time or resource intensive. Two formats, the Crisis Planning Model and FEMA's *Emergency Management Guide for Business & Industry*, presented in the following sections, illustrate these features and the larger processes of crisis planning.

CRISIS PLANNING MODEL

Crisis planning involves establishing and maintaining functional communication networks and relationships with important constituencies, developing crisis teams, specifying spokespersons, and establishing preset responses. Coombs (1999b) synthesized 15 components of a comprehensive crisis management plan (CMP) from the crisis communication and management literature (see Table 9.1). The CMP is a strategic document carefully prepared and maintained as a master guide for framing, overseeing, and tracking a systematic crisis management and response process (Barton, 2001). In essence, the CMP is largely a communication plan, outlining whom to contact, when, and how.

The first three components include background information and instructions on how the plan is to be used. The cover page includes revision dates, assurances of confidentiality, and document number, and the

Table 9.1
Coombs's Fifteen Characteristics of a Crisis Management Plan

1. Cover page	Basic information, revision dates, assurances of confidentiality, and document number.
2. Introduction	Introduces plan; highlights importance of crisis plan.
3. Acknowledgment	Removable page requiring employee signature, ensuring that they have read and understand the plan.
4. Rehearsal dates	Indicates when plan has been practiced.
5. Crisis management team (CMT)	Identifies the incident commander, team members, how to activate the plan.
6. Contact sheet	Contact information (phone numbers, e-mails, addresses for all persons and agencies involved in the plan, including outside groups such as fire, police, hospitals, regulatory agencies).
7. Crisis risk assessment	Overview of types of crisis assumed to be possible, including primary features and level of risk assessment.
8. Incident report	Sheets to record important features of crisis, decisions, who was contacted (when and how).
9. Proprietary information	Identification of parameters of disclosure (i.e., types of information that cannot be disclosed without top management approval).
10. CMT strategy worksheet	Provides prompts and guidelines for message construction (i.e., audiences, message goals, specific contingencies, background, etc.).
11. Secondary contact sheets	List of secondary audiences who may need to be contacted, along with contact information.
12. Stakeholder contact worksheet	Lists of procedures to be used when responding to a stakeholder contact (such as media inquiry) and details regarding nature of the contact.
13. Business resumption plan.	Details regarding how business will resume under specific contingencies (i.e., equipment destroyed, facilities closed, employees harmed, etc.).
14. Crisis control center	Identification of locations/facilities for management of the crisis (both off-site and on-site).
15. Postcrisis evaluation	Details regarding how crisis management plan will be evaluated.

Source: Adapted from *Ongoing Crisis Communication: Planning, Managing, and Responding,* by W. T. Coombs, 1999, Thousand Oaks, CA: Sage.

introduction highlights the importance of a crisis plan. It is notable that Coombs (1999b) viewed the CMP as a sensitive document that includes proprietary information and recommended that distribution be limited and controlled. He recommended, for example, that employees sign a separate document (see Item 3) indicating they have received a CMP copy, have read it, and understand it. This signatory provision encourages employees to take crisis planning seriously and to follow the plan in the case of an incident. Plans should also be numbered to ensure that all plans are returned in the case of updates and that missing copies can be tracked.

The fifth component of the CMP involves specification of the crisis management team. A crisis management team is a coordinating structure bringing together participants with the necessary expertise and resources (Littlejohn, 1983). These teams, described in more detail in chapter 10, typically include senior management and employees with expertise in legal, public affairs, communication, operations, finance, security, medical liaison, victim and family liaison, and others as appropriate to the specific event (Nudell & Antokol, 1988, p. 35). The team should be run by an "incident commander" with specialized training in crisis response. Teams should be constituted during the precrisis period and should meet regularly to review plans and contingencies. Team members should also know their individual responsibilities and be familiar with the CMP. Typically, a crisis team includes public relations practitioners, legal counsel, top management, a crisis spokesperson, and other personnel such as human resources, security, operations, finance, or marketing, as needed (Dilenschneider & Hyde, 1985).

The public relations literature suggests that in almost all cases a single designated spokesperson should be the principal or initial source for crisis-related messages (Burson, 1995; Dilenschneider & Hyde, 1985; Hearit, 1995; Small, 1991). Although the designated spokesperson usually has other members of the team respond to technical questions, he or she retains final authority for the message. This ensures consistency of messages, reduces confusion and rumors, and enhances organizational credibility (Gottschalk, 1993). In cases in which multiple agencies are involved in managing a crisis, such as the recent letter-borne anthrax episode, precrisis clarification of the spokesperson role is particularly important. Because the crisis spokesperson will deal with an aggressive press, he or she should also receive media training (Katz, 1987).

Although some observers disagree, the chief executive officer (CEO), as the organization's formal symbol of authority and control, is usually the most credible crisis spokesperson. There appears to be an implicit need to hear reassurances from designated and recognized authority figures during times of crisis (Seeger, Vennette, Ulmer, & Sellnow, 2002). During a crisis, a CEO may also provide the initial interpretations of an equivocal event necessary for initial sensemaking. Lee Iacocca's credibility and skill as a communicator was instrumental in managing a variety of crises for the Chrysler Corporation (Seeger, 1994). There are instances, however, when a CEO is not familiar or comfortable with the press, when he or she is not an effective communicator, and when it may not be appropriate to expose the CEO to probing media questions. When Microsoft faced antitrust charges, it chose to limit the public statements of CEO Bill Gates, due to his close association with the charges (Barton, 2001). In cases such as these, another senior officer of the organization may take on the role of spokesperson. Benson (1988) concluded that the spokesperson should also be willing to confront the media when its portrayal is unfair or overly sensational. As explored in chapter 13, a strong, credible, and articulate leader is a particularly valuable crisis management asset.

This fifth component of the CMP also specifies how and by whom the plan is activated. Some plans include codes to signal that a crisis has occurred and that particular remedial actions should be taken. Most schools, for example, have lock-down and evacuation codes that can be announced over a public address system to notify teachers of specific actions they should take in a crisis. These codes inform only the appropriate individuals, so that alarm is not created among students or so that an intruder is not alerted.

The next seven components of the CMP contain worksheets and guidelines for creating a response within preestablished philosophies and policies. Worksheets have several advantages. They assist the crisis team in crafting an appropriate response within an uncertain and stressful context. They describe preestablished structures and procedures that help maintain chains of command, two-way communication, and a high level of coordination. A worksheet may include prompts and cues to remind crisis managers of important contingencies, issues, audiences, and resources. Plans should include telephone trees for employees, FAX numbers, and e-mail distribution lists. Worksheets may help structure a response, such as a sample press release, or letters to employees. School crisis plans often include a sample public address statement regarding the death of a student or teacher and age-appropriate suggestions and guidelines for how teachers might discuss grief and provide counseling. Worksheets also help the organization keep detailed records of the how the crisis developed and key decisions that were made—something Coombs (1999b) has suggested is often important for postcrisis legal disputes.

Component 6 involves an outline of various types of crises, an assessment of their associated risk, an evaluation of the probability of occurrence and possible scope of harm, and a description of how these events are expected to develop (Coombs, 1999b). Risk assessment allows crisis managers to develop what Mitroff (1988) described as a "crisis portfolio," response repertoires for different crisis scenarios. As described in chapter

3, crises of specific types develop in broadly similar ways. An understanding of these general forms may reduce some of the uncertainty associated with a particular crisis.

The CMP also should outline proprietary information policies and guidelines (see Component 9). During crisis, organizations are usually under intense media pressure to provide information on scope of harm, consequences, and possible cause. Failure to be open in these circumstances may create the general perception that the organization has something to hide. In fact, most guidelines for crisis response suggest that the organization should be quick to respond and as open as possible (Wilcox, Ault, & Agee, 1986). It is relatively easy in these circumstances for organizations to inadvertently disclose proprietary information. Organizations sometimes violate employee privacy by identifying who was associated with a crisis. Information regarding victims should only be disclosed after careful checks that all family members have been personally contacted. Even then, careful consideration must be given to releasing this information sensitively and respectfully. The CMP should also include information-disclosure guidelines.

The CMP also gives careful consideration to crisis stakeholders. Worksheets for communicating with stakeholders should be used to ensure that the organization initiates appropriate contacts and tracks responses to stakeholders. During the stress and uncertainty of a crisis, it is easy to overlook important stakeholders or to misplace or ignore an important inquiry. Failure to communicate with a stakeholder can significantly enhance harm. In the case of toxic spills, for example, organizations are often required to contact regulatory agencies within a very narrow time frame. There is also a natural tendency to withdraw during a crisis. Often, this means that the decision makers on a crisis team are cut off from important sources of information (Gouran, 1982). Maintaining connections with stakeholders, both in terms of initiating contact and receiving information, is critical to maintaining a flexible response to the dynamic conditions of the crisis. Some plans call for closely monitoring the media to provide feedback on how the crisis is being portrayed, whereas other plans have preestablished contracts with clipping and video-monitoring services to track media coverage.

The last three components of the CMP involve resumption of business, establishment of crisis control centers, and postcrisis evaluation. Business resumption has become an increasingly important aspect of crisis management. In general, the longer business is disrupted, the greater the level of crisis-induced harm (Coombs, 1999b). A business resumption plan details how the organization will initiate restart of operations given various crisis-induced constraints, such as loss of equipment, personnel, or facilities (Myers, 1999). This may entail provisions for moving or even outsourcing operations, contacting suppliers and customers, and arranging for emergency backup systems. Phone and computer lines may need to be rerouted. In cases of extreme acts of violence, an office or a facility may become a crime scene. In these cases, law enforcement must complete its investigations; often the scene must be cleaned and/or repaired by specialized crews before business can resume. General guidelines should also be in place for various aspects of disrupted business, such as late payments, continued pay and health benefits for employees, or postponement or moving of important events. Finally, psychological counseling is sometimes an important part of business continuity. In some cases, employees may simply be too emotionally distraught to immediately return to work without some professional support, which is often covered by insurance programs or by various employee assistance programs. Counseling is also a manifestation of the organization's concern and commitment to the well-being of employees and may add a human element to the crisis.

Coombs (1999b) also suggested that the CMP should specify the crisis control center features. These may include specialized equipment, computers, telephones, Internet service, FAX, televisions, VCRs, a press room and a conference room, the CMP, and information in the form of manuals, blueprints, organizational charts, contact information, directories, product information, and records (Barton, 2001; Fearn-Banks, 2002; Meyers & Holusha, 1986). A crisis center may be especially important when an event makes company offices and resources inaccessible. In these cases, the crisis team should know when and where to gather. Contingencies should also consider communication and logistics needs. A copy of the CMP should also be available offsite. Organizations sometimes develop reciprocal support agreements with other organizations, allowing access to facilities in the case of a disaster. Schools, for example, may need to evacuate students to another facility in the case of a fire or hostage situation and arrange for parents to pick up their children at this alternative site.

The last component of the CMP is postcrisis evaluation. Crisis, as described earlier, should create learning. Through careful and systematic evaluation of their response, organizations can reformulate their understanding and assessment of risks and refine their plans. Part of this postcrisis assessment is a review of alternative "What if?" scenarios. This ensures that the organization does not structure its future response plan in a way that is only attuned to the last crisis it experienced and so that postcrisis assessment does not become merely a case of self-congratulation. Nudell and Antokol (1988) have developed an 18-point postcrisis checklist that includes such items as adequacy of resources, control center, supplies, accuracy of reporting and information system, effectiveness of liaisons, rumor control, training, and the overall effectiveness of the crisis management team (pp. 52–53).

The CMP model is a comprehensive approach to crisis planning, with a particular focus on the communicative dimensions of crisis management: maintaining channels of communication with key stakeholders, audience analysis, and strategic-message preparation. As such, the emphasis is largely on creating the resources and capacities to respond appropriately and successfully in a postcrisis environment. Coombs (1999b) argued for a simplistic approach so that the plan itself is neither very complex nor inaccessible.

FEMA'S EMERGENCY MANAGEMENT GUIDE

An extensive body of resources, including a variety of planning guides, is available from FEMA, the principle federal agency for disaster management and relief. The agency was created in 1979 by combining a number of disaster-related services. FEMA defines emergency management as the dynamic "process of preparing for, mitigating, responding to and recovering from an emergency." In the past decade, the agency has placed greater emphasis on proactive strategies, such as planning and insurance, as opposed to reactive responses, such as cleanup and rebuilding. Crisis planning is critical, but not sufficient to successful emergency management. In addition, "Training, conducting drills, testing equipment and coordinating activities with the community are other important functions" (FEMA, 2001). FEMA has devised a number of planning aids for communities, families, and groups, covering a wide range of principally natural disasters, such as hurricanes, floods, tornadoes, blizzards, earthquakes, and fires. More recently, technological disasters, such radiological accidents, hazardous-materials spills, and terrorism

Table 9.2
Outline of FEMA Emergency Management Guide for Business and Industry

STEP 1. ESTABLISH A PLANNING TEAM. Individual or group in charge of developing emergency management plan.
    1.1 Form the team. Size contingent on the facility's operations, requirements, and resources: upper/line management; labor, human resources; engineering/ maintenance; safety, health, environmental affairs; public information office; security; community relations; sales/marketing; legal; finance/purchasing.
    1.2 Establish authority structure. Led by CEO or plant manager. Clear lines of authority, although not so rigid as to prevent free flow of ideas; define authority and structure of the planning group.
    1.3 Issue mission statement. Define purpose of plan, indicating involvement of entire organization.
    1.4 Establish schedule and budget.
STEP 2. ANALYZE CAPABILITIES AND HAZARDS. Information about current capabilities, hazards, emergencies, and vulnerability analysis.
    2.1 Current state. Current internal plans and policies: evacuation; fire; safety/health program; environmental policies; security procedures; insurance; plant-closing policy; hazardous materials plan; etc.

(Continued)

Table 9.2 (continued)

2.2 **Meet with outside groups.** Government agencies, community organizations/ utilities; potential emergencies, plans, available response resources; community emergency management office; fire department; police department; emergency medical services; American Red Cross; utilities; neighboring businesses, etc.

2.3 **Identify codes and regulations.** Occupational safety/health; environmental regulation, fire/seismic codes, transportation regulations, corporate policies.

2.4 **Identify critical products, services and operations.** Company products, services, facilities, equipment needed to produce them; products/services provided by suppliers, especially sole-source vendors; lifeline services, such as electrical power, water, sewer, gas, telecommunications, transportation; vital operations, equipment, personnel.

2.5 **Identify internal resources and capabilities for emergency.**

   2.5.1 Personnel: Fire, hazardous-materials team, emergency medical services, security, emergency management group, evacuation, public information officer.

   2.5.2 Equipment: Fire-protection/suppression, communications, first aid, emergency supplies, warning, emergency power, decontamination equipment.

   2.5.3 Facilities: Emergency operating center, media briefing area, shelters, first aid, sanitation facilities.

   2.5.4 Organizational capabilities: Training, evacuation plan, employee-support system.

   2.5.5 Backup systems: Payroll, communications, production, customer services, shipping and receiving, information systems support, emergency power, recovery support.

2.6 **Identify external resources.** Local emergency management office, fire department, hazardous materials response organization, emergency medical services, hospital, local/state police, community service organizations, utilities, contractors, suppliers of emergency equipment, insurance carriers.

2.7 **Insurance review. Review all policies.**

2.8 **Vulnerability analysis.** Probability and potential impact of each emergency, assigning probabilities, estimating impact, and assessing resources.

2.9 **List potential emergencies.** All possible emergencies, identified by internal/external sources, both community/facility based; historical; geographic; technological human error; physical; regulatory.

2.10 **Estimate probability.** Likelihood of each event.

2.11 **Assess potential impact.** Human, property, business.

2.12 **Assess internal and external response resources.** Determine whether additional resources/capabilities needed, training, equipment, mutual-aid agreements, specialized contractors.

(Continued)

Table 9.2 (continued)

STEP 3. DEVELOP THE PLAN.
    3.1 Plan components.
        3.1.1 Executive summary. Brief overview of purpose, emergency management policy, authorities and responsibilities of key personnel, types of emergencies that could occur, where response operations will be managed.
        3.1.2 Emergency management elements. Approach to elements of emergency management: Direction and control, communications, life and safety, property protection, community outreach, recovery and restoration, administration and logistics.
        3.1.3 Emergency response procedures. Checklists to assess situation; protect employees, customers, visitors, equipment, records, assets; recover business. Specific situational procedures: Warning employees/customers, communicating with personnel/ community responders, conducting an evacuation/accounting for all persons, managing response activities, activating and operating an emergency operations center, fighting fires, shutting down operations, protecting records, restoring operations.
        3.1.4 Support documents and emergency call lists. Building/site maps indicating: Utility shutoffs; water hydrants/main valves/lines; gas main valves/lines; electrical cutoffs/substations; storm drains; sewers; location of each building; floor plans; alarm and enunciators; fire extinguishers/suppression systems; exits, stairways, escape routes; restricted areas; hazardous materials; high-value items.
        3.1.5 Resource lists. Emergency equipment, supplies, services, mutual-aid agreements.
    3.2 Development process.
        3.2.1 Identify challenges and prioritize activities. Goals milestones, tasks, responsibilities, problem areas, resource shortfalls.
        3.2.2 Write plan. Determine format, establish timeline, develop and review drafts, print/distribute.
        3.2.3 Establish training schedule.
    3.3 Coordinate with outside organizations. Inform agencies; determine requirements for reporting emergencies and incorporate into procedures; set protocols for turning control over to outside agencies, and determine procedures for outside response.
    3.4 Maintain contact with other corporate offices. Determine emergency notification requirements; mutual assistance and support; names, telephone numbers, and pager numbers of key personnel.
    3.5 Review, conduct training and revise.
    3.6 Seek final written approval.

(Continued)

Table 9.2 (continued)

    3.7 **Distribute plan.** Number all copies and pages; require signature; distribute appropriate sections to outside agencies (chief executive/senior managers, emergency response organization, company headquarters); have key personnel keep copy at home.

STEP 4. IMPLEMENT THE PLAN. Reduce vulnerability, integrate into company operations, train, evaluate plan.

    4.1 **Integrate into company operations.** Make emergency planning part of corporate culture; build awareness, educate, train personnel; test procedures; involve management, departments, community in the planning process; make emergency management part of day-to-day operations.

    4.2 **Training, drills and exercises.** Train all employees as appropriate; periodic discussions to review procedures, technical training equipment, evacuation drills, full-scale exercises.

    4.3 **Employee training.** Individual roles/responsibilities; threats, hazards, protective actions; notification, warning, communications procedures; means for locating family; emergency response procedures; evacuation, shelter, accountability; location/use of emergency equipment; emergency shutdown procedures.

    4.4 **Evaluate and modify the plan.** Conduct annual formal audit after each training drill/exercise, after each emergency, when personnel/responsibilities change, when layout or design of the facility changes, when policies or procedures change; brief personnel on changes.

Source: Adapted from *Emergency Management Guide for Business & Industry,* by the Federal Emergency Management Agency (FEMA), 2003, retrieved from http://www.fema.gov/library/bizindex.shtm

have been added to the list. FEMA has also developed an elaborate and comprehensive disaster planning model for business and industry (see Table 9.2) designed to help organizations prepare for a range of adverse events such as fire, hazardous-materials incidents, flood, hurricane, tornado, earthquake, communications failure, radiological accident, civil disturbance, or even the loss of a key supplier or customer. By virtue of planning, "business and industry can limit injuries and damages and return more quickly to normal operations if they plan ahead" (FEMA, 2001, www.fema.gov/library/biz1.htm).

Unlike the CMP, the process offered by FEMA is not a communication-based approach per se. Rather, FEMA's view of business emergency management is grounded in coordination between groups and agencies and the creation of a set of cooperative relationships to bring appropriate resources to bear on a crisis. This focus is perhaps due to FEMA's larger mission of community-based disaster management as a "collaborative process" using consensual approaches to risk identification, mitigation, and elimination (FEMA, 2002, www.FEMA.gov). Emphasis is placed on codifying and organizing information, sharing information among various agencies and groups, and establishing precrisis relationships, procedures, and structures for creating a coordinated response. For example, FEMA suggests that the crisis team should be broad based and inclusive of a wide set of stakeholders. A broad-based team has several advantages: it "encourages participation and enhances investment in the process; enhances the visibility and stature of the planning process; provides for a broad perspective on the issues" (FEMA, 2002, www.FEMA.gov). In Step 2, the analysis of hazards and capabilities, crisis planners are encouraged to meet with a wide array of government, community, social service, and neighborhood groups. Such collaboration is encouraged to create broad insight, enhance capacity for risk identification, and develop cooperative relationships. Others have made similar observations. In a study of school crisis plans, the scope of each plan was related to the number of groups participating in planning (Seeger et al., 2001).

The emphasis on collection and codification of information is evident in Step 2, Analyze Capabilities and Hazards, and in Step 3, Develop the Plan. This emphasis reflects a recognition that emergencies are often precipitated by unforeseen or poorly understood risks and are associated with high levels of uncertainty. Clarifying risks during planning can reduce the frequency of crisis. Collecting information in planning stages for use during an actual emergency reduces the uncertainty of the event and the response time and is the heart of the planning process.

The analysis of risk (see Item 2.9) is broad based and includes a systematic review of historical, geographic, technological, human error, physical, and regulatory risk areas. Historical analysis asks what previous emergencies have occurred in the community, the company, or the facility. This may include severe weather, utility outages, work stoppages, hazardous-material spills, or other events. An analysis of the geographic region identifies location or proximity-based risks: floodplains, seismic faults, dams and proximity to hazardous materials, transportation routes, and airports. Technological interdependence has become an increasingly important risk area for organizations. In assessing technological interdependence risks, organizations should ask, What could result from a process or system failure? This may include power, water, transportation, communication, computer, and heating or cooling failures. Most crises are initially described as the consequence of human error. FEMA suggests that two human error issues be explored: (1) What emergencies can be caused by employee error? and (2) Are employees trained to respond appropriately? In the increasingly common cases of workplace violence, issues of employee background and psychological stability are often involved. Factors in human error include training, maintenance, carelessness, misconduct, substance abuse, and fatigue. Risks associated with the physical nature of facilities include aspects of design, construction, lighting, equipment layout, evacuation routes, and hazardous and combustible materials. Finally, with regard to regulatory risks, FEMA encourages organizations to identify and become familiar with relevant emergency or hazard regulations. This includes issues of prohibited access to the facility, chemical releases, explosions, and building collapses. A comprehensive analysis is also recommended for the organization's current risk mitigation and crisis response capabilities. Organizations, accordingly, should determine their ability to respond to the risks identified (see Item 2.5, Table 9.2) and assess the ability of external groups to assist in the response to a crisis (see Item 2.6, Table 9.2). Contingent upon the outcome of these assessments, organizations are encouraged to develop new internal or external response capacities.

The central features of the FEMA emergency management plan are procedures, structures, and bodies of information designed to create coordination and reduce uncertainty and response time. These factors, outlined in Step 3, Develop the Plan, include both general orientations to particular forms of crisis as well as specific checklists and guidelines to formulate a response. The checklists and guidelines recommendations are essentially the same as those presented in the CMP approach. In both cases, checklists and guidelines ensure a systematic and complete response.

Emergency procedures should specify how the facility will respond to particular kinds of emergencies. FEMA recommends a series of checklists that can be quickly accessed by senior management, department heads, response personnel, and employees. Procedures should outline sequential responses to emergencies (see Item 3.1.3, Table 9.2). Additional lists for notification of all appropriate individuals and agencies, both internal and external to the organization, and detailed maps and blueprints indicating a wide range of mitigation and strategic resources and locations are recommended (see Item 3.1.4, Table 9.2). Finally, crisis mitigation resources, including lists of employees, emergency equipment, supplies, expertise, both internal and external to the organization, should be included, as well as copies of any mutual-aid agreements with other organizations (see Item 3.1.5, Table 9.2).

One of the interesting features of the FEMA Model is the emphasis placed on implementation, maintenance, and training (see Step 4, Table 9.2). Although many approaches suggest that the planning process is finished once the completed crisis response document is distributed, FEMA recommends a more dynamic view. Emergency management, in this sense, is an ongoing managerial process. FEMA's recommended steps include integration of the plan into company operations, including ongoing programs to build awareness; testing procedures; involving management; and making emergency management part of day-to-day operation. FEMA also notes that integration may require a change in the larger corporate culture. A variety of training activities is also proposed, including training all appropriate employees in response procedures and providing technical training on equipment, procedures, or in specialized areas such as first aid, as appropriate (see Item 4.3, Table 9.2). In addition, evacuation drills, tabletop walk-throughs, and full-scale exercises are recommended. Finally, comprehensive recommendations are offered for ongoing evaluation and modification of plans. FEMA notes that, "a mitigation plan is obsolete almost as soon as it is completed. We do not live in a static world and communities are constantly changing" (FEMA, 2002). Crisis plans, therefore, should be reviewed, modified, or reaffirmed at least on an annual basis (see Item 4.4, Table 9.2). In addition, reviews should be undertaken after each emergency and following personnel, responsibility, facility, or other procedural changes to the organization.

FEMA's model of business and industrial emergency management planning is comprehensive, integrative, and community based. It adopts egalitarian, risk-sharing, and uncertainty-reduction assumptions in an effort to create cooperative relationships, greater understanding of risks, and enhanced mitigation-response capacity. Although the FEMA model is based on realistic assumptions about most emergencies, it is perhaps overly optimistic about the relative openness most organizations are able or willing to adopt. In fact, the relationship between many organizations and their larger communities with regard to risk remains largely adversarial. Many managers are reluctant to discuss risks with the community for fear of "airing dirty laundry." Organizations are often reluctant to publicly disclose information about toxic materials or risky technologies. For many organizations, crisis-induced threat creates retraction and withdrawal from stakeholders, enhanced efforts to withhold information, and suspicion of outside groups and agencies.

The other dominant characteristic of FEMA's model is its detail and comprehensiveness. The process identifies an exhaustive set of factors associated with risk and an inclusive set of response contingencies and strategies. The FEMA model reaches across hierarchical and divisionalized organizational boundaries in identifying risks, attending to threats, and creating responses capacities. In some cases, however, this detailed approach may impede efforts at effective planning by contributing to the perception that crisis planning is too complicated and resource intensive. It may also risk creating a plan that is detailed and precise in its recommendation but lacking flexibility in its application. Complex and comprehensive plans are also more difficult to update and maintain. Streamlined approaches, such as the CMP, may be most appropriate for some organizations in some contexts, whereas the detailed and exhaustive methodology of FEMA's Emergency Management Guide may be appropriate in others. What is perhaps most important is that all organizations undertake some form of crisis planning.

ADDITIONAL FEATURES

In addition to the provisions outlined in the CMP and by FEMA, other approaches and issues to crisis planning and management have been developed. Myers (1999), for example, has developed a business-continuity model based on streamlined contingency planning. Rather than detailed contingencies, his framework emphasizes developing a "worst case scenario" under the assumption that anything less could be handled within that framework. Mitroff and Anagnos (2001) created a series of templates and decision trees to assist in developing a crisis management capability. This includes strategic activities undertaken before, during, and after a crisis. They argued that crisis plans and manuals are often useless because they fail to take into account larger and more general issues and contingencies. Many planning models are also specific to crisis type. Toxic-spill recovery plans emphasize timely containment, recovery, and/or treatment of the spill materials. Plans for responding to an outbreak of food-borne illness require immediate identification of the source of contamination and notification of public health officials and the public. Plans for responding to floods include predictions and forecasts; creation of mitigation structures and activities, such as dikes and pumps; and procedures for evacuation and protection of critical resources. These and other approaches suggest a number of additional considerations and contingencies. Among these is a best-practice approach to crisis management.

Meyers and Holusha (1986) have matched a wide variety of best practices to specific types of crises. The practices they describe follow a largely problem-solving format that includes information collection, problem identification and definition, generating options for a solution, evaluation of solutions, and implementation, followed by steps to prevent any recurrence of the crisis. This approach emphasizes the critical role of both decisional vigilance and openness in crisis management. Fearn-Banks (2002) recommends that best practices of maintaining a reputation for openness, honesty, and credibility are particularly important to successful crisis management (pp. 480–481).

A number of observers have suggested that positive precrisis relationships with stakeholders are instrumental in helping organizations recover from crisis (Seeger & Ulmer, 2001; Ulmer, 2001). Barton (2001) argued that a healthy forward-looking organization creates an environment in which credible employee communications exist long before a crisis. Organizations, based on their reputation, image, and social legitimacy, may develop "reservoirs of good will" that they may draw on for support during a crisis. Credibility and a record of positive accomplishments, ethical conduct, good corporate citizenship, or even extended networks of interdependence are important when organizations face crisis. Chrysler, for example, was able to draw on extensive networks of support in lobbying for federal loan guarantees during a near bankruptcy (Seeger, 1994). Malden Mills engendered great support from the community following a devastating fire, largely because of the CEO's previous record of corporate responsibility. Larger and older organizations may enjoy some insulation from failure due to their extensive networks of mutual dependence on suppliers, community groups, employees, customers, stockholders, and other stakeholders (Perrow, 1984). This insulating effect is enhanced when the organization has a positive image, a record of credibility, and a reputation for responsiveness. Sometimes the initial response to a crisis assists in bolstering an organization's image and building support. Ford CEO Bill Ford's initial response to a plant explosion generated an outpouring of good will. Ford, the grandson of Ford Motor Company's founder, visited hospitalized workers and their families and expressed a deep personal concern for their well-being. He was widely praised in the media and by workers for his response.

Diversity of audiences is also an important factor in the larger issue of organization communication, including crisis communication (Cheney, 1991). Organizations face multiple and diverse audiences with conflicting values, norms, expectations, and interests. Messages directed to these audiences inevitably must balance these factors. For example, an organization's postcrisis statement that crisis victims will receive full and rapid restitution may be by viewed negatively by stockholders, whose economic interests may be damaged by such a response. Cultural diversity also plays an important role. Cultures have widely divergent views about the nature of risk and the care and compensation of victims and have different expectations regarding organizational responsibility. These views and values are often reflected in laws, regulations, and responses to crises. Pinsdorf (1999) cited the example of a Japanese Airlines disaster that precipitated the company president's resignation and the maintenance chief's suicide (p. 74). The Bhopal, India, Union Carbide disaster was associated with culturally specific views regarding risk, fate, and destiny (Seeger & Bolz, 1996). As organizations become increasingly global, the level of cultural complexity increases exponentially.

A final consideration in planning concerns the basic structure of a planned response. Although an increasing number of corporations have formal crisis management plans in place, many companies continue to focus their planning solely on operations, rather than on communication strategies. Clearly, few crises can be resolved without attention to operations. However, the afflicted organization's reputation, throughout the urgent period of the crisis, is largely determined by how the organization communicates. Moreover, as reflected in the CMP and FEMA approaches, coordination achieved through carefully planned communication structures and procedures is instrumental to the reduction of harm. Some crisis management formats segment the operations and communication, whereas others maintain one unified plan that addresses both operational and communication issues.

Regardless of the approach, contingencies regarding both operations and communication are important, and close coordination should occur between these activities.

SUMMARY

Planning is universally advocated as the most important crisis management activity an organization can undertake. Fink (1986) noted that all organizations, regardless of size, industry, culture, or type, should have crisis plans: "There are no exceptions, merely differences of degree" (p. 54). Despite this fact, not all organizations plan for a crisis or maintain their plans, leaving themselves open to the possibility of increased crisis-induced uncertainty and higher levels of harm. A variety of structural and psychological factors limit the ability and motivation to plan for crisis. The Crisis Planning Model and FEMA's *Emergency Management Planning Guide* are two approaches to crisis management that broadly represent the steps organizations can take to be prepared.

Crisis plans should be contextualized and adapted to the industry and the organization. Planning should assess risks, develop new repertoires and response capacities, involve a variety of stakeholders, and be practiced and updated regularly. Crisis plans do not guarantee that organizations will avoid crisis or harm. They do, however, decrease uncertainty and stress and increase the ability of the organization to respond more quickly and in strategic ways.

CHAPTER 10

Crisis Teams and Decision Making

A central factor in preparing for and managing a crisis involves creating a crisis management team (CMT). CMTs are typically developed to bring together various kinds of technical and response expertise within an established authority structure to create a crisis response capacity. They are involved with constructing the organization's larger understanding of risk and risk mitigation, with crisis planning and preparation, and in making decisions about how to respond. After a crisis, the CMT collects data and processes information to promote organizational learning.

CMTs are principally decision-making and coordinating structures designed to function under the stress and uncertainty of the crisis. By virtue of their design, teams are often better able to function under these difficult conditions. A team composed of various members with different specialties brings together broader perspectives, enhancing the team's information-processing capacity. Moreover, crisis is often a context in which close coordination between a variety of agencies and departments is required. CMTs serve this coordinating function.

This chapter outlines the characteristics and functions of CMTs. First, an examination of characteristics of crisis teams is provided, including composition of crisis teams and incident command structures. Second, principals of crisis decision making are examined. CMTs represent a critical crisis management capacity and are often instrumental to successful resolution of a crisis.

COMPONENTS OF CRISIS TEAMS

The crisis literature contains a variety of general recommendations regarding CMTs and their components and processes. Generally, organizations create crisis teams with cross-functional specialists, including lawyers, accountants, information technology specialists, emergency-response professionals, security personnel, public relations and marketing professionals, finance managers, human resource managers, medical liaison personnel, victim and family liaison personnel, and others (Coombs, 1999b; Dilenschneider & Hyde, 1985; Nudell & Antokol, 1988). Moreover, members' appointments to a CMT is based on the representation and perspective they bring. Managing a major financial crisis would require members with financial background but might also draw on members of the organization's audit committee. Some kinds of organizations may choose to appoint union members to a CMT. Issues of diversity should also be addressed in team composition. Companies facing charges of sexual harassment often bring in senior female executives to help manage the organization's response (Snyder, 2001). Weick (1995) suggested that various perspectives are required to match the forms of uncertainty the organization faces. Diversity and a variety of perspectives, then, are required for an appropriate response. In short, CMTs should be made up of sufficiently diverse perspectives and backgrounds so that the organization may both notice warning cues and respond effectively.

Other observers have offered more specific recommendations for CMT membership. For instance, Barton (2001) suggested that crisis management teams be comprised of "an attorney, media relations manager, several technical experts from various departments of the company, a finance/controller manager, the information technology manager, and an expert on public affairs" (p. 207). Attorneys play an important role on a CMT by managing legal liability during a crisis. They may also be able to identify legal issues related to various kinds of risks. During a crisis event, an attorney may help protect the organization from additional legal liability and, through attorney-client privilege, may protect certain privileged kinds of information and communication. The public relations coordinator is responsible for creating public statements, giving advice to the spokesperson regarding media relations, and assisting in meeting the information needs of organizational stakeholders. Technical experts bring specific capacities and skills to solve particular crisis-related problems. These can include a variety of technical areas, such as hazardous-spill mitigation, engineering and operations management, logistics, security, health and medical expertise, mental health counseling, and a variety of other areas. Security is often important in protecting property, controlling access, and protecting safety. Financial expertise is important because crisis often requires both the purchasing of additional goods and services and tracking losses. Coombs (1999b) argued that team members need to understand conflict resolution, how to cope with uncertainty and ambiguity, vigilant decision making, argumentation, and listening skills to be effective. "In the ideal world," he said, "the crisis team members would be selected through a combination of trait evaluation and functional area" (p.

150). The CMT should be large enough to represent all the needed content experts, but small enough to operate as a team in which all members are able to participate. CMTs of 20 or 30 members are probably too large to operate efficiently.

Crisis teams are generally established during the precrisis stage and involve members from many parts of the organization and their designated alternates. Alternate members are important because crisis may make a representative from a critical content area unavailable. Littlejohn (1983) suggested a matrix approach to selecting members so that a "crisis manager can select from various functional divisions those personnel possessing the most appropriate skills and abilities to handle the situation" (p. 13). In this way, the team may be matched to the specific contingency. In addition, the CMT should be as consistent as possible and should meet regularly to review and update plans, consider emerging threats, and assess response capacity. Meeting regularly allows members to plan for a crisis and to become familiar with one another. This may reduce uncertainty and ensure smooth operations during an event.

At times, members of the crisis team may come into conflict regarding the organization's preparation or response strategy, particularly given the high stress and uncertainty associated with a crisis event. Fitzpatrick and Rubin (1995), for instance, described the potential conflict between public relations officers and legal counsel following a crisis. Public relations advice typically focuses on "(1) stating the company policy on the issue (if appropriate), (2) investigate the allegations, (3) be candid, (4) voluntarily admit that the problem exists, if true, then (5) announce and implement corrective measures as quickly as possible" (p. 22). The traditional legal strategy is, "(1) say nothing; (2) say as little as possible and release it as quietly as possible; (3) say as little as possible, citing privacy laws, company policy, or sensitivity; (4) deny guilt and/or act indignant that such charges could possibly be made; or (5) shift or, if necessary, share the blame with the plaintiff" (p. 22). Fitzpatrick and Rubin argued that at times organizations can use a mixed strategy that includes some denial of responsibility, while expressing general remorse for the crisis. In crisis decision making "Both the risk of legal liability and the need to protect the organization's reputation must be considered" (p. 23). Their analysis of sexual-harassment cases suggests that organizations most often used a legal strategy. In most cases, the legal strategy involved the spokesperson denying guilt and/or acting indignant. In sexual-harassment cases, the dominance of legal strategies is "shortsighted and costly" (p. 31), whereas a more collaborative approach to crisis communication is often more effective.

Some researchers have suggested that the head of communication or public relations should serve as the head of the crisis management team (Fearn-Banks, 2002; Ferguson Devereaux, 1999). In other cases, the chief executive officer (CEO) is the most appropriate CMT leader. Coombs

(1999b) indicated that an incident commander, with specialized training in emergency response and crisis decision making, serve as the CMT leader. The requisite skills and background of potential leaders should be taken into account. In one case in which a crisis team was being developed, the director of public relations blurted out that his CEO had a drinking problem that was exacerbated during high stress. Obviously, in this case, the CEO was a poor choice to head a CMT. Moreover, crisis teams are best when matched to the type of organization and its likely areas of risk. Two examples illustrate how different CMT membership and structure is dependent on the type of organization and the crisis situation.

The Society for Healthcare Strategy and Market Development (2002) provided recommendations for assembling a crisis team designed for health care crises. It noted that during a crisis "several disciplines will be required for effective communications" (p. 25). Some members of the crisis team, such as legal counsel or outside communication specialists in particular areas, should be available on an as-needed basis. In hospital crises, they suggested that organizations have a crisis communication coordinator, an internal communication coordinator, an external media coordinator, a patient-family coordinator, a medical adviser, legal counsel, an outside communication council, a support staff, a Web staff, and a historian (p. 26). Medical crises often require close coordination with outside agencies—such as emergency medical services and police and fire departments—and careful communication with the public, particularly when unknown risks are involved. Failure to communicate effectively with the public may result in medical facilities being overwhelmed by the "worried well." The medical CMT should have access to both credible medical information and effective channels for communicating that information. In addition, the specific nature of the medical emergency will determine a variety of other technical issues that may need to be addressed by the CMT.

School districts, following the recent rash of shooting incidents, developed crisis plans and associated CMTs. In Ohio, for example, state law mandated that school crisis teams consist of the superintendent of the schools, the director of pupil personnel, a counseling facilitator, the Safe and Drug Free Schools coordinator, the school psychologist, the school nurse supervisor, and a media specialist (www.middletowncityschools. com/pdf/Crisis-Protocols.pdf). Seeger, Barton, Heyart, and Bultnick (2001) found that in Michigan school CMTs were comprised mainly of school administrators at the school and district levels, as well as such content specialists as security personnel, school psychologists, and teachers. In addition, some Michigan schools had specialized teams for different kinds of crisis activities. For instance, one school had a standing bomb-search team that examined school properties in the case of a bomb threat. These individuals had received specialized training in bomb identification and were familiar with the school grounds. Some schools and some districts had specialized grief-counseling teams that had also received special training. In both cases, these standing teams allowed for a more immediate response. In general, for Michigan schools, Seeger et al. found that crisis management teams were fundamentally the responsibility of central administration, the district superintendent, or the building superintendent.

CRISIS COMMAND STRUCTURES

Regardless of the kinds of crisis or the specific configuration of the CMT, issues of authority, responsibility, and command are important. In general, sorting out authority should occur before an event. At times, large-scale crises such as terrorism, natural disasters, or fires, require larger efforts and the close coordination of many different agencies. The Federal Emergency Management Agency (FEMA) has noted that these kinds of emergencies often require coordination of a variety of resources, technical skill, and response capacity. Some kinds of disasters may require heavy construction equipment for rescue and recovery or specialized equipment such as pumps or generators. Medical emergencies often require close coordination with a variety of medical facilities and experts. Those managing natural disasters often call on the Humane Society to care for displaced pets and animals. Frequently, these resources often must be transported long distances to the disaster site, creating logistic complications.

In multiagency crises, authority structures may become confused, disrupting coordination and slowing the response. In these cases, many organizations implement a unified incident command structure to coordinate the crisis management teams and crisis management efforts of different groups and agencies (see Figure 10.1). The FEMA unified command structure is widely used by state emergency-management agencies.

An incident command structure provides structure to the coordination process. FEMA's incident command structure is designed principally for a large-scale crisis, such as terrorism or a natural disaster. In these cases, the top of this structure features a unified command that coordinates the actions of police, fire, emergency-management departments, and other agencies and groups as appropriate to the crisis through a liaison officer. A public information officer and a scribe are also part of the unified command structure. The command structure is hierarchically and divisionally ordered, with fire, law enforcement, and medical services each being assigned specific responsibilities. Support services (planning, logistics, and finance/administration) are also structured into the incident command structure.

Once an incident has occurred, local government emergency-response agencies will respond to the scene and appropriate notifications to local, state, and federal authorities will be made. Designated officials will take control of the incident scene from local, state, and federal agencies. The incident command structure initially established at the scene translates into a

Figure 10.1
FEMA's Unified Command Structure

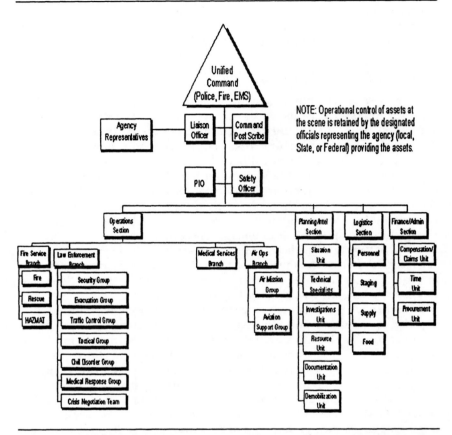

Source: From Federal Emergency Management Agency (FEMA). Unified Command Structure. Retrieved September 10, 2003 from http://www.fema.gov/rrr/conplan/ conpln4p.shtm.

unified command structure. This unified command structure then expands to accommodate support units composed of the agency representatives that are necessary to crisis and consequence management operations.

The unified command structure clarifies both areas of responsibility and authority relationships. This is particularly important given the stress and uncertainty that arises during a crisis. A preset understanding regarding who is responsible for what and who reports to whom removes a critical form of uncertainty and speeds effective response. Although most organizational CMTs are unlikely to adopt the FEMA system, a similar preevent understanding of authority, responsibility, and command is appropriate. Clear lines of authaority, responsibility, and reporting relationships—such as those outlined by FEMA—help to reduce conflict between agencies and ensure that appropriate resources are available to manage an event.

FUNCTIONS OF CRISIS TEAMS

In addition to issues of membership, CMTs also fulfill a variety of functions as part of crisis planning and preparation, crisis response, and post-crisis adaptation and learning (Barton, 2001; Coombs, 1999b; Fearn-Banks, 2002; Ferguson Devereaux, 1999; Littlejohn, 1983). Coombs, for instance, suggested that the CMT "is responsible for (a) creating a crisis management plan, (b) enacting the crisis management plan, (c) dealing with any problems not covered in the crisis management plan" (p. 63). Littlejohn described three CMT functions. First, the crisis team is responsible for carrying out a crisis audit, "a tool that assists managers in systematically analyzing their environment, identifying potential issues, assessing their impact and probability of occurrence, and setting priorities among them for planning purposes" (pp. 15–16). An audit represents a formalized risk assessment that allows the team to both reduce risk and plan in a risk-specific way. Second, once an organization has determined potential areas of risk, the CMT can move to contingency planning. This contingency planning involves introduction, objectives, assumptions, trigger mechanisms, and action steps (p. 16). In essence, the CMT manages the planning process described in chapter 9. This participation in the planning processes ensures that the CMT is familiar with the plan. Moreover, as part of the planning process, the CMT will have worked through various crisis scenarios, drills, and exercises. Third, a crisis team is responsible for managing the actual crisis event. At this point, the crisis team will likely work closely with upper management, including the CEO. Managing the event involves signaling the crisis and activating the plan, notifying all appropriate groups and agencies, collecting information and making initial responses, initiating preset responses and contingencies, and being flexible in light of the dynamics of the situation. Maintaining flexibility requires that the CMT engage in decision making within the highly uncertain, threatening, and restricted time frame of the crisis. The ability to make effective decisions under these conditions is one of the most important features of the CMT.

CRISIS DECISION MAKING

Crisis decision making is different from noncrisis decisional contexts. Crisis creates a particularly high level of uncertainty and an associated need for information, while contracting the amount of time available to decision makers (Gouran, 1982). Careful and systematic examination of a problem, leisurely evaluation of options, and determined consideration of various viewpoints are often impossible during a crisis.

Groups are particularly useful in crisis decision making for three reasons. First, group decisions often create a greater likelihood that someone will have the requisite skills or knowledge necessary to solve a particular problem. In this case, group members are able to pool their resources and contribute more information. In other instances, the complexity of the problem may be such that no one person has the functional expertise to solve the problem. Individuals working in groups are able to complement one another in the problem-solving process. For instance, different group members may have differing kinds of information about the problem or different perspectives on the issue itself. These differences may allow examination of a crisis from several angles or viewpoints. Second, groups have a greater capacity to correct errors and fallacies in judgment. Group members often critique and refine individual preferences and predispositions. Consequently, critical evaluation of premises and assumptions is generally enhanced in groups. This may be particularly important during crisis, in which the initial impulse is sometimes to react without full consideration of the consequences. Finally, groups create a redundant capacity. The reality of many crises is that some redundancy is often necessary. Some members of the group may be unavailable, inaccessible, or distracted.

Maintaining Decisional Vigilance

Vigilance is a quality of systematic and mindful group decision making. Decision makers are said to be vigilant when they consider a wide pool of alternative courses of action, survey objectives and values implicated by the decision, and weigh costs and risks associated with negative outcomes. Moreover, intensive searches for new information; taking into account new information, even when it clashes with their own beliefs; reexamining positive and negative consequences of alternatives; and making provisions for implementing choices are also characteristics of vigilant groups (Gouran, 1982). Decisional vigilance, however, works best when team members have considerable time and do not face significant external pressure. Crisis obviously does not offer this optimal decisional scenario. Crisis decision making puts tremendous stress and pressure on the CMT. In many cases, the team must make decisions immediately, without a clear understanding of the nature or scope of the crisis. This may cause a quick rush to judgment without adequate consideration; in other cases, a kind of decisional paralysis may set in, in which decision makers cannot act. The question for crisis decision makers is how to maintain decisional vigilance in the less-than-optimal decisional conditions of crisis.

Functional Decision Making and Crisis

Improving decisional quality has been a focus of much inquiry in a variety of fields. One approach that has emerged is a systematic and rational methodology for group decisions known as functional decision theory (FDT). FDT seeks to describe the group functions and processes associated with decisional vigilance and effectiveness. Gouran and Hirokawa (1983), for example, described five communication activities that are associated with vigilant groups. Communication among members should function to (1) show understanding of the matters to be resolved, (2) determine the characteristics of a successful alternative choice, (3) identify a pool of relevant alternative choices, (4) assess and evaluate the alternatives, and (5) assist in selecting the best alternative.

This approach has been applied to help understand both effective and ineffective group decisions. For instance, Hirokawa and Scheerhorn (1986) identified five factors of ineffective decision making: (1) inadequate assessment of the problem, (2) inappropriate goals or objectives for dealing with the problem, (3) improper assessment of the consequences, (4) an inadequate information base, and (5) invalid reasoning from the information base. Effective groups, in contrast, evaluate opinions and assumptions more thoroughly than ineffective groups. Moreover, effective groups analyze possible solutions and their consequences completely. Effective groups base decisions on reasonable and fully examined premises. Faulty leadership, including leadership that is too directive, is also a factor in ineffective decision making (Hirokawa & Pace, 1983).

Several models have been proposed for helping groups make effective decisions within the time-restricted conditions of crisis. Heath (1995, 1998), for example, described a model he called crisisthink, designed to enable the user to focus on three elements of effective problem solving and crisis management. Crisis is a condition of inadequate information and restricted time and resources. Decision makers, therefore, should focus on methods for addressing these inadequacies. Heath (1995) proposed three questions: (1) How do I get more information? (2) How do I get more time? and (3) How do I conserve/save more resources? In this way, the limitation on the specific abilities of the CMT to make decisions is addressed. These three questions suggest that effective crisis decision making involves gaining the best possible information about the crisis, gaining as much time as possible to deploy appropriate resources during the crisis, and understanding the best possible way to conserve resources following the crisis. Although the exigencies following a crisis are typically different, these questions provide crisis decision makers some areas to focus on in their postcrisis decision making. In this case, these decision-making questions are broad in their application yet specific in terms of how decision makers should attend to crisis problem solving (Heath, 1995).

Other models have adopted basic principles and structures of effective decision making in the context of a crisis (Seeger & Gouran, 2002). The crisis decision model provides a prescriptive, rational approach to crisis decision making, using a decision tree (see Figure 10.2). Although not every feature of the model is applicable to every crisis, a complete understanding of the model will help decision makers better manage exigencies of crisis decision making.

From the outset, decision makers will either identify or fail to recognize the warning signs of the crisis. If they identify the crisis and take the appropriate preventative actions, there may be no crisis. Gouran (1982) advised that if the group averts the crisis it should ask, "Were the measures taken actually effective, was the failure of the crisis to materialize the result of chance factors, or was there simply a misreading of the signs?" (p. 179). In other words, could there be some other reason why the crisis was avoided?

If decision makers fail to perceive the crisis or if their preventative actions prove to be ineffective, then the decision makers are forced into crisis management. When decision makers must deal with a crisis, they must answer the question, "What should we do?" (Gouran, 1982, p. 181). To answer this question, members must identify necessary issues and information. Important information may then be collected. In the next stage, the crisis team must assess the time available for collecting and processing information. In this case, the team must either take whatever time it has to engage in information collection or immediately begin implementing the least-risky solution. It is important, however, that crisis teams continue the evaluative process after selecting the least-risky solution. The least-risky solution may fail to contain the crisis. Once a crisis team has selected a course of action, contingency plans should be developed, even though the plans feature alternatives other than those preferred. Once the contingency plans are in place, the crisis team should move toward implementation of the preferred alternative. At this point, the crisis team may have two additional steps to consider. The first step is preliminary testing and reconsideration. Through communication, the CMT can receive feedback about the proposed solution. If the feedback is negative, the group may reevaluate its choice. Following reevaluation, the group should be ready to implement its plan. After the plan has been implemented, the CMT should then assess the outcome. If the solution has been ineffective, the team should try to assess why it failed. Similarly, if the solution has been effective, the team should try to identify the specific reasons for success.

Although the crisis decision model systematically addresses the limitations imposed by crisis, it may in some cases fail to accommodate the chaotic conditions of a crisis. In crisis situations, decision makers can sometimes only react. There is no time for systematic consideration of information or alternatives. Moreover, these reactions sometimes are later judged

Figure 10.2
The Crisis Decision Model

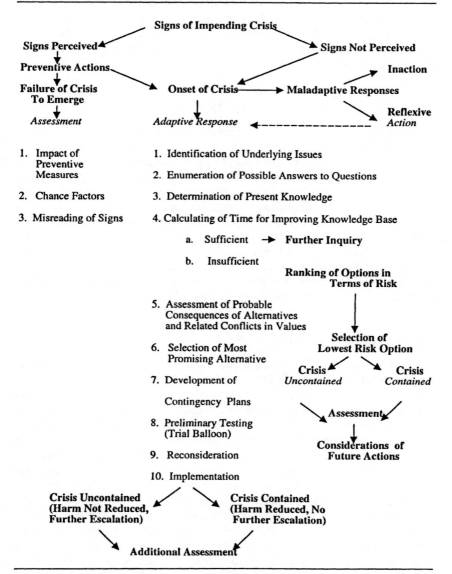

Source: From Functional Decision Making under the Conditions of Crisis, by M. W. Seeger and D. S. Gouran, 2002. Paper prepared for the U.S. Centers for Disease Control (CDC).

as appropriate responses. Following the fire at Malden Mills, CEO Aaron Feuerstein did not engage in systematic evaluation of the problem. Rather, he and his team of senior executives merely reacted to the situation out of core values in deciding to continue to pay workers and announcing immediately that he would rebuild the plant. His reflexive response, however, reduced the uncertainty of the crisis and stimulated an outpouring of stakeholder support.

CRISIS TEAMS AND UNCERTAINTY REDUCTION

A primary part of the decisional processes described above is information collection. Information collection is central to effective responses because crises are by definition highly equivocal and dynamic and break existing structures and patterns. Moreover, there is a tendency for organizational authority systems to contract and withdraw when threatened, thus effectively shutting down channels for critical information. The CMT's goal should be to remain open and to collect as much information as possible about the nature of the crisis, about cause and consequences, and about the response of stakeholders—and it must do so under the chaotic conditions of crisis. The CMT must also communicate effectively with stakeholders and promote crisis-related organizational learning. Each of these functions is discussed below.

Collecting Information

Following a crisis, the organization must mobilize immediately to collect information. This includes basic information about what happened, the scope of the harm, how the crisis developed, who was affected, and what responses are being initiated. Crisis however, often disrupts routine channels of communication, making it difficult to answer these questions. Because of the information vacuum, crisis is also a time of speculation and rumor. The CMT must be particularly vigilant with regard to checking facts and ensuring that information is accurate. The 9/11 attack, for example, was initially reported to be an accident. Organizations often send individuals directly to the scene to verify facts. Sometimes, however, the scene is inaccessible or the necessary information is unavailable. Following the 9/11 attacks, for example, there was much speculation about air quality at the World Trade Center (WTC) site. Information about the kinds of potentially toxic materials stored in the WTC, however, was destroyed in the attacks. It is also important to recognize that a crisis, particularly a major crisis, has many manifestations. Any single perspective is likely to be an incomplete picture. In other cases, participants in a disaster, believing that disclosing information about the crisis and its cause could increase their vulnerability, may be reluctant to share information. They may distort facts, downplay the levels of harm, or simply withhold important details.

Determining Cause

One function of the CMT is to work with other agencies in determining the cause. Crisis management is about moving from the unknown to the known through information processing (Egelhoff & Falguni, 1992). Processing information enables the CMT to make decisions about how to move forward, what actions to take, and what messages to communicate to stakeholders. The process of determining cause emphasizes information collection.

Determining cause often involves very detailed and systematic investigations during the postcrisis stage. It may involve examining records, taking eyewitness testimony, reconstructing accident sites, interviewing survivors, and listening to experts (Ray, 1999). Often, a great deal of information must be processed to identify a plausible explanation for what went wrong. As described in chapter 8, questions of cause are often related to liability and to the degree of damage done to the organization's image. The CMT should be cognizant of these related issues and should work to ensure that determination of cause is done in a systematic, open, and credible manner. This usually requires being forthright and cooperative with investigators and open and honest with stakeholders. It may also require the CMT to protect sources of information (crash sites; audiotapes and videotapes; organizational records, including computerized records; and other data sources) so that they are available for a postcrisis inquiry. The CMT must also keep careful records of its own operations during the management of the crisis, an activity usually assigned to a designated scribe. These goals, however, must be balanced against the need to protect proprietary information.

Monitoring the Public

A major part of managing a crisis is monitoring the public and various stakeholders to ensure that the CMT is receiving adequate feedback about the responses of stakeholders and so that any developing rumors can be addressed. Feedback may take the form of media reports, including those of television, radio, and print media; direct calls from the public or from the media; and Internet activity, including e-mail and online discussion groups. Organizations often contract with clipping services, video-monitoring services, or public-opinion polling organizations to provide feedback. News reports and media attention may give the organization an understanding of how its stakeholders are interpreting the crisis and how the organization's response is being received. However, some stakeholder groups may be difficult to identify and assess, because new stakeholders often emerge from a crisis. Monitoring the public is a dynamic process, but one that is often critical to the CMT's success.

Disseminating Information to Stakeholders

The CMT is also responsible for providing information to stakeholders via the media, usually through the public relations department. Crisis creates an extreme information vacuum, and stakeholders immediately seek information. Since an intense information deficiency about a significant issue is the primary condition for the development of rumors, disseminating information in these conditions may help limit rumors. In general, the closer or more direct the impact, the greater the need for information. CMTs may be responsible for establishing telephone hot lines for stakeholders, making sure that the representatives for the organization have adequate information to communicate to stakeholders. They may also be responsible for providing regular press releases and updates to local and national media. Depending on the scale of the crisis and the level of harm, press conferences should be held at least daily, perhaps more often. Accommodation should be made both for the print and broadcast media. Images and background video are particularly important to television coverage and may help the CMT show the organization functioning normally.

As discussed earlier, crisis often disrupts the normal channels of communication, making it difficult to disseminate important information to the public. In many instances, adaptive communication processes have developed to ensure that crisis information is disseminated (Sellnow, Seeger, & Ulmer, 2002). Radio stations may abandon their typical format and take calls about the crisis. In other cases, flyers have been disseminated with information about missing persons, resources for recovery, and information about risk mitigation. Cellular phones have been instrumental in many crises. The Internet has become an invaluable resource for disseminating information during crises. Unlike television and radio, however, the Internet does not allow for instantaneous dissemination of information. Evidence suggests that relatively few turned to the Internet during the 9/11 attacks (Jones & Rainie, 2002). In fact, one popular Internet search engine shut down for the first several hours after 9/11 and posted a notice telling users to watch television.

The CMT's role in disseminating information during a crisis is not merely one of providing access to information. Communication in these instances is reassuring to the public, particularly if the spokesperson is a well-known and credible figure. The mere fact that information is available and that organizational leaders are communicating may be reassuring and may create the impression of openness and accessibility. New York mayor Rudy Giuliani's press conferences following the 9/11 attacks often included very little new information. Nonetheless, he continued to hold them at regularly scheduled intervals. By doing so, he created a reassuring public presence and an impression of openness.

PROMOTING CRISIS VIGILANCE

As discussed in chapter 9, one of the principal hurdles facing crisis practitioners is getting organizations to take crisis planning and preparation seriously (Mitroff, 2001). CMTs have a fundamental role in helping organizations learn about crises, understand their risks, and prepare accordingly. CMTs, for example, may conduct drills and exercises not only to test and refine plans but to signal to the organization the importance of crisis planning. In postcrisis examinations of cause, CMTs can help refine these understandings and cultivate more effective responses. The CMT's prominence within the larger organization will signal the relative importance of crisis vigilance. Having senior executives serve on the team, holding regular meetings, and openly discussing risk are important to developing an organizational culture of crisis vigilance.

SUMMARY

This chapter examined the role of crisis teams in preparing for and responding to organizational crises. The CMT is responsible for creating the crisis plan, implementing it, analyzing the event, and promoting learning about crisis and risk. Crisis teams are also responsible for making decisions about how to manage the crisis under conditions of high uncertainty, threat, and restricted response time. Although organizations can respond to crises effectively without a CMT, these structures enhance the probability that crisis will be avoided when possible. The CMT also helps to ensure that the organization will be vigilant and agile in its response in those cases in which a crisis is unavoidable.

CHAPTER 11

Communication and Risk

Risk is an essential element in the study of crisis communication. Crises prove the presence of risk and heighten the public's perception of risk. For example, the environmental risk of oil transportation in the pristine waters of Alaska was verified by the *Valdez* spill. The unthinkable terrorist assaults on 9/11 validated airport-security risks. Since the eruption of these and other crises, the general public is increasingly aware of the potential for disasters in both industries. Future decisions related to oil transportation and airport security must be made in light of a fuller understanding of the risks.

If the general public perceives that an activity generates excessive risk, it may resist that activity. Resistance may come through established channels, such as political influence, or through spontaneous channels, such as protests and boycotts. For example, public protests of proposed nuclear power plants intensified greatly after the Three Mile Island incident. To avoid or resolve such controversy, organizations must engage in strategic risk communication. The challenges in these circumstances are compounded by the fact that, according to Williams and Olaniran (1994), "the opposing sides of the issue are judged with differing standards by the general public in regard to what is trustworthy." Organizations seek to resolve angst over a risk issue by maintaining or earning the public's trust. Mather, Stewart, and Ten Eyck (2000) described public trust in risk situations as the sum of three factors: "confidence, altruism, and similarity" (p. 13). Trust for organizations is equated with credibility in the following explanation:

You are credible to the extent that I think you know what you are doing.
You are credible to the extent that I think you have my interest at heart.
You are credible to the extent that I think you are like me. (p. 13)

Organizations tend to emphasize their competence, particularly technical, whereas opposing social activists tend to emphasize altruism in their messages (Mather et al., 2000).

When organizations rely on scientific evidence to establish their credibility regarding a risk issue, the situation becomes even more complex. Using technical or scientific data often results in a "perceived bad fit between scientists' and lay audiences' risk judgments" (Griffin, Neuwirth, & Dunwoody, 1995, p. 201). Typically, the organization is seen as less than trustworthy, because it stands to profit by the introduction of a risky technology or process while the public bears the brunt of the risky outcomes. Moreover, organizations often come across as technologically arrogant, stating risk in unequivocal terms and dismissing any criticism as not scientific. If organizations are to earn the trust or legitimacy of their stakeholders, they must engage in effective risk communication. The problem is that most organizations have not "figured out how to do business when their trust is questioned" (Mather et al., 2000, p. 13). The recognition of this knowledge gap has resulted in considerable research in risk communication. Entire academic journals and interdisciplinary organizations are now dedicated to furthering our understanding of what constitutes both effective and ethical risk communication (Pidgeon, Hood, Jones, Turner, & Gibson, 1992).

This chapter begins by defining risk and exploring the tensions organizations face as they attempt to establish a connection with the public when considering risk issues. In addition, the influence organizations have over risk-related policies affecting them is explored. Finally, some best practices of organizations involving effective internal and external risk communication are identified.

DEFINING RISK COMMUNICATION

"Risk communication," Heath (1995) suggested, "deals with risk elements, whether they are appropriately tolerable, and risk consequences" (p. 257). Covello (1992) defined risk communication as "the exchange of information among interested parties about the nature, magnitude, significance, or control of a risk" (p. 359). Risk communication, in early stages, is most closely associated with crisis sensing and threat assessment. This area of research also focuses on media reporting of environmental hazards associated with industrial activities and with health-related messages (Heath, 1995; Covello, 1992).

Crisis communication involves the sending and receiving of messages "to prevent or lessen the negative outcomes of a crisis and thereby protect the organization, stakeholders, or industry from damage" (Coombs, 1999b, p. 4). As such, it is part of the larger crisis management function. Emergency public information, most often associated with natural disasters, is designed to "protect health, safety, and the environment by keeping the

Figure 11.1
Distinguishing Features of Risk Communication and Crisis Communication

Risk Communication	Crisis Communication
Risk centered; Projection about some harm occurring at some future date	Event centered; Specific incident that has occurred and produced harm
Messages regarding know probabilities of negative consequences and how they may be reduced	Messages regarding current state or conditions; Magnitude, immediacy, duration, control/remediation, cause, blame, consequences
Based on what is currently known	Based on what is known and what is not known
Long term (pre-crisis)	Short term (crisis)
Message preparation (i.e., campaigns)	Less preparation (i.e., responsive)
Technical experts, scientists	Authority figures, emergency Managers, technical experts
Personal scope	Community or regional scope
Mediated; Commercials, ads brochures, pamphlets	Mediated; Press conferences, press releases, speeches, Web sites
Controlled and structured	Spontaneous and reactive

public informed" and "to restore public confidence in the organization's ability to manage an incident" (p. 4).

One of the principal distinctions between crisis communication and risk communication concerns their origins. Crisis communication typically is associated with public relations and is grounded in the effort to manage public perceptions of an event so that harm is reduced for both the organization and stakeholders. Crisis communication has also begun to draw more heavily on the need to communicate during public emergencies, such as earthquakes, floods, and hurricanes (Sellnow, Seeger, & Ulmer, 2002).

Risk communication and crisis communication may be distinguished on a number of levels. Some of these distinctions are presented in Figure 11.1. Although there are areas of overlap, principle distinctions include the fact that crisis communication is about an event that has occurred, whereas risk communication is a projection of what might happen. Risk communication tends to be focused within carefully planned media campaigns; crisis communication is spontaneous and focused around a single spokesperson.

For an applied definition of risk communication, scholars frequently turn to the National Research Council's (NRC's) extensive 1989 report (Diana &

Heath, 1995; Pidgeon et al., 1992; Rimal, Fogg, & Lora, 1995; Williams & Olaniran, 1994). The NRC (1989) defines risk communication as "an interactive process of exchange of information and opinion among individuals, groups, and institutions" (p. 2). The appealing aspect of this definition is that it concisely establishes risk communication as an interaction among all stakeholders. As such, the NRC encourages organizations to view their stakeholders as active participants rather than as passive bystanders in the risk communication process. Moreover, risk is perceptual and involves "beliefs, attitudes, judgments and feelings, as well as the wider social or cultural values and dispositions that people adopt, towards hazards and their benefits" (Pidgeon et al., 1992, p. 89). Hazards should be seen as anything that threatens individuals physically or threatens possessions they value.

Rimal et al. (1995) have identified four aspects of risk directly relevant to the field of communication. First, communication is central to any effort to identify cultural meaning and to "determine a collective course of action" (p. 320). Specifically, consensus-seeking and negotiation skills are necessary to achieve a collective action. Second, risk situations often require decision making in stressful times and under uncertain conditions. As described in chapter 10, understanding group decision making and how issues are framed is central to effective risk management. Third, risk situations involve the use of communication to alter beliefs and thereby change behaviors. Finally, risk issues involve communication at multiple levels. Individuals, organizations, industries, and governments may all be involved in a single risk issue. Knowledge of communication at all of these levels is needed to fully explore a risk situation.

COMMUNICATING RISK MESSAGES TO THE PUBLIC

An organization's understanding of risk must be based on both task and culture (Chess, 2001). The task environment focuses on risk issues related to the production or service. In general, the task environment involves "exchanges between the environment and the focal organization (the organization under study) largely in terms of resources." The cultural circumstances are far more inclusive, embodying the "rules, norms, roles, and expectations that can affect organizations independent of resources" (p. 181). When organizations are mindful of their larger cultural environment, their consideration of risk includes the symbols, cognitive systems, and normative beliefs that are socially constructed by the members of their extended environment. Recognizing and responding to the cultural environment involves enactment. As Chess explained, "[O]rganizations' perceptions of their reality are shaped by what companies choose to notice in their external environments and how they understand events" (p. 181). As an organization monitors perceptions of risk in its environment, through boundary spanning and environmental monitoring, it must continuously reformulate risk-related messages.

Organizations must also be proactive in the public interpretation of information related to risk issues (Diana & Heath, 1995). The relationship between public relations practitioners and technical experts is a vital link in this interpretation process. Diana and Heath explained that "most public relations practitioners lack the technical expertise required to understand, evaluate, and explain technical matters." There is an assumption that "culture, values, attributions of responsibility, and interests employed in risk interpretations are more important than mere availability of data" (p. 211). However, some form of technical expertise is needed to assist public relations officials in constructing risk communication. Incorporating technical experts as "interpreters" of risk data can enable the lay public to "avoid drawing simplistic conclusions" (p. 211). In addition to their technical knowledge and contacts within professional networks, technical experts are often part of the larger community in which risk issues are debated (Diana & Heath, 1995). As such, they often understand the public's frustration with emerging risk issues. Diana and Heath offered five suggestions for integrating technical experts into the risk communication process. First, public relations practitioners should realize that technical experts, in addition to being confident in their assessment of particular risk issues, are typically employed by or have contacts with the industry, giving them a proindustry bias. Second, integrating these experts in venues where they can communicate face-to-face with less-knowledgeable individuals can provide a more comprehensive view of the issue. Third, technical experts should be given the training and access needed to communicate actively about risk issues in their communities. Fourth, technical experts should be used in the issue management process to alert public relations practitioners when an issue is beginning to reach a controversial stage. Finally, public relations professionals should help technical experts capitalize on their "professional approach to risk issues." Because they often perceive that the "industry is willing to regulate its activities in the public interest," technical experts "tend to critique news reports and commentary" (p. 211). This activity can yield helpful information for public relations practitioners.

Although these strategies have the potential to enhance risk communication, such messages cannot be fully understood without an explanation of the tensions organizations face when attempting to establish a favorable connection with the public. Figure 11.2 illustrates three common tensions that exist between the public and organizations regarding the degree to which the public should be involved in making risk decisions. First, the degree to which the public can or should engage in a dialogue with organizations is often contested. Second, tension arises over whether or not an organization's messages should seek to persuade the public. Third, an organization's public relations efforts can vary from quelling outrage to garnering a modicum of public interest in a risk issue.

Figure 11.2
Tensions in Connecting with the Public

	Dialogue	
Technosphere	--	Demosphere
	Persuasive	
Informative	--	Persuasive
	Public reactions	
Indifference	--	Outrage

Dialogue

Chess (2001) has challenged the assumption that the role of organizations in risk communication is to protect the public rather than to involve them in decision making about risks affecting their safety and health. He described the contrast between protection and connection as content-oriented risk communication versus process-oriented risk communication. When organizations take a content-oriented approach to risk communication, they "constrain individuals' decisions about risk by limiting the range of choices available." By delimiting their consideration and communication of available options regarding risk, organizations reduce their ethical responsibility to simply "getting the numbers right" in their external messages (p. 180). Witte (1995) disputed the ethicality of such selective communication. She argued that "any risk message, by virtue of presenting certain facts to the exclusion of others (because of time or other constraints) will influence its audience in some manner. There is no such thing as a neutral risk message" (p. 251). To counteract this tendency toward selective communication, Chess proposed a process-oriented approach that emphasizes social responsibility on the part of the organization. In this manner, "interactions between corporations and their organizational environments" become the "impetus for risk communication" (p. 180).

Risk identification within an organization functions best when employees at every level in the organization participate, through a dialectical process, in developing a knowledge base related to risk (Mitroff & Anagnos, 2001; Weick & Sutcliffe, 2001). Juanillo and Scherer (1995) clarified this point. They distinguished between two general paradigms of risk communication, depicted in the "Dialogue" continuum of Figure 11.2. The traditional approach to risk communication is linear. Heath (1995) characterized this view as dominated by technical communicators who prefer "a linear, hypodermic communication process, whereby technical information can be injected into non-technical audiences" (p. 269). Traditional risk communication is designed primarily for communication to stakeholders outside the organization. Experts determine risk levels and explain to a less-informed public the degree to which a product, process, or program is safe. Success, in the classical risk communication sense, was based on the degree to which popular behaviors and attitudes "harmonize with scientific-technocratic values and principles" (Juanillo & Scherer, 1995, p. 287). Although this end is reasonable, it includes several problematic assumptions. First, scientists are seen as the only "accurate, objective," and "value-free" source of information (p. 287). Second, classical risk communication models assume that technical rationality is superior to other forms of reasoning. Third, the public and employees are at lower levels of the hierarchy. The result is a kind of technological arrogance that potentially alienates audiences. Moreover, the credibility of risk communicators is reduced in those cases in which technological projections of risk are demonstrated to be inadequate.

Juanillo and Scherer (1995) proposed a dialectical view of risk communication that actively and mutually engages the public. They see technical experts as "extenders" of risk-based evidence, rather than as the only source of such information. Similarly, Williams and Olaniran (1998) insisted that, for risk communication to function in the "most beneficial manner, [the] exchange is best viewed by experts as a dialogue instead of a monologue" (Risk Communication, para. 7). The ultimate goal for risk communication is a public dialogue emphasizing the "interests, knowledge and values prevailing in each community" (Diana & Heath, 1995, Introduction). The eventual goal is that, within each community, a "risk democracy" will emerge (Heath, 1995, p. 255). The passage of the federal Right-to-Know Act of 1986 clearly established the public's right and need to know what risks they are facing (Williams & Olaniran, 1994). Finally, this dialogue should both elucidate just technical facts and account for the cultural values of a community.

In addition, a solely technocratic approach to risk communication may impede organizational learning. Within organizations, reliance on technical experts alone may have the unanticipated and undesirable consequence of "dumbing down" the rest of the organization. Weick and Sutcliffe (2001) explained that skilled technical expertise allows other members to "quit thinking." They added, "The better the person is, the worse it is for the organization. All the education flows to the person who already knows the most" (p. 123). Decisions are deferred to the technical experts, and broader understanding is neither generated nor disseminated. The dialectical approach to risk communication emphasizes multiple perspectives based on a free flow of information and open access to communication channels and resources.

Glicken (1999) provided a helpful context for understanding the tension between the technosphere and the demosphere (see Figure 11.2). She also proposes a series of pragmatic steps organizations can take to make their decision making and risk communication more inclusive of risk stake-holders. The philosophy known as technocracy reflects a bias in govern-ing toward "technically trained experts [who] rule by virtue of their specialized knowledge and position in dominant political and economic institutions." From the time of Roosevelt's New Deal, technocracy has offered a "politics of expertise." The perceived advantage to this approach was that experts could "separate information from emotion and values and make appropriate social decisions based on abstract principles of the social sciences" (p. 301). Clearly, the technocracy had little interest in the lay public's opinions. In the technosphere, decision making is restricted to individual cognitive knowledge "based on technical expertise" (p. 301).

The shift toward a more democratic view of risk communication began in the 1960s, when special interests reemerged as a notable political force. Ques-tions regarding risk then expanded from technicality and efficiency to include a view that considered the "appropriateness of policies affecting the public" (Glicken, 1999, p. 301). Whereas a dominant technosphere used cognitive knowledge to debate correctness, the reemerging demosphere considered the appropriateness or goodness of policies, welcoming the consideration of experience or value-based knowledge to the decision-making arena.

There are three advantages to including public participation in decision making. First, an inclusive approach increases the competence of decision makers because the public provides information on matters that affect it. In short, public contribution allows for a more considered approach to decision making. Second, an inclusive approach offers "greater legitimacy through greater accountability" (Glicken, 1999, p. 303). Specifically, "the legitimacy of a decision is higher when the process by which that decision is reached is perceived to be fair and when the decision can be said to represent the desires of stakeholders or constituencies" (p. 303). Third, inclusive decision making reflects the "proper conduct of democratic societies" (p. 304).

Specific recommendations may help organizations function effectively in the demosphere (Glicken, 1999). First, "participants must feel that their participation or input will make a difference" (p. 318). Organizations that take a "tell and sell" approach, where persuasion rather than inquiry is dominant, are unlikely to create the impression that participant comments were valued. Second, if concerned parties do not believe their representa-tion was adequate, they are unlikely to support a decision. Third, these processes of risk sharing must involve interested parties from the outset. Glicken recommended that organizations undertake some form of out-reach as early in the decision-making process as possible. Failure to do so will result in the assumption that the organization is simply trying to sell a decision it has already made. Finally, creating understandings of risk through the demosphere requires a considerable time commitment. Pub-lic relations campaigns, community meetings, and other forms of outreach take considerable time and effort.

Even when organizations follow these steps, they may still encounter difficulties. A particular issue may be a "hot topic" in the minds of stakeholders. Perceptions of the risk associated with an issue may be swayed by the media or by unrealistic fears. An individual or interest group may view the invitation to participate in a dialogue as an opportunity to disrupt the decision-making process. Conversely, people may emerge from the discussion process with the unrealistic expectation that all of their suggestions will be acted on by the decision makers. Despite this potential for frustration or failure, the inclusive dialogue approach offers an important step forward in the practice of risk communication.

Purpose

Two additional weaknesses in the demosphere model are illustrated in the "Purpose" continuum of Figure 11.2. Rowan (1995) observed that the democratic approach equated "fair process" with "fair product" (p. 303). Truth, it is assumed, will eventually emerge, as long as a concerned public has access to risk-related information. Acquiring such information is necessary, but not sufficient, to keep government and industry in check. Similarly, balanced participation in the discussion of risk is certainly appropriate but does not "assure careful problem analysis" (p. 303). More importantly, Rowan cautioned against a view of the democratic approach that "tries to outlaw an important communication skill: persuasion" (p. 303). Persuasion in this context represents a legitimate method of generating agreement (Johannesen, 2001). The problem is that many risk communicators rush to persuasion before fully listening to and understanding the concerns and values of stakeholders. Effective risk communication based in the demosphere model should be mutually accommodating, seeking understanding between organizations and their stakeholders.

Public Reactions

The third continuum included in Figure 11.2 addresses the two extreme reactions the public may have regarding risks. The public may be indifferent to an organization's risk communication or, for a variety of reasons, people may become outraged. This "social amplification of risks" plays an important role in influencing hostile reactions (Griffin et al., 1995, p. 207). Social amplification occurs when agencies such as "groups of scientists, the mass media, government agencies and politicians, as well as activists groups within a community" seek to heighten the public's awareness of a given hazard (Pidgeon et al., 1992, p. 114). Such messages, however, sometimes employ fear appeals that actually backfire (Witte, 1995). A characteristic irony of risk communication, then, is that "the richest, longest lived, best protected, most resourceful civilization, with the highest degree of

insight into its own technology is on its way to becoming the most frightened" (Slovic, 1987, p. 281).

There is compelling evidence of a fundamental disconnect between
"risks that kill people" and public perceptions of risk (Sandman, 2000, p. 3).
The threat of a hazard alone is not sufficient to generate public alarm. Sandman proposed that "risk, as perceived by the public, is the outcome of hazard plus the outrage surrounding an issue. Failure to account for this
outrage factor in risk analysis produces risk estimates that do not reflect
public opinion. Sandman pointed out that the public typically assigns an
unnecessarily high degree of risk to hazards that involve a high degree of
outrage. Conversely, the public tends to assign dangerously low levels of
risk to hazards involving little outrage. The media is a major influence on
public outrage and, consequently, on the public's risk perception. Sandman
explained that "when outrage is low, media coverage is typically light and
policy procedures are discounted—though when outrage is high, media
coverage is intense and policy procedures take center stage" (p. 3).

Risk communication often requires the balance of two seemingly contradictory goals (Witte, 1995). First, risk communication must induce sufficient
fear in the public to motivate people to take action. Second, risk communication seeks to prevent "panic and/or outrage among those faced with
environmental and/or technological risks" (p. 230). The public's response
to risk messages is determined by a variety of factors. Research based on
health communication campaigns, for example, indicates that "the probability of exposure to health risks, the unpleasantness of the outcome, and
the individual's perception of his or her ability to achieve recommended
behavioral changes are all important message factors leading to behavioral
modification" (Griffin et al., 1995, p. 206). Personalizing a risk issue can also
make the information more influential. Griffin et al. (1995) explained: "[T]he
assumption is that telling a story about an individual to illustrate a pattern
will make information more vivid, more colorful and thus more memorable" (p. 208). In a study of risk communication concerning contaminated
tap water, the "perception of personal risk from the hazard correlated most
directly with relative level of risk when subjects read personalized leads
and were not given headlines that stressed the risk" (p. 222).

Key components in fear appeals or risk messages include perceived
threat, severity of the threat, probability of the threat's occurrence, self-
efficacy, and response efficacy (Witte, 1995). Initially, people must perceive
that a threat exists before any response can occur. The greater the perception of severity, the more attention a risk issue receives. Public interest in a
risk issue is also intensified by the probability that a hazard will affect
their lives. Self-efficacy refers to perceived control. If people feel there is
little they can do to avert a hazard, they have little motivation for action.
When people perceive that a risk is severe but that there is little or nothing
they can do to avoid it, they are likely to engage in defensive avoidance

behavior such as denial or evasion of the issue. Successful risk communication messages, then, include a measure of response efficacy. This form of efficacy reassures the public that, if they take a series of prescribed steps, they will reduce the risk. Previous research indicates that "when perceived threat and perceived efficacy were high, people were motivated to control the danger" (p. 237). If, however, perceived threat is high and perceived efficacy is low, people are more likely to engage in fear-management strategies, such as denial or avoiding the issue. In these cases, they may also engage in reactive behaviors, such as angry protests, that appear illogical to technical experts. For example, residents in rural Minnesota became fearful of health hazards related to a high-voltage power line that was under construction in their county. Although no specific health threat had been identified, rumors of deformed children and increased cancer rates swirled around the county. Legal efforts to stop construction of the power line failed, and the power company largely ignored what it felt were unfounded concerns. The fear and frustration of local residents inspired them to begin toppling the unguarded power line towers with dynamite. Eventually, the power line was built, but only after the company incurred millions of dollars in added costs. Periodic assaults still occur on the power line structure.

Witte (1995) explained that "too often, it appears that risk messages contain information about the threat only, with no information (or information is given too late) about how to avert harm from or minimize exposure to the threat" (p. 250). Moreover, trying to "minimize a perceived serious catastrophic threat while neglecting the efficacy of recommended responses in averting harm from the threat can inadvertently produce fear control responses" (p. 236). After the explosion at the Chernobyl nuclear reactor, for example, European countries responded with messages emphasizing the superior safety of their reactors. Yet, public opinion polls indicated that nearly half of the public still wanted specific information "about what to do in the event of an [nuclear] accident, as well as what to do currently to minimize potential harms from the hazard" (p. 236).

Maximizing danger control and minimizing fear responses on the part of the public are facilitated by strategies for risk communication:

a) developing communication infrastructures and adopting practices, such as citizen's councils, for soliciting and responding to community sentiments; b) training technical experts in place of public relations practitioners as spokespersons on technical issues; and c) encouraging open-door practices whereby the public can scrutinize plant permits and operating standards. (Heath, 1995, p. 258)

Heath added that if organizations "do not have a track record of responsible performance, the community has reason to doubt their ability and willingness to protect the environment and the health of their neighbors" (p. 258).

RISK COMMUNICATION TO INFLUENCE POLICY

Gaining public trust is only one of several objectives associated with risk communication. Organizations must also exert influence on audiences such as politicians, regulatory agencies, and industry peers in order to secure favorable policies and standards. In this section, the role of risk communication in influencing government policy and industry standards is discussed.

Government Policy

Public pressure for political action in the form of regulation is most likely to occur when public outrage is high. Although managing such public impressions is expensive, failure to address the outrage at its inception can result in increasingly intense adversarial postures. Sandman (2000) summarized this situation succinctly: "The point is that while it does take time and money to manage outrage, if done in the beginning, it leads to a better understanding of hazards associated with the outrage" (p. 5). In a study of a proposed incineration plant, for example, the advocates of the project failed to engage the public in a dialogue regarding risk at the outset of the project. Had they done so, they would have been able to debate the hazards of the project on their ground. By failing to initiate this dialogue, the project's advocates found themselves embroiled in a protracted and unpleasant public debate between the city and the county (Renz, 1996). Sandman (2000) advised organizations that it is "much more productive to invite comments and criticism early when outrage is not increasing and potential opponents can be part of the decision-making process" (p. 5).

Active engagement in the process of forming public opinion and public policy is increasingly a requirement for organizations. Crable and Vibbert (1985) argued that "organizations, having no 'authority' over public policy, are limited to exerting 'influence' over policies enacted by [governmental agencies]" (p. 4). To do so, they engage in issues management to "generate and nurture issues until they result in favorable policy" (p. 3). Such external organizational communication as paid advertising on a controversial issue may actually "enrich public policy dialogue" by alerting both the public and the media to relevant information that might otherwise be overlooked (Heath, 1997, p. 227). "Industry and government," noted Curwood (2000), "must become more proactive" in their approaches to risk communication, seeking areas that could be potentially harmful or beneficial, instead of waiting for a crisis to emerge" (p. 6). Ideally, such proactive measures will lead to the development of more inclusive and impartial policies and laws related to risk issues.

Industry Standards

In addition to public policy, organizations are influenced by industry-wide risk communication. The public's perception of risk can be dramatically influenced by a single crisis. For example, both Three Mile Island and the Tylenol poisonings profoundly influenced the procedures and standards in their relevant industries. If an organization responds insufficiently or incompetently to crisis, the public is likely to view the organization as socially irresponsible. When one organization experiences a crisis, the perceived level of risk for the entire industry also rises. Mistakes made by one company can produce indirect costs for other companies in the same industry (Slovic, 1987). Moreover, "Different companies in the same industrial sector and in the same geographic area can function at different evolutionary stages" in the risk communication process (Chess, 2001, p. 186). Some companies are highly innovative in devising risk communication systems, whereas others lag. These laggards are often motivated by "strategy rather than values" (Chess, 2001, p. 186). Successful or legitimate organizations build trust with their risk stakeholders by finding congruence between the social values that are implied by the organization's actions and the norms or standards that are upheld in the community with which the organization interacts. The risk communication shared by innovators can, however, alter the expectations of the risk stakeholders in the organization's relevant environment.

The expectations of a community may shift toward the positions offered if progressive risk communication includes partnerships between the industry and community rather than secrecy or a one-sided, highly technical form of risk communication. These shifting expectations may create gaps between communities' expectations and less-proactive organizations. The pressure, then, is for the reluctant organization to improve its risk communication to meet industry standards.

BEST PRACTICES FOR MANAGING RISK EFFECTIVELY

As awareness and study of risk communication increase, organizations are acknowledging the need to adopt procedures that ensure effectiveness in identifying and communicating about risk issues. Current research emphasizes a series of best practices for both internal and external risk communication.

Internal Communication

Risks often originate within an organization. These risks also include forms of systemic error such as interactiveness and tight coupling, described in chapter 1. Pidgeon et al. (1992) observed that the behavioral causes of accidents and disasters "involve not just individual slips and lapses, but also...patterns of management and organizational failings such as failures of communication, information handling, coordination and error diagnosis" (p. 97). Any systematic effort to reduce risk must include an analysis of organizational limitations and failings. These "organizational and management factors" create "critical blind-spot[s] in the current risk assessment practice" (p. 97).

Accurate and efficient communication among employees is essential to identifying risks and preventing crises. Employees who are active in the process of generating and acting on risk-related information are more likely to act in ways that avert or interrupt crises or potential crises (Mitroff & Anagnos, 2001; Weick, 1995, 2001). Communication plays an essential role in the identification and implementation of risk management programs (Chess, 2001; Frohwein & Lambert, 2000) and in the identification of specific warnings and crisis cues.

Significant evidence exists that "far in advance of their actual occurrence, all crises send out a trail of early warning signals" (Mitroff & Anagnos, 2001, p. 40). Because employees are directly engaged in the treatment of the product, well ahead of the technical experts much higher in the hierarchy, they are likely to be the first to see the errors and signs of potential problems. Mitroff and Anagnos concluded that many crises could be avoided if organizations advocated open communication related to safety and change rather than a fear of punishment for errors. They insist that "humans can pick up the most minute signals when it is in their interest, whether to satisfy curiosity, imagination, or security needs" (p. 105). As part of this open communication, they suggested that "except in cases of criminal malfeasance or negligence, blame and fault-finding are not to be encouraged" (p. 42). Instead, organizations should encourage employees to recognize and share openly even the most subtle signs that all is not well within the organization.

Some organizations are seeking to instill values that promote internal identification and communication of risks. Some chemical companies, for example, use spokespersons with technical expertise "to instill in technical and operations plant personnel the corporate culture that their managements do not tolerate pollution" (Heath, 1995, p. 271). The key to this cultural shift is that these organizations "stress to operations workers that they are responsible for assuring compliance rather than being expected to cover up environmental problems or covertly contribute to them by sloppy operations or by committing illegal actions." Ideally, this culture "empowers employees to improve plant operations" through open communication within the plant and with the public (p. 271).

Similarly, Weick and Sutcliffe (2001) proposed a means for developing an organizational culture that creates mindfulness concerning risk and crisis.

This mindfulness or risk vigilance is further fortified by a reward system favoring open communication regarding risk. These are designed to produce a "safety culture" (p. 127). This culture requires that management's beliefs, values, and actions be communicated throughout the organization in credible, consistent, and salient ways. Such a culture changes behavior by empowering employees to both notice risk and communicate warnings.

External Communication

Beyond the philosophical tensions concerning efforts to connect to stakeholders, organizations must contemplate the specific strategies for external messages. Several recommendations regarding these strategies are provided in the risk communication literature. For instance, Rowan (1995) has advocated a move away from narrow comparisons and toward a rhetoric of risk communication. Much of the current research regarding risk communication focuses on comparisons of how one risk type compares to another. Pidgeon et al. (1992) pointed out that the comparisons used in explaining risk levels to the public fail to account for the distinctions people hold between "personal safety" and "threat to society" (p. 102). Slovic (1987) agreed:

[S]tatements such as, "the annual risk from living near a nuclear power plant is equivalent to the risk of riding an extra three miles in an automobile," give inadequate consideration to the important differences in the nature of the risks from these two technologies. (p. 280)

There are severe limitations in this focus. Relying on risk comparisons, said Rowan (1995), "wrongly suggested to practitioners that risk communication with the public is a matter of knowing 'what answers people get wrong on the risk quizzes life offers' and teaching them the correct answers" (p. 313). Rowan advocated a shift from "focusing on specific message *forms*, such as comparisons" to "helping practitioners analyze risk situations and achieve certain *goals*" (p. 313). In essence, this involves a shift toward rhetorical sensitivity rather than technical formulas for constructing crisis messages. Although "rules" of effective crisis communication are necessary, they require contextual understanding and analysis of the situation. When citizens become angry or hostile, for example, the practitioner's emphasis must shift from technical message construction to a situation analysis. A rhetorical focus, then, enables risk communicators to identify the obstacles in the situation and match the message accordingly. The result is a message that may better fit the audience's needs. The ultimate goal of this rhetorical perspective is to "provide practitioners with a highly refined sense of the ways in which risk communication is likely to go awry and the communication options that are available for addressing or avoiding these difficulties" (p. 316). In short, a rhetorical view of risk communication gives practitioners the sensitivity to, and set of tools for, a situational analysis they typically lack.

SUMMARY

Risk is an inevitable component of modern technological society and organizational life. Communicating about risk to the general public is complex because of the diverse perceptions the public has about risk. To function effectively, organizations must constantly monitor their environments to detect and respond to public frustration or fear related to their products and services. Ideally, organizations seek to form cooperative relationships with their stakeholders so that all parties subjected to the risk have direct input in any risk- or thresholds-related decisions. Forming these connections may create tensions between the organization's goals and public sentiment. When the public reaches a level of outrage regarding a risk issue, organizations must respond to the public outcry while seeking to secure favorable polices from regulatory agencies. Crisis situations regarding risk give organizations an opportunity to lobby on behalf of their industry for tolerance or for what they see as needed reform. If organizations wish to manage risk effectively, they need to consider revising both their internal and external communication practices. Internally, organizations must create an atmosphere intolerant of unnecessary risk. Employees must be trained to identify and report looming risks to appropriate levels of leadership in the organization. The organization must then respond vigilantly. Finally, organizations must maintain external communication that is responsive to the fluid nature of public opinion and to the fluctuating levels of risk.

PART IV

The Role of Crisis

CHAPTER 12

Crisis and Ethics

Questions of values and ethics have become increasingly important to organizations, to stakeholders, and to the larger society within which they exist. These questions relate not only to products and services, but also to processes, technologies, employees, decisions, and the basic form, nature, and culture of organization. Ethical questions, however, are highly equivocal and increasingly characterized by competing values of both organizations and stakeholders. These competing values are most strongly felt during a crisis, when questions of wrongdoing, negligence, responsibility, and blame arise and when victims of a crisis are often powerless and vulnerable. Moreover, crisis often makes the organization's fundamental ethical stance highly visible. Ethical issues are associated with crisis at all stages of development and are the principle factor in ethics scandals. We suggest that maintaining an ethical stance regarding crisis requires discussing and clarifying values so that they may be taken into account both when planning for and when responding to a crisis.

This chapter provides a brief overview of organizational ethics and discusses particular ethical imperatives associated with organizational crisis. Crisis, by virtue of threatening conditions and restriction of time for reflection, is a context of great moral imperative. We describe five ethical perspectives, or frameworks, that are particularly salient to crisis, including issues of organizational responsibility and responsiveness, the virtues of organizational leaders, humanistic values and the ethics of care, issues of organizational legitimacy, and truthfulness and significant choice.

ETHICS AND ORGANIZATIONS

Interest in organizational ethics has exploded as a consequence of several widely publicized cases of wrongdoing. These include instances of insider trading, price fixing, fraud, executive misconduct, harmful products and services, deception and lying, discrimination, sexual harassment and mistreatment of employees, illegal dumping and polluting, and irresponsible environmental management (Jackall, 1988; Valesquez, 1982; Werhane, 1985). In fact, contemporary American society is increasingly mired in ethical scandals at all levels, including the ranks of top executives. These wrongdoings are compounded by an attitude of seeming indifference or arrogance on the part of many organizations and their leaders. Many executives are willing to rationalize unethical conduct, ignore basic standards of morality, and avoid personal responsibility as part of doing business. The result has been closer scrutiny of many executives, combined with a reduction in the overall credibility, reputation, and moral standing of many organizations. Moreover, employees and the general public are increasingly cynical regarding the moral foundation of organizations and institutions.

Ethical issues are fundamental to organizations, to both their normal operations and to the abnormal conditions of a crisis (Seeger, 1997). Ethics concerns the essential judgments of good and bad, right and wrong, desirable and undesirable, acceptable and unacceptable, legitimate and illegitimate, worthy and unworthy. These judgments influence perceptions, decisions, attitudes, choices, and actions. Ethics also concerns accepted standards of moral conduct in a society, community, or culture. Lying, deception, and dishonesty are ethically suspect, for example, partly because they undermine the fundamental ability of individuals to interact with one another in meaningful and predictable ways. Ethics and norms regarding basic honesty and truthfulness, then, are necessary for individuals to work together.

Specific instances of ethical failure, such as the Archer Daniels Midland price-fixing scandal, the deception and consumer harm caused by tobacco companies, the Enron scandal, and the sex-abuse scandal in the Catholic Church, have dramatically demonstrated the scope of ethical problems in organizations. In fact, as described in chapter 3, the ethics scandal is a particularly common and damaging crisis type. Crises based in ethics compromise the fundamental legitimacy of the organization. Moreover, many other spectacular failures and crises, such as the Exxon *Valdez* oil spill, the Jack-in-the-Box crisis, the Bhopal Union Carbide disaster, and the Three Mile Island accident are often associated with serious moral lapses. These kinds of events have helped to make questions of right and wrong more central to organizational inquiry (Seeger, 2002).

Ethics are based on shared values—the specific ideals, norms, and goals that exist throughout a given society, culture, or community (Beyer & Lutze,

1993). In many democratic societies, for example, the ideals of individual freedom of expression, equality of treatment and opportunity, and self-determination are widely shared and used to make a variety of judgments regarding ethics. Moreover, values of individual freedom and self-determination complement values of private ownership and property rights, private business and industry, and the unrestricted movement of capital. Private business and industry, the pursuit of profit, and capitalistic economic systems are associated with democracy. Free trade and capitalistic reforms in communist countries, for example, are often justified on the grounds that they create economic opportunity and lead to political freedom.

Three specific features of values are particularly important to questions of organizational ethics (Seeger, 1997). First, values exist in a hierarchy and compete for saliency in any particular context or decision, including organizational decisions (Jaksa & Pritchard, 1988). Making ethical judgments involves sorting out and balancing competing values. Organizations, for example, often must balance basic values of profitability against issues of employee well-being, safety, and security. Ethical dilemmas develop when these conflicting values or ethical positions are relatively equal, forcing a choice between two comparatively desirable or undesirable, good or bad, right or wrong choices (Seeger, 1997). The North American Free Trade Agreement, for example, has allowed the city of Toronto, Ontario, Canada, to export million of tons of its municipal garbage to Michigan landfills.

A second characteristic of values is that no single value or set of values is universal. Values vary widely from individual to individual, context to context, organization to organization, and culture to culture. Values important during times of normalcy and stability may not be as salient during the threat and uncertainty of crisis. Crisis also tends to activate new values and standards, some of which may be entirely novel for the organization. Some organizations value innovation and creativity; others emphasize stability and predictability. Some organizations encourage values of free expression, whereas others actively seek to "screen out dissenting voices and ideas" (Pinsdorf, 1999, p. 99). As organizations have become more diverse and globalized, the values of their stakeholders have become similarly diverse. This is particularly pronounced as organizations have moved into developing countries and cultures. Some of the *maquiladors*, manufacturing facilities located on the United States-Mexico border, have been forced to confront traditional values related to gender roles. These have come into conflict with the goals of diversity and gender equity common to many progressive U.S. corporations. The hierarchical and competing nature of values accounts for the fact that values are so often the basis of serious disagreement and conflict.

The third feature of values concerns the fact they are highly dynamic in terms of hierarchical position and saliency. Values change dramatically over time in response to changing social needs, perceptions, ideologies, under-standings, and events (Seeger, 1997). Environmentalism is a very recent development, particularly as it is manifest as an organizational ideal. For example, the existence of so-called nuisance species, such as the wolf and coyote, is now actively debated by the agricultural industry. Affirmative action, equal representation, and diversity are relatively recent organiza-tional values. The 9/11 tragedies changed a variety of social values, creating a new emphasis on security and safety, reducing the prominence of privacy and civil liberties, and reinvigorating patriotism. Part of the process of orga-nizational learning as described in chapter 2 involves adjusting organiza-tional value systems in response to new understandings.

Organizations also have unique values, norms, ideals, and ethical stan-dards encoded into a corporate culture. These are the unique social struc-tures, processes, beliefs, and relationships manifest in part because of the industry, technology, physical context, and history of the organization. Cultural values are unique adaptations to contingencies and opportuni-ties that clarify the organization's preferred "shoulds and oughts" for members (Putnam & Cheney, 1985). Much of the socialization process for new members involves abandoning individual morals and values as the basis of ethical judgments and replacing them with organizationally based ethics and values (Jackall, 1988). In many ways, members of an organiza-tion are forced to modify, or in some cases even abandon, their own sense of right and wrong and good and bad to accommodate the organization's value system.

Communication is in several ways particularly critical to organizational ethics (Seeger, 1997). It is through communication that members come to learn the basic ethical standards for their organization. Sometimes this occurs formally, through ethics-training programs, codes of ethics, value statements, or executive speeches. Often, ethics and values are transmit-ted informally through processes of socialization, modeling, observation, and trial and error. Formal leaders have a particularly prominent respon-sibility for modeling ethical standards. By observing which behaviors are rewarded, punished, praised, or critiqued, for example, members come to learn what is valued within an organization. In addition, communication is necessary to identify the various values inherent in a particular situa-tion and to determine the specific hierarchy of values for that context. Conrad (1993) noted:

It is through discourse that individuals develop their own views of morality; through discourse that organizations develop and inculcate core values and ethi-cal codes; and through discourse that incongruities within individual and organi-zational value-sets are managed and contradictions between the value sets of different persons are negotiated. (p. 2)

Communicating, discussing, debating, challenging, and seeking clarification are particularly important in the process of clarifying ethics and in making ethical judgments (Seeger, 1997). "To be ethically responsible," Pauchant and Mitroff (1992) noted, "one must engage in an external conversation with others and with self" (p. 193). In the absence of these conversations, values remain unclear, confused, and equivocal; little consensus develops about which values are dominant in a particular context; and the probabilities of making an ethically suspect judgment and inviting criticism are enhanced (Seeger, 1997).

A final way in which communication is related to organization ethics is in accounting for actions. As described in chapter 9, these processes are often highly visible in postcrisis contexts, when organizations must explain, justify, and defend their actions. These accounts, strategies of apologia, and image restoration are often elaborate and draw on larger questions of cause and responsibility. In some cases, where the accounts, explanations, and defenses are perceived as inadequate, organizations are forced to publicly commit to changes. Often, this involves adhering to a higher ethical level. In fact, organizational ethics have been spurred on by some dramatic cases of court-ordered ethics programs for companies with long-term records of illegal and unethical conduct.

Ethics and Crisis

Ethical questions arise whenever an action has the potential to adversely affect another person. Crises are by definition large-scale, nonroutine problems that have the potential to profoundly affect the organization and its stakeholders. Seeger and Ulmer (2001) have argued that organizational crises almost always include ethical issues—including questions about wrongdoing, intent, cause, blame, and responsibility—and usually place stakeholders in the role of victim. Moreover, crisis is a moment where the organization's core values are starkly displayed, usually through the lens of the media. Crisis strips an organization's ethical framework to its core elements and makes these available for close public scrutiny (Seeger & Ulmer, 2001). The recent Enron bankruptcy, for example, brought into sharp focus the company's values and culture of freewheeling partnerships, high profits, deceptions, and simple greed. Executives were forced to defend and justify their actions in the press and before congressional hearings. A similar public accounting was forced on the tobacco industry when executives were compelled to justify their actions and explain years of deception during congressional hearings (Ulmer & Sellnow, 1997). In contrast, at Malden Mills and Cole Hardwoods, long-standing values of commitment to workers and the community, a record of philanthropy, and a record of good corporate citizenship came to the forefront during times of crisis (Seeger & Ulmer, 2001). These values helped the companies respond to devastating fires in both ethically appealing and effective ways.

Ethical issues are related to organizational crisis at all stages of development. Questions of value are always present during precrisis. Organizations that systematically violate fundamental social values, for example, are more likely to experience crisis. Pauchant and Mitroff (1992) argued that crisis-prone organizations are managed by individuals who fail to take responsibility. "To be ethically responsible," they noted, "means being responsible not only to oneself, accepting one's limitations, but also to others, accepting their limitations and perspectives" (pp. 192–193). Organizations that ignore and violate stakeholder or social values are more likely to experience a radical mismatch with the environment. In contrast, organizations that are responsible and responsive to stakeholders may have more success adapting and avoiding crisis. Moreover, records of good social conduct establish "reservoirs of good will" that may be drawn upon during an actual crisis (Ulmer, 2001). Organizations that establish patterns of virtuous conduct before a crisis may be able to respond in a morally appealing manner. Particularly important values during precrisis are social responsibility and responsiveness (Sethi, 1987). In addition, valuing free-flowing information and ideas, as well as disagreement and dissent, are important to early crisis warning (Seeger, 1997). Organizations that quash disagreement, punish employees for identifying problems and expressing concerns, and cultivate a climate in which upward communication is infrequent and distorted are more likely to miss precrisis cues and warnings. In some cases, administrators discourage employees from communicating about problems so they may maintain plausible deniability in the case of a crisis.

During the crisis stage, organizations are expected to act responsibly, particularly with regard to humane treatment of victims. Crisis-induced harm often affects employees, members of the community, customers, and suppliers, both directly and indirectly. Organizations have some moral obligations to these "crisis stakeholders," to limit and offset harm where possible, to provide information about the nature of the harm, and to compensate for damage. Often, however, organizations are reluctant to respond to victims for fear of creating or enhancing legal liability. In such cases, organizations may deny or diffuse responsibility or shift blame to others. Responsiveness is particularly important during the crisis stage, but it is often overwhelmed by legal posturing that reduces moral and ethical obligations to mere questions of monetary damages. In many cases, organizations require victims to sign settlement agreements promising not to sue as a condition of receiving assistance.

During postcrisis, organizations must provide accounts of cause and blame and assurances that similar events will not occur again. As described in chapter 8, accountability—providing a reasonable and complete explanation about cause, blame, and responsibility—is necessary for resolution and image restoration. Accountability is often coupled with strategies of apologia to create a comprehensive postcrisis response. Values associated with openness, honesty, and truthfulness are particularly important in the postcrisis stage, as are forgiveness and healing. A response grounded in honesty may help to bolster the organization's overall image and legitimacy. In some cases, organizations are able to build on long-established values and virtues to help move out of the postcrisis stage quickly and in a way that leads to renewal.

Finally, crisis not only makes values and ethical stances visible, it may also help to clarify values. Participants in a crisis often report that the event helped them understand more clearly what is important. Often, these descriptions focus on the importance of personal and family safety and security. Lost property is usually described as unimportant and replaceable. Crisis also creates opportunities for support and outreach in ways that build relationships and community. Many organizational crises, repeated in the media or in the stories members tell, even become morality plays. A morality play encodes important values and ethical lessons in a structure that encourages communication and learning. It includes a dramatic narrative with a familiar structure leading to a moral lesson. The morality play developed as a stylized form of medieval drama designed to teach moral lessons through abstractions of good and evil. These abstractions facilitated learning through clearly right-and-wrong moral stances. The term has come into contemporary usage to refer to dramatic public events in which fundamental lessons of morality are publicized, usually through the media. As with the classic dramatic structure, good and evil are clearly presented, along with the consequences of unethical acts. Recent ethics scandals, such as Wall Street insider trading, the Enron bankruptcy, and the Catholic Church sex scandal have been described as contemporary morality plays. Morality plays may promote vicarious organizational learning regarding issues of values and morality. Organizations, seeing the dramatic consequences of unethical behavior, may modify their actions and structures to avoid similar scandals. Cases such as Enron indicate that moral lessons are often part of the larger story of a crisis.

ETHICAL PERSPECTIVES ON CRISIS

Although ethics are endemic to all instances of organizational crisis, four sets of values and norms are particularly relevant: ethical traditions, guideposts, clusters of related values, and associated standards. As such, they offer specific moral perspectives, or frames, within which ethical judgments may be made (Johannesen, 1996). They clarify the standards that are most salient within a crisis context. These include (1) responsibility and responsiveness, (2) virtue ethics, (3) humanistic values and the ethics of care, (4) organizational legitimacy, and (5) truthfulness and significant choice. These perspectives, along with their implications for crisis, are described in greater detail below.

RESPONSIBILITY AND RESPONSIVENESS

Responsibility is a broad ethical concept that refers to the fact that individuals and groups have morally based obligations and duties to others and to larger ethical and moral codes, standards, and traditions (Johannesen, 1996). In addition, those who are free to choose to behave in a particular way are then responsible for the consequences of their behavior. This articulation between freedom and responsibility is the basis of many moral and legal codes. Among other things, the relationship between freedom and responsibility assumes that individuals may be held morally accountable or forced to give an accounting of their actions when there is reason to believe that the action was unethical. Responsibility, therefore, has important implications for how individuals or organizations communicate following a crisis.

Responsibility has several additional implications. For example, organizations are part of society and have obligations to support the general development and health of society. Values such as honesty, equality, and fair and equal treatment of individuals, are in the best interest of society (Seeger, 1997). Organizations, therefore, have an obligation to uphold these basic social values. Moreover, many organizational ethicists argue that equality and fairness are simply the "right" way to behave. A "good corporate citizen" is responsible to the community, involved in the community, and works to improve and protect the community. Moreover, organizations "have a responsibility to devote some of their resources to helping to solve some of the most pressing social problems, many of which corporations helped to cause" (Buchholz, 1990, p. 299). Corporation must also uphold important social values and make ethically appropriate choices and decisions regarding safety and security. An organization that places the community at risk and that does not take appropriate safeguards with dangerous products or processes has failed to meet its moral responsibility to the community.

The concept of corporate social responsibility was first formalized in the general "community chest" movement of the early nineteenth century. The American Association for Community Organization was formed in 1918 to provide coordination and standardization of community-based philanthropy. The association solicited funds from organizations to help support community-based social programs. Eventually, the movement evolved into the United Way of America and retains its tradition of fundraising on the work site for charitable community organizations (Heald, 1970). The community chest movement acknowledged corporate responsibility and promoted a sense of good corporate citizenship through broad-based philanthropy.

Corporate social responsibility, however, has been criticized as promoting a set of narrow and self-serving corporate values and confusing the profit-seeking goals of private organizations. In determining what causes to support, for example, organizations often become mired in arguments over competing values (Buono & Nichols, 1995). These arguments confuse organizational goals and complicate efforts to be socially responsible (Seeger, 1997). Moreover, according to Buchholz (1990), "business executives have little experience and incentive to solve social problems" (p. 301). An alternative to these traditional approaches to corporate social responsibility (CSR I) is corporate social responsiveness (CSR II). CSR II emphasizes organizational openness and willingness to respond to and accommodate social issues and concerns. Responsiveness requires a dynamic, adaptive relationship between the organization and society. In being responsive, an organization is open to concerns from the community, anticipates issues, and responds proactively. A responsive stance might include using procedures, technologies, and materials that do not jeopardize the safety of the community and creating procedures and polices to protect the community in times of crisis. Responsiveness also requires methods and procedures designed to promote openness. Some school districts, for example, have instituted community safety-tip lines designed to enhance the schools' ability to be responsive to student safety and security issues.

In addition to a community-based notion of responsibility, organizations are also morally and legally responsible for the outcomes they create. As described in chapter 3, harms induced by defective products, negligent use or poor maintenance of equipment, poor selection of employees, lack of skill or training, unsafe processes and procedures, or unsafe transportation of materials are probably the most-common sources of organizational crises. As noted earlier, discussions of responsibility over the specific causes of harm often dominate postcrisis stages as part of the efforts to determine legal liability. Frequently, these discussions become mired in divisive arguments and legal bickering that extend the harm.

Responsibility, in many ways, is the fundamental moral principle from which other more-specific ethical frameworks flow. It concerns the basic relationship and attendant obligations and commitments that exist between an organization and its larger community, stakeholders, and environment. These obligations are often complex and competing and represent a common source of ethical ambiguity and dilemmas. Responsibility, as an ethical principle for crisis, relates most directly to precrisis obligations to avoid or reduce the possibility of harm to stakeholders and to complex postcrisis questions of accountability.

CREDIBILITY AND VIRTUE

We have argued that organizational behavior in a precrisis environment is particularly important to the development of a crisis. In planning for a crisis, for example, an organization can create relationships with external groups and agencies. These relationships may help an organization respond more effectively and resolve a crisis more quickly. Establishing networks with external groups, professional associations, trade groups, and governmental and regulatory agencies facilitates crisis sensing. An organization's record of conduct established before a crisis is particularly important in determining how an organization is perceived and judged following a crisis. Organizations that establish patterns of ethical or virtuous conduct during precrisis are more credible and able to more effectively leverage important resources, including the goodwill and support of stakeholders, during a crisis.

One approach to understanding the relationship of precrisis conduct to postcrisis response is virtue ethics (Seeger & Ulmer, 2001; Slote, 1992). This perspective represents a more complete representation of morality than many other approaches grounded in ethical codes or standards. Virtue ethics emphasize the character of a person "independent of the rightness of their actions or the consequences of their actions" (Louden, 1992, p. 28). Virtues are moral or ethical traits, established patterns of conduct derived from a person's internal character, rather than externally driven or imposed. Aristotle regarded a moral virtue as "a form of obedience to a maxim or rule of conduct accepted by the *agent* [italics added] as valid for a class of recurrent situations" (Smith, 1946, p. xiv). For organizations, virtues are expressed most directly and visibly through the decisions and behaviors of top executives, particularly during times of unrest, confusion, or moral uncertainty. In this way, organizational leadership is closely associated with both virtues and crisis.

Virtues require two elements. First, the focus is on character as a pattern of conduct, including motivation and intent in making ethical judgments (Slote, 1992). The focus is on the virtuous or exemplary person who is admirable or praiseworthy and who personifies ethical traits such as generosity, thoughtfulness, honesty, hard work, loyalty, and perseverance. Second, the description of these traits or virtues emphasizes their essential moral features rather than external moral obligations, laws, rule-based "oughts," the restrictions outlined in professional codes, or contractual commitments (Slote, 1992, p. 89). The virtuous person acts in a virtuous way not because laws or professional codes of conduct dictate such action, but because he or she recognizes this as the right way to behave. A virtuous person, then, can be expected to act in a predictably moral or ethical way regardless of the context. More important, perhaps, is the fact that the virtuous person or manager models credibility and suitability behavior. Leadership during crisis is particularly important in framing the initial meaning, reducing equivocality, and setting a tone for the response. This process, described more fully in chapter 13, also establishes the overall moral tone for the crisis response. A chief executive officer (CEO) or senior manager who responds to a crisis in a virtuous or ethically appealing way serves as a model for others. Moreover, because virtues are traits and do not necessarily require time for reflection and analysis, they allow for a more immediate response within the compressed time frame of a crisis. A virtuous manager in a crisis acts in an ethical way out of instinct, without privileging the legal or economic consequences of his or her actions.

For example, in the case of the deadly 1999 explosion at Ford Motor Company's Rouge River manufacturing complex, William Clay Ford, Jr., CEO of Ford and grandson of the company founder, visited injured workers and their families to offer his personal condolences. His visit, occurring only hours after the explosion, was a human expression of concern and support that appeared to come from a deep personal sense of commitment to Ford workers. Ford described the injured workers as part of the extended "Ford family" and expressed his personal sympathy and support. Milt Cole, owner of a small lumberyard in Indiana, experienced a devastating fire that essentially destroyed all of his equipment, facilities, and 1.5 million board feet of warehoused lumber. Even as the fire burned, however, Cole made an immediate and unequivocal commitment to continue to pay his workers as he rebuilt the plant. Cole's response was rooted in a personal sense of commitment to his workers and an instinctual entrepreneurial response to rebuild. Probably the best-known case of a virtuous response to an organizational crisis involved the owner of the textile company Malden Mills. Aaron Feuerstein was 79 when a fire threatened to destroy the company that had been in his family for three generations. As the fire continued to burn, Feuerstein stepped forward to make an unequivocal commitment to continue to pay his workers, even though the future of his company was unclear. Credibility, clear moral foundations, and a record of virtuous leadership may function much like a crisis plan, creating relationships and structures for support during a crisis and helping to clarify the organization's initial response.

HUMANISTIC ETHICS OF CARE

Humanism as a philosophical standpoint and value system cultivates an appreciation of the uniqueness of the human condition. Among the unique and essential features of humanity are the capacity to reason and think rationally and the ability to make ethical judgments. Therefore, behaviors, decisions, and processes that support these aspects of humanity would be considered ethical (Johannesen, 1996). Johnstone (1981) also noted that "a humanistic ethic requires that the individual be responsive in his or her actions to the impact that they might have on the humanity of those affected by the act" (p. 180). Humanism is the basis of much of the corporate-responsibility movement described earlier. The initial focus of the community

chest movement involved efforts to help those in need: the sick, the home-
less, the poor, the unemployed.

A humanistic orientation also requires that organizations be sensitive to
the harms that may be caused by their operations, including what would
happen in a crisis. Humanism, then, requires that organizations not only
seek to avoid harming others, but also to be prepared and to consider the
possibility of a crisis. This preparation, as described in chapter 9, includes
consideration of how harm could be limited and how victims would be
cared for after a crisis. In this way, humanism "advocates the social support and welfare of humankind, particularly those individuals facing
hardship, and often guides efforts to assist victims following a crisis"
(Seeger & Ulmer, 2001). This assistance may involve medical care, emergency shelter, counseling, and care of families when employees have been
injured. Following the death of an employee due to an organizational accident or workplace violence, many organizations provide financial assistance to the family. Psychological counseling for victims, their families,
and others affected is often part of a crisis response. A humanistic ethic for
crisis, then, requires attending to the physical, psychological, and emotional needs of those affected.

An additional humanistic orientation with implications for crisis is the
ethic of care. Care was initially described as a feminist reaction to traditional male-centered ethics of justice, usually framed in inflexible codes or
laws that emphasize rights. Carol Gilligan (1982) argued that because
women typically have stronger relational orientations and sensitivities, a
female morality emphasizes the needs and well-being of others. According
to Gilligan, morality is an essential responsibility to support and nurture
others, rather than a function of the rights of individuals. While a rights
approach might involve the application of a static set of impersonal and
inflexible rules, laws, and codes, care involves a set of flexible interpersonal
responses and accommodations. Compassion, nurturing, and empathy are
manifestations of a moral sense of relational responsibility, where individual interests and those of others intersect. These responses vary, based on
context and need. Care involves a highly individualized and flexible set of
moral obligations. Manning (1992) noted that the ethic of care specifically
requires a caring response to those whose need creates a human obligation
to respond. Care, in this sense, concerns attending to the needs of others
who suffer hardship, loss, and physical and emotional harm. In this sense,
the ethic of care has particular relevance to issues of crisis or disaster in
which victims have suffered physical and emotional harm.

Caring responses to large-scale crises are often undertaken by relief agencies, such as the American Red Cross. The Red Cross provides medical
assistance, food, shelter, counseling, and short-term financial assistance for
disaster victims. The Red Cross defines its mission as "the service of humanity" by "providing relief to victims of disasters" and helping people "pre-

vent, prepare for and respond to emergencies" (American Red Cross, 2002, www.redcross.org/home/). The Red Cross has been responding to human suffering and the need for care and support created by disasters, wars, and crises for more than one hundred years.

The ethics of humanism and care can be one of the most uplifting aspects of a crisis. Crisis often creates an opportunity for organizations and other groups and agencies to respond in humane and caring ways, to nurture others, and to ethically respond to human suffering. The 9/11 terrorist attacks were met with an outpouring of support from around the country and the world. The response was so strong and so immediate that it threatened to overwhelm the ability of agencies such as the Red Cross and the Federal Emergency Management Agency to cope with the influx of donations. Financial and blood donations, support of rescue agencies, scholarships for the children of victims, campaigns designed to encourage people to visit New York, and expressions of sympathy in a wide variety of venues helped to reaffirm a fundamental sense of a community of support and care. Among the programs was the Twin Towers Fund, established specifically to assist the families of the emergency workers, police officers, and firefighters who lost their lives in the disaster (http://www.twintowersfund.org). This program, along with many others, was an expression of a deep human drive to help others when they experience a devastating crisis. Such efforts may help the givers to vicariously participate in the recovery and renewal.

ORGANIZATIONAL LEGITIMACY

Legitimacy, as described in chapter 8, involves the normative evaluation of an organization by external groups and constituencies. External groups assess the degree to which an organization is operating in a just and worthy manner, consistent with larger social values. External groups, stakeholders, and communities pressure organizations to explain and justify their activities according to the "prevailing norms" of that larger community. In this way, organizations become "impregnated with community values" (Perrow, 1970, p. 191). Organizations are viewed as legitimate when they "establish congruence between the social values associated with or implied by their activities and the norms of acceptable behavior in the larger social system of which they are a part" (Dowling & Pfeffer, 1975, p. 122). Legitimacy, therefore, is conferred on the organization by external groups and agencies. In this way, organizations are pressured to conduct themselves in ways that are judged by these groups as ethical. Legitimacy as a general assessment of the appropriate and ethical conduct of an organization is associated with crisis in three ways: (1) in general assessments of the organization's image and reputation, (2) in postcrisis assessment and justification of the organization, and (3) in the case of ethics scandals as the genesis of crisis.

In order to create a sustained impression that an organization is legitimate, it must establish and continually reestablish a perception that it is operating in a manner consistent with and supportive of general social norms and values. Legitimacy is established by sustained communication seeking to persuade stakeholders that the organization is worthy of a positive assessment (Metzler, 2001). This general assessment of legitimacy is established in three broad domains: normative, through secondary outcomes, and through linkages (Seeger, 1997).

Organizations are expected to operate in a manner consistent with social norms. "Role performance" disputes over legitimacy develop when a discrepancy arises between organizational performance and social expectations (Metzler, 2001, p. 322). These discrepancies arise over profitability and fiscal responsibility, rational operations, and a variety of specific norms, such as environmentalism and fair treatment of employees. Enron, for example, lost legitimacy because it failed to comply with basic norms of accounting practice. The restaurant chain, Denny's, faced a crisis because it failed to comply with basic norms regarding the fair and equal treatment of minority customers. With regard to secondary outcomes, organizations make sustained arguments about the positive outcomes they create, such as jobs, contributing to tax bases, support of families and communities, and philanthropic activities. Pharmaceutical companies conduct image-advertising campaigns to emphasize their efforts to cure debilitating diseases, such as Alzheimer's, AIDS and diabetes. The tobacco industry has been one of the largest philanthropic contributors to the arts. Such activities are designed to enhance the impression that the organization is creating positive outcomes and thus is legitimate. Finally, in terms of linkages, organizations develop specific connections to legitimate organizations and individuals. These linkages may take the form of interconnecting boards of directors, advisory boards, or other associations. Organizations, for example, may be perceived as legitimate by creating connections to legitimizing individuals. Exxon appointed a prominent environmental scientist to its board of directors following the *Valdez* oil spill as a way of enhancing its legitimacy. General Motors, faced with criticism in the 1970s and 1980s over its operations in apartheid South Africa, appointed a prominent African American minister, the Reverend Leon Sullivan, to its board of directors.

The general impression regarding legitimacy is particularly important to an organization's ability to withstand a crisis. As discussed earlier, a positive reputation or strong sense of legitimacy represents a "reservoir of good will" that the organization may draw on in times of crisis. A legitimate organization is one that is worthy of support and has demonstrated its values to stakeholders. Stakeholders are thus willing to support the organization by speaking out, choosing to do business with the organization, and providing important resources. The "visit New York" campaign that followed 9/11 sought to draw on the larger perception that New York deserved support in its time of crisis.

As discussed in chapter 8, arguments over legitimacy are also often a significant part of the postcrisis stage. Crises are often dramatic and public, placing organizations "on the defensive" to demonstrate their legitimacy (Brummer, 1991). As part of the postcrisis assessment of blame and responsibility, organizations must also reestablish legitimacy. This loss of legitimacy following a crisis is critical to larger issues of organizational stability.

In cases of extreme inconsistency between expectations for appropriate conduct and actual behavior, the organization may experience a legitimacy crisis. These crises usually involve serious ethics scandals or perceptions of severe misconduct that fundamentally compromise legitimacy and managerial credibility and ultimately lead to a loss of public support. Important constituencies, such as customers and stockholders, often react to ethics scandals by withholding support and boycotting products. Overcoming these perceived radical incongruities between expectations and behavior often involves not only a sustained discourse of justification or explanation but often requires significant changes in the organization and its management. In this way, corrective actions discussed earlier, are designed to reestablish legitimacy by clearly and publicly demonstrating that the organization has learned from its wrongdoing.

Legitimacy crises are surprisingly common. The *Dateline NBC* General Motors C/K7 pickup scandal involved an instance in which a television news program rigged a fire on a pickup truck in order to demonstrate that these trucks were excessively prone to postimpact fires. *Dateline*, in its 1992 segment "Waiting to Explode," passed the footage off as an accurate demonstration and failed to give viewers any indication that the fires were staged. In this case, *Dateline* operated in a manner fundamentally inconsistent with the basic journalistic norms for accuracy, honesty, and full disclosure. Under threat of a multimillion-dollar lawsuit, *Dateline* aired a full public apology and made changes to its news staff and procedures (Ulmer, 1999). The sex-abuse scandal in the Catholic Church also involved a fundamental incongruity between norms of appropriateness and the conduct of certain priests and church officials. In this case, the priests and church officials appeared to be operating in contradiction to both traditional religious doctrine regarding protecting the innocent and laws against sexual abuse of minors. Many observers have suggested that the Catholic Church may suffer a serious reduction in its fund-raising as a consequence of the scandal. Moreover, the Church has been slow to adopt the kinds of serious corrective actions that would demonstrate that they have learned from their transgressions.

Legitimacy as a general normative evaluation of an organization is associated with almost all crises. In some cases, such as the *Dateline NBC* report or the Catholic Church scandal, it is the awareness of severe normative and value incongruity that triggers the crisis. Legitimacy is also a fundamental factor in the ability of the organization to recover. Organizations that are seen as "just and worthy" enjoy more support. A perception that an organization is not operating in a legitimate manner, however, may enhance the damage. Finally, corrective action is often necessary to realign organizations with social norms and reestablish legitimacy.

TRUTHFULNESS AND SIGNIFICANT CHOICE

As discussed earlier, a fundamental value-based norm of human interaction is truthfulness and honesty. Without some basic level of honesty in our interactions with others, it is impossible to coordinate activities, have meaningful relationships, or work toward common goals. Honesty and the development of trust are basic to all effective work relationships. The ethics of truthfulness and honesty are complex, however, as individuals seek to balance honesty with other values and consequences. For example, brutal honesty may create serious psychological harm to others. In fact, life-management lies, or so-called white lies, are used by everyone as ways of managing interpersonal relationships and perceptions (Bok, 1979, p. 58). Lying may be judged as ethically acceptable in order to avoid serious harm, to promote safety, or to avoid some risk. Political leaders often withhold information for reasons of national security and defense. Diplomats frequently parse words and subtly shade the truth to promote international harmony. Although the Federal Trade Commission protects consumers from most blatant lies, advertisers regularly portray products and services inaccurately in order to accentuate their appeal (Seeger, 1997).

Truthfulness, honesty, deception, and even lying become even more complex moral issues during a crisis. Bok (1979), for example, has suggested that the threat inherent in a crisis situation may provide a moral justification for lying or withholding information, particularly if doing so will save a life. In the case of a large-scale threat to public or national security, officials may withhold information from the public and justify these actions on the grounds that they are preventing panic and protecting public safety. Moreover, said Bok, "for those confronted with a crisis, there is little time to reflect on the consequences of various choices, making moral reasoning in such contexts more difficult" (p. 108). Crisis, when it creates a threat to survival, restricts human choice in much the same way as coercion. In these cases, individuals may effectively lose their freedom to choose. "Survival alone counts," in these contexts, and "lying may be justified on the grounds of a large survival value" (p. 113). Bok pointed out, however, that individuals are very quick to use "crisis" as a justification for lying. Too often, Bok wrote, "the word crisis becomes a sufficiently elastic term to suit every occasion for lies" (p. 121).

Deception is problematic in part because it restricts the freedom of the person being deceived. Lies place the liar in a power position over others by restricting the accuracy of the information to which others have access (Bok, 1979). Moreover, lying and deception deny the deceived the ability to make reasoned and informed choices. In the Union Carbide Bhopal disaster, for example, the company sought to manage the public perception of its insecticidal products by describing them as benign "plant medicines." This subtle description helped to reduce the level of public apprehension regarding the facility. This also meant that residents could not make fully informed choices about risks. Enron's deceptive accounting practices denied investors information about the real financial status of the company. They were unable to make fully informed choices about the value of company stock.

Withholding information as a form of deception may also deny individuals the ability to make informed judgments. This deception is more common in crisis than direct lies. Because crisis is a public event that places the organization under close scrutiny, the media often pressures the organization to release information very quickly. Organizations may choose to withhold information or temporarily postpone its release for a variety of ethically justifiable reasons. Airlines usually have policies mandating that families of victims be notified before passenger lists are disseminated to the press. School crisis plans sometimes include provisions to protect the privacy of students. Warnings about the possibility of terrorist threats, bomb threats, or general threats of violence have traditionally been withheld from the general public on the grounds that panic might result. In the post 9/11 context, however, pressure to notify the public of such threats led to new national policies and warning procedures. Organizations also may justify withholding proprietary information—information about products or processes that may compromise competitive position or increase legal liability. The ethical justification for withholding information on the grounds that it is proprietary is much more tenuous, particularly if the information is relevant to the ability of stakeholders to understand and make decisions about the crisis.

The idea that honesty and truthfulness are related to informed decision making and reasoning has been developed further in the concept of significant choice. In democratic systems, Nilsen (1974) noted, "the good is served by communication that insures adequate information, diversity of views, knowledge of alternative choices and their possible consequences" (p. 72). Therefore, debate, argument, disclosure of information, and solicitation of alternative views promote the ability of individuals to make rational choices about significant issues. The tobacco industry's systematic deception regarding the dangers of smoking included withholding information, releasing information designed to confuse the issue, and making knowingly false statements (Ulmer & Sellnow, 1997). This failure to be truthful about the dangers of smoking denied consumers critical information necessary to informing their decisions about smoking. The tobacco industry "illustrates some disturbing realities concerning how organizations can use their public discourse to diminish the deliberative ability" of audiences (Ulmer & Sellnow, 1997, p. 230). In another disturbing case, management for Jack-in-the-Box used a strategy of ambiguity during its *E. coli* crisis to privilege financial interests and stakeholders over others (Ulmer & Sellnow, 1997). Strategic ambiguity has been identified as a common organizational response used during postcrisis to diffuse and confuse responsibility. Strategic ambiguity may deny stakeholders access to information they need to make choices. Alternatively, in some cases, maintaining truthfulness and preserving choice during a crisis may require ambiguous responses. In the case of the Red River Valley floods, described in chapter 8, residents were misled, albeit unintentionally, by overly confident projections of water crests that did not reflect the uncertainty inherent in the system.

The ethics of significant choice have been bolstered by the emergence of the right to know as an information-based ethic (Seeger, 1997). The right to know suggests that individuals have rights to specific information about the risks they face, particularly when those risks are a function of agencies or organizations. The Occupational Safety and Health Administration, as part of its larger mission of mitigating workplace risks, has developed the Hazardous Communication Standard. This policy requires that chemical importers, manufacturers, and distributors notify workers exposed to hazards. In 1986, Congress passed the Community Emergency Planning and Right to Know Act. This act requires many organizations to disclose information regarding the amount and type of hazardous substances they release. The act is based on the premise that members of a community have a right to know what chemicals they may be exposed to and that this knowledge is necessary for effective emergency planning.

Ethics of truthfulness and honesty are complex, particularly within the high consequence-high uncertainty context of a crisis. During a crisis, information has a specific utility in empowering individual choice and decision making and in reducing or containing the level of harm. Withholding information, deceiving, use of strategic ambiguity, being certain when the situation does not merit certainty, or even lying to the public, therefore, require careful and specific moral justification. Moreover, such justification must go beyond the elastic definition of crisis to weigh the consequences of such dishonesty. Typically, such moral justification can only be made on the grounds of reducing or limiting additional harm, such as protecting life, avoiding panic, or protecting the privacy or psychological well-being of victims. In many instances, the severity of a crisis is significantly enhanced by the perception that the organization has been dishonest or withheld information for self-serving reasons. In contrast, the perception that the organization has been open, honest, and forthcoming with all relevant information may reduce the seriousness of a crisis and ultimately bolster the organization's image.

ADDITIONAL ETHICAL PERSPECTIVES

In addition to the five ethical frames outlined above, a number of other ethical perspectives and traditions may inform moral reasoning and decision making during crisis. Principles of equality are often relevant in post-crisis contexts, when stakeholders expect fair and equal treatment. Strategic ambiguity, for example, privileges some crisis stakeholders and concerns over others. Crises precipitated by charges of sexual harassment or discrimination, such as the Mitsubishi Motors Corporation case of 1996, are grounded in ethics of fairness and equality. When crises are international in nature, intercultural values often become important. The postcrisis investigation of the crash of Egypt Air Flight 990 was characterized by a high level of misunderstanding of cultural norms and values. Several cases of crisis have involved sweatshop working conditions in foreign manufacturing plants. Wal-Mart, K-Mart, Kathy Lee Gifford's apparel line, and the Nike Corporation have all experienced crises precipitated by this intersection of international values. The specific nature of the crisis may invigorate other specific ethics, values, and standards. The sex-abuse scandal in the Catholic Church involved a variety of religious principles and codes, including vows of celibacy for priests and provisions for protecting children. Religion often becomes part of the postcrisis process of healing, as described in chapter 8. Sometimes, the religious convictions of managers influence the crisis response. Aaron Feuerstein attributed much of his virtuous response to the teachings of Orthodox Judaism. Environmental ethics are usually associated with hazardous-material spills. As this discussion illustrates, crisis is a complex moral domain where a wide variety of values and ethics intersect in unanticipated and dynamic ways. New ethics, values, and standards often emerge as a consequence of crisis, forcing organizations to traverse entirely new moral territory. The need to find a path through such territory may compound the harm, particularly if the organization has not previously considered and clarified its moral foundations.

CONCLUSION

Crisis is a high consequence-high uncertainty context that challenges the ability of decision makers to engage in moral reasoning. Crises create complex and equivocal ethical and moral issues for both organizations and their stakeholders. Values clash, and often there is no time to consider the various ethical dimensions and consequences of a decision. During a crisis, the organization's basic moral stance is often publicly displayed and critiqued. At the same time, however, many important ethical issues are dismissed using the elastic justification of a crisis context. In many instances, ethical issues are overlooked or ignored during a crisis, causing additional harm and leaving the organization open to further criticism. In other cases, it is a serious lapse in ethical judgment on the part of organizational participants or senior managers that precipitates a crisis, calling into question the basic legitimacy of an organization. The ethical issues of crisis, as with ethics in other contexts, involve balancing and prioritizing a set of competing values. This requires discussing and debating moral issues in a way that allows for their full exploration. Doing so before a crisis may help the organization respond in a more ethically appealing manner.

CHAPTER 13

Crisis and Leadership

Leadership processes are closely associated with both organizational successes and dramatic failures. Leaders inculcate and personify many of the organization's values and set the overall tone and direction of the organization. During a crisis, a leader often becomes the organization's public face, playing a critical role by providing information and explaining the crisis to stakeholders and the larger public. Crisis frequently requires that leaders respond to accusations of wrongdoing, justify and explain choices, and offer personal assurances that problems will be corrected. Leadership frequently frames the larger meaning of the crisis, which may be necessary for followers to begin the initial sensemaking process that ultimately leads to coordinated, harm-reducing actions. In addition, the leader may establish an overall tone for the crisis by remaining calm, personifying authority and control, and reinforcing core values. Leadership, therefore, is one of the most important and most visible organizational roles in the aftermath of a crisis.

This chapter examines the role of leadership in preparing for and responding to crises. Within the extensive body of leadership research are several orientations to effective crisis leadership. What follows is a discussion of the importance of leadership to the successful management of crisis. First, general guidelines for effective crisis leadership in terms of both form and content are proposed. Second, leadership theories are examined for implications regarding crisis, including leader traits, styles, contingencies, and symbolic leadership. Specific functions of leadership during crisis are also explored. Chaos theory and leadership virtue ethics are proposed as larger methods for approaching crisis leadership. This chapter concludes with a summary of crisis leadership and a review of implications for leadership and crisis management.

GUIDELINES FOR CRISIS LEADERSHIP

Leadership, because of its visibility and the uncertainty of the situation, has a particularly important role in framing the initial meaning of a crisis trigger event. Hearing from a leader helps to reduce some of the crisis-induced uncertainty, confusion, and perceived threat (Seeger, Vennette, Ulmer, & Sellnow, 2002). In addition, leaders play a critical role in setting the tone and initial trajectory of the organizational response (Weick, 1988). Specific guidelines and recommendations for crisis leadership have been offered (Coombs, 1999b; Mitroff, 2001; Valle, 2001). These guidelines concern both what leaders should communicate and how they should communicate in the aftermath of a crisis.

Form Recommendations

Form recommendations concern what a leader should do after a crisis. For instance, showing concern for victims and visiting the scene of the event is often identified as a basic leader response to a crisis. (Coombs, 1999b). When Exxon chief executive officer (CEO) W. D. Stevens failed to visit the scene of the *Valdez* spill, many of the crisis stakeholders were frustrated. Conversely, when Aaron Feuerstein stood in front of his burning textile manufacturing plant and pledged to rebuild, he symbolized his commitment in the face of the disaster. Visiting the scene of the crisis is often a critical step for effective crisis leadership. President George W. Bush's visit to ground zero following the 9/11 attacks illustrated to New Yorkers that the city was safe and that he was personally connected to the devastation. President Jimmy Carter visited the Three Mile Island nuclear power plant, even before the crisis was fully contained. Leaders, by visiting the scene, provide symbolic attention and often direct media attention to the crisis. Active attention of the leader may provide comfort and reassurance to those affected, help reconstitute a sense of normalcy, and help leverage resources for mitigation. CEOs, by virtue of their status, are perceived to be "in charge," and their visible involvement in the response signals that the event is being taken seriously. On the other hand, a CEO's visit may sometimes be inappropriate. The CEO of Union Carbide, Warren Anderson, was arrested by the Indian government when he tried to visit the site of the Bhopal explosion. In this case, Anderson symbolized for Indians the failure of Union Carbide to operate safely. In other cases, the visits of officials may distract workers from recovery efforts. Visiting the scene is generally an effective form of crisis leadership, provided other contingencies are taken into account.

In addition to visiting the scene, having a formal leader designated as a crisis spokesperson is important. Typically, the CEO serves as spokesperson, but occasionally, as described in chapter 10, this responsibility falls to another prominent manager or crisis team leader. The nature of crisis, associated communication exigencies, and the relative communication skills of the executives are important considerations in selecting a spokesperson. Harry Pearce, for example, was part of the General Motors (GM) legal counsel when *Dateline NBC* attacked GM for selling supposedly defective pickup trucks. In a news conference successfully rebutting *Dateline's* accusations, Pearce offered a well-crafted argument accusing *Dateline* of deception. Pearce's skill in building an argument using a variety of data sources was particularly important in this crisis. Regardless of who is selected, the spokesperson should go out of his or her way to be open and accessible. Mayor Rudy Giuliani's daily press conferences following the 9/11 attacks enhanced his status as an effective crisis leader by signaling his openness and demonstrating his active involvement and personal control of the situation. In general, a leader should be visible, attentive, open, and responsive during a crisis.

Content Recommendations

In addition to issues of form, several important content issues concern the communication of leaders during a crisis (Coombs, 1999b; Mitroff, 2001; Valle, 2001). Content refers to the actual response the leader provides following a crisis. Use of a single spokesperson such as the CEO, for example, helps to create a unified message. Moreover, leaders' responses should be honest, open, and communicated as quickly as possible. Leaders are often criticized for delayed responses to crisis. An immediate and open response has a greater probability of resolving the crisis quickly. However, leaders should also recognize that these statements might become public commitments to a particular interpretation and course of action. After the 9/11 attacks, the CEO of brokerage company Cantor Fitzgerald made public statements regarding his desire to continue to pay salaries to those workers killed in the World Trade Center tragedy. It soon became evident that Cantor Fitzgerald was in a precarious financial position and might not be able to fulfill those obligations. The CEO recanted and as a consequence was severely criticized. Eventually, the company was able to fulfill the obligations it had made to the workers' families, but the early, albeit supportive and honest, response created additional confusion and conflict in the midst of an already threatening and chaotic situation.

Clearly, leadership can have a positive or negative impact on the development of a crisis. Leadership can be a positive force by helping to frame the meaning of a crisis event, expressing appropriate concern and support, overseeing mitigation, coordinating support, and facilitating timely, open communication. In many cases, however, crisis leadership is characterized by strategies minimizing harm, denying responsibility, and shifting the blame, as was the case with W. D. Stevens, of Exxon, and Kenneth Lay, of Enron. In these cases, the CEO's response to the crisis reduced the organization's credibility and compounded the harm. In contrast, responses such as Aaron Feuerstein's and Mayor Giuliani's exemplify a positive form of crisis leadership. These responses reduce confusion and help create support for the crisis recovery.

These examples are helpful in providing models of effective and ineffective crisis leadership. They also point to some specific behaviors that are helpful during a crisis. The larger question regarding what constitutes effective crisis leadership is more fully addressed through an examination of the three major approaches to organizational leadership: traits, style, contingency, and symbolic leadership and through the functions of crisis leadership (see Table 13.1).

ORGANIZATIONAL LEADERSHIP

Leadership, from a variety of perspectives, is a large and diverse area of study. Despite this, much about this critical process remains unclear (Smircich & Morgan, 1982). Generally, leadership is described as the process of influencing others to achieve goals (Northouse, 2001; Yukl, 2002). Leaders personify organizations, motivate followers, clarify the desired methods of operation, frame events in meaningful ways, and provide a vision of where the organization is moving. Whether though direc-

Table 13.1
Factors in Crisis Leadership

Leadership Approach	Crisis Leadership Functions/Characteristics
Traits	High tolerance for stress and uncertainty.
	Experience with crisis.
	Communication skills.
	Decisiveness.
	Credibility/virtue.
Style	Directive, decisive and authoritarian.
	Open to information, input, feedback and critique.
Contingency	Flexible, matched to the dynamics of the crisis.
	Task oriented with regard to crisis response.
	Relational focus with regard to stakeholder needs.
Symbolic	Acts toward crisis in a way that frames meaning and leads to harm reduction.
	Maintains responses that match inherent uncertainty of the situation.
	Provide information, comfort support, and reassurance.
	Serves as a symbol of order and authority.
	Serves to leverage resources.

tives, charisma, or by example, leaders play an important role in setting the direction of an organization and specifying how the organization achieves its goals. The popularity of autobiographical books by such recognized corporate leaders as Lee Iacocca and, more recently, Jack Welch, suggests that understanding effective leadership is important to understanding larger questions of organizational effectiveness. Success is generally attributed to leaders based on the belief that they are directly in control of their organizations. Moreover, leaders are frequently terminated because they are personally blamed for organizational crises or failures. A change in leadership is often used to signal organizational change and provide new direction in the wake of a scandal or crisis.

Systematic investigation into organizational leadership generally began with trait approaches that emphasized the leader's identifiable characteristics. Interest in leadership styles soon followed. Contingency approaches emerged in an effort to connect leader style to the specific situation. Recently, researchers have begun exploring the symbolic dimensions of leadership. Each of these approaches has implications for understanding how leadership functions in crisis.

Leadership Traits

The trait approach is grounded in the notion that leadership is tied to personal qualities, identifiable characteristics, or traits. These traits may include a drive to take responsibility, originality in problem solving, willingness to tolerate frustration, and the ability to influence others (Stogdill, 1974). Early research into leader traits focused on the general abilities of leaders as well as personality characteristics (Barge, 1994). General abilities emphasize things such as high intelligence, greater knowledge, and more technical competence. Personality characteristics include qualities such as alertness, emotional control, extroversion, initiative, insightfulness, integrity, originality, self-confidence, and sense of humor. Leaders and followers, then, are distinguished from one another by the inherent traits they possess and the characteristics they personify. Leader traits, according to this view, are not context specific. That is, the traits of leader effectiveness are universal for all conditions of leadership.

This notion of universal leader traits has been challenged on a number of grounds. The traits of effective leadership described in this approach are either very general skill sets or are general physical attributes bordering on stereotypes. For example, leaders are most often identified as tall men of moderately high intelligence who have strong social skills. Moreover, the importance of specific traits appears to vary widely with context. For instance, a leader with certain attributes, such as a sense of humor or strong social orientation, might be more important in some group or organizational contexts than in others. Because crisis management is a narrower subset of leadership, it is useful to delineate a set of traits that logically might be more important during a crisis.

As discussed throughout this book, crisis managers must deal with the confusion and uncertainty of crisis situations. Crisis leaders, then, need the ability to both resolve and function under conditions of confusion and uncertainty. Traits such as high tolerance for stress and calmness are particularly important in crisis. Calmness in these contexts is sometimes described as infectious. In addition, the ability to see situations from diverse perspectives, a sense of personal control, a sense of responsibility to stakeholders, and self-confidence are traits of effective crisis leadership. During a crisis, leaders are often called on to be public spokespersons and must be agile in their response to the media. Crisis leaders must be able to act quickly under conditions of high stress and uncertainty. These traits emphasize the importance of critical thinking as well as self-confidence in decision-making ability. One very specific trait of effective crisis leadership is previous experience with a crisis. Leaders and managers who have experienced a crisis may be more comfortable with the uncertainty and stress of the situation. Crisis leaders with a well-developed sense of personal integrity and values may also be able to act more decisively during crisis. In this way, the trait approach to crisis management is closely tied to a virtue ethics. Virtues, as discussed in chapter 12, are character traits that leaders may use to make quick decisions during a crisis.

Leadership Styles

The style approach to leadership focuses on the specific sets of related behaviors leaders exhibit. Styles generally vary according to consideration of structural and task issues, such as work assignments, organization, and task definition, and consideration of social issues, such as cohesion, trust, and liking. In general, three major leadership styles have been described: authoritarian, democratic, and laissez-faire (Northouse, 2001; Yukl, 2002). Authoritarian leaders exhibit high levels of direct control. These leaders usually develop clear and rigid reporting relationships and make decisions quickly, generally without the benefit of consultation or input from followers. In this way, authoritarian decision making is sometimes judged as more decisive, resolute, and directive. Democratic leaders, in general, share responsibility and authority with others through consensus and participatory decision methods. Democratic leaders generally solicit input, information, and opinions from followers. The decision-making process under democratic leadership often takes longer, with more potential for conflict. However, more information and perspectives are brought to the decision-making process under democratic styles. The conflict may enhance the critique of information and the quality of decisions. Finally, laissez-faire leaders are nondirective and delegate a significant amount of authority to others. Laissez-faire leaders are usually described as nonleaders who tend to abdicate their supervisory and management duties. Laissez-faire leaders typically have high levels of trust that subordinates will accomplish the task appropriately with little or no supervision. In extreme cases, laissez-faire leaders may become disconnected from the responsibilities of their organization.

Democratic leadership styles are generally preferred during the day-to-day operations of most organizations. These methods empower employees and create greater problem-solving capacity throughout the organization. In addition, they make fuller use of the insights, information, and creativity of followers. A more authoritarian style, in contrast, may be appropriate for crisis situations. Crises typically demand quick decisions under threatening circumstances. Leaders often have to act quickly following a crisis to contain harms and to ensure that subordinates have a clear sense of how the organization is responding. Moreover, there may be some benefit to creating an impression of decisiveness and reiterating authority during the confusion and uncertainty of crisis. Followers generally are willing to grant leaders more authority and control in threatening circumstances. The quality of decisions, however is still a function of the amount and quality of information accessed. Regardless of the style, leaders should actively resist the urge to cut themselves off from important sources of information during a crisis. Even during the restricted time frame of a crisis, leaders should take time to closely consult followers and stakeholders.

Contingency Theory

Contingency theory is based on efforts to match leadership styles to the task situation. It assumes that particular patterns or styles of leader behavior will be effective in some situations but not others. Fiedler (1967), for example, described leader situations according to three task elements: leader-member relations, task structure, and position power. Leader-member relations may be good or bad. Tasks may be structured or unstructured. Leaders may have high or low position power. He suggested that these factors created a continuum of situations ranging from highly favorable to leadership, to highly unfavorable to leadership. Leaders with high task orientations, such as authoritarian or directive styles of leadership, are more successful when the situations are either very favorable or very unfavorable to the leader. The middle ranges of somewhat favorable, according to Fiedler, are best matched to a leader with a more relationally orientated style, such as is often found in democratic leadership styles.

Contingency theory provides support for several of the previously discussed approaches to crisis leadership in that more-directive leadership or authoritarian styles appear to be better suited to crisis situations. Crisis is a

challenging leadership environment. Task situations are generally unstructured, and relations with followers are often strained. Moreover, the leader's
authority is often confused. Crisis also creates a reduced time frame for consultation, building consensus, and explaining and justifying decisions and
actions. Relationship dimensions of leadership, however, are also important
during crisis. For instance, leaders who fail to pay attention to important
relationships after a crisis may overlook important stakeholder needs. These
may in turn complicate the ability to resolve a crisis. Supportiveness, understanding, expressions of concern, and empathic responses are some of the
most salient aspects of postcrisis leadership. Moreover, effective crisis leadership often reaffirms core values and relationships. The contingencies of crisis leadership are, therefore, particularly complex, requiring a strong task
orientation while also attending to important relational concerns. Contingency views also emphasize the need to maintain leader flexibility in light of
what is an inherently dynamic and equivocal situation. Unforeseen issues
almost always arise during a crisis, calling for additional contingent behaviors on the part of the leader.

Symbolic Leadership

A fourth approach to leadership has recently emerged that emphasizes
the qualitative and symbolic dimensions of the leader's activities. The
interpretive and cultural approach suggests that organizations are constructed from symbolic processes. Leaders, then, are strategic conductors
or framers of organizational meaning (Fairhurst & Starr, 1996; Pfeffer,
1981; Smircich & Morgan, 1982). Leaders play an important role in creating and maintaining meaning in organizations through framing of events
and through the personification of meaning systems and core values. For
instance, Schein (1991) discussed the important role of founders in the
development of organizational meaning and culture. Founders often
make decisions based on their own cultural history and experiences. The
organization's basic culture, then, is often determined by the personality,
perspective, and values the founder brings to the day-to-day activities of
managing. These are passed on to subsequent generations of leaders. The
industry, physical location, nature of the product, and the technology also
play an important role in determining the organizational culture.

The management of the culture by subsequent generations of leaders of
the organization is accomplished through strategically identifying and
personifying organizational values, rituals, myths, and symbol systems.
The symbolic dimensions of leadership involve defining social action and
framing meaning for stakeholders. Framing, according to Fairhurst and
Starr (1996), is the leader process of determining "the meaning of a subject...to make sense of it, to judge its character and significance" (p. 3).
Framing involves the assertion of a particular interpretation of an event

over other interpretations. Leaders thus help interpret organizational activities and provide a vision for where the organization is going and what action members should take. Leaders have a powerful role in creating the corporate culture and its attendant meaning systems. They can have a strong impact on how organizational members view what they are experiencing in the organization. In addition, leaders are in a position to articulate clear value positions for the organization. How organizational leaders label and act toward events or situations, for example, influences the meaning organizational stakeholders have for the situation. Because meaning often is a precursor for coordinated action, framing is often necessary for followers to begin taking strategic action. This need for meaning is greater in chaotic situations such as crises.

Symbolic crisis leadership involves acting toward an event in a way that frames meaning and facilitates harm-reducing action, while maintaining responses that are sufficiently general to match the inherent uncertainty of the situation. This represents a significant challenge for leaders facing a crisis. As discussed earlier in this chapter, participants in a crisis look to leaders to reduce uncertainty, clarify meaning, and provide information, comfort, support, and reassurance. How a leader behaves during a crisis early in its development will have a profound impact on how the organization and its stakeholders view the event. From this perspective, it is important to examine how leaders enact a situation and its impact on the tenor of the crisis as it develops.

Moreover, leaders must also be aware that their interpretations must compete with other interpretations of the crisis. The leader's interpretation of the crisis must be compelling in the sense that it is plausible, coherent, and facilitates appropriate action. Smircich and Stubbard (1985) referred to the winner of this competition as the individual who can reach "critical mass" in terms of acceptance of his or her beliefs. This critical mass depends on persuasion and interpretation much more than on the objective facts (p. 733).

Beyond enactment, a leader is a symbol of order and authority. As a consequence, merely being present, visibly engaged, and accessible during a crisis is reassuring. Moreover, symbolic leadership may be necessary to leverage harm-reducing resources. Leaders, by virtue of their positions, can often gain access to resources that would not otherwise be available. Even during precrisis, a leader may provide symbolic attention to issues of crisis planning and thus encourage followers to take planning seriously. In addition, leaders who are successful in managing a crisis—such as Mayor Giuliani, or Montgomery, Maryland's, chief of police, Charles Moose, who led the Washington, D.C., sniper investigation—symbolize successful crisis responses and consequently may increase their own credibility, visibility, and stature. Aaron Feuerstein, widely praised for his commitment to workers and the community and acknowledged by President Bill Clinton in a state of the union address, is often called on to comment on issues of corporate responsibility. These leaders all came to symbolize successful crisis management.

These theoretical orientations to the complex aspects of organizational leadership are useful not only for the routine, day-to-day functioning of leaders but also for the aberrant and novel conditions of crisis. As discussed in chapter 1, crises immediately create high levels of threat and surprise and restrict response time. New stakeholders arise and become prominent in the wake of a crisis. Similarly, stakeholder needs for information and communication differ following a crisis. In essence, the constraints and expectations for leadership in crisis situations are typically quite different than those required for routine operations. Moreover, effective leadership is clearly a central process in the successful management of a crisis.

Functional Approaches

In addition to the approaches described above, it is also possible to characterize crisis leadership by examining what leaders actually do during crisis events. Mayor Giuliani, for example, was widely praised for his leadership following the 9/11 attacks on the World Trade Center. Not only was Giuliani accessible to the media, but he remained both calm and decisive in what was one of the most stressful and threatening crises to ever strike the United States. Giuliani was attentive to the needs and concerns of victims, yet vigilant and directive in his efforts to restore order.

In a speech at the University of Minnesota, Giuliani described six principles of leadership that guided his management of the 9/11 crisis (speech given September 16, 2002, University of Minnesota). First, he suggested that leadership in such situations is most effective when it is supported by a philosophy, religion, set of beliefs, or ideology that is clearly evident to followers. These beliefs promote clarity and may help followers understand what to do. Such values-based responses are similar to the concepts of virtue ethics described in chapter 12. Second, Giuliani emphasized the importance of optimism. Optimism, he noted, is forward-looking, promotes calmness, and reduces maladaptive reactions. Crisis leadership, in this way, is prospective, projecting recovery and promoting followers to work for renewal. Throughout the crisis, Giuliani remained confident that the city would recover from the event and encouraged residents to return to normal as soon as possible. He personally asked business leaders and New York–based performers to return to normal operations. In addition, Giuliani concluded that an effective crisis leader must be courageous and manage the inevitable fear associated with the crisis. Fear may be debilitating, slowing responses and reducing the credibility followers place in the leader and in remedial actions. One memorable video clip of the World Trade Center collapse showed Mayor Giuliani calmly leading his staff away as the buildings fell behind him. He was reportedly looking for a safer location to set up his crisis-coordinating efforts. The fourth principle Giuliani described is preparation. "It really is up to leaders to think about this [preparation] all the time. That's the responsibility of a leader prepare, prepare, prepare, prepare again. Think about the worst that could happen" (speech given September 16, 2002, University of Minnesota). Effective preparation and planning, as described in chapter 9, requires commitment from top management. A fifth principle is teamwork. Teamwork allows for the application and coordination of specialized skills and knowledge to the management of the crisis. Simply stated, crisis leaders must rely on others. A final key skill in crisis leadership, according to Giuliani, is communication. Crisis communication is not only about words, but also "about actions, deeds, examples" (speech given September 16, 2002, University of Minnesota). In other words, the behavior of the leader during crisis has important symbolic dimensions.

In addition to the six functions described by Mayor Giuliani, other leadership functions are associated with the stages of precrisis, crisis, and postcrisis. A list of these crisis leadership functions is presented in Table 13.2.

During precrisis, for example, a leader's primary crisis responsibilities involve preparation, usually through the crisis management planning process described in chapter 9 and through developing a positive image and reputation. This reputation is helpful in enhancing credibility, legitimacy, and the organization's overall "reservoir of good will" that can then be drawn on during a crisis. Moreover, the leader is responsible for establishing and maintaining an appropriate level of risk vigilance within the organization. This may involve, for example, empowering employees to both recognize and call attention to deficiencies or emerging risks. Followers should be encouraged to communicate warnings. Leaders may also publicly advocate risk vigilance, invest in programs of risk reduction, and make issues of risk and threat part of the organization's overall decision-making process.

The crisis management aspects of leadership are most visible during the crisis phase. This is the point at which followers may have lost standard sensemaking and interpretive structures and at which the leader must provide some clarity regarding the situation. Effective crisis leadership at this stage is often value driven, grounded in core beliefs and established virtues. Initially, the leader must activate the crisis management plan, with its attendant structures and processes, and work to both contain and reduce harm. He or she must also engage in symbolic activities, such as framing the meaning of the event and expressing concern for those harmed, while remaining calm and conveying a sense of order and control. As part of this process, it is important that the leader remain visible through activities such as tours of the site, meeting with families, and regular press conferences. A variety of instrumental functions during the cri-

Table 13.2
Functions of Crisis Leadership

Precrisis
    Maintains risk vigilance
    Prepares and helps others prepare
    Establishes positive image, credibility and reputation
    Develops instrumental communication channels with stakeholders
Crisis
    Initiates response/activates crisis plan
    Facilitates mitigation of harm
    Serves as spokesperson
    Expresses sympathy for those harmed
    Frames meaning
    Remains accessible and open
    Facilitates information flow
    Acts decisively
    Coordinates/links with crisis team and other groups and agencies
    Re-connects with stakeholders
    Maintains decisional vigilance
    Prioritizes activities and resources
    Communicates (reaffirms or activates) core values
    Pays symbolic attention to the crisis
    Maintains appropriate flexibility
    Facilitates renewal via public commitments
Postcrisis
    Offers explanations and/or apologies
    Facilitates investigations
    Commits to appropriate changes/signals willingness to change
    Creates prospective vision
    Participates in memorializing and grieving
    Facilitates learning
    Tells the story of the crisis

sis stage concern decision making, setting priorities, maintaining decisional vigilance, coordinating with the crisis teams and with other groups,
and facilitating flows of information. Although basic decisions may be
part of the crisis plan, the dynamic nature of the crisis will create unforeseen issues and problems. An effective crisis leader is decisive, acting
quickly and establishing priorities for actions and resources. James Lee
Witt, former director of the Federal Emergency Management Agency
(FEMA), suggested that crisis is essentially "a series of decisions you have
to make quickly, under intense pressure, with little chance to reflect or
research" (Witt & Morgan, 2002, p. 23). At the same time, however, the cri-

sis leader should remain open and accessible to followers, stakeholders, and sources of information and remain appropriately flexible and equivocal in light of the uncertainty of the crisis situation.

The crisis, then, is a time of competing demands and conflicting priorities. The leader is called on to do many things quickly, yet to be vigilant and careful in making choices and decisions. The leader must frame the meaning of the crisis and facilitate renewal through public commitments yet should maintain strategic flexibility. In addition, a crisis leader may be expected to be everywhere and do everything during a crisis. In the days following the World Trade Center attacks, Mayor Giuliani held press conferences at least daily; helped to coordinate recovery efforts, information collection, and contributions; met with visiting dignitaries from around the world; visited ground zero dozens of times; made a number of strategic decisions; and attended hundreds of funerals and memorial services.

These exceptional demands on the crisis leader begin to dissipate during the postcrisis stage. The leader engages in a number of symbolic and instrumental activities associated with recovery and renewal. Leaders may offer apologies and explanations as part of the image restoration processes. Renewal is usually initiated by a leader's compelling postcrisis vision. Leaders may be called on to testify about the event and their crisis management efforts. The leader helps the organization and other groups to learn from the crisis by retelling the story of the crisis, summarizing lessons, and reiterating important discoveries. He or she may offer a prospective postcrisis vision for the organization. Leaders also signal willingness to change and make appropriate commitments to change.

One of the signals of change that sometimes occurs during the postcrisis stage is a change in leadership. Shifts in top management are often important symbols of change, particularly when the crisis was precipitated by some failure in leadership or when the leader failed to manage the crisis successfully. In other cases, however, the leader is judged as a hero for the crisis management efforts. Mayor Giuliani was widely praised for his efforts following 9/11 and was described as "America's mayor." This praise occurred despite the fact that prior to 9/11 Giuliani had been criticized for his vigorous law enforcement efforts that were described by some as overly zealous and compromising civil rights.

This example reaffirms the fact that crisis leadership is highly contingent. Leader symbols, activities, styles, and traits appropriate during the routines of business as usual may not be suited for a crisis situation. Moreover, crises types, as described in chapter 3, vary widely. The kinds of leadership appropriate for an industrial accident will be different from those needed for an ethics scandal or financial crisis. In addition, leadership tends to be judged in retrospect by the outcome of the crisis. When a crisis is resolved successfully, leaders tend to get at least some of the credit, but crises that spin out of control also tend to be associated with the leader.

CHAOS THEORY AND CRISIS LEADERSHIP

As discussed in chapter 2, chaos theory (CT) has particular utility for understanding crisis. CT is also useful for understanding leadership in modern organizational contexts characterized by high levels of uncertainty, interactive complexity, and change. Wheatley (1999), for example, suggested that effective organizational leaders functioning within these contexts must abandon traditional notions of order and chaos. Organization is "a continual process where a system can leap into chaos and unpredictability" and yet be held stable within the parameters of order and predictability (p. 11). From this perspective, leaders should recognize that the organizational shape is more often a function of general concepts and values rather than invariable rules and structures. Effective leadership, in these circumstances, emphasizes contingent responses, flexibility, and accommodation while adhering to central principles of order, core values, and key relationships. Effective leadership, then, is a dynamic, accommodating, and value-based process rather than a static system of controls and constraints.

This emphasis on values and relationships suggests that communication and relational development are the critical processes of a chaos-based view of leadership. Accordingly, leaders should engage with the organization's environment in ways that lead to the development of relationships with key stakeholders (Wheatley, 1999, p. 37). Moreover, clarification and articulation of core values helps to create a basis of order for complex and chaotic organizations. These core values are reflected in the organization's culture. Values may take on fractal patterns, manifest throughout the organization's basic "ways of doing business." According to Wheatley, a kind of value-based "self-similarity is found in its people, in spite of the complex range of roles and levels" (p. 132). Leaders should work to manage their organizations and motivate employees through conceptual understanding and broad systems of meaning, not through narrow rules or structures. These values and relationships may have particular value as strange attractors helping to reconstitute order following a crisis. The leader's job is to activate, make explicit, or privilege these values and relationships in ways that contribute to the reemergence of order and a return to normalcy. Guiding visions, clear values, and underlying organizational beliefs are the basic touchstones of order that individuals can use to shape and coordinate their behavior, even during a crisis.

CT also emphasizes the interconnectedness between the organization and its larger environment, including stakeholders. The value-based attractors discussed above function both within and outside of the organization. Organizations have specific value-based relationship with stakeholders that serve as the basis for the organization's legitimacy. As discussed earlier, legitimacy is a function of primary and secondary outcomes the organization creates, such as products and jobs, or linkages to values and to other legitimate organizations, or by virtue of operating according to norms of acceptable conduct. In many ways, organizations can be understood as complex networks of claims and obligations, mutual interdependencies, and responsibilities with stakeholders. This network, established long before a crisis, can serve as source of critical support during a crisis. A leader's job is not only to nurture this network before a crisis, but also to activate the network during a crisis.

Leaders should regularly work during precrisis to demonstrate their value to stakeholders. This includes cultivating a positive image, building and protecting a positive reputation, and ensuring consistency. Effective leaders also work to expand the basis of their legitimacy by creating mutually beneficial networks or support. They should consistently remind stakeholders of core values and reiterate the value premise of the organization. By doing so, the leader builds the broad-based legitimacy and reservoir of goodwill that may be drawn on during a crisis.

A CT-based view of leader effectiveness during a crisis, then, emphasizes the development of resilient organizational processes in a precrisis environment. The development and communication of core values and cultivation of positive stakeholder relations are necessary for both responding quickly and effectively. Moreover, they are instrumental to recovery and ultimately to renewal.

LEADER VALUES AND VIRTUES

The ethical frameworks detailed in chapter 12 emphasize the role of leadership virtues during organizational crisis. Ethical issues are endemic to leadership whenever choices have consequences for employees, members of the community, stockholders, suppliers, customers, and a variety of other stakeholders. In fact, organizational leaders have extensive networks of ethical and moral obligations concomitant to the scope, size, and nature of their organizations. Leaders are representatives of various groups and have associated obligations to represent the needs, concerns, interests, and values of those groups.

Leadership virtues and character serve as predictable standards for conduct. Leadership helps determine which behaviors will be privileged and valued and helps to establish and maintain the organization's larger ethical climate. Virtue ethics focus on the pattern of the leader's behavior in the role as leader and its relationships to accepted standards for integrity, honesty, truthfulness, and responsiveness. Virtues, and the values they embody, then become forces of organizational order and predictability. This view of leader virtues, however, differs somewhat from the trait theories discussed earlier in that virtues are not necessarily innate. Rather, they are derived through experience, practice, and learning. In fact, a number of researchers have described the process of moral development as one in which individuals learn to follow more-principled standards of ethical conduct.

One way in which learning about ethics occurs is through modeling. Leaders serve as models for moral conduct for followers and other observers. Leaders have particular responsibilities for modeling and establishing an organization's ethical climate and moral tone (Simms & Brinkmann, 2002; Seeger & Ulmer, 2003). Leaders are role models who regularly demonstrate standards and virtues in both the routines of organizational life and in the critical incidents that organizations sometimes encounter. The routine ethical standards and norms of organizational life are acted out and reaffirmed on a day-to-day or routine basis. These may involve short-term efforts to resolve contained ethical problems in the organization, such as correcting isolated incidents of discrimination, dealing with cases of sexual harassment, or addressing petty theft. Through these routine efforts and sustained discussion of values and standards, moral work climates are created. Occasionally, however, a nonroutine incident occurs with greater moral weight, such as during a crisis (Seeger & Ulmer, 2003). These episodes create the opportunity for the leader both to publicly demonstrate moral conduct and to learn (Sitkin, 1996). Crises often take on a significant moral character and serve as opportunities to clearly display and reaffirm ethics for both organizational members and stakeholders. Crises also sometimes create clear opportunities for moral choice regarding such things as treatment of victims, compensation, and acceptance of responsibility. Character is often developed through these moral challenges and choices.

Virtue ethics, and the study of character, can be important in understanding crisis responses. Johannesen (2001) explained that "virtues guide the ethics of our communication when careful or clear deliberation is not possible" (p.11). Since crises are typically characterized by uncertainty and equivocality, basic values and virtues should have an impact on how leaders instinctively respond to crises. Critical to this notion is the fact that leader virtues are typically established before the crisis. From this perspective, leaders often have little time and information to create a response. Hence, virtue ethics provides a useful approach to understanding how leaders may respond to crises quickly. Moreover, virtuous responses may compel and motivate followers. As Mayor Giuliani suggested, responding from a clear moral or value perspective promotes clarity by signaling what is important and creating a common basis for action.

Lessons regarding the role of virtues may be found in examples, however rare, of ethical responses to a crisis (Seeger & Ulmer, 2001). We have described as virtuous the responses of Malden Mills owner Aaron Feuerstein and Cole Hardwoods owner Milt Cole. Although organizational crises are typically characterized by accusations of wrongdoing and responsibility, these two CEOs responded almost spontaneously from well-established personal value systems. Both Feuerstein and Cole responded immediately from value positions, reducing the uncertainty regarding the crisis and the potential harm for stakeholders. In both instances, these leaders built postcrisis responses on a strong sense of corporate responsibility, community, and employee commitments established long before the crisis. Phil Knight, CEO of Nike, responded to criticism of company manufacturing practices with comprehensive changes to ensure the safety of workers. Although this response was much less spontaneous, the sweeping nature of the changes indicated a fundamental commitment to be responsible to the health and safety of workers. Similarly, the Schwan's food-borne illness case, described in chapter 7, was a response to a crisis based on a fundamental set of values and relationships. In this case, the relationships and values concerned a long-term commitment to customers. Witt noted that leaders who know, practice, and communicate their values are able to act more decisively in the face of a crisis, in part because they have a clear sense of what is most important (Witt & Morgan, 2002).

Virtue ethics provide a much-needed ethical grounding for understanding the role of leadership in crisis. As noted in chapter 12, crisis is a moment of high moral tension at which questions of value take on added significance. This is in part a consequence of the vulnerability of stakeholders during a crisis. Moreover, this view provides linkages between leadership during normal business operations and crisis situations. Virtue ethics suggest that character and values are cultivated and developed over time, often long before the crisis begins. The crisis situation then exposes the leader's character and values in highly dramatic and public ways. From this perspective, values serve to link crisis leadership to the routines of organizational leadership. The relationships that leaders have with stakeholders prior to a crisis and the core values they advocate and enact have direct implications for how the leader responds in the aftermath of a crisis. Moreover, a leader who has cultivated relationships and a positive image with stakeholders has additional resources available for responding to a crisis.

CONCLUSION

Leadership is a critical process in the management of crisis. During a crisis, leaders play a particularly important role in making sense of and framing the events for both internal and external stakeholders. By remaining calm and acting from value positions, leaders may respond more effectively. Leadership theory, including trait, style, and contingency theory, suggests a variety of features, behaviors, and processes that have particular relevance to crisis. Moreover, the symbolic approach to crisis leadership is particularly important given the high uncertainty of a crisis. Crisis leadership may also be described by what leaders actually do in these situations. This includes specific behaviors during precrisis, crisis, and postcrisis. Chaos theory and virtue ethics suggest that leaders facing crisis may be able to respond effectively by activating core values and key relationships. These values and relationships should be cultivated before the crisis. Doing so also creates a reservoir of good will that may help the organization respond more effectively to a crisis.

CHAPTER 14

The Role of Crisis in Society

Crises are an inevitable stage in the organizing process. Although no sensible or rational organization would invite crisis, there is ample evidence to suggest that the extreme discomfort and uncertainty that cause organizations to abhor crises also offers opportunities that may benefit organizations and society. The 9/11 terrorist attacks, for example, were forces of significant social change. Lapses in surveillance inspired the federal government to seek greater coordination among the Central Intelligence Agency (CIA) and the Federal Bureau of Investigation (FBI) and increase its ability to sense threats and respond more effectively. Changes were also made to enhance the communication networks and coordination among the nation's agricultural, shipping, immigration, emergency management, and customs agencies. The horrific acts of 9/11 inspired sweeping changes that, in the flow of typical government bureaucracy, would never have been possible. Although the crisis deeply scarred America, the ongoing learning and adaptation have already initiated significant changes in broader notions of risk, methods for avoidance, and effective response. Thus, crises have an intrinsic capacity for inducing learning and innovation.

In this chapter, we explore crises as an impetus for meaningful, sometimes beneficial, and often broad-based change. We begin with a description of three conditions that are essential to establishing a progressive mind-set related to crises. From this progressive mind-set, we propose five ways for reenvisioning crises: threat, dialogue, power, control, and responsibility.

EMERGING FROM CRISES WITH A PROGRESSIVE
MIND-SET

Previous chapters outlined a view of complex systems as dynamic, unpredictable, and even chaotic, in which small variance has disproportional and nonlinear impact. This perspective is essential to understanding and evaluating the complexities that circumscribe most crises. Under these conditions, organizations are best served through what is described as an inclusive mind-set. Inclusive mind-sets require that organizations clarify and act on a central value structure of social responsibility that considers stakeholder needs. This inclusive mind-set views crisis as (1) a force for social change that is potentially positive, (2) a recognition that the organization's environment is continuously changing, and (3) an acceptance of the irrational nature of crises. We discuss each of these elements below.

Crisis as a Force for Social Change

Chapter 2 suggests that uncertainty is inherent to all complex systems, including organizations. Although chaos theory has only recently been introduced into the study of crises, this perspective offers a soberly pragmatic view of the dynamic and nonlinear nature of organizations. Specifically, chaos theory asks to what extent any organization can impose order on a complex and dynamic environment. Employees, investors, and other stakeholders typically seek organizational stability and its associated predictability. Employees, for example, purchase homes, invest in pension programs, and plan their future based largely on the stability of their employers. Each of these aspects of the employees' lives is in jeopardy when their company is threatened by an extreme disruption, such as a crisis. The uncertainty and anxiety experienced by an organization during a crisis reaches deeply into the lives of employees. When factories close as a consequence of an explosion or when jobs are lost due to financial scandals, unions, politicians, the media, and employees themselves are quick to denounce the organization and its leadership for failing to account for the needs of stakeholders. Yet, to focus on the crisis itself is to miss a larger frame. Social systems are inherently dynamic. Holding to a specific form of stability for a prolonged period of time is in essence a failure to account for the shifting nature of society. Wheatley (1999) has suggested that this stability exists only to the degree that an organization can "provide the energy to reverse the decay" that is natural to organizing (p. 19). How then does an organization account for the dynamic nature of the environment? More specifically, what role do crises play in the entropy inherent to organizing? Answers to these questions are based on the particular perspective taken to understand organizations.

As established in chapter 2 chaos theory does not reject the notion of order. Order is inherent to any complex system. A fundamental difficulty, however, is in perceiving and understanding that order, particularly as it shifts. Most modern conceptualizations of organizations emphasize the process character of these systems. Organizations are in continual accommodation of environmental inputs and contingencies.

Imposing an inflexible form of order by exerting resources to maintain that order in some static way for prolonged periods of time is inconsistent with the fundamental facts of organizing. Deetz, Tracy, and Simpson (2000) captured this sentiment:

Success in business or by any organization today cannot be achieved by formula. Positive outcomes result from luck and unpredictable changes in tastes and markets as well as from creativity, hard work, and good management. Frequently, the best we can hope for is to increase the chances of being at the right place at the right time and being ready to meet the challenges once there. (p. ix)

In short, organizations achieve enduring success through a willingness and ability to monitor their environment and to adapt as best they can to meet the evolving demands of a dynamic context. The essential management perspective, then, is sensitivity to environmental contingencies, and the essential management function is flexibility.

As discussed in chapter 6, organizations that fail to adequately monitor their environments and evolve accordingly risk missing the emerging cues or prodromes that serve as indicators of an impending crisis (Fink, 1986). Although in theory all crises appear to throw off some warning signals, in practice not all are predictable. The complexity of systems, the impact of small variances and nonlinear interactions makes predicting many crises impossible. It is not possible, therefore, to offer a formula for averting all crises. Instead, we advocate an attitude or mind-set of vigilance, readiness, and flexibility. Organizations should prepare for crises, be willing to recognize and accept the warning signs, and, perhaps most importantly, exhibit a willingness to learn and engage in novel corrective actions to resolve the crisis. With this perspective, crises serve as a force for social change in two ways: (1) organizations that are unwilling to change are forced to do so in the aftermath of a crisis, or (2) crises clarify the path for organizations that are constantly seeking to evolve in response to dynamic environments. In either case, crises inspire changes that reflect a dynamic and evolving environmental context. The continuous adaptive processes that are fostered by crises are described below.

Continuous Adaptive Process

The organizational-change literature is replete with cases and theoretical perspectives admonishing organizations to avoid complacency, static assumptions, and narrow paradigms (Deetz et al., 2000; Rogers, 1995). Continual research and development for new products and innovative models of existing products and services is essential to organizations seeking to remain competitive in a global economy. Fadlike management models rise and fall in popularity. Changes in personnel, technology, and reporting relationships in most organizations is so frequent as to become routine. Mergers and acquisitions are the norm. Yet, substantial change in the fundamental organizational structures or notable transformations in the way an organization relates to stakeholders remains rare. Unlike organizational changes associated with product development, technology, management techniques, or corporate affiliation, crises are often a catalyst for this extensive change. This point was described in detail as part of the postcrisis communication stage outlined in chapter 8 and in the review of ethical issues associated with crises in chapter 12.

Simply put, crises often shock organizational systems out of complacency and into the pursuit of radical learning, restructuring, and realignment of basic assumptions. Crisis resolution often requires original solutions based on changes in both internal and external functions (Brinson & Benoit, 1996; Seeger, 1997; Sellnow, Ulmer, & Snider, 1998; Ulmer, 2001). For organizations to reestablish legitimacy, these changes must also meet the needs, expectations, and values of stakeholders. Crises ultimately serve as an impetus for the realignment of the organization with the values and needs of society.

All crises do not result in this radical change, however. In some cases, crises can inspire organizations to reaffirm long-standing core values. As we described in chapter 8, organizations such as Malden Mills and Cole Hardwoods responded to their crises with a form of value-based renewal that allowed them to regain stability and move forward. In fact, a clearly articulated set of values and a well-developed sense of responsibility are important to both avoiding crisis and recovering more successfully. In other cases, however, organizational crises are fostered principally by an organization or industry failure to perceive changes in the environment and keep pace with those changes. This failure sometimes results in organizational structures and value systems that are simply incapable of responding effectively to crisis. In a few cases, the organization simply does not survive the crisis.

From this perspective, organizations that suffer crises are not necessarily immoral, insensitive, poorly managed, or irrational. They may not even be complacent. Crises are a natural and ongoing force of social change. Although many crises are the consequence of a few unscrupulous individuals, many more are the result of honest managers seeking to maintain a stable organization in a highly dynamic and increasingly complex atmosphere. Many are distracted, overworked, undertrained, and facing competing and often unrealistic expectations for continual growth and profitability. They make mistakes, overlook issues that later turn out to be significant, or fail to understand a critical contingency. Although crises serve as clear indications that organizational change is needed, they do not always offer clear indications for the direction of the change. Thus, as Perrow (1984) indicated, organizations can actually intensify crises through attempts to resolve them. The rapid expansion of technology has created tightly coupled relationships among organizational components, other seemingly unrelated organizations, and the environment. In the past, one part of an organization could fail without having an impact on the entire organization or the people living in the surrounding community. In the current organizational environment, however, the likelihood of one failure remaining isolated is far less common. These tightly coupled relationships produce what Perrow described as an "interacting tendency" that transfers the consequences of a crisis far beyond the immediate surroundings (p. 4).

This principle of tightly coupled systems and normal accidents is strikingly apparent in flood-mitigation efforts. For example, communities in western Minnesota, frustrated by recent flooding, began a series of ambitious flood-relief efforts in the mid-1990s. Dozens of seemingly unrelated projects in communities along three different river systems were completed. Water was diverted, dikes were raised, and several dams were constructed. Residents watched with pride as spring floods were steered around their communities. Simultaneously, farmers downriver watched in horror as water six feet deep pooled over fields that had resisted spring flooding for three or four generations. Millions of dollars in crops were lost. Several farmers were forced to leave farms that had been in their family for generations. The communities upriver were guilty of what Perrow (1984) cautioned against: "[T]rying to fix the systems in ways that only make them riskier" (p. 4). When events are viewed as isolated occurrences, or one-time mistakes or oversights, there is a strong tendency to implement shortsighted or limited solutions.

This explanation introduces an apparent paradox in crisis management. We know that crises require change. Often these changes produce better organizations that are more responsive to stakeholders. There is a persistent danger, however, that one form of resolution may serve as a prodrome for a potentially more intense future crisis. The resolution to this paradox requires a fundamental shift in the way we view crises. Specifically, accepting the irrational or illogical aspects of crises provides a more practical understanding of these events.

Accepting the Irrational Nature of Crises

If crisis-induced changes are to be beneficial, those changes must acknowledge the complex web of dynamic and nonlinear interactions and interdependencies that develop among organizations and their environments. As discussed above, the failure to do so may lead organizations to enact innovations that later create additional harm. Perrow's (1984) advice is helpful. He suggested that organizations carefully contemplate the externalities of their actions. Externalities are "the social costs of an activity (pollution, injuries, anxieties) that are not reflected in the price of the activity" (p. 341). For example, nuclear power plants were sold to the public in the 1970s and 1980s with claims of lower energy costs. This claim did not consider externalities such as the added risk to the public, the expense of disposing of spent fuel, and the cost of disassembling plants at the completion of their life span. Nor did advocates of nuclear power provide a comprehensive explanation, externalities included, of competing alternatives, such as solar energy. The energy crisis of the 1970s ushered in the rapid implementation of nuclear technology without a thorough consideration of the ultimate costs and alternatives. A number of crises have resulted, including the accidents at Three Mile Island and Fermi II, the leaching of contaminate mine tailings into the Colorado River in Utah, and the simmering conflict over long-term storage of nuclear waste.

Achieving full consideration of the interactions and externalities related to crisis resolution requires that managers, public officials, community leaders, and other stakeholders adopt a comprehensive perspective in considering crisis-induced changes. In the tradition of some postmodern literature, organizations must open the margins so that the outcomes for all relevant stakeholders are fully considered in the crisis resolution process (Calas & Smircich, 1999). This perspective is only possible, however, if crises are viewed as inevitable and constant forces of social change.

Initially, expanding the margins of crisis management has the potential to empower individuals whose voices are typically silent. For example, postcrisis inquiry into the 9/11 attacks revealed a failure by the FBI to heed the warnings of agents who voiced concerns about suspicious individuals seeking flight instructions. As the crisis investigation intensified, one agent was asked to testify before Congress. She was given immunity from retaliation in hopes that she would speak freely. The agent revealed that she had been concerned with management procedures that suppressed warnings long before the crisis. The crisis, from the perspective of critical theory, served as a form of "emancipation" (Miller, 1999, p. 120). When Congress enabled this agent to express her concerns, she was able to bring attention to what she saw as an oppressive organizational condition. Ultimately, her testimony created the momentum for establishing more thorough consideration of the knowledge provided by agents. The agency has the potential to expand its margins in a way that will enhance its awareness and crisis-sensing capacity.

This perspective is in sharp contrast to a more linear view of crisis. If crises are viewed as the result of an unfortunate error or oversight, then the organization's only task is to ferret out those who made the error, eliminate them, and return to the status quo. This limited view frames crises as momentary aberrations that, if it were not for human error, could be avoided. From this perspective, the existing power structure remains in place to define, delimit, and diminish the crisis. Essentially, in this case, all that is needed is a well-crafted apology and thoughtful strategies of image restoration. Although such strategies are an essential part of crisis management, crisis resolution reaches far beyond these techniques and time frames. Rather, image restoration is merely the initial step in constructing a full meaning of a serious crisis event. Organizations that embrace the crisis as a significant opportunity for learning are much more likely to adopt comprehensive solutions based on a more complex understanding of both risk and their environment. In these cases, crises have greater potential to bring about renewal.

By proposing an expansive view of crisis stakeholders and the potential social and organizational benefits that can be derived from crises, we are also advocating a revised narrative of organizational crises. In short, a change in the way organizations respond to crises is predicated on a change in the way people think and talk about risk and crisis. A number of researchers have suggested that organizational reality is "mediated through its discursive practices, particularly through the articulation of narrative discourse" (Mumby, 1988, p. 114). Sensemaking as an organizational process is rooted in the interpretation and explanations members exchange with one another. The stories members share and the ways they share them are reflections of the existing power structures. These power structures are both reified and reproduced through discourse. Moreover, the narrative structure of organizational discourse "strives for closure by portraying events as essentially moral dramas—dramas in which a particular set of values are given legitimacy and authority" (Mumby, 1988, p. 114). Changes in these narratives, in the privileged values and authorities, and in the larger methods of sharing interpretations are evidence of the organization's learning process (Huber, 1996). Crises produce intense dramas that severely challenge legitimacy. Ideally, crises foster new paradigms and perspectives leading to poststructural analysis: "to think 'the unthinkable'; to move, as it were 'outside the limits'; and to consider taken-for-granted knowledge-making operations under very different premises" (Calas & Smircich, 1999, p. 657). For this type of beneficial change to occur, organizations must consider both an expanded set of stakeholders and the externalities of their actions. The narrative, then, expands beyond preserving an existing structure and extends to seeking a resolution that truly engages the organizations in a socially legitimate relationship with its members, its community, its industry, and its relevant environment.

This expanded view of crisis addresses several issues related to the larger role and position of organizations in society. For example, as discussed in chapter 4, organizations have the potential to emerge from crisis with an enhanced public presence and with a more responsive structure. As described in chapter 12, crises can advance a set of core organizational values that favor social responsibility and legitimacy over issues of profitability. Specifically, four forms of improvement may result from this inclusive point of view (see Figure 14.1). First, an inclusive point of view regarding crisis may enhance the public sphere of discourse and debate (Goodnight, 1989). The term *public sphere* describes a forum for public dialogue and debate regarding those policies and procedures that affect the common good. Risk communication, for example, is one element of this public sphere. As we outlined in chapter 9, when organizations fail to engage the public in a meaningful discussion regarding risk, they become disconnected from the public's concerns and values. In this manner, the public sphere is diminished. Failing to confer with stakeholders who are directly affected by organizational decisions is both unwise and irresponsible. An inclusive view of crisis management calls for meaningful dialogue among stakeholders regarding risks and strategies for crisis resolution. The risk-sharing view, for example, advocates frank discussion and open exchange so that stakeholders and organizations may mutually understand the risks (Heath, 1997).

Second, as organizations grow in size and complexity, their responsiveness to public concerns is often compromised. Organizational leaders become further insulated from the concerns of employees, clients, and customers. Global organizations risk replacing local or regional concerns and responsiveness with a more generalized, diluted, and multinational set of priorities. This perspective inherently overlooks the needs of local communities, ignores place-based contingencies, and disregards provisional perspectives. Organizations cannot benefit from the learning and change opportunities of crises unless they reconsider their fundamental relationship to their environment. Such reconsideration bases legitimacy on the organization's ability to establish or reestablish a responsive relationship with a diverse set of stakeholders.

A third consequence of this view is that it encourages organizations to move beyond viewing crises as merely financial or economic issues. Clearly, organizations cannot regain stability nor legitimacy if they are not profitable

Figure 14.1
Crisis as Resolving Social Issues

Threats to Society	*Parallel Opportunities*
Diminishing public sphere	Crisis as public dialogue
Bureaucratic insensitivity	Crisis as restructuring
Financial exigencies	Ethical and environmental evolution
Greed and irresponsibility	Reasserting legitimacy

and economically viable. Still, viewing crises as only a matter of financial costs and gains is akin to treating symptoms without addressing their cause. When companies view calamities from a ledger rather than from the perspective of human suffering, they cannot make gains in solidifying or preserving their social legitimacy. In fact, those organizations that are perceived as only protecting narrow financial interests during a crisis typically receive closer scrutiny and criticism. Taking a purely financial perspective on a crisis is itself a symptom of a failure to consider the larger relationship between an organization and its stakeholders. These limited perspectives on crisis lead to bickering with stakeholders and an extended period of conflict.

An inclusive view of crisis management also deters organizations from making decisions based on immediate or short-term financial gains. Organizations often react to crisis in ways that are subsequently judged as ineffective or inadequate. A cash crisis for a retailer may lead to additional loans without consideration of the underlying factors that created the crisis. An episode of employee violence may result in dismissal and legal action, without consideration of the failure in hiring practices or working conditions that prompted the episode. By reconsidering blind spots that preceded the crisis, organizations can make comprehensive efforts to improve operations. From this perspective, the goal becomes one of learning, long-term recovery, and renewal rather than short-term resolution and protection of the status quo.

In summary, crises, although disrupting and harmful in the short term, are also a natural and ongoing force of social change. Rather than aberrations, crises often draw attention to the need for organizations to adapt to better fit the complex and dynamic contexts in which they function. In this manner, crises are often positive influences on organizational change. This positive change, however, is only possible if organizations engage in a crisis narrative that broadens the margins to embrace a diverse set to stakeholders. This narrative is an expression of a willingness to make meaningful long-term changes in the organization and to carefully consider the broad impact of these changes. The following section clarifies this perspective by proposing a means for reenvisioning crisis.

REENVISIONING CRISIS

The inclusive view of crisis and crisis management requires organizations to reconsider many long-standing assumptions and belief systems regarding risk and crisis. As discussed earlier, many of these assumptions concern the tension between stability and change. Moreover, these assumptions also concern long-standing notions of managerial power, privilege, and prerogative. Such reconsideration, however, can profoundly affect the way organizations both plan for and manage crises. Crisis can be reenvisioned in five specific ways (see Figure 14. 2).

Figure 14.2
Reenvisioning Crisis

From	To
Threat to stability	Opportunity for change
Restricted communication	Public dialogue
Control	Irrepressibly dynamic environment
Preserving power structures	Adapting to a dynamic system
Short-term profitability	Long-term social responsibility

Reenvisioning Crisis as Opportunity

Viewing crises as solely and unequivocally the sudden demise of an organization is unnecessarily narrow and potentially paralyzing. Lerbinger (1997) reminded us that the Chinese symbol for crisis "signifies opportunity as well as danger" (p. 51). Crises have the potential to improve relations through the influence of a common threat, to change the topic and tone of communication, and to reduce resistance to change. Managers facing crises should be willing to "seize the opportunity to restructure company thinking" (p. 51). Following this philosophy, crises have the potential to transform companies into more responsive, efficient, and effective competitors matched more appropriately to their environment.

Throughout this book, we have emphasized the importance of organizational learning. Crises present a compelling need for learning and create an intense opportunity for learning. If organizations embrace the opportunity to acquire new knowledge and to enact new strategies, they can emerge from crises with renewed vitality and increased competitive advantages. Sitkin (1996) goes so far as to argue that "failure is an essential prerequisite for effective learning and adaptation" (p. 541). Although panic and defensiveness may be natural reactions to crisis, both thwart the kinds of learning that turn crises from disaster into opportunities for renewal.

Nike serves as a recent example of an organization that enacted consequential changes based on a crisis. Throughout most of the 1990s, Nike was criticized for manufacturing shoes in Third World countries under sweatshop conditions. Initially, Nike denied all allegations of mistreating workers or creating inappropriate working conditions. However, evidence of abuse and media attention continued to intensify. Eventually, boycotts of Nike's goods began to take a serious toll on the company's profits. In response, Phil Knight, Nike's CEO, announced in May 1998 that the company would make sweeping changes to ensure the safety of its workers. First, he pledged to improve air quality by switching from toluene, a chemical that is potentially harmful to workers' lungs, to water-based cements for shoe construction. Second, Knight made a commitment to remain steadfast in refusing to hire workers under the age of 18 at Nike's shoe factories and under 16 at its garment and equipment factories. Third, Knight offered to continue exploring an acceptable means for independent monitoring of factory working conditions. Knight also pledged to offer employees educational programs, including "middle and high school equivalency course availability for all workers in Nike footwear factories" (Sellnow & Brand, 2001, p. 288). In his fifth initiative, he outlined his plans to expand the microenterprise loan program that enabled families in Vietnam, Indonesia, Pakistan, and Thailand to start "small businesses such as pig farming and the making of rice paper" (p. 640).

This comprehensive response clearly reflects the learning and growth that can emerge from crisis. Criticism of Nike's global manufacturing procedures was sharply curtailed as critics praised the company for its bold stand against abuse. For example, Simon Billenness, senior analyst for a Boston-based mutual fund specializing in socially responsible companies, described Nike as a "bellwether" for human rights (Ramey, 1998, p. 11). Nike's employees were given enhanced opportunities for personal safety and enrichment not previously available. Knight also set a new industry standard. American companies that did not follow Nike's example set themselves up for the same regimen of criticism that Nike had previously endured. This crisis in public image, then, became an opportunity to improve working conditions in the entire sporting-goods industry.

Companies such as Malden Mills, Cole Hardwoods, and Nike illustrate the potentially positive side of crisis as an opportunity for learning, growth, and renewal. These organizations were able to frame their crisis responses in ways that envision opportunity rather than merely seeing crisis as a wholly negative event to be resolved as quickly and cheaply as possible. Unfortunately, such responses to crisis remain comparatively rare as organizations seek to shift blame, protect the status quo, and avoid responsibility whenever a threat erupts into a crisis.

Reenvisioning Crisis Communication as Dialogue

The tendency to restrict communication during crisis situations is an almost visceral reaction of most managers. Veteran public relations counselor Alfred Geduldig advised, "Once a crisis has run its course in the media, it is likely to reemerge in court...statements made and actions taken during the early stages of the crisis come back to haunt the organization years later" (International Association of Business Communicators, 1995, p. 250). Similarly, Marcus and Goodman (1991) pointed out that, whereas some leaders are forthcoming in crisis events, others have "consistently denied wrongdoing, even in the face of overwhelming evidence to the contrary, perhaps because their lawyers have warned that admissions could be used against them in court" (p. 282). A fundamental tension exists in a crisis between stances that encourage full, detailed, and rapid disclosure and positions that favor secrecy, withholding information, strategic ambiguity, and incremental disclosure. Clearly, organizations must monitor their public statements closely during a crisis, given their increased vulnerability in our highly litigious society. Still, there is an equally compelling need for organizations that have failed in some manner to accept responsibility for their errors and to compensate those who were harmed by the crisis (Benoit, 1995a). Such admissions and compensations are essential elements of social responsibility and ultimately of crisis resolution (Heath, 1997).

Several studies offer clear evidence that reticence on the part of organizations to admit wrong often serves to intensify a crisis. For example, Dow Corning's initial failure to publicly admit some responsibility in its breast implant crisis inhibited the company's crisis recovery efforts. Dow Corning continued to lose ground with the public until, after a prolonged delay, it admitted that it had "mishandled the situation, and promised to behave more appropriately in the future" (Brinson & Benoit, 1996, p. 39). In a similar case, Sears intensified the severity of claims that it overcharged its auto repair customers, in part by attempting to deny all wrongdoing. Benoit (1995b) explains that "corporate attorneys may have recommended denying the problem existed to avoid litigation, but this position could not have been expected to restore Sears' image" (p. 99). In these cases, and many others, the companies floundered in their crisis management efforts until they admitted that changes were necessary.

Two additional points regarding this postcrisis openness require clarification. First, we do not contend that an organization should accept blame for a crisis when it genuinely believes it is not responsible for the harm. Organizations can and should exonerate themselves when denial is in order. Claims that Pepsi-Cola had produced cans of Diet Pepsi with spent syringes inside, for example, were false. Yet the rumor spread widely. The company responded swiftly and decisively with an advertisement campaign debunking the rumor (Fearn-Banks, 2002). These claims were quite simply false. The situation obviously did not call for Pepsi-Cola to publicly reconsider and correct flaws in its bottling procedures. The case of GM C/K7 pickups and *Dateline NBC* similarly illustrates the need for organizations to vigorously and publicly defend themselves when wrongfully charged. The assessment of claims about wrongdoing should be done carefully and fully, however, to ensure that the organization is not in the wrong.

Second, organizations should not disregard the legal consequences of their public statements. Public statements become part of the public record and can be held against organizations. Organizations can, however, express remorse and publicly consider possible means for correcting and improving a situation without announcing that the company is fully responsible for a crisis. For example, Schwan's offered to pay the hospital expenses for its customers who presumed their *Salmonella* infection stemmed from Schwan's products well before the source of the contamination was verified. In the end, an outside company was found to be responsible for the outbreak. Had Schwan's waited weeks for the State Health Department to finalize its report, the company would certainly have had a far more difficult time regaining customer confidence (Sellnow et al., 1998). Similarly, Aaron Feuerstein's response to the fire at Malden Mills did not discount questions of responsibility. Rather, Feuerstein's commitments redirected the focus of debate to the well-being of workers.

Reenvisioning Internal Power Structures

In chapter 4, the epistemic role of crisis was explored. Crises, it was argued, reveal information and weaknesses that were previously overlooked or ignored. Organizations develop blind spots in their policies and procedures by seeking positive knowledge (Knights, 1992). Positive knowledge is a form of self-fulfilling feedback that allows organizations to maintain and reify existing beliefs and structures, even when these structures are outdated and begin to fail. Certainly, stability in an organization's systems and hierarchies is necessary. Positive knowledge, however, can preserve, solidify, or institutionalize weaknesses. Thus, many organizational structures and assumptions become wasteful, inefficient, and prone to catastrophic failure over time. These weaknesses are often exposed by crises.

Greg Brenneman, who is credited with helping to turn Continental Airlines from a dysfunctional, bankrupt company into one of the top five U.S. airlines for key performance, is brutally honest in his appraisal of power structures that lead organizations into crises. He noted, "I have never seen the team that managed a company into a crisis get it back on track" (Brenneman, 2000, p. 100). Brenneman offered this pragmatic portrayal of what he typically sees in organizational hierarchies facing crisis:

Managers who have gotten a company into a mess are usually mired in a puddle of overbrained solutions. They can't see any way out either. In fact they have many ways of saying, "If the solution were simple, we would have already thought of it." On top of that, they usually have trouble accepting responsibility for and reversing the poor decisions they made in the past. (p. 100)

Brenneman's stark description offers an explanation for some of the inconceivable reactions managers have had to crises. Exxon's lethargic, if not arrogant, response to the *Valdez* oil spill is a clear example of an organization's leadership failing to enact appropriate solutions to a crisis. Similarly, Sears' leadership continued to deny that its auto repair services were corrupt even after their mechanics were recorded by concealed video cameras making unnecessary repairs. Northwest Airlines' management refused to capitulate to their pilots' demands for higher wages even though the company had experienced record profits for several years. The company's management was certain the pilots would not actually strike. The pilots did strike, and Northwest Airlines was forced to concede to all of the pilots' demands after losing an estimated $223 million (Cowden & Sellnow, 2002).

The changes in the internal structure of organizations are not simply a means of punishing those who led the company into a crisis. Offering individuals as scapegoats for a crisis does not in itself provide assurance to the public nor does it ensure that the organization has changed. For meaningful correction to occur, organizations must adapt the core of the knowledge structures that guide them (Von Krogh, Roos, & Slocum, 1994). In this manner, crises have the potential to promote learning and strategic change in the organization's culture.

Crisis creates the opportunity to reshuffle existing power structures and hierarchical relationships in important ways. In some cases, for example, aspects of the organization that are able to successfully manage the crisis may establish their value. In other cases, components of the organization associated with the onset of the crisis may lose status. In this way, the power structure of the organization may shift to reflect a revised organizational agenda and new understandings of the environment.

Reenvisioning External Control

In reconsidering control, questions regarding the degree to which an organization influences or controls its environment emerge. In contrast, much contemporary organizational theory suggests that the environment extends a high level of influence on the form, structure, operations, culture, and ultimately the success of organizations (Pfeffer & Salancik, 1978). The organization's environment as filtered and manifest through a variety of perceptional and mediating processes has a profound and irrefutable influence on organizations. Crises serve as compelling evidence of this influence. The environment is most often the ultimate source of crisis-inducing threat. Moreover, when organizations struggle to maintain equilibrium in an ever-changing world, as Perrow (1984) explained, they may enhance the probability of a catastrophic failure. Organizations can exert control on their environments for some period of time, but disruption, as described in chaos theory, is an inevitable feature of organized systems. From this perspective, then, disorder is the ultimate product of order.

Successful organizations do not follow prescribed and static maps. Rather, they continually rewrite them. Wheatley (1999) drew parallels between organizational stagnation and equilibrium: "[T]he search for organizational equilibrium," she suggested, is a "sure path to institutional death, a road to zero trafficked by fearful people." Borrowing from systems theory, she noted that "equilibrium is the end state in the evolution process" (p. 76). Conversely, "disturbances could create disequilibrium, but disequilibrium could lead to growth" (p. 79). In this way, disruption of stability is necessary for reconstituting the system at higher levels of operations. Crises in this way include important generative elements for the renewal of the system.

Wheatley (1999) explained further that communicative processes are necessary to embracing the renewal:

Information must actively be sought from everywhere, from places and sources people never thought to look before. And then it must circulate freely so that many people can interpret it. The intent of this new information is to keep the system off-balance, alert to how it might need to change. An open organization doesn't look for information that makes it feel good, that verifies its past and validates its present. It is deliberately looking for information that might threaten its stability, knock it off balance, and open it to growth. (p. 83)

This explanation of the role of disequilibrium-inducing information is essentially the same as organizational learning, described in chapter 2. Similarly, chaos theory advocates embracing the nonlinear and dynamic aspects of complex systems. Predictive patterns and static structures cannot be imposed for extended periods of time. Rather, chaos theory demands that the observer remain open and responsive to new forms of order and to the inevitable changes in the environment. Seeking to limit and contain these dynamic forces is likely to create a significant mismatch between the organization and its environment and enhance the probability of serious crisis. Rather, organizations need to seek out the margins, provide opportunities for the expression of dissenting views, and encourage debate and discussion that questions the status quo.

Reenvisioning Corporate Responsibility

Throughout this text we have been careful to avoid portraying crises as necessarily the product of corruption or incompetence. Corrupt leadership and incompetent management are certainly all-too-common sources of crisis. But many well-meaning and well-managed organizations also fall into crisis. Crisis strips away and makes evident the organization's core values and sense of integrity. Often, this serves to accentuate preexisting value systems. Malden Mills responded to its crisis by continuing its long established pattern of community and employee support. Enron executives, on the other hand, responded to the crisis by denying knowledge and responsibility of wrongdoing and fleeing the company with as much personal profit as possible before its collapse. This response also reflected a set of long-standing company values.

As discussed in chapter 12, organizations have ethical responsibilities and moral obligations to communicate openly with stakeholders. Deception during crisis is both unethical and counterproductive. The prolonged period of postcrisis examination inevitably reveals the actions that organizations take as crises unfold. Recent cases of corporate corruption, for example, saw many executives cashing out on their stock options in the face of an impending collapse in stock values. *BusinessWeek* chronicled the pattern of corruption:

Even while shareholders were losing millions of dollars, executive after executive seemed to be cashing in on an unsupervised lottery. At now bankrupt telecom provider Global Crossing Ltd., Chairman Gary Winnick sold $735 million in company stock from 1999 to last November. At Enron, Chairman Lay sold more than $100 million in stock over the past three years—even while publicly insisting that he wasn't cashing out. The same was true at Tyco, where CEO Kozlowski and his chief financial officer unloaded more than $500 million of stock, quietly selling it back to the company, a trick that allowed them to delay public disclosure of their sales. (Arndt, Zellner, & McNamee, 2002, p. 34)

This pattern of abuse has lead to a crisis in the confidence of investors. The intensity of these crises became so great that Congress issued subpoenas to executives, managers, and accountants in hopes of restoring order to the financial turmoil. President Bush addressed the issue by observing that the actions of these executives has "tarnished our entire free enterprise system" and that "the federal government will be vigilant in prosecuting wrongdoers to ensure that investors and workers maintain the highest confidence in America's business" ("Bush Assails Corporate Responsibility," 2002, p. A4).

These executives responded to troubled times by taking all they could get. They showed limited regard for the harm they caused to employees, investors, and to the American economy as a whole. Some were simply shameless and failed to acknowledge even the slightest sense of personal responsibility. Now that their actions have been exposed, some face severe financial penalties and likely jail time. In each case, these executives lost touch with the basic standards of responsibility described in chapter 12. The utter disregard they demonstrated for others brought public humiliation and has damaged the credibility of corporate America. In such cases, organizations cannot regain social legitimacy unless they fully reconsider the impact that their actions may have on the well being of stakeholders. Henry Paulson, Jr., CEO of Goldman Sachs, captured this point in his discussion of the current investment scandal: "Integrity is the cornerstone, if not the bedrock, upon which all financial markets are based" (Arndt et al., 2002, p. 35). Organizations that face crisis situations without a willingness to carefully consider the needs and values of stakeholders are destined for failure.

One positive consequence of the current crisis in confidence will inevitably be a renewed emphasis on basic notions of responsibility. Managers will be forced to be more honest, transparent, and responsive in their financial reportings so that investors may make more informed choices. Investors will be more active and boards of directors more involved. Employees who blow the whistle on managerial wrongdoing will inevitably receive more attention and protection. Employees will be given more freedom and choice in terms of their retirement investment opportunities. Regulatory agencies will be more vigilant. The consequences of decisions for communities and for the larger economy will be more carefully examined. Responsibility is a managerial obligation that transcends the stages and phases of precrisis, crisis, and postcrisis or the various forms a crisis might take.

CONCLUSION

An impressive body of literature exists to advise organizations on the steps for avoiding crises. In contrast, the view outlined here suggests that crises are an inevitable part of the organizing process. As organizations seek to establish and protect their stability, they face the inevitable consequence of disruption, failure, wrongdoing, collapse, and disasters. The probability of these events occurring is increasing. This escalation suggests that crisis management will become an increasingly common function of modern management. In fact, crisis management is becoming the essential function of long-term organizational success.

We have explored the many ways in which organizations can recognize and avoid risk and more effectively plan for, manage, and learn from crises. We have argued for reenvisioning crises as events that have a dual character: they create great harm *and* they have the potential to benefit both organizations and stakeholders. Crises have the capacity to destroy companies, devastate communities, and disrupt industries. They also have the capacity to create new opportunities for organizations and their stakeholders; to revitalize institutions; to shed outdated assumptions, technologies, and approaches; and to activate core values. When organizations approach crises with a willingness to communicate openly and honestly, a willingness to be flexible and to consider new organizational structures, a sense of responsibility and values, and with a strong public image and reputation, they have the potential to emerge at a higher level of order and functioning. From this perspective, crises are both signs of decay and opportunities for renewal.

References

Allen, W. M., & Caillouet, R. H. (1994). Legitimation endeavors: Impression management strategies used by an organization in crisis [Monograph]. *Communication Monographs, 61,* 44–62.

American Red Cross. (2002). Retrieved September 9, 2002, from http://www.redcross.org/home/

Anderson, J. (2000, July 6). Flood relief organizations say cleanup nearly done. *The Forum,* p. B1.

Andriole, S. J. (1985). *Corporate crisis management.* Princeton, NJ: Petrocelli Books.

Anfuso, D. (1994). Deflecting workplace violence. *Personnel Journal, 73,* 66–67.

Angeles, M. (1997, May 13). It's okay to be angry, health experts tell victims. *The Herald,* p. 15.

Arndt, M., Zellner, W., & McNamee, M. (2002, June 24). Restoring trust in corporate America. *BusinessWeek,* 30–35.

Auf Der Heide, E. (1989). *Disaster response: Principles of preparation and coordination.* Portland, OR: Book News.

Baird, J. (2002, April 16). Oakport no longer an island. *The Forum,* p. A8.

Barge, J. K. (1994). *Leadership: Communication skills for organizations and groups.* New York: St. Martin's Press.

Barton, L. (2001). *Crisis in organizations II.* Cincinnati, OH: South-Western College Publishing.

Benoit, W. L. (1995a). *Accounts, excuses and apologies.* Albany, NY: State University of New York Press.

Benoit, W. L. (1995b). Sears' repair of its auto service image: Image restoration discourse in the corporate sector. *Communication Studies, 46*(1 & 2), 89–105.

Benoit, W. L., & Brinson, S. L. (1994). AT&T: Apologies are not enough. *Communication Quarterly, 42*(1), 75–88.

Benoit, W. L., & Dorries, B. (1996). Dateline NBC's persuasive attack on Wal-Mart. *Communication Quarterly, 44*(4), 463–477.

Benoit, W. L., & Lindsey, J. J. (1987). Argument strategies: Antidote to Tylenol's poisoned image. *Journal of the American Forensic Association, 23,* 136–146.

Benson, J. A. (1988). Crisis revisited: An analysis of strategies used by Tylenol in the second tampering episode. *Central States Speech Journal, 39*(1), 49–66.

Berger, C. R., & Bradac, J. J. (1982). *Language and social knowledge: Uncertainty and interpersonal relations.* London: Edward Arnold.

Beyer, J., & Lutze, S. (1993). The ethical nexus: Organizations, values, and decision-making. In C. Conrad (Ed.), *The ethical nexus* (pp. 23–45). Norwood, NJ: Ablex.

Billings, R. S., Milburn, T. W., & Schaalman, M. L. (1980). A model of crisis perception: A theoretical and empirical analysis. *Administrative Science Quarterly, 25,* 300–316.

Bok, C. (1979). *Lying.* New York: Vintage Books.

Brenneman, G. (2000). Right away and all at once: How we saved Continental. In *Harvard business review on crisis management* (pp. 87–118). Boston: Harvard Business School Press.

Brinson, S. L., & Benoit, W. L. (1996). Dow Corning's image repair strategies in the breast implant crisis. *Communication Quarterly, 44*(1), 29–41.

Brown, J. S., & Duguid, P. (1996). Organizational learning and communities of practice: Toward a unified view of working, learning, and innovation. In M. D. Cohen & L. S. Sproull (Eds.), *Organizational learning* (pp. 58–82). Thousand Oaks, CA: Sage.

Brummer, J. J. (1991). *Corporate responsibility and legitimacy: An interdisciplinary analysis.* New York: Greenwood Press.

Buchholz, R. A. (1990). The evolution of corporate responsibility. In J. M. Shafritz (Ed.), *Essentials of business ethics* (pp. 298–310). New York: Penguin.

Buono, A. F., & Nichols, L. (1995). *Corporate policy, values, and social responsibility.* New York: Praeger.

Burson, H. (1995, December). Damage control in a crisis. *Management Review,* 42–45.

Bush assails corporate responsibility in radio address. (2002, June 30). *Fargo Forum,* p. A4.

Butz, M. R. (1997). *Chaos and complexity: Implications for psychological theory and practice.* Washington, D.C.: Taylor & Francis.

Calas, M. B., & Smircich, L. (1999). Past postmodernism? Reflections and tentative directions. *Academy of Management Review, 24,* 649–671.

Centers for Disease Control and Prevention (CDC), Food Safety Office. (2002). Retrieved August 15, 2002, from http://www.cdc.gov/ncidod/dbmd/diseaseinfo/foodborneinfections_g.htm#foodbornedisease

Centers for Disease Control and Prevention (CDC), Food Safety Office. (2003). Retrieved May 7, 2003, from http://www.cdc.gov/foodsafety/default.htm

Cheney, G. (1991). *Rhetoric in an organizational society.* Columbia: University of South Carolina Press.

Chess, C. (2001). Organizational theory and stages of risk communication. *Risk Analysis, 21,* 179–188.

Cohen, M. D., & Sproull, L. S. (Eds.). (1996). *Organizational learning.* Thousand Oaks, CA: Sage.

Comfort, L. K. (1999). *Shared risk: Complex systems in seismic response*. Oxford, England: Elsevier Science.

Comfort, L. K., Sungu, Y., Johnson, D., & Dunn, M. (2001). Complex systems in crisis: Anticipation and resiliance in dynamic environments. *Journal of contingencies and crisis management, 9*(3), 144–158.

Condon, P. (1997, April 19). River swallows Forks streets. *The Forum*, p. A1.

Conrad, C. (Ed.). (1993). *The ethical nexus*. Norwood, NJ: Ablex.

Coombs, W. T. (1995). Choosing the right words: The development of guidelines for the selection of the appropriate crisis-response strategies. *Management Communication Quarterly, 8*(4), 447–476.

Coombs, W. T. (1999a). Information and compassion in crisis responses: A test of their effects. *Journal of Public Relations Research, 11*(2), 125–142.

Coombs, W. T. (1999b). *Ongoing crisis communication: Planning, managing, and responding*. Thousand Oaks, CA: Sage.

Covello, V. T. (1992). Risk communication: An emerging area of health communication research. In S. A. Deetz (Ed.), *Communication Yearbook 15* (pp. 359–373). Newbury Park, CA: Sage.

Cowden, K., & Sellnow, T. L. (2002). Issues advertising as crisis communication: Northwest Airlines' use of image restoration during the 1998 pilots' strike. *Journal of Business Communication, 39*, 194–221.

Crable, R. E., & Vibbert, S. L. (1985). Managing issues and influencing public policy. *Public Relations Review, 11*, 3–16.

Curwood, S. (2000). Guarded communication. In E. Mather, P. Stewart, & T. Ten Eyck (Eds.), *Risk communication in food safety: Motivating and building trust.* (pp. 1–10). East Lansing, MI: National Food Safety and Toxicology Center, Michigan State University.

Cushing, S. (1994). *Fatal words: Communication clashes and aircraft crashes*. Chicago: University of Chicago Press.

Davidson, A. (1990). *In the wake of the Exxon Valdez*. San Francisco: Sierra Club Books.

Deakin, E. (1989). *Oil industry profitability in Alaska; 1969 through 1987*. Alaska, Department of Revenue.

Deetz, S. A., Tracy, S. J., & Simpson, J. L. (2000). *Leading organizations through transition: Communication and cultural change*. Thousand Oaks, CA: Sage.

Department of Transportation (DOT). (1999). *1999 status of the nation's highways, bridges, and transit: Conditions and performance report*. Retrieved August 1, 2002, from http://fhwa.dot.gov/ohim.hiqsep00

Devine, T. M., & Aplin, D. G. (1988). Whistleblower protection: The GAP between the law and reality. *Howard Law Journal, 31*, 223–239.

Diana, C., & Heath, R. L. (1995). Working with technical experts in risk management. *Public Relations Review, 21*, 211.

Dilenschneider, R. L., & Hyde, R. C. (1985). Crisis communications: Planning for the unplanned. *Business Horizons, 28*, 35–38.

Doughty, R. A. (1993). The need for a crisis plan is illustrated in responding to two accidents. In J. A. Gottschalk (Ed.), *Crisis response* (pp. 345–365). Detroit, MI: Visible Ink Press.

Dowling, J., & Pfeffer, J. (1975). Organizational legitimacy: Social values and organizational behavior. *Pacific Sociological Review, 18*, 122–136.

Egelhoff, W.G., & Falguni, S. (1992). An information-processing model of crisis management. *Management Communication Quarterly, 5*(4), 443–484.

Eisenberg, E.M. (1984). Ambiguity as strategy in organizational communication [Monograph]. *Communication Monographs, 51,* 227–242.

Eisenberg, E.M., & Goodall, H.L.J. (1997). *Organizational communication: Balancing creativity and constraint* (2nd ed.). New York: St. Martin's Press.

Eisenberg, E.M., & Riley, P. (1991). Organizational culture. In F.M. Jablin & L.L. Putnam (Eds.), *The new handbook of organizational communication: Advances in theory, research, and methods* (pp. 291–322). Thousand Oaks, CA: Sage.

Eisenberg, E.M., & Witten, M.G. (1987). Reconsidering openness in organizational communication. *Academy of Management Review, 12*(3), 418–426.

Epler, P. (1989, October 22). Blueprint for disaster: Despite years of warnings from its field staffers about Alyeska's poor oil spill preparedness, the DEC did next to nothing, department leaders put no real heat on Alyeska. *Anchorage Daily News,* p. A1. Retrieved September 9, 2003, from http://www.adn.com/evos/stories/ev265.html

Epstein, E.E., & Votaw, D. (1978). *Rationality, legitimacy, responsibility: Search for new directions in business and society.* Santa Monica, CA: Goodyear Publishing.

Exxon *Valdez* Oil Spill Trustees Council. (2002). Retrieved October 10, 2002, from http://www.oilspill.state.ak.us

Fairhurst, G.T., & Starr, R.A. (1996). *The art of framing.* San Francisco: Jossey-Bass.

Fearn-Banks, K. (2002). *Crisis communications* (2nd ed.). Mahwah, NJ: Erlbaum.

Feder, B.J. (1994). Obscure company gains unwelcome prominence. *The New York Times,* p. A23.

Federal Emergency Management Agency (FEMA). (2001; updated 2003, February 12). *Emergency management guide for business & industry.* Retrieved August 25, 2003, from http://www.fema.gov/library/bizindex.shtm

Federal Emergency Management Administration (FEMA). (2002). Retrieved September 9, 2002, from http://www.fema.gov

Federal Emergency Management Administration (FEMA). (2003). *Unified command structure.* Retrieved September 10, 2003, from http://www.fema.gov/rrr/conplan/conpln4p.shtm

Ferguson Devereaux, S. (1999). *Communication planning: An integrated approach.* Thousand Oaks, CA: Sage.

Fiedler, F.E. (1967). *A theory of leadership effectiveness.* New York: McGraw-Hill.

Fink, S. (1986). *Crisis management: Planning for the inevitable.* New York: AMACOM.

Fitzgibbon, J.E., & Seeger, M.W. (2002). Audiences and metaphors of globalization in the Daimler Chrysler AG merger. *Communication Studies, 53*(1), 40–55.

Fitzpatrick, K.R., & Rubin, S.M. (1995). Public relations vs. legal strategies in organizational crisis decisions. *Public Relations Review, 21*(1), 21–33.

Freedy, J.R., Kilpatrick, D.G., & Resnick, H.S. (1993). Natural disasters and mental health: Theory, assessment, and intervention. *Journal of Social Behavior and Personality, 8,* 49–103.

Freeman, R.E. (1984). *Strategic management: A stakeholder approach.* Marshfield, MA: Pitman Publishing.

Frohwein, H.I., & Lambert, J.H. (2000). Risk of extreme events in multiobjective decision trees,: Pt. 1: Severe events. *Risk Analysis, 20,* 113–124.

Froslie, E. H. (2002, April 14). Now in Florida, Owens recalls the flood like it was yesterday. *The Forum*, p. A22.

Gaunt, P., & Ollenburger, J. (1995). Issues management revisited: A tool that deserves another look. *Public Relations Review, 21*(3), 199–210.

Gilligan, C. (1982). *In a different voice: Psychological theory and women's development.* Cambridge, MA: Harvard University Press.

Gilmour, D. (1997a, April 10). Red to hit 39–39.5 feet; suffering encircles metro area. *The Forum*, pp. A1, A14.

Gilmour, D. (1997b, April 17). River passes 100-year-old mark early this morning; FM prays, piles sandbags. *The Forum*, pp. A1, A9.

Gilmour, D. (2000, December 6). Living with Red: Flood protection for population centers needs immediate attention, report concludes. *The Forum*, p. C3.

Gilmour, D. (2002a, April 14). The nation's poster child for flood recovery. *The Forum*, pp. A21, A23.

Gilmour, D. (2002b, April 15). Learning from the past. *The Forum*, pp. B1, B2.

Gleick, J. (1987). *Chaos: Making a new science.* New York: Viking.

Glicken, J. (1999). Effective public involvement in public decisions. *Science Communication, 20*, 298–327.

Goodnight, T. G. (1989). Toward a social theory of argumentation. *Argumentation and Advocacy, 26*, 60–70.

Gottschalk, J. A. (Ed.). (1993). *Crisis response.* Detroit, MI: Visible Ink Press.

Gouran, D. S. (1982). *Making decisions in groups: Choices and consequences.* Glenview, IL: Scott, Foresman.

Gouran, D. S., & Hirokawa, R. Y. (1983). The role of communication in decision-making groups: A functional perspective. In M. S. Mander (Ed.), *Communications in transition: Issues and debate in current research* (pp. 168–185). New York: Praeger.

Gouran, D. S., Hirokawa, R. Y., & Martz, A. E. (1986). A critical analysis of the factors related to decisional processes involved in the Challenger disaster. *Central States Speech Journal, 37*, 119–135.

Government Printing Office (GPO). (1989). Investigation of the Exxon Valdez oil spill, Prince William Sound Alaska, oversight hearings before the subcommittee on Water, Power, and offshore energy resources of the Committee on Interior and Insular Affairs, House of Representatives, Serial No. 101-5, Part I. Washington, D.C.: GPO.

Grand Forks recalls '97 flood disaster. (2002, April 18). *The Forum*, p. A18.

Greenberg, B. S., & Gantz, W. (Eds.). (1993). *Desert storm and the mass media.* Cresskill, NJ: Hampton Press.

Greenberg, B. S., Hofschire, L., & Lachlan, K. (2002). Diffusion, media use, and interpersonal communication behaviors. In B. S. Greenberg (Ed.), *Communication and terrorism: Public and media responses to 9/11* (pp. 3–16). Cresskill, NJ: Hampton Press.

Griffin, R. J., Neuwirth, K., & Dunwoody, S. (1995). Using the theory of reasoned action to examine the impact of health risk messages. In B. R. Burleson (Ed.), *Communication Yearbook* (Vol. 18, pp. 201–228). Thousand Oaks, CA: Sage.

Guth, D. W. (1995). Organizational crisis experience and public relations roles. *Public Relations Review, 21*(2), 123–136.

Hayles, N. K. (1990). *Chaos bound: Orderly disorder in contemporary literature and science*. Ithaca, NY: Cornell University Press.

Heald, M. (1970). *The social responsibility of business: Company and community 1900–1960*. New Brunswick, NJ: Transaction Books.

Hearit, K. M. (1995). "Mistakes were made": Organizations, apologia and crises of social legitimacy. *Communication Studies, 46*(1 & 2), 1–17.

Hearit, K. M. (1996). The use of counter-attack in apologetic public relations crises: The case of General Motors vs. Dateline NBC. *Public Relations Review, 22*(3), 233–248.

Hearit, K. M. (1997). On the use of transcendence as an apologia strategy: The case of Johnson Controls and its fetal protection policy. *Public Relations Review, 23*.

Heath, R. L. (1995). Corporate environmental risk communication: Cases and practices along the Texas Gulf Coast. In B. R. Burleson (Ed.), *Communication Yearbook* (Vol. 18, pp. 255–277). Thousand Oaks, CA: Sage.

Heath, R. L. (1997). *Strategic issues management: Organizations and public policy challenges*. Thousand Oaks, CA: Sage.

Heath, R. J. (1998). The Kobe earthquake: Some realities of strategic management of crises and disasters. *Disaster Prevention and Management, 4*(5), 11–24.

Hermann, C. F. (1963). Some consequences of crisis which limit the viability of organizations. *Administrative Science Quarterly, 8*(1), 61–82.

Hilgers, D. (1997a, April 11). Ready for the Red. *The Forum*, pp. A1, A12.

Hilgers, D. (1997b, April 12). Rising Red round two. *The Forum*, pp. A1, A12.

Huber, G. P. (1991). Organizational learning: The contributing processes and the literature. *Organizational science, 2*, 88–115.

Hirokawa, R. Y., & Pace, R. (1983). A descriptive investigation of the possible communication-based reasons for effective and ineffective group decision-making. *Communication Monographs, 50*, 363–379.

Hirokawa, R. Y., & Scheerhorn, D. R. (1986). Communication in faulty group decision making. In R. Y. Hirokawa & M. S. Poole (Eds.), *Communication and group decision-making* (pp. 63–80). Beverly Hills, CA: Sage.

Huber, G. P. (1996). Organizational learning: The contributing processes and the literatures. In M. D. Cohen & L. S. Sproull (Eds.), *Organizational learning* (pp. 124–162). Thousand Oaks, CA: Sage.

Ice jam could worsen flood. (1997, April 8). *The Forum*, p. A10.

Ice, R. (1990, November). *Is anybody there?: Defining "corporate" apologia*. Paper presented at the annual meeting of the National Communication Association, Chicago, IL.

Ice, R. (1991). Corporate publics and rhetorical strategies: The case of Union Carbide's Bhopal crisis. *Management Communication Quarterly, 4*(3), 341–362.

International Association of Business Communicators (IABC). (1995). *Crisis communication*. San Francisco: IABC Communication Bank.

Jablin, F. M. (1979). Superior-subordinate communication: The state of the art. *Psychological Bulletin, 36*, 1201–1222.

Jackall, R. (1988). *Moral mazes: The world of corporate managers*. London: Oxford University Press.

Jaksa, J. A., & Pritchard, M. S. (1988). *Communication ethics methods of analysis*. Belmont, CA: Wadsworth.

Janis, I. (1972). *Victims of groupthink: A psychological study of foreign decisions and fiascoes*. Boston: Houghton Mifflin.

Jensen, V. J. (1987). Ethical tension points in whistleblowing. *Journal of Business Ethics, 6,* 321–328.

Johannesen, R. L. (1996). *Ethics in human communication* (4th ed.). Prospect Heights, IL: Waveland Press.

Johannesen, R. L. (2001). *Ethics in human communication* (5th ed.). Prospect Heights, IL: Waveland Press.

Johnson, D., & Sellnow, T. L. (1995). Deliberative rhetoric as a step in organizational crisis management: Exxon as a case study. *Communication Reports, 8,* 54–60.

Johnstone, C. L. (1981). Ethics, wisdom, and the mission of contemporary rhetoric: The realization of human being. *Central States Speech Journal, 32,* 177–188.

Jones, S. (1989, October 15). Blueprint for disaster: Empty promises. *Anchorage Daily News,* p. A1. Retrieved September 9, 2003, from http://www.adn.com/evos/stories/ev264.html

Jones, B. L., & Chase, W. H. (1979). Managing public issues. *Public Relations Review, 5,* 3–23.

Jones, S., & Rainie, L. (2002). Internet use and terror attacks. In B. S. Greenberg (Ed.), *Communication and terrorism: Public and media responses to 9/11* (pp. 27–38). Cresskill, NJ: Hampton Press.

Juanillo, N. K., & Scherer, C. W. (1995). Corporate environmental risk communication: Cases and practices along the Gulf Coast. In B. R. Burleson (Ed.), *Communication Yearbook* (Vol. 18, pp. 278–299). Thousand Oaks, CA: Sage.

Katz, A. R. (1987, November). 10 Steps to complete crisis planning. *Public Relations Journal,* 46–47.

Kauffman, S. A. (1993). *Origins of order: Self organization and the nature of history.* New York: Oxford University Press.

Keil, L. D. (1994). *Managing chaos and complexity in government.* San Francisco: Jossey-Bass.

Kernisky, D. A., & Kernisky, I. F. (1998). We sell bad meat...but they really lied: The case of Food Lion v. ABC's PrimeTime Live—A legal/ethical conundrum. In M. W. Seeger (Ed.), *Free Speech Yearbook* (Vol. 36, pp. 61–71). Annandale, VA: Speech Communication Association.

Knights, D. (1992). Changing spaces: The disruptive impact of the new epistemological location for the study of management. *Academy of Management Review, 17,* 514–536.

Knutson, J. (2002, April 14). Ravaged city boosted by $171 million in federal aid. *The Forum,* pp. A21–22.

Kreps, G. A. (1984). Sociological inquiry and disaster research. In R. E. Turner & J. F. Short, Jr. (Eds.), *Annual Review of Sociology* (pp. 309–330). Palo Alto, CA: Annual Reviews.

Kuebelbeck, A. (1994, December 2). Schwan's wants home court. *The Marshall Independent,* pp. A1, A13.

Lerbinger, O. (1997). *The crisis manager: Facing risk and responsibility.* Mahwah, NJ: Erlbaum.

Littlejohn, R. F. (1983). *Crisis management: A team approach.* New York: AMACOM.

Louden, R. B. (1992). *Morality and moral theory.* New York: Oxford University Press.

Lovejoy, L. J. (1993). Villian and victims of product tampering. In J. A. Gottschalk (Ed.), *Crisis response* (pp. 175–185). Detroit, MI: Visible Ink Press.

MacDonald, J. (1997, April 12). Bad gauge reading leaves unanswered questions. *The Forum*, p. C3.

Mandelbrot, B. B. (1977). *Fractals: Form, chance, and dimensions.* San Francisco: W. H. Freeman.

Manning, R. C. (1992). *Speaking from the heart: A feminist perspective on ethics.* Lanham, MD: Rowman & Littlefield.

Marcus, A. A., & Goodman, R. S. (1991). Victims and shareholders: The dilemmas of presenting corporate policy during a crisis. *Academy of Management Journal, 34,* 281–305.

Mather, E., Stewart, P., & Ten Eyck, T. (2000). *Risk communication in food safety: Motivating and building trust.* East Lansing, MI: National Food Safety and Toxicology Center, Michigan State University.

Matthews, M. K., White, M. C., & Long, R. G. (1999). Why study the complexity sciences in the social sciences? *Human Relations, 25,* 439–461.

McCoy, C. (1989, July 6). Broken promises—Alyeska record shows how big oil neglected Alaskan environment. *Wall Street Journal,* pp. A1, A4.

Metzler, M. S. (2001). The centrality of organizational legitimacy to public relations practice. In R. L. Heath (Ed.), *Handbook of Public Relations* (pp. 321–334). Thousand Oaks, CA: Sage.

Meyer, A. D. (1982). Adapting to environmental jolts. *Administrative Science Quarterly, 27,* 515–537.

Meyers, G. C., & Holusha, J. (1986). *When it hits the fan: Managing the nine crises of business.* Boston: Houghton Mifflin.

Middleton city schools crisis plan. Retrieved September 10, 2003, from http:// www.middletowncityschools.com/pdf.crisisprotocols.pdf

Mileti, D. S., & Sorensen, J. H. (1990). *Communication and emergency public warning.* ORLN-6609. Washington, D.C.: Federal Emergency Management Administration.

Miller, K. (1999). *Organizational communication: Approaches and processes.* Belmont, CA: Wadsworth.

Mitroff, I. I. (1986). Teaching corporate America to think about crisis prevention. *Journal of Business Strategy, 6,* 40–48.

Mitroff, I. I. (1988, Winter). Crisis management: Cutting through the confusion. *Sloan Management Review,* 15–19.

Mitroff, I. I. (2001). Crisis leadership. *Executive Excellence, 18,* 19–22.

Mitroff, I. I., & Anagnos, G. (2001). *Managing crises before they happen: What every executive and manager needs to know about crisis management.* New York: AMACOM.

Muchlinski, J. (1994, November 14). Carlson helps Schwan's reopen ice cream plant. *Marshall Independent,* pp. A1, A13.

Mumby, D. K. (1988). *Communication and power in organizations: Discourse, ideology, and domination.* Norwood, NJ: Ablex.

Murphy, P. (1996). Chaos theory as a model for managing issues and crises. *Public Relations Review, 22(2),* 95–113.

Myers, K. N. (1999). *Managers guide to contingency planning for disasters.* New York: John Wiley & Sons.

Nakra, P. (2000). Corporate reputation management: "CRM" with a strategic twist. *Public Relations Quarterly, 45*, 35–43.

National Research Council (1989). *Improving risk communication.* Washington, D.C.: National Academy Press.

Near, J. P., & Micelli, M. P. (1986). Retaliation against whistleblowing: Predictors and effects. *Journal of Applied Psychology, 71*, 137–145.

Newspaper: No evidence feds bungled flood forecast. (1997, May 19). *The Forum,* p. C1.

Nilsen, T. R. (1974). *Ethics of speech communication* (2nd ed.). Indianapolis: Bobbs-Merrill.

Normann, R. (1985). Developing capabilities for organizational learning. In Johannes M. Pennings Associates (Ed.), *Organizational strategy and change* (pp. 217–248). San Francisco: Jossey-Bass.

Northouse, P. G. (2001). *Leadership: Theory and practice.* Thousand Oaks, CA: Sage.

Nudell, M., & Antokol, N. (1988). *The handbook for effective crisis management.* Lexington, MA: Lexington Books.

Pantera, T. (2002a, April 16). Painful lessons. *The Forum,* pp. A1, A8.

Pantera, T. (2002b, April 16). Spring of '97 sturs up a flood of memories. *The Forum,* pp. A1, A22.

Pauchant, T. C., & Mitroff, I. I. (1992). *Transforming the crisis-prone organization.* San Francisco: Jossey-Bass.

Payne, D. (1989). *Coping with failure: The therapeutic uses of rhetoric.* Columbia: University of South Carolina Press.

Pearson, C. M., & Clair, J. A. (1998). Reframing crisis management. *Academy of Management Review, 23*(1), 59–76.

Perrow, C. (1970). *Organizational analysis: A sociological view.* Belmont, CA: Brooks/Cole.

Perrow, C. (1984). *Normal accidents.* New York: Basic Books.

Perrow, C. (1999). *Normal accidents* (2nd ed.). New York: Basic Books.

Perrow, C. (2001). *Normal accident theory and the terrorist attack of 9/11/01.* Paper presented at the conference "Emerging Diseases: Crisis Communication in Public Health, Atlanta, GA."

Pfeffer, J. (1981). Management as symbolic action: The creation and maintenance of organizational paradigms. In L. L. Cummings & B. M. Staw (Eds.), *Research in organizational behavior* (Vol. 3, pp. 1–52). Greenwich, CT: JAI Press.

Pfeffer, J., & Salancik, G. (1978). *The external control of organizations.* New York: Harper & Row.

Pidgeon, N., Hood, C., Jones, D., Turner, B., & Gibson, R. (1992). Risk perception. In The Royal Society (Ed.), *Risk: Analysis, perception, and management* (pp. 89–134). London: The Royal Society.

Pinsdorf, M. K. (1987). *Communicating when your company is under siege.* Lexington, MA: Lexington Books.

Pinsdorf, M. K. (1995). Flying different skies: How cultures respond to airline disasters. *Public Relations Review, 17*(1), 37–56.

Pinsdorf, M. K. (1999). *Communicating when your company is under siege: Surviving public crisis.* Lexington, MA: Lexington Books.

Plantly, E., & Machaver, W. (1952). Upward communication: A project in executive development. *Personnel, 28*, 304–318.

Produs, J. (1997, April 24). Finger pointing begins in Forks. *The Forum*, p. A7.

Putnam, L. L., & Cheney, G. (1985). Historical developments and future directions. In T. W. Benson (Ed.), *Speech communication and the 20th century* (pp. 130–156). Carbondale: Southern Illinois University Press.

Quarantelli, E. I. (1988). Disaster crisis management: A summary of research findings. *Journal of Management Studies, 25*, 273–385.

Ramey, J. (1998, May 13). Nike CEO vents at presentation of new anti-sweatshop efforts. *Women's Wear Daily, 175*(95), 11.

Ray, S. J. (1999). *Strategic communication in crisis management: Lessons from the airline industry*. Westport, CT: Quorum Books.

Renz, M. A. (1996). Ethics and the communication of risk technology. In J. A. Jaksa & M. S. Pritchard (Eds.), *Responsible communication: Ethical issues in business, industry, and the professions* (pp. 245–265). Cresskill, NJ: Hampton Press.

Reynolds, B. (2002). *Crisis and emergency risk communication*. Atlanta, GA: Centers for Disease Control and Prevention.

Rimal, R. N., Fogg, B., & Lora, J. A. (1995). Moving toward a framework for the study of risk communication: Theoretical and ethical considerations. In B. R. Burleson (Ed.), *Communication Yearbook* (Vol. 18, pp. 320–342). Thousand Oaks, CA: Sage.

Roberts, K. H., & O'Reilly, III, C. A. (1974). Failure in upward communication: Three possible culprits. *Academy of Management Journal, 17*, 205–215.

Robertson, R., & Combs, A. (Eds.). (1995). *Chaos theory in psychology and the life sciences*. Mahwah, NJ: Erlbaum.

Rogers, E. M. (1995). *Diffusion of innovations* (4th ed.). New York: Free Press.

Rowan, K. E. (1995). What risk communicators need to know: An agenda for research. In B. R. Burleson (Ed.), *Communication Yearbook* (Vol. 18, pp. 300–319). Thousand Oaks, CA: Sage.

Rubonis, A., & Bickman, L. (1991). Psychological impairment in the wake of disaster: The disaster-psychopathology relationship. *Psychological Bulletin, 109*, 384–399.

Sandman, P. (2000). Open communication. In E. Mather, P. Stewart, & T. Ten Eyck (Eds.), *Risk communication in food safety: Motivating and building trust*. East Lansing: National Food Safety and Toxicology Center, Michigan State University.

Schein, E. (1991). The role of the founder in the creation of organizational culture. In P. Frost, L. Moore, M. Louis, C. Lundberg, & J. Martin (Eds.), *Reframing organizational culture* (pp. 14–25). Beverly Hills, CA: Sage.

Schuetz, J. (1990). Corporate advocacy as argumentation. In R. Trapp & J. Schuetz (Eds.), *Perspectives on argumentation* (pp. 272–284). Prospect Heights, IL: Waveland Press.

Schultz, P. D., & Seeger, M. W. (1991). Corporate centered apologia: Iacocca in defense of Chrysler. *Speaker and Gavel, 28*(1–4), 50–60.

Schwan's cleared of wrongdoing, but probe continues. (1995, October 19). *The Marshall Independent*, pp. A1, A14.

Seeger, M. W. (1986a). The Challenger tragedy and search for legitimacy. *Central States Speech Journal, 37*(3), 147–157.

Seeger, M. W. (1986b). Free speech and institutional restraint. *The Free Speech Yearbook, 25*, 11–21. Washington, D.C.: National Communication Association.

Seeger, M.W. (1994). *I gotta tell you: Speeches of Lee Iacocca.* Detroit: Wayne State University Press.

Seeger, M. W. (1997). *Ethics and organizational communication.* Cresskill, NJ: Hampton Press.

Seeger, M.W. (2002). Chaos and crisis: Propositions for a general theory of crisis communication. *Public Relations Review, 28*(4), 329–337.

Seeger, M. W., Barton, E., Heyart, B., & Bultnick, S. (2001, Fall). Crisis planning and crisis communication in public schools: Assessing post-Columbine responses. *Communication Research Reports,* 375–383.

Seeger, M. W., & Bolz, B. (1996). Technological transfer and multinational corporations in the Union Carbide crisis in Bhopal, India. In J. A. Jaksa & M. S. Pritchard (Eds.), *Responsible communication: Ethical issues in business, industry, and the professions* (pp. 245–265). Cresskill, NJ: Hampton Press.

Seeger, M. W., & Gouran, D. S. (2002, July). *Functional decision-making under crisis conditions.* Paper presented at the Risk Communication Workshop on Effectively Communicating Protective Actions and Exposure Information During an Incident Involving a Release of Radioactive Material, Las Vegas, NV.

Seeger, M. W., Sellnow, T. L., & Ulmer, R. R. (1998). Communication, organization and crisis. In M. E. Roloff (Ed.), *Communication Yearbook* (Vol. 21, pp. 231–275). Thousand Oaks, CA: Sage.

Seeger, M. W., Sellnow, T. L., & Ulmer, R. R. (2001). Public relations and crisis communication: Organizing and chaos. In R. L. Heath (Ed.), *Handbook of Public Relations* (pp. 155–165). Thousand Oaks, CA: Sage.

Seeger, M. W., & Ulmer, R. R. (2001). Virtuous responses to organizational crisis: Aaron Feuerstein and Milt Cole. *Journal of Business Ethics, 31,* 369–376.

Seeger, M. & Ulmer, R. R. (2003). Explaining Enron: Communication and responsible leadership. *Management Communication Quarterly, 17,* 1, 58–85.

Seeger, M., W., Vennette, S., Ulmer, R. R., & Sellnow, T. L. (2002). Media use, information seeking, and reported needs in post crisis contexts. In B. S. Greenberg (Ed.), *Communication and terrorism: Public and media responses to 9/11* (pp. 53–63). Cresskill, NJ: Hampton Press.

Seely, L. (1995, February 4). Schwan's plaintiffs reach agreement. *The Marshall Independent,* pp. A1, A5.

Sellnow, T. L. (1993). Scientific argument in organizational crisis communication: The case of Exxon. *Argumentation and Advocacy, 30,* 28–42.

Sellnow, T. L., & Brand, J. D. (2001). Establishing the structure of reality for an industry: Model and anti model arguments as advocacy in Nike's crisis communication. *Journal of Applied Communication Research, 31,* 278–295.

Sellnow, T. L., & Seeger, M. W. (1989). Crisis messages: Wall Street and the Reagan administration after Black Monday. *Speaker and Gavel, 26,* 9–18.

Sellnow, T. L., Seeger, M. W., & Ulmer, R. R. (2002). Chaos theory, informational needs, and natural disasters. *Journal of Applied Communication Research, 30,* 269–292.

Sellnow, T. L., Ulmer, R. R., & Snider, M. (1998). The compatibility of corrective action in organizational crisis communication. *Communication Quarterly, 46*(1), 60–74.

Senge, P.M. (1990). *The fifth discipline: The art and practice of the learning organization.* New York: Doubleday.

Senge, P.M., & Kleiner, A. (Eds.). (1994). *The fifth discipline fieldbook: Strategies and tools for building a learning organization.* New York: Doubleday.

Sethi, S.P. (1987). A conceptual framework for environmental analysis of social issues and evaluation of business response patterns. In C.M. Falbe (Ed.), *Business and society: Dimensions of conflict and cooperation.* Lexington, MA: Lexington Books.

Shirvastava, P. (1987). *Bhopal: Anatomy of a crisis.* Cambridge, MA: Ballinger.

Shirvastava, P., Mitroff, I.I., Miller, D., & Miglani, A. (1988). Understanding industrial crises. *Journal of Management Studies, 25*(4), 285–303.

Sievers, S. (1994a, October 28). Schwan's: Plant could reopen Tuesday. *The Marshall Independent,* p. A1.

Sievers, S. (1994b, November 19). Judge: Schwan's free to settle with its customers. *The Marshall Independent,* pp. A1, A9.

Sievers, S., & Yost, D. (1994, October 8). Illness tied to Schwan's. *The Marshall Independent,* pp. A1, A5.

Simms, R.R., & Brinkmann, J. (2002). Leaders as moral role models: The case of John Gutfreund at Solomon Brothers. *Journal of Business Ethics, 35,* 327–339.

Sitkin, S.B. (1996). Learning through failure: The strategy of small losses. In M.D. Cohen & L.S. Sproull (Eds.), *Organizational learning* (pp. 541–578). Thousand Oaks, CA: Sage.

Sitkin, S.B., Sutcliffe, K.M., & Weick, K.E. (1999). Organizational learning. In R.C. Dorf (Ed.), *The technology management handbook* (pp. 7–76). Boca Raton, FL: CRC Press.

Slote, M. (1992). *From morality to virtue.* New York: Oxford University Press.

Slovic, P. (1987). Perception of risk. *Science, 236,* 280–286.

Small, W. (1991). Exxon Valdez: How to spend billions and still get a black eye. *Public Relations Review, 17*(1), 9–26.

Smart, C.F. (1985). Strategic business planning: Predicting susceptibility to crisis. In S.J. Andriole (Ed.), *Corporate crisis management* (pp. 9–21). Princeton, NJ: Petrocelli.

Smart, C.F., & Vertinsky, I. (1977). Designs for crisis decision units. *Administrative Science Quarterly, 22,* 640–657.

Smircich, L., & Morgan, G. (1982). Leadership: The management of meaning. *Journal of Applied Behavioral Studies, 18,* 257–273.

Smircich, L., & Stubbard, C. (1985). Strategic management in an enacted world. *Academy of Management Review, 10,* 724–736.

Smith, J.A. (1946). *The Nicomachean ethics of Aristotle* (Introduction, pp. vii–xxviii). New York: E.P. Dutton & Co.

Snyder, D.A. (2001). The role of communication management in the enactment of two sexual harassment cases in the public domain. Unpublished doctoral dissertation. Wayne State University.

Society for Healthcare Strategy and Market Development (2002). *Crisis Communications in healthcare: Managing difficult times effectively.* Chicago: Author.

Staw, B.M., Sandelands, L., & Dutton, J. (1981). Threat-rigidity effects in organizational behavior: A multilevel analysis. *Administrative Science Quarterly, 26,* 501–524.

Stewart, I. (1989). *Does God play dice? The mathematics of chaos.* Middlesex, MA: Penguin Books.

Stogdill, R.M. (1974). *Handbook of leadership.* New York: Free Press.

Sturges, D. L. (1994). Communicating through crisis: A strategy for organizational survival. *Management Communication Quarterly, 7*(3), 297–316.

Susskind, L., & Field, P. (1996). *Dealing with an angry public: The mutual gains approach to resolving disputes.* New York: Free Press.

Sutcliffe, K. M. (2001). Organizational environments and organizational information processing. In F. M. Jablin & L. L. Putnam (Eds.), *The new handbook of organizational communication: Advances in theory, research, and methods* (pp. 197–230). Thousand Oaks, CA: Sage.

Tsoukas, H., & Papoulias, D. B. (1996). Creativity in OR/MS: From technique to epistemology. *Interfaces, 26*(2), 73–79.

Turner, B. (1976). The organizational and interorganizational development of disasters. *Administrative Science Quarterly, 21,* 378–397.

Twin Towers Fund. (2001). Retrieved November 15, 2002, from http://www.twintowersfund.org/

Tyler, L. (1997). Liability means never being able to say you're sorry: Corporate guilt, legal constraints and defensiveness in corporate communication. *Management Communication Quarterly, 11*(1), 51–73.

Ulmer, R. R. (1999). Responsible speech in crisis communication. In M. W. Seeger (Ed.), *The Free Speech Yearbook, 37,* 155–168. Washington, D.C.: National Communication Association.

Ulmer, R. R. (2001). Effective crisis management through established stakeholder relationships: Malden Mills as a case study. *Management Communication Quarterly, 14*(4), 590–615.

Ulmer, R. R., & Sellnow, T. L. (1997). Strategic ambiguity and the ethic of significant choice in the tobacco industry's crisis communication. *Communication Studies, 48*(3), 215–233.

Ulmer, R. R., & Sellnow, T. L. (2000). Consistent questions of ambiguity in organizational crisis communication: Jack in the Box as a case study. *Journal of Business Ethics, 25*(2), 143–155.

Valesquez, M. (1982). *Business ethics: Concepts and cases.* Englewood Cliffs, NJ: Prentice-Hall.

Valle, M. (2001). Crisis, culture, charisma. In W. E. Rosebach & R. L. Taylor (Eds.), *Contemporary issues in leadership* (5th ed.). Cambridge, MA: Westview Press.

Von Krogh, G., Roos, J., & Slocum, K. (1994). An essay on corporate epistemology. *Strategic Management Journal, 15,* 53–71.

Weick, K. E. (1979). *The social psychology of organizing* (2nd ed.). New York: McGraw-Hill.

Weick, K. E. (1988). Enacted sensemaking in crisis situations. *Journal of Management Studies, 25*(4), 305–317.

Weick, K. E. (1993). The collapse of sensemaking in organizations: The Mann Gulch disaster. *Administrative Science Quarterly, 38,* 628–652.

Weick, K. E. (1995). *Sensemaking in organizations.* Thousand Oaks, CA: Sage.

Weick, K. E. (2001). *Making sense of the organization.* Malden, MA: Blackwell.

Weick, K. E., & Ashford, S. J. (2001). Learning in organizations. In F. M. Jablin & L. L. Putnam (Eds.), *The new handbook of organizational communication: Advances in theory, research, and methods* (pp. 704–731). Thousand Oaks, CA: Sage.

Weick, K. E., & Bougon, M. G. (1986). Organizations as cognitive maps: Charting ways to success and failure. In H. P. J. Sims & D. A. A. Gioia (Eds.), *The thinking organization*. San Francisco: Jossey-Bass.

Weick, K. E., & Sutcliffe, K. M. (2001). *Managing the unexpected: Assuring high performance in an age of complexity*. San Francisco: Jossey-Bass.

Werhane, P. (1985). *Persons, rights, and corporations*. Englewood Cliffs, NJ: Prentice-Hall.

Wheatley, M. J. (1999). *Leadership and the new science: Discovering order in a chaotic world*. San Francisco, CA: Berrett-Koehler.

Wilcox, D. L., Ault, P. H., & Agee, W. K. (1986). *Public relations strategies and tactics*. New York: Harper & Row.

Williams, D. E., & Olaniran, B. E. (1994). Exxon's decision making flaws: The hypervigilant response to the Valdez grounding. *Public Relations Review, 20*(1), 5–18.

Williams, D. E., & Olaniran, B. A. (1998). Expanding the crisis planning function: Introducing elements of risk communication to crisis communication practice. *Public Relations Review*, [Online], 24. Available:

Williams, D. E., & Treadaway, G. (1992). Exxon and the Valdez accident: A failure in crisis communication. *Communication Studies, 43*, 56–64.

Witt, J. L., & Morgan, G. (2002). *Stronger in broken places: Nine lessons for turning crisis into triumph*. New York: Times Books.

Witte, K. (1995). Generating effective risk messages: How scary should your risk communication be? In B. R. Burleson (Ed.), *Communication Yearbook* (Vol. 18, pp. 229–254). Thousand Oaks, CA: Sage.

Yukl, G. A. (2002). *Leadership in organizations* (3rd ed.). Englewood Cliffs, NJ: Prentice Hall.

Zent, J. (2002, April 17). Three-way race for flood plan. *The Forum*, pp. A1, A18.

Author Index

Allen, 92
Anderson, 158, 240
Andriole, 164
Anfuso, 165
Angeles, 155
Antokol, 169
Arndt, 12, 272
Auf Der Heide, 32

Barge, 241
Barton, 55, 163, 165, 169, 172, 174, 182, 186, 191
Benoit, 5, 10, 16, 58, 76, 92, 102, 144, 145, 146, 155, 268
Benson, 165, 172
Beyer, 220
Billings, 91, 112, 126
Bok, 234, 235
Brenneman, 269
Brinson, 268
Brown, 36, 38, 42
Brummer, 142, 233
Buchholz, 226, 227
Buono, 227
Butz, 21, 28, 31, 33, 34

Calas, 262, 263
Cheney, 76, 183
Chess, 204, 206, 213, 214

Cohen, 18, 37, 38, 40, 41
Comfort, 25, 28, 31, 104
Conrad, 222
Coombs, 45, 46, 47, 49, 51, 55, 65, 75, 85, 88, 96, 97, 143, 144, 145, 155, 163, 164, 169, 170, 172, 173, 174, 175, 186, 187, 191, 202, 240
Covello, 11, 70, 202
Cowden, 270
Crable, 11, 148, 212
Curwood, 212
Cushing, 62

Davidson, 116, 117, 118, 120, 121
Deakin, 116
Deetz, 133, 259
Devine, 110
Diana, 203, 205, 207
Dilenschneider, 171
Doughty, 166
Dowling, 66, 142, 231

Egelhoff, 197
Eisenberg, 39, 174
Epstein, 142

Fearn-Banks, 18, 54, 174, 182, 187, 191, 268
Ferguson Deveraux, 187, 191

Fiedler, 245
Fink, 85, 102, 143, 164, 165, 167, 184, 259
Fitzgibbon, 39, 41
Fitzpatrick, 51, 187
Freedy, 149, 150
Freeman, 133
Frohwein, 214
Froslie, 156

Gaunt, 11
Gilligan, 232
Gleick, 28, 33
Glicken, 207, 208
Goodnight, 264
Gottschalk, 163, 164, 169, 171
Gouran, 9, 15, 26, 41, 87, 173, 191, 192, 193, 194, 195
Greenberg, 87, 129, 130
Griffin, 202, 209, 210
Guth, 85, 96, 165

Hayles, 28, 29
Heald, 226
Hearit, 16, 58, 76, 142, 143, 152, 155, 171
Hermann, 8
Hilgers, 153, 154
Hirokawa, 193
Huber, 18, 21, 36, 38, 39, 40, 86, 147, 156, 263

Ice, 76, 144

Jablin, 111
Jackall, 220, 222
Jaksa, 221
Janis, 14, 15
Jensen, 82
Johannesen, 74, 209, 225, 229, 254
Johnson, D., 68
Johnstone, C., 25, 104
Jones, B.L., 68
Juanillo, 206, 207

Katz, 171
Kauffman, 29, 32
Keil, 21, 29, 35

Kernisky, 58
Knights, 81, 269
Knutson, 159
Kreps, 10

Lerbinger, 266
Littlejohn, 171, 187, 191
Louden, 228
Lovejoy, 166

Manning, 230
Markus, 131
Mather, 201, 202
Matthews, 28, 29, 30, 31, 32
Metzler, 92, 232
Meyer, 105
Meyers, 6, 45, 46, 47, 48, 52, 54, 59, 60, 167, 174, 182
Miller, 262
Mitroff, 47, 48, 49, 55, 163, 164, 167, 169, 172, 182, 199, 206, 214, 242, 241
Muchlinski, 135
Mumby, 263
Murphy, 7, 18, 21, 28, 29, 32, 33, 34, 86
Myers, 166, 169, 173, 182

Nakra, 143
Near, 89
Nilsen, 235
Normann, 36
Northouse, 242, 244
Nudell, 163, 169, 171, 174, 186

Pauchant, 5, 8, 9, 14, 85, 87, 88, 93, 94, 95, 96, 97, 102, 110, 133, 163, 167, 223, 224
Payne, 150
Pearson, 55
Perrow, 5, 6, 12, 13, 14, 28, 50, 108, 109, 113, 115, 119, 120, 183, 231, 261, 262, 270
Pfeffer, 39, 66, 67, 69, 246, 270
Pidgeon, 202, 204, 209, 214, 215
Pinsdorf, 14, 165, 221
Putnam, 222

Quarantelli, 10, 165

Ray, 35, 50, 63, 85, 88, 96, 97, 165
Renz, 212
Rimal, 204
Robertson, 28
Rogers, 259
Rowan, 209, 215
Rubin, 52, 187
Rubonis, 149, 150

Sandman, 210, 212
Schein, 246
Schuetz, 65, 74, 143
Schultz, 76, 144
Seeger, 4, 6, 7, 13, 18, 21, 25, 26, 29, 32,
    37, 66, 68, 73, 85, 86, 88, 96, 129, 130,
    133, 142, 143, 151, 152, 165, 167, 171,
    172, 179, 182, 183, 188, 189, 194, 195,
    220, 221, 222, 223, 224, 226, 228, 230,
    232, 234, 238, 240, 254, 262
Sellnow, 72, 75, 76, 143, 148, 198, 203,
    260, 267, 269
Senge, 21, 36, 37, 38, 79
Sethi, 224
Sitkin, 36, 41, 42, 103, 150, 254, 266
Slote, 228
Slovic, 210, 213, 215
Small, 66, 171
Smart, 31, 105
Smircich, 22, 242, 246, 247

Stewart, 30
Stogdill, 243
Sturges, 85
Susskind, 51
Sutcliffe, 21, 22

Tsoukas, 81
Turner, 9, 13, 37, 42, 85, 88, 89, 90, 92,
    93, 95, 96, 97, 102, 106, 108, 110, 166
Tyler, 51

Ulmer, 35, 51, 58, 96, 101, 129, 133, 151,
    152, 182, 223, 224, 233, 235, 236, 260

Valesquez, 222
Von Krogh, 80, 81, 147, 270

Weick, 8, 17, 18, 19, 21, 22, 23, 24, 25,
    26, 27, 37, 38, 67, 71, 87, 90, 97, 102,
    112, 130, 131, 132, 146, 148, 186, 206,
    207, 214, 240
Werhane, 220
Wheatley, 252, 258, 270, 271
Wilcox, 66, 173
Williams, 62, 152, 201, 204, 207
Witt, 250, 255

Yukl, 242, 244

Index

Airline disasters, 35, 42, 50, 54, 55, 62, 63, 64, 73–74, 96, 149, 166
Airline Security, 31, 37
Airlines: American, 91; Aloha, 37; Continental, 267; Egypt, 237; general, 7, 10, 15, 22, 32, 37, 52, 235, 267; Japanese, 184; Northwest, 7, 30, 270; Valujet, 7, 91, 112
Alaska, 25, 113–42, 167, 201
Alyeska, 114, 116, 117–21
Andersen, Arthur, 74
Anderson, Warren, 26, 242
Anthrax, 35, 109, 148, 171
Apologia, 16, 76, 77, 144, 223, 225; defined, 76–77. *See also* Image restoration
Archer Daniels Midland, 222
Attractors, strange, 29, 34–55, 252

Belief structures, 90, 105–106, 112; regarding risk, 115–15
Bhopla, India, 7, 13, 26, 30, 43, 72, 87, 131, 133, 183, 222, 235, 242
Bifurcation, 7, 29, 30–31, 32, 80, 86, 90, 102, 103, 112, 126; defined, 30–31; in chaos theory, 30–36; as system breakdown, 30–31
Bil Mar Foods, 15, 57

Bioterroism, 59. *See also* Anthrax
Blame, 36, 46, 50–52, 61, 68, 75, 77, 86, 94–95, 102–103, 122, 128, 144, 151–51, 155, 164, 187, 214, 219, 223, 233, 241, 243, 267–68
Bush, President George, 242, 272

Care, ethic of, 232
Carter, President Jimmy, 242
Catholic Church, 7, 23, 222, 225, 233, 237
Centers for Disease Control, 11, 35, 46, 57, 128, 135, 195
Challenger Shuttle, 6, 7, 12, 15, 26, 30, 35, 41, 73, 90–1, 97, 109, 131, 147
Chaos theory, 3, 16–19, 28–36, 58, 80, 103, 239, 255, 260, 270–71; defined, 28; and leadership 252–1; crisis communication and, 34
Chemical Spills, 17, 53, 63, 269; and oil spills, 62
Chernobyl, 6, 10, 102, 20F
Chrysler, 7, 27, 34, 39, 41, 59–60, 172, 182
C/K7 Pickups, 7, 233
Cole Hardwoods, 32, 223, 254, 260, 267
Cole, Milt, 151, 229, 254

Columbine High School, 7, 106
Communication, 14, 16, 17, 18, 25, 27,
    30, 34–36, 39, 45, 51, 54, 59, 62–83,
    64–82, 88, 89, 92, 94, 127, 133, 136,
    144, 150, 157, 166, 168, 169, 172, 188,
    196, 198, 203, 257, 266, 267; and
    crisis (See crisis: communication);
    and the crisis stage, 125–37; and
    decision making, 193–F3; defined,
    65; effective, 150, 188, 273; as envi-
    ronmental scanning, 66, 109,
    10E–10F; as epistemic, 80; and
    ethics, 222–203, 225, 253, 267; and
    functions of, during crisis, 19, 67,
    70; ineffective, 14, 62; and issue
    management, 68, 143; and leader-
    ship, 241–40, 249; and the precrisis
    stage, 105–23; and the postcrisis
    stage, 125–58; and risk (see risk
    communication); role of, in crisis,
    19–20, 64–82
Community Emergency Planning and
    Right to Know Act, 236
Continuous Adaptive Process, 159, 257
Coordination, 6, 12, 35, 39, 59, 62–83,
    67, 71, 72–93, 92, 157, 172, 178, 183,
    185, 188, 214, 255; and crisis com-
    mand structures, 189, 214, 249
Creutzfeldt-Jakob, 11
Crisis: cause, 12–35; characteristics of
    organizational, 15–17; command
    structures, 189–89; communication,
    11, 17–20, 65–82, 202, 203–206, 215;
    components of, management
    teams, 186; and crisis planning,
    163–82, 169, 170–72; decision
    model, 191, 195; defined, 4, 7–11;
    development, 85–104; ethics,
    219–36; factors in, planning, 167–67;
    functions of, management teams,
    166–65, 191; interactive, manage-
    ment, 96; leadership (see leader-
    ship); management, 9, 19, 20, 43, 46,
    56, 65, 70–75, 85, 87, 96, 131–30, 136,
    138–37, 146, 148, 163–83, 182–81,
    202, 244, 248; management models,
    88, 93–94; management teams, 16,
    185–97; models of, planning,

169–80; organizational, 15, 17–19,
    21–63; planning, 16, 20, 53, 70, 75,
    142, 163–E3, 191, 199, 247; proac-
    tive, management, 96; reactive,
    management, 96; sensing, 126, 202,
    228, 262; stage, the 125–27; state of,
    planning, 164–84; types, 45–64

Dateline, 56, 58, 233, 241, 270
Decay, 7, 29, 42, 99, 105–108, 112–11,
    118–18, 123, 167, 258, 275
Decision making. See Crisis, decision
    model
Developmental stages, 3
Development of crisis, 94, 95, 105. See
    also crisis: development
Dialogue, 37, 67, 79, 80, 205–207, 209,
    264, 266, 267
Dispersants, 25, 114–33, 119, 122–123

Earthquakes, 9–10, 48–49, 55–56, 164,
    168, 175, 203
E. coli. 7, 15, 30, 50, 57–58, 73, 10F, 236
Egypt Air, Flight 990, 237
Emergencies, 168, 175–79, 189, 203,
    231
Enactment, 3, 18, 22–48, 36, 67–68, 80,
    90, 97, 131–30, 135, 204, 247
Enron, 7, 14, 23, 37, 60, 74, 77, 90, 106,
    128, 151, 222, 223, 225, 232, 235, 241,
    271–272
Environmental scanning, 66–70
Equivocality, 18–19, 22–43, 27, 53, 67,
    80, 132, 228, 254
Explanative messages, 76–77, 105, 10F,
    112–113
External communication, 215–14
Exxon Valdez, 85, 102–123, 128, 148,
    165, 167, 222, 232, 242–39, 269

Failure in foresight, 85, 88–108
Fargo, ND, 73, 153–77
Federal Emergency Management
    Agency, 73, 164, 166–67, 175,
    178–82, 186, 189–89, 232, 252
Feuerstein, Aaron, 148, 151, 196, 229,
    237, 242, 242, 247, 254, 269
Firestone, 7, 23, 102

Floods, 49–50, 55, 77, 85, 153, 160, 164, 168, 175, 182, 203, 236, 261
Food and Drug Administration, 56, 106, 135
Foodborne illness, 57, 135
Ford Pinto, 7
Ford, William Clay, 229
Forgetting, 40, 142, 149–49, 157–56
Fractals, 29, 33

Giuliana, Rudy, 199, 241
Grand Forks, ND, 55, 72–93, 77, 154–77
Grieving, 75, 77, 78, 158, 252

Healing, 225–25, 141–40, 148–152, 157–58
Hurricane Andrew, 11, 56
Hurricane Mitch, 4

Iacocca, Lee, 61, 171, 243
Image restoration, 17, 76, 92, 103, 142, 144–64, 151, 155, 223, 225, 251, 263
Incident command, 170–69, 185, 188–87
Incubation, 17, 19, 89–90, 95, 105–109, 112, 119,123
Informational environment, 18, 22, 24, 68
Informational input, 22–43, 25, 27
Investigations, 41, 58, 96–97, 102–103, 135, 174, 197, 252
Issue Management, 11–32, 19, 66–68, 205

Jack in the Box, 7, 57, 222, 236
Johnson & Johnson, 53, 56–57, 75, 165
Leadership: contingency, 242–41; functions of, 242; styles, 243–43; symbolic, 239–38, 242–41, 246–49, 255; traits, 242–42
Learning, organizational, 3, 12, 18–19, 21, 36–38, 40, 42–63, 53, 56, 59, 66–67, 79, 86, 92, 103, 144, 150, 156, 185, 196, 207, 222, 225, 266, 271
Legitimacy, 4–5, 7, 10, 16, 48, 66, 69–70, 75–76, 92–F3, 97, 99, 131, 141–42, 147, 151, 155, 182, 202, 208, 219–18, 225, 231, 232–32, 238, 249, 252–51, 260, 263–65, 272

Listeria, 15, 50
Logansport, IN, 151
Lying, 222, 234–54

Mad Cow Disease, 7, 11
Malden Mills, 25, 53, 10F, 148, 151, 183, 196, 223, 229, 254, 260, 267, 269, 271
Mann Gulch, 26
Media: attention, 8, 58, 78, 112, 150, 198, 242, 266; campaigns, 167; coverage, 8, 59, 71, 112, 142, 173, 20E
Memorializing, 67, 75, 77–78, 82, 252
Microsoft, 48, 172
Mindfulness, 214–13
Moose, Chief Charles, 247
Morality Play, 225
Morton Thiokol, 15, 73, 98

NASA, 6, 15, 35, 41, 73, 90, 98, 131, 147
National Oceanic and Atmospheric Administrations Weather Service, 153–75
National Transportation Safety Board, 12, 92, 96
Normal Accident Theory, 12, 28
Normalcy, 4, 6, 75, 78–79, 82, 96–97, 104, 126, 129, 221, 242, 252
Normal, new, 86, 104
Norms, 8–9, 12–33, 15–16, 27, 31, 37, 66, 70, 75, 81, 88–92, 96, 103–107, 109, 10F–10, 117–16, 142–41, 164, 183, 204, 213, 222, 222, 225, 231, 232–32, 237, 253–52

Occupational Safety and Health Administration (OSHA), 106, 236
Oil Spills, 49, 62, 99, 105, 113, 115, 118

Pepsi-Cola, 270
Post Crisis, 142, 170, 252
Pre-crisis, 142
Prince William Sound, 62, 113–12, 116, 119
Public Relations, 16, 19, 65–66, 68, 122–21, 144, 165, 168, 171, 186–86, 198, 203, 205, 208, 20F, 267

Red Cross, American, 4, 168, 176, 232, 231
Red River, 141, 152–52, 156–55, 159, 236
Renewal, 3, 6–7, 18, 29, 32–53, 35–36, 43, 67, 103, 141–40, 149, 151–50, 159–58, 164, 225, 231, 248, 252–49, 253, 260, 263, 265–67, 271, 275
Requisite variety, 23, 25
Responsibility, 5, 8, 10, 16, 20, 23, 36, 41, 46, 49, 51, 55, 62–83, 68, 74, 86, 92, 94, 96, 102, 131–30, 135–34, 142–43, 152, 164, 166, 181, 183, 187, 189–89, 205–206, 219–18, 233, 242–39, 243–42, 248–47, 254–73, 257–58, 260, 264, 266–69, 271, 272–93; diffusion of, 51, 76, 103, 224, 236; ethics, 60, 222–23, 229–28; responsiveness, 226, 227
Risk communication, 11, 20, 66–67, 70, 201–202, 205–11, 215–14, 262; crisis communication, 70, 164, 203; defined, 202, 204

Salmonella, 50, 57, 134–53, 138, 269
Scapegoats, 5, 61, 76, 86, 270
Schools, 50, 52, 61, 10E, 165, 167, 172, 174, 188–87, 227
School shootings, 7, 61, 106
Schwans, 52–73, 57, 85, 125, 133–57, 255, 270–269
Self Organizing, 31–52, 80, 102–103
Sensemaking, 8, 17–19, 21–43, 26–28, 36, 43, 66–67, 79, 82, 97, 102, 105, 112, 129–29, 133, 142, 146, 171, 239, 249, 263
Sensitive Dependence on Initial Conditions, 29
Sexual Harassment, 23, 60, 186–85, 222, 237, 254
Short Response Time, 75
Significant Choice, 219, 234, 236
Stakeholders, 6, 9, 11, 16, 21, 27, 36, 45–46, 48–49, 52–75, 60, 64, 66, 69–75, 80–82, 94–95, 99, 126, 131–37, 142–41, 145–49, 160, 163, 166, 170, 173–92, 179, 181–82, 186, 196–96,

202–204, 207–209, 213, 215–14, 219, 221, 223–22, 227–26, 231–30, 235–35, 239–38, 242, 244–66, 252–53, 260, 260–65, 272–93
Strategic Ambiguity, 67, 71, 74–75, 236–35, 270
Strategies of crisis response, 16, 51, 75–76, 92, 102, 144–64, 155

Teams, Crisis, 16, 20, 169, 185–87, 191, 193–F2, 196–95, 199, 252
Terrorism, 49, 51, 59, 63, 146, 168, 178, 189
Threat, 4, 6–11, 14–17, 20–23, 25–27, 34–36, 45, 48, 50, 58, 60, 64, 66, 68–69, 71, 75, 87–88, 90–91, 97, 99, 103–11, 126, 128–28, 134–54, 138–37, 144, 149, 160, 164, 166–66, 178, 181, 187–86, 191, 196, 199, 202, 204, 20E–20F, 215, 219, 221, 229, 231, 233–33, 242–39, 245, 248–47, 257–58, 264, 266–67, 270–71
Threat rigidity, 9, 112
Three Mile Island, 6–7, 102, 201, 213, 222, 242, 262
Tight Coupling, 12–33, 28, 99, 108–109, 213
Trigger event, 4, 86, 90, 97, 99, 103–106, 10F–10, 123, 126, 129–30, 134, 138, 167, 242
Truthfulness, 219–18, 225, 234, 236, 253
TWA Flight 800, 8
Twin Towers, 231
Twin Towers Fund, 231
Tylenol, 53, 56–57, 10F, 148, 165, 213
Typology, of crisis, 45, 54, 144, 146, 155

Uncertainty, 7, 16, 18, 21–42, 27, 35, 45, 64, 66–67, 70–71, 74, 82, 87, 97, 99–103, 105, 122, 125–25, 129–28, 135, 138–37, 148, 163–82, 173, 179–79, 184–E5, 190–89, 196, 199, 221, 228, 236–35, 242, 242, 244–63, 247, 251–50, 254–73, 257, 260
Union Carbide, 7, 13, 26, 43, 72, 87, 131, 133, 183, 222, 235, 242

Unlearning, 39–40, 147, 156

Values, 8, 14, 24, 33–34, 48, 52, 54, 60,
   66, 75, 79, 89, 91, 10F, 115–14, 131,
   133, 137–37, 142, 183, 192, 196,
   204–205, 207–209, 213, 215, 219–25,
   231, 232, 234, 237–37, 244, 246, 248,
   252, 252–53, 260, 263–64, 271–73
Valujet, 7, 91, 112
Vicarious learning, 24, 39, 77, 106, 142,
   146, 148, 157
Victims, 4–6, 11, 17, 41, 51, 53, 56, 74,
   77–78, 87, 92, 129, 132, 141, 144,
   149–48, 154, 156–55, 173, 183, 219,
   224, 232–29, 235–34, 242, 248, 254

Virtue Ethics, 3, 151, 219, 225, 228–27,
   239, 242, 244, 248–47, 253–53

Watkins, Sherron, 90
Welch, Jack, 61, 243
West Nile Virus, 63
World Trade Center, 23, 27, 46, 53, 59,
   78–79, 91, 129, 151, 196, 241, 248,
   251

Y2K, 183, 219, 224, 232–29, 235–34,
   242, 248, 254

About the Authors

MATTHEW W. SEEGER is Associate Professor of Communication at Wayne State University, Detroit.

TIMOTHY L. SELLNOW is Professor of Communication at North Dakota State University, Fargo.

ROBERT R. ULMER is Associate Professor of Speech Communication at the University of Arkansas, Little Rock.

CPSIA information can be obtained at www.ICGtesting.com
Printed in the USA
LVOW071109240113

317081LV00006B/78/P